Building Distributed
Applications with ADO

Building Distributed Applications with ADO

William Martiner
David Herion
James Falino

Wiley Computer Publishing

John Wiley & Sons, Inc.

NEW YORK · CHICHESTER · WEINHEIM · BRISBANE · SINGAPORE · TORONTO

Publisher: Robert Ipsen

Editor: Robert M. Elliott

Managing Editor: Micheline Frederick

Text Design & Composition: SunCliff Graphic Productions

Designations used by companies to distinguish their products are often claimed as trademarks. In all instances where John Wiley & Sons, Inc., is aware of a claim, the product names appear in initial capital or ALL CAPITAL LETTERS. Readers, however, should contact the appropriate companies for more complete information regarding trademarks and registration.

This book is printed on acid-free paper. ∞

Published by John Wiley & Sons, Inc.

Published simultaneously in Canada.

This publication is designed to provide accurate and authoritative information in regard to the subject matter covered. It is sold with the understanding that the publisher is not engaged in professional services. If professional advice or other expert assistance is required, the services of a competent professional person should be sought.

Library of Congress Cataloging-in-Publication Data:

Martiner, William, 1967–
    Building distributed applications with ADO / William Martiner,
James Falino, David Herion.
        p.   cm.
    "Wiley computer publishing."
    Includes index
    ISBN 0-471-31701-2 (pbk. : alk. paper)
    1. Application software--Development.   2. Electronic data
processing--Distributed processing.   3. Data structures (Computer
science) 4. ActiveX. I. Falino, James, 1964–   . II. Herion,
David, 1968–   .   III. Title.
QA76.76.A65M389   1999
005.1--dc21   98-51575
                                                                    CIP

Printed in the United States of America.

10 9 8 7 6 5 4 3 2 1

Contents

Acknowledgments

Thanks to the good people at GARPAC Corporation: Joe Dahan and Phu Luong, who make work a pleasure to come to everyday. I'd also like to acknowledge the support of my parents, family, and friends, who have endured so many of my cancelled plans and missed engagements. Thanks for your patience; I love you all.

—*Jim Falino*

Special thanks to my wife and family for their support during this project. Also, thanks to the Philly Branch of Xerox Connect for their help and for constantly listening to me expound on the great aspects of ADO 2.x development.

—*Dave Herion*

I would like to extend special thanks to the folks at RTIS, in the Lexis-Nexis family of companies and Wingspan Technology. Thank you all for the opportunity to work with great people on interesting projects and to use these powerful new technologies. Also, thanks to my family, friends, and colleagues, who have been (again) puzzled at my disappearance while I wrote another book. Yes, I'm still here; thanks for waiting.

—*Bill Martiner*

We would all like to thank the staff at Wiley Computer Book Publishing for their work. Thanks also goes out the people at Microsoft for all their assistance during the writing of this book and for producing tools that make a developer's job easier and more productive.

Finally, a special thanks to Juan Valdez and all the coffee growers of the world, without whose efforts this book would, truly, never have been possible.

—*All*

Introduction

The ambitious goal of this book is to help you to develop robust client/server and Internet applications quickly, easily, and powerfully. This goal cannot be achieved on the Microsoft platform without a solid understanding of the power, flexibility, and ease-of-use of ActiveX Data Objects (ADO). ADO, in conjunction with OLE DB, has matured into the all-purpose way to access data of every conceivable type. Whether the data is relational, hierarchical, flat, or existing in such diverse providers as the file system and Web sites, ADO has a simple, standardized means of accessing it based on the component object model (COM).

Although ODBC had the same lofty goals, its implementation has never been easy, most likely because the ODBC API is rather cryptic for the average programmer and proved to be a needlessly cumbersome tool even for the advanced. A "wrapper" of some sort was sorely needed to provide a layer of abstraction from the API, while maintaining a level of performance close to that of native ODBC calls. Based on that need, ADO (and its predecessors DAO and RDO) was born. And with version 2.0, ADO's credo of "universal data access for the masses" has finally been realized.

As you will see in the coming pages, ADO provides much more than a "dumbing down" of data access. Since it is based not directly on ODBC, but on OLE DB, ADO represents a new generation of data access, and has simply become the common language of all data in the new Microsoft platform.

As this data access structure has moved to center stage, it has seen incredible growth in power and utility. Today, ADO touches most aspects of business-distributed application development; from where you can deploy data structures to the types of data that you can work with to the way that you think about software development and the way that you do your job.

Even the timing of this release emphasizes ADO's importance. As companies rebuild systems like never before, Windows NT platform tools and services such as ADO, COM,

MTS, and SQL Server are being taken very seriously, and ultimately are finding their way into a corporate America previously devoted to "Big Iron."

The Age of Reconstruction

For the majority of companies, the late-1990s marked a period in which IS managers had to make, arguably, the most significant decisions of their careers. This has been due to several contributing factors, forcing them to decide either to completely rewrite existing systems or to invest huge sums of money into applications with perhaps only a limited lifespan.

The most obvious of these factors is the computer Armageddon known as the Year 2000 bug, or Y2K. Y2K issues have forced the hand of many IS mangers regarding the life of the applications they maintain, decisions they might otherwise have forestalled. Y2K alone has companies literally racing against the clock to evaluate the available tools on the market. For some, it's more cost-beneficial to build Y2K departments, hire high-priced consultants, and patch the existing system. This choice is typically made when the application is either too monolithic, too new, or time is too short to consider a new system. Those with smaller, cheaper, PC-based systems, on the other hand, have been scouring the market either for a replacement or the right tools with which to rewrite the application in-house.

Another contributing factor to this period of reconstruction is the explosion of the World Wide Web. As companies jockey for their piece of the Internet, major decisions are being made regarding if and how to integrate existing systems. For many, the answer is a complete Web solution. For others, a combination of Web and non-Web-based functionality is what's needed. But in most cases, some presence on the Internet must be instituted. Thus, Web development departments are becoming more commonplace and often end up spearheading the company's new software development direction.

While the Y2K and Internet factors are probably the most significant stimuli for major decision making, there are other issues that compound the need for movement. The exponential growth of the hardware industry (and corresponding reduction in prices) is chief among them. Can you believe that today the typical business PC has a 350MHz Pentium II processor, 96 megabytes of RAM, 8.0 gigabytes of storage space, a 15" monitor, a CD player, a 56K modem, a sound card with speakers, and sells for under $1,500? It was just seven years ago that I purchased my first PC, and that same $1,500 bought me only a 386SX 20MHz, with 2 megabytes of RAM (expandable to 4, thank you), a 500-megabyte hard drive, and a 14" monitor. Amazing!

The average employee today essentially has yesterday's mainframe on his or her desk. That, of course, factors into the question of whether to build a new system and which tools to use. As the PC gets more powerful, more and more processing is being offloaded from the server and given either to the client or to another supporting server. In the early nineties, when this growth first began, departmental systems were sprouting everywhere, as companies were able to make their data much more accessible. Often, they were small XBase file/server systems that reported on data downloaded from a mainframe.

Today, the PC has become so powerful that it is often used as a server—hosting a relational database and supplanting the mainframe. Actually, the flexibility of PC-based systems allow for an infinite number of possible designs by using techniques such as creating multiprocessor machines, clustering servers, implementing one or more application servers between client and data server, putting user-interface logic on the client, or using very "thin" clients with little to no logic locally, and more. This movement from host-based systems to distributed client/server computing has spawned new thoughts in the area of software design.

Programming practices are also certainly changing as developers look for ways to spread the processing among available resources and to make systems stand the test of time. Most seem to agree that object orientation, business objects, design patterns, and the Universal Modeling Language (UML) are keys to achieving that end. And companies like PeopleSoft and SAP have been very successful at installing enterprisewide CORBA-based applications on the Unix platform that tout these features. Microsoft, on the other hand, has its own thoughts on the subject.

Distributed interNet Applications

To Microsoft, the future lies in what it has (currently) coined Distributed interNet Applications (DNA). DNA proposes applications that are at least three-tier, with user-interface, business objects, and data services physically (or possibly just logically) separated. However, it is the business objects that are responsible for the bulk of the applications logic.

In DNA, the client should do nothing more than present data to the user, and the data server should do nothing more than perform data-related services like query and update data. The business objects take on more responsibility than ever before, with roles including establishing security, controlling transactions, accessing data and stored procedures through ODBC, and passing data back to clients.

The beauty of this architecture is that it insn't language or network specific. An appropriately designed distributed application should be able to access multiple, disparate (cross-LAN/Internet and even to disconnected) data stores, employ business objects created in multiple languages, communicate across multiple network protocols, and be able to scale up or down as needs change.

With its emphasis on simplifying application development, Microsoft seems to be asking the following questions: Why should Web development be any different from other types of development? Why do I need Unix operating systems and cryptic scripting languages to program for Internet publication? Isn't HTTP just another network protocol serving up bytes of data to and from client machines?

If that all seems like theory that will never meet reality, you owe it to yourself to investigate the new and improved Windows NT services like Internet Information Server (IIS), Microsoft Index Server, Microsoft Transaction Server (MTS), and Microsoft Message Queue Server (MSMQ). These services, in conjunction with ActiveX Data Objects (ADO), ActiveX Server Pages (ASP), XML, and Component Object Model (COM) round out the most significant pieces of the DNA development puzzle.

Universal Data Access

Both ADO and MTS represent the maturation of important ideas. ADO represents the fulfillment of the never-realized dream of ODBC: easy, robust, and universal data access.

MTS is a technology that enables developers to follow through on the promises of n-tier application development. Together, they are the most advanced method of data access and management that the Windows platform provides.

Much has been written about MTS enabling the developer to work with COM objects more easily and safely. However, its power is only fully realized when it is used to manage properly constructed COM objects. Therefore, this book is about not only the individual importance of ADO and MTS; it also concentrates on the powerful synergy of the ADO/COM object structure used in the context of MTS. In concert, these two technologies create efficiencies and capabilities in database application development that would be impossible using either alone.

Microsoft continues to try to bring sophisticated application development to the masses by emphasizing simplicity in all of its development tools. That's not to say a child of four can build a multitiered client/server application using Microsoft tools, but the learning curve to do so gets less steep every year. If you know DAO and RDO, ADO is very easy to learn. If you don't, it's still easy, thanks to the hierarchical nature of the object model. And the server-side tools are all built in such similar ways that learning one gives you a head start on learning all of the others.

How This Book Is Organized

In an effort to achieve our goal of enabling you to develop distributed client /server applications using Microsoft's technologies, this book is organized into three parts, each emphasizing the importance of ADO in the overall design of Distributed interNet Applications.

The first part of the book deals with the subject of ADO. It begins with a look at the use of OLE DB as a blueprint for universal data access, then immediately moves to the basic structure and implementation of ADO as a practical means of using the powerful OLE DB technology. After the basics of ADO are presented, the different types of data that can be accessed with ADO are detailed. This discussion begins by using ADO to access traditional ODBC data sources and extends to nontraditional data sources such as Microsoft Index Server data. This section concludes with the use of ADO on the Web, concentrating on the use of RDS to marshal sets of data to a client application over the Internet.

The second part covers the practical use of ADO in conjunction with Microsoft's Windows NT middle-tier services. It begins by taking a step back to detail the basics of distributed client/server architecture, development with COM/DCOM and the Visual Studio set of tools. Then the individual discussion will cover two of these essential server-side services—Microsoft Transaction Server (MTS) and Microsoft Message Queue Server (MSMQ). These areas will begin with a look at MTS's ability to manage multiple requests for server resources and allow normal, COM-based solutions to operate at new performance thresholds. This discussion moves to the ability to create both component and database transactions with MTS, which gives developers the opportunity to create a new generation of truly robust data management solutions. Since these transactions are so crucial to large database implementations, this section also details the transaction monitoring tools that MTS provides. The MTS section ends with a discussion of using MTS to implement exacting levels of security in a business application.

As powerful as Transaction Server is, it does make some bold assumptions as to the state of its environment. For instance, it assumes that both client and server are available at all times, and that both are running the same operating system. That's a fair assumption in most cases, but there are circumstances when this might not be possible. And that's where the technology of message queuing can be utilized. Microsoft Message Queue Server provides message queuing capabilities to connectionless and even disparate systems to bridge the communication gap that can be left by networks and offline applications.

The last section of the book ties the first two together in a powerful, reusable, real-world example, amplified by discussions of using these two technologies to create optimized application architectures. It begins with a general discussion of the methodologies that must be used to expose efficiencies of MTS-based database access and its practical uses. The discussion turns to lengthy code examples that show the powerful combination of COM and ADO implemented in business applications. This section illustrates the advantages of working with COM and ADO, as well as the challenges inherent to its implied object-relational mapping.

Chapter Outlines

Chapter 1 begins by looking at where ADO fits into Microsoft's plan to provide universal data access to all levels of application development and how OLE DB aids in that endeavor. Next, the object model of ADO is overviewed as a guide to those without prior knowledge of data access objects.

In Chapter 2, we take a much more in-depth look at the basics of the object model to facilitate learning the more advanced ADO features described throughout the book. You'll start by performing simple tasks such as opening an ADO connection and using the OLE DB provider. Gradually, the topics become more advanced to include working with ADO 2.0 events and asynchronous operations.

Chapter 3 proves that the ADO Recordset object is worthy of a chapter of its own. New features introduced with the release of version 2.0, like disconnected Recordsets and persisting Recordset data locally, are covered, using plenty of Visual Basic and ASP examples. These features alone make ADO a much more powerful, yet flexible client/server data access tool because they give you the ability to offload some server processing to another tier.

With the basics under your belt, Chapter 4 broadens your ADO knowledge by explaining ADO's "unusual" capabilities, such the capability to build and maintain database structures, including tables, indexes, and stored procedures, and to tap into nontraditional data sources like Microsoft Index Server. You'll learn how similar it is to query either the hierarchical file system of your company's intranet or a relational database like SQL Server. The key lies in that ADO, in conjunction with OLE DB, provides a layer of abstraction that enables you to use the same interface no matter what type of data you need to access.

In Chapter 5 you'll learn about Remote Data Services (RDS), a variant of ADO that allows data communication over HTTP, the protocol on the Internet. RDS also allows client-side caching of data and the ability to invoke server-side COM components from the client, two features that enable your Web applications to enjoy the same power as traditional client/server applications.

After five chapters of ADO, you'll be itching to start developing a large scale client/server application using your new found skills. But you won't need your ADO skills for Chapter 6, because it, the start of the second part of the book, is required reading to lay the foundation of the concepts necessary to achieve the book's goal. After a backgrounder on *n*-tier component development and COM/DCOM, we provide an overview of MTS and MSMQ to whet your appetite for the next two chapters.

Chapter 7 is an in depth look at MTS, Microsoft's answer to the lack of a transaction monitor on the PC level. You'll learn how MTS, in conjunction with ADO, solves the performance and server resource problems typically faced by distributed applications. You also learn how MTS simplifies the developer's role by abstracting the complexity inherent to these types of applications. A sample sales order entry system is developed with Visual Basic and SQL Server to illustrate how business objects created under MTS differ from traditional "stateful" objects.

Chapter 8 examines how to add message queuing functionality to the MTS-enabled component application developed in Chapter 7. The chapter begins with a discussion of the need for connectionless communication with guaranteed delivery and the role it plays in solving today's business problems. You then are shown how to manage queues, send and receive messages, and trap for errors.

Chapter 9 begins the third and final part of the book. This is where you can apply much of what you've learned about building a distributed application with ADO. A description of an application framework is presented first, followed by the start of the development of a sophisticated ADO-based and MTS-enabled application.

While the earlier chapters focused on the concepts of the technologies, Chapter 10 is chockful of novel ideas, proven techniques, and the source code to back them up. We encourage you to steal whatever you can carry! It is here that you learn about using ADO and MTS to retrieve, add, update, and delete data using production-ready code. This chapter also describes how optimistic and pessimistic locking can be implemented in a distributed system, with a stateless server. Chapter 11 follows by covering the common implementation of complex issues such as parent-child object relationships and transaction processing.

Who Should Read This Book?

Modesty (and the desire for a clear conscience) prevents us from saying that this book is a must-read for every man, woman, and child walking the Earth. So, royalties notwithstanding, the fact is that this book was written for a specific, yet growing audience, which includes:

- Professional client/server application developers who, like the authors, have been struggling with fledgling data access technology and eagerly awaiting the advancements that ADO and the Microsoft Windows NT Services represent. Ideally, this group will have some knowledge of an object-based programming language, such as Visual Basic, COM technology, and client/server architecture. However, we consider only a cursory understanding of Visual Basic and COM a prerequisite for understanding the concepts presented.

- Mainframe developers who would like to learn how to create large-scale, client/server applications on the PC level, a departure from the traditional host-based architecture.

- XBase, Access, and other PC programming language developers who have been creating departmental file/server applications and would like to learn how make them scale like never before, while leveraging their ability to work with relational data.

Because the technologies covered in this book can be used from any application development language that supports COM objects, it is also valuable to developers from a large number of backgrounds. In short, *Building Distributed Applications with ADO* is of interest to any developer who wishes to work with data under the Microsoft platform.

Road Map for Readers

If you are already a seasoned COM-based application developer using ADO and are just interested in learning the new technologies now available to you, you might consider Chapter 1 and part of Chapter 2 to be light reading as they cover the basics of ADO. Aside from that, every other chapter offers enough fresh ideas in application development that we would not recommend glossing over any one of them.

What Tools Will You Need?

This book utilizes several Microsoft development tools and operating system services. They are listed here separately, but many of them can be obtained through the installation of Visual Studio 6.0 (developer tools) and the Windows NT 4 Option Pack (server-side services). From a cost standpoint, we recommend a Microsoft Developer Network (MSDN) subscription if you can afford one. The quarterly updates, beta products, and international versions make it well worth the investment. Consult the following Web site for more details: msdn.microsoft.com/developer.

To follow the book's examples, you will need the following software: MS Windows NT Server (or Workstation) 4.0, ADO 2.01+, MS Visual Basic 5.0+, MS SQL Server 6.5+, and the MS Windows NT 4.0 Option Pack. (Note: Windows NT 5 will ship bundled with these tools, so the Option Pack will no longer be necessary.)

From the Option Pack, install the following tools: Internet Explorer 5.0+, MS Transaction Server 2.0, Internet Information Server 4.0+ (includes Active Server Pages 1.0+), MS Message Queue Server 1.0+, and Microsoft Index Server.

What's on the Web Site?

The *Building Distributed Applications with ADO* Web site contains the complete set of Visual Basic and ASP source code presented in the book, as well as any future updates or errata. The address is: www.wiley.com/compbooks/martiner.

Summary

This book was written by professional developers for professional developers. It's the kind of book we'd add to our own libraries, because it answers the question: How do we make sense of all of the tools available to build powerful, scalable Windows applications? We hope that you'll view ADO, COM, and the Windows NT Services as we do: essential tools for developing sophisticated, yet maintainable applications into the twenty-first century.

PART
One

Unleashing ActiveX
Data Objects

It's time to get out of the starting gate and running. You'll do that in this part of the book by beginning with OLE DB and ADO. ADO has been around for a while; almost two years to be exact. In that time it has matured from infancy into a credible set of data access interfaces that can be used for all kinds of application development. While this book is about developing distributed applications, you'll first drill down into ADO so you have a foundation for its usage in larger application contexts. Below is a summary of each chapter in Part 1.

A Roadmap for Your Journey

Chapter 1: OLE DB, A Blueprint for Data Access. In Chapter 1, you'll find out Microsoft's vision for universal data access and how it impacts all levels of application development. You'll receive a general understanding of OLE DB, which provides the underlying system-level interfaces to ADO. Further, you'll scratch the surface of ADO by learning about the ADO object model and the purpose of each ADO object. If you're new to OLE DB and ADO, this chapter will provide you with good background information as you go on to learn ADO in the following chapters. If you've already worked with ADO, then you may want to consider this chapter a light read if you're familiar with the concepts discussed.

Chapter 2: Learning ADO Basics. In Chapter 2, you'll get out of the starting gate. Here you'll learn about not all, but the essential, yet basic features of each ADO object. You'll explore topics as simple as opening an ADO Connection, using OLE DB providers, and more complex topics such as working with ADO 2.0

events and asynchronous operations. If you're new to ADO, this chapter gets you off the ground with ADO; without it, you'll flounder in a sea of code. If you've worked with ADO already, you'll find some material in this chapter familiar. However, the chapter is full of information that applies to ADO 2.0 and operations of which you may not be aware.

Chapter 3: Getting the Most Out of Recordsets. In Chapter 3, you'll explore the robust feature set of the ADO Recordset. While you learned Recordset basics in Chapter 2, here you'll learn about the not so basic. The discussion in Chapter 3 involves features that are entirely new to the ADO Recordset. You'll explore features such as disconnecting Recordsets from a Connection, using XML with ADO, and how to persist Recordset data. Many of the features you'll explore will be shown in the context of a variety of scenarios from client/server Visual Basic development to examples of the Recordset on the Web with Active Server Pages and DHTML. The playing field is leveled in this chapter since most of the discussion revolves around ADO 2.0 features. If you're novice or experienced, you'll be ready to take advantage of exciting ADO 2.0 features after digesting this chapter.

Chapter 4: Unusual ADO: Executing DDL with ADOX and Using ADO with Non-traditional Data Sources. In this chapter, you'll expand your understanding of using ADO to create and maintain a database and to query information from the Microsoft Index Server Provider. First, you will see how extender objects to ADO can be used to build tables and indexes. Then you'll examine how applications built using Microsoft Index Server rely on using familiar ADO objects. At the same time, however, you'll learn about what to be aware of when using less traditional OLE DB providers.

Chapter 5: Using Remote Data Services in Web Applications. In Chapter 5, you'll learn about Remote Data Services (RDS) and its role in World Wide Web applications. Essentially, RDS is a technology that allows client-side caching of data and the ability to invoke server-side COM components from the client. Whether novice or experienced, you'll benefit from generous code examples and clear explanation about the advantages and disadvantages of RDS.

OLE DB, a Blueprint for Data Access

If you are a person who likes change, it's an exciting time to be an application developer. Every developer in the IT industry, regardless of whose technology he or she uses to build applications, stands awed by the speed at which new technology enters the landscape.

The same is true for Microsoft developers, particularly in the area of data access technologies. Many, especially those who use Visual Basic as a development tool, have used Microsoft's Data Access Objects (DAO) and Remote Data Objects (RDO) to handle the data access portions of their application development. Of course, many other means of data access exist as well, such as ODBC API-based libraries and third-party data access components. Wouldn't it be nice if there were only one data access tool for all application development? That's right, a single set of interfaces for accessing data from diverse sources; a single set of interfaces that you the developer could learn and continue to use to deepen your understanding as you work on project after project.

That's precisely the vision behind Microsoft's Universal Data Access strategy. Actually, this is not a new strategy; it was developed over two years ago. But in the future, more developers will be using tools that take advantage of Microsoft's Universal Data Access strategy. This strategy will necessitate that you learn a new set of interfaces for accessing data. But once you do, you can breathe a sigh of relief because your investment is in rich and powerful tools that will be championed by Microsoft for years to come.

Universal Data Access

Some years ago, someone (probably in Redmond, Washington, Microsoft's home) coined the phrase "data access for the masses" to describe Microsoft's Universal Data

Access strategy. Perhaps it alluded to the bygone open-door immigration policy of the United States when the country opened its door to the "huddled masses" from abroad. Whether the allusion was purposeful or not, Universal Data Access represents an open-door policy for vendors, developers, and customers to benefit from enterprise applications that utilize diverse data sources.

Behind this strategy are some assumptions rooted in the idea that technology should give business strategic, competitive advantages. After all, what good is technology if it doesn't allow business to function smarter and more efficiently?

Throughout the 1980s and 1990s, as PC-based application development grew, it produced a new landscape for the storage of data. It is not uncommon for corporate and even midsized businesses to store critical information in a variety of places, including file-system databases, data servers such as Oracle or SQL Server, mainframe storage mediums and even less robust storage structures such as e-mail systems, spreadsheets, and the like.

How many midsized businesses and even departments within corporations have mission-critical data stored in spreadsheets while other information is located in a variety of databases? The numbers might surprise us. Despite attempts at standardization, the speed of conducting business and the overall evolution of PC-based application development produced this situation.

Continuing today, businesses have still more diverse means of storing information that is critical to their enterprises. Many users need access to information from remote locations. Also, the complexity of information used for presentation continues to grow. So the reality in the marketplace today is this: Most businesses utilize *diverse* sources for the storage of their data.

Leave the Data Where It Lives

With this in mind, one of the major aims of Universal Data Access is to allow businesses to continue to use their diverse mediums of data storage. Universal Data Access does not imply that businesses should migrate their data to a common data store. Quite the contrary! It means that Microsoft will provide businesses with the technology they need to access data from any storage medium. This is a powerful and unique concept, one that is in direct contrast with competing data access technologies based on the notion that corporations must migrate their data to a common store so it can be presented in the desired fashion.

The ability to access data from diverse sources is achieved by you the developer when you use ActiveX Data Objects (ADO). ADO is a set of Component Object Model (COM) interfaces that give you a robust capability to do all your data manipulation tasks: create cursors of numerous different types, handle transactions, execute and create stored procedures, and much more. This set of ADO interfaces is remarkably lean, yet powerful. And the message to you is this: Use this set of interfaces for all your data access needs. Don't worry about learning another ODBC API-based library or another third-party vendor's data access objects. All you need is ADO for all your projects.

Furthermore, Universal Data Access is broad in its implementation. Its end product is not just a set of COM objects, but much more. It is a platform, services, and developer tool initiative. Look for more Microsoft developer tools to seamlessly integrate ADO into their respective products. We see this in Visual Basic 6.0 with the incorporation of improved data-bound technology and the inclusion of technologies like Data Classes. Also, Visual Studio 6.0 includes an ADO-based Data Environment, an object-based environment that uses ADO for rapid design-time development and runtime data access. Moreover, look for other Microsoft system services to take advantage of ADO, such as COM and extended services for Internet development.

Then consider the practical implications of Universal Data Access:

- You can tell your clients that there is no need to absorb the cost of migrating portions of their enterprise data for presentation purposes. You can tell them that they will save money by investing in your firm's technical expertise.

- You and your clients will enjoy a technology that includes growing industry support, and that will be a major part of Microsoft's vision for years to come. Furthermore, it is a technology that does not lock your clients into a vendor's limited, proprietary set of interfaces. Since Universal Data Access is implemented through COM, you have a set of generic, open interfaces with which to work.

- You can expect to take advantage of Universal Data Access when you use just about any Microsoft developer tool because Universal Data Access is also a developer tool initiative, not just a data access initiative.

- You can apply this technology to numerous application development contexts. Since Universal Data Access is implemented as a set of COM objects, you can use it for Web-based application development as well as file server and tiered, client/server development.

- You can reduce your learning curve for doing data access because you learn ADO once and then deepen your understanding as you work with it over time.

- Universal Data Access also recognizes your client's two most important requirements: reliability and performance. You can assure your clients that the technology you are using is reliable and optimized for small and large applications alike.

OLE DB, the Blueprint

So what exactly is OLE DB and how does it fit into the Universal Data Access strategy? Just as an architectural blueprint specifies how a housing developer is to build a house, OLE DB is a blueprint or specification that defines how Microsoft data access works. Specifically, the OLE DB specification is characterized by the following:

- OLE DB exists as a system-level programming interface in much the same way as its forerunner, the ODBC API.

- OLE DB is an open specification designed to build on the success of ODBC by providing an open standard for accessing all kinds of data. Whereas ODBC was created to access relational databases, OLE DB is designed to access any data store. For example, you can use it to access relational and nonrelational data sources, including mainframe, ISAM/VSAM, and hierarchical databases. And you can access less traditional file storage systems such as e-mail systems and file-system stores such as text, graphical data, and more.

- OLE DB defines a collection of COM interfaces that encapsulate various database management system services (more on these later).

In practice, however, the blueprint metaphor falls a bit short. Not only does OLE DB define how Universal Data Access works, it is also the underlying set of interfaces that make it work. Much could be written about the underlying programming interface of OLE DB, but the focus of this part of the book is to teach you about the practical nature of working with ADO.

With this in mind, let's take a brief look at the architecture of OLE DB. As you do so, you'll learn about the basic components that make OLE DB work. Again, chapters could be written on the internal functionality and relationships of OLE DB components, and in the next section, you'll be exposed to the foundational knowledge that a developer should understand. For those of you with a burning desire to learn more, you can find a fuller explanation of OLE DB components at www.microsoft.com/data/oledb.

Universal Data Access Architecture

OLE DB's system-level interfaces are implemented as COM objects that provide data management services. When you hear that OLE DB is a platform initiative, this is what it means. These interfaces enable you to create or use other software components that implement the Universal Data Access platform.

While OLE DB interfaces provide the core data access management services at a system level, ADO exposes application-level interfaces that are derived from OLE DB interfaces. ADO, based on Automation, is a database programming model that allows developers to write applications over OLE DB data from any language, including VB, Java, VBScript, JavaScript, and C/C++.

OLE DB services are provided through three types of components: data providers, services, and consumers (Figure 1.1). Each plays a unique role in an OLE DB application.

Data Providers

Data providers are components that represent data sources such as relational databases, ISAM files, spreadsheets, and more. Providers expose information uniformly, using a common abstraction called the Rowset. The OLE DB Rowset is a system-level interface that is capable of exposing the functionality derived from the provider (Figure 1.2). Herein lies part of the power of OLE DB. Diverse providers each have different storage structures and data manipulation capabilities. Think of the differences between a simple text file and the file structure and capabilities of an RDBMS system. Yet each provider exposes its functionality to a common OLE DB interface, the Rowset. So, how much functionality must a provider expose? Must a provider for a text file provide all the robust functionality necessary for an RDBMS? No! Each provider exposes as much functionality as makes sense for that provider. The exposed functionality manifests itself in a Rowset.

This is not as simple as it sounds, so OLE DB incorporates the use of Service components that play a key role in how a common interface can be derived from diverse providers.

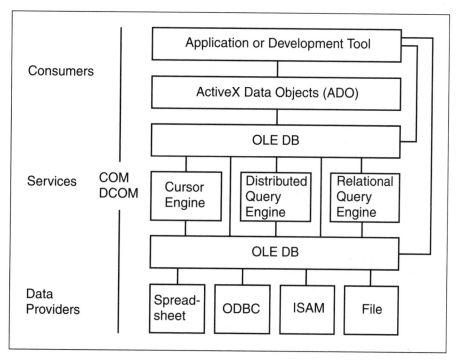

Figure 1.1 OLE DB components fall into three categories: data providers, services, and consumers.

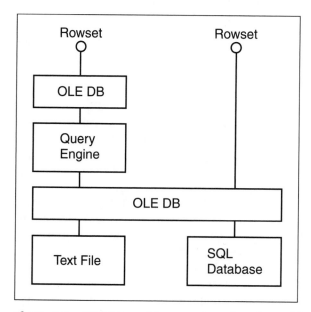

Figure 1.2 OLE DB provides a common interface while maintaining the ability to access diverse data providers.

Services

Providing a common interface to diverse data providers that contain mission-critical data is not an easy task. As an application developer, you want a common interface, so that when you work with differing data providers, you can use the "common" interface with all its properties, methods, and events that you're accustomed to. So how can common interfaces expose the appropriate functionality for diverse providers?

The answer is relatively simple, in concept anyway. Service components are used to extend the natural functionality exposed by a provider, so you can understand service components as an extension to a provider. For example, Figure 1.2 shows how an OLE DB query engine (service component) is used by OLE DB to expose a Rowset for a simple text provider. By using the query engine as a service component, the resulting Rowset contains all of the robust functionality that the application requires, without imposing high overhead on the provider itself. However, OLE DB does not force you to use service components for providers that expose more robust functionality.

In its role as an extender of functionality, service components themselves are both providers and consumers. They are providers in that they are used by OLE DB to expose data (in the sense of object properties and methods) in the form of a Rowset. They are a consumer in that they consume OLE DB data from data providers. Let's summarize:

- Service components are extenders for OLE DB providers.

- Service components are used by OLE DB to expose the proper, robust functionality you require, even when the provider itself may lack the required functionality.

- Service components are used by OLE DB as both a consumer and provider. They consume common interfaces from OLE DB data providers, so they can provide extended functionality to other consumers.

Why is there a need to extend anything? What needs extending? Remember, data providers expose only the functionality that makes sense for the provider within an accepted, standard minimum set of functionality.

Specifying the level of functionality as limited to the collective functionality among all possible data providers does not give you a very rich data access API. Further, this approach limits the ability of the data provider to expose innovative extensions natively. On the other hand, requiring a rich level of functionality would force a simple data store (such as a text file) to implement, in full or in part, a relational engine on top of its data, such as ODBC requires. Such barriers would prevent many types of simple data from participating in universal data access.

This makes OLE DB attractive for the data provider, but we can't stop there. In order to be generic, the application would have to be filled with extensive conditional code to verify whether a particular set of functionality was supported. In many cases, the application would be forced to implement extensions internally to compensate for data stores that could not support extended functionality natively.

As you've seen, to solve this problem, Universal Data Access provides a component architecture that allows individual, specialized components to implement discrete sets of database functionality, or "services," on top of providers. Thus, rather than forcing each data store to provide its own implementation of extended functionality, or forcing generic applications to implement database functionality internally, service components provide a common implementation that any application can use when accessing any data store. The fact that some functionality is implemented natively by the data store, and some through service components, is transparent to the application.

Consumers

This brings us to the next concept, consumers. A consumer is any piece of system or application code that consumes an OLE DB interface. This includes OLE DB components themselves (typically, service components) and ADO components. For example, the native OLE DB Rowset object provides the underlying interface to create a cursor from a data source. In order to work with a Rowset, you may create an ADO Recordset object. Once the Recordset is created, you could use it to fetch rows, update rows, and the like. In this capacity, the ADO Recordset acts as a data consumer, because it consumes the underlying OLE DB Rowset's interface (Figure 1.3).

Component Cooperation

Part of the genius of OLE DB is its component-based nature, which provides very efficient, flexible application development models. OLE DB accomplishes this by its component-based services model. Rather than having a prescribed number of intermediary layers between the application and the data, OLE DB requires only as many components

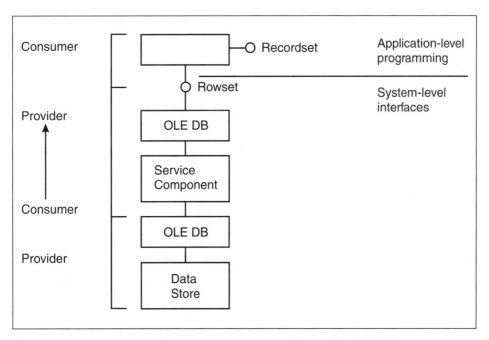

Figure 1.3   An ADO Recordset acts as a consumer of the native OLE DB Rowset.

as are needed to accomplish a particular task. Consider the ways in which OLE DB can stretch to accommodate four possible scenarios.

- The data lives in an RDBMS, for which there currently exists an ODBC driver, but no native OLE DB Provider. Fortunately, the application uses ADO to communicate with the OLE DB Provider for ODBC, which then loads the appropriate ODBC driver. The driver passes the SQL statement to the DBMS, which retrieves the data.

- The data lives in SQL Server 7.0 or another data source, for which there is a native OLE DB Provider. The application uses ADO to talk directly to the OLE DB Provider for Microsoft SQL Server.

- The data resides in Microsoft Exchange Server, for which there is an OLE DB Provider, but which does not expose an engine to process SQL queries. Remember, according to OLE DB, the provider should not have to implement functionality too robust for its type of data. So, the application uses ADO to talk to the Microsoft Exchange data provider and calls upon an OLE DB query processor component to handle the querying.

- The data resides in the Windows NT file system in the form of documents. Data is accessed using a native OLE DB Provider over Microsoft Index Server, which indexes the content and properties of documents in the file system to enable efficient content searches.

In each of these scenarios, ADO, in conjunction with OLE DB components, were able to satisfy the query requirements of an application. And in each case, the data remained in its original database or storage medium.

Putting Theory to Work

The preceding just scratched the surface of OLE DB architecture. There are a number of OLE DB system-level components that are used in addition to the Rowset mentioned. If you were involved in the business of writing your own data providers and/or service components, a much deeper look into OLE DB components would be of prime importance. However, this part of the book is about how developers can use ADO to build applications. As you've just seen, ADO acts as a consumer of OLE DB interfaces, such as the Rowset shown in Figure 1.3.

At this point, it's important that you understand a number of things about OLE DB, so that you can appreciate to a further extent how rich ADO is. Let's review some key points:

- Because OLE DB does not impose a strenuous set of expectations for providers, they can expose common interfaces. These common interfaces also remain consistent and uniform for you, the ADO developer. This means that your learning curve is short—especially if you've worked with DAO or RDO—and that your investment will prove to be well worth your while as you use common ADO interfaces time and again.

- Because extended provider functionality is furnished through service components that are transparent to the application programming interface, you, the ADO developer, can write code for applications that use or do not use service components with the same ease.

- Because OLE DB data access is implemented as a component technology, applications can quickly, and with minimal difficulty, be changed to access other data stores.

- Because OLE DB components take care of the lower-level database access tasks, you can focus your energy on the custom requirements of the application.

Comparing DAO, RDO, and ADO

Many Microsoft developers have used DAO and RDO objects. If you've used either, you will certainly find many similarities with ADO properties and methods. Clearly, as ADO was engineered, the former object models were considered. So, those of you who have used DAO and/or RDO will find the move to ADO a fairly easy process. But even if you have not used DAO or RDO, you'll find that learning ADO is not a daunting task.

You may, however, be asking: Why start using ADO if I haven't before? One good reason, already mentioned, is that ADO is *the* data access object into which Microsoft will pour its energy for the foreseeable future. Microsoft will no longer make any significant enhancements to either the DAO or RDO models. In fact, since the release of Visual Basic 5.0 in March 1997 (when RDO 2 was released), Microsoft has continued to embellish only ADO. Also, ADO is positioned to be a reliable and powerful development tool for all sorts of projects from desktop productivity databases to multitiered applications.

ADO 2.0 represents the third release of the product. The first exposed basic client/server functionality and introduced developers to the world of OLE DB through the OLE DB Provider for ODBC. It was targeted at developers who used Active Server Pages in Web applications. ADO 1.5, the next major release (which shipped with IIS 4.0 and Internet Explorer 4.0) focused on integration of RDS. It added some of the features that developers missed from RDO 2.0. The feature set of ADO 2.0 is designed to provide for the data access needs of the developer using Visual Studio. ADO 2.0 implements or exposes the most interesting features of RDO 2.0 and adds others that users have not seen in the past.

Finally, both DAO and RDO are implemented over ODBC, which means that they are limited to accessing SQL data sources. On the other hand, since ADO is based on the OLE DB specification, the ADO object model can be used to access non-SQL sources. Figure 1.4 shows how ADO differs from DAO and RDO with respect to dependence on ODBC. ADO can use ODBC to access SQL data sources if no OLE DB data provider is available for that source. However, with the supply of more providers all the time, straight ADO/OLE DB data access is being more fully realized.

Getting to Know ADO

As mentioned already, you'll find that working with ADO is easy because, essentially, it is a fairly slim set of COM objects that act as consumers over OLE DB data. Each object

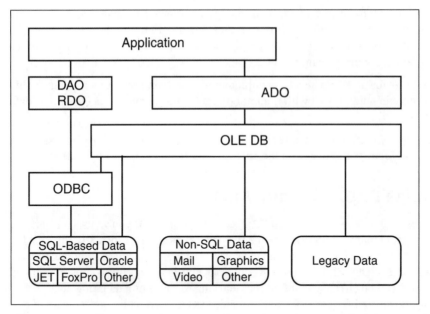

Figure 1.4 Unlike DAO and RDO, ADO is not dependent on ODBC for accessing a data source.

has a unique purpose and noncomplex sets of properties, methods, and events. Though these objects are not terribly complex, you'll find them to be extremely powerful.

Since its release in early 1997, the overall ADO object model has not changed much, but with each release, Microsoft makes each of the objects more robust by adding new properties and methods, and by making existing interfaces more stable and capable.

Let's take a look at the ADO object model and the purpose of each object. As you can see in Figure 1.5, the ADO object model is fairly simple; there are only a handful of objects to master. The objects are implemented in a nonstrict object collection hierarchy. The topmost object, the ADO Connection, contains an Errors collection, which in turn contains Error objects. The Connection also contains Command objects, each of which contains a Parameters collection that contains Parameter objects. The Connection object also contains Recordset objects, each of which maintains a Fields collection that houses Field objects.

 The ADO object model also contains a Properties collection that belongs to the Connection, Command, Recordset, and Field objects. The Properties collection and Property objects will be discussed in the next chapter.

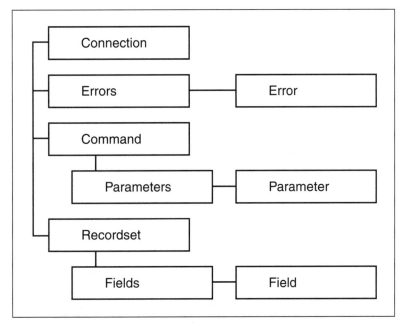

Figure 1.5   The ADO object model is a simple, yet powerful object hierarchy for data access.

The Connection Object

The Connection object has one primary purpose: to enable you to open a connection to a data source. A Connection object represents a unique session (an underlying OLE DB interface) with a data source. With the Connection object, you can access simple data sources such as files on a server or more robust sources like an RDBMS system. Since the Connection object has a fairly narrow function, it has few collections, properties, and methods. You'll explore the use of those properties and methods in the next chapter, but for now it's important to understand that, practically speaking, the Connection object gives you, the programmer, several benefits:

- It allows you to open a connection to a data source with the Open method.

  For SQL data sources that do not have an OLE DB Provider, connections can be opened using the OLE DB Provider for ODBC.

  For SQL and non-SQL data sources that do have a specific OLE DB Provider, connections can be opened using the provider for that data source.

- It allows you to execute SQL statements or stored procedures with the Execute method.

- It allows you to establish transactions for data updates with the use of the transaction methods BeginTrans, CommitTrans, and RollbackTrans.

In the following code example, the Open method establishes a connection to a SQL server database using an ODBC DSN.

```
Sub ConnectionExample()

    Dim objConn as ADODB.Connection
    Set objConn = New ADODB.Connection

    'Open a Connection

    objConn.Open "DSN=ADOBook", "sa", ""

    'Find out if the attempt to connect worked.

    If objConn.State = adStateOpen Then
        'Connection succeeded
    Else
        'Connection failed - handle appropriately
    End If

    'Close the connection and destroy it

    objConn.Close
    Set objConn = Nothing

End Sub
```

 The preceding code example and subsequent examples were written in Visual Basic.

The Errors Collection and Error Object

When you work with ADO objects, you can cause provider errors. As each error occurs, one or more Error objects are placed in the Errors collection. When another ADO operation generates an error, the Errors collection is cleared, and the new set of Error objects are placed in the Errors collection. You use the Error objects to provide the proper error trapping for your application.

It's important to understand that the errors that are supplied to the Errors collection are provider errors—errors specific to the provider being used. This is different from runtime errors that can occur. Runtime errors are not returned to the Errors collection, but to the exception-handling means that your application provides, such as the Err object in Visual Basic. For example, if you wrote some code that was navigating through a Recordset and you tried to read a field value, when the Recordset contained no records, an ADO error would result and be passed to the runtime handler.

The following code shows a loop that enumerates Error objects in the Errors collection, providing useful debugging information via Error object properties. Later, you'll

examine more code and an approach to using the Errors collection for handling antici-
pated and unanticipated data provider errors.

```
Sub ErrorsCollectionExample()

    Dim objConn As ADODB.Connection
    Dim colErrs As ADODB.Errors
    Dim objError As ADODB.Error
    Dim strError As String

    Set objConn = New ADODB.Connection

    On Error GoTo Error_ErrorsCollectionExample

    'Try and open a connection using a DSN that doesn't exist.
    'This will produce a provider reported error

    objConn.Open "MissingDSN", "sa", ""

Exit_ErrorsCollectionExample:
    Exit Sub

Error_ErrorsCollectionExample:

    'Loop through each Error object in the Errors collection
    'and display properties

    Set colErrs = objConn.Errors
    For Each objError In colErrs
        With objError
            Debug.Print .SQLState
            Debug.Print .NativeError
            Debug.Print .Description
        End With
    Next

End Sub
```

The Command Object

You'll find that the Command object is one of the most useful ADO objects. With it, you
can do a number of necessary and powerful tasks:

- Execute SQL statements or stored procedures. This is particularly important
  since queries that modify data, when executed in this fashion, do not require the
  overhead of a cursor (Recordset).

- Define and execute parameterized queries that use input and output parameters.

- Use a Command object to source a Recordset.

As you can see, you use the Command object for a variety of data manipulation tasks. It is an easy-to-learn object interface. In the next code sample, the Execute method of a Command object updates a table in a SQL Server database.

```
Sub CommandExample()

    Dim objCommand As New ADODB.Command

    'In this example, set the command object connection using
    'a connection string

    objCommand.ActiveConnection = "DSN=ADOBook;UID=sa;PWD=;"

    'Set the command text and specify that it
    'is a SQL statement

    objCommand.CommandText = "INSERT INTO Customers " & _
        "(cuCustID, cuCompanyName) VALUES " & _
        "(10057, 'Any Company')"
    objCommand.CommandType = adCmdText

    'Execute the command
    objCommand.Execute

End Sub
```

The Parameters Collection and Parameter Object

Many providers support parameterized commands. These are commands where the desired action is defined once, but parameters are used to alter some details of the command. For example, a SQL SELECT statement could use a parameter to define the matching criteria of a WHERE clause.

You can use a Parameter object to define input parameters, but you can also use it to return output values. For example, if you wanted to query the database to find the GPA of a student based on his or her ID number, you could execute a stored procedure with a Command object and return the GPA in a Parameter object. Using Command and Parameter objects in this fashion is powerful and more efficient than doing the same operation with a Recordset.

In the next example, an input parameter is used to restrict the rows returned when a Command is executed. The filtered rows are returned to a Recordset. In the next chapter, you will learn about the use of parameters for both input and output operations.

```
Sub ParameterExample()

    Dim objCommand As New ADODB.Command
    Dim objRecordset As New ADODB.Recordset
    Dim objParameter As ADODB.Parameter
```

```
'Set the command object connection using a connection
'string

objCommand.ActiveConnection = "DSN=ADOBook;UID=sa;PWD=;"

'Set the command text and specify that it
'is a stored procedure

 objCommand.CommandText = "StoredProcedureName"
 objCommand.CommandType = adCmdStoredProc

'Create a parameter for the stored procedure

Set objParameter = _
    objCommand.CreateParameter("ParamName", adInteger, _
    adParamInput, , 50)
objCommand.Parameters.Append objParameter

'Create a recordset by executing the parameterized command

Set objRecordset = objCommand.Execute

'Loop through the recordset and print the first field

Do While Not objRecordset.EOF
    Debug.Print objRecordset(0)
    objRecordset.MoveNext
Loop

'Close and destroy the recordset

objRecordset.Close
Set objRecordset = Nothing

End Sub
```

The Recordset Object and Fields

The Recordset is the most robust of all the ADO objects. It has two overall purposes:

- It allows you to retrieve row-based data (an in-memory cursor) from a data source so you can make the data available to some presentation sources such as a Web page or an application interface.

- It allows you to retrieve rows for data modification—editing, inserting, and deleting.

Though that doesn't sound very robust, and these two points may seem fairly simple, the Recordset is the most richly dressed of the ADO objects. It provides numerous properties, methods, and events that are geared at a full-featured object for presenting and modifying data.

In this example, the procedure creates a Recordset and enumerates the Fields collection.

```
Sub EnumerateFields()

    Dim objRecordset As ADODB.Recordset
    Dim objField As ADODB.Field

    Set objRecordset = New ADODB.Recordset

    'Open the recordset, specifying a SQL statement
    'and a connection string resulting in the creation
    'of an implicit connection

    objRecordset.Open "SELECT * FROM Customers", _
        "DSN=ADOBook;UID=sa;PWD=;"

    Debug.Print "Customer Fields:" & vbCr

    'Loop through each Field object in the
    'Fields collection and display some properties

    For Each objField In objRecordset.Fields
        Debug.Print "Name: " & objField.Name & vbCr & _
            "Type: " & objField.Type & vbCr & _
            "Value: " & objField.Value
    Next objField

    'Close the recordset and destroy it

    objRecordset.Close
    Set objRecordset = Nothing

End Sub
```

Yes, this example is simplistic, but don't let that skew your thoughts about the Recordset. ADO 2.0's Recordset object underwent significant changes with respect to its features. Here are some of the highlights you'll explore in Chapters 2 and 3:

- Opening Recordsets and using cursor types.

- Using Recordset sorting and filtering.

- Exploring standard and expanded data modification features.

- Using Recordset events and paging mechanisms.

- Disconnecting Recordsets from a connection and persisting Recordset data.

- Creating hierarchical Recordsets.

From Here

This chapter presented the vision for Universal Data Access, an overview of OLE DB architecture, and a brief introduction to ADO objects. As the code samples demonstrated, writing ADO code is not complex. The key to developing applications using ADO is to achieve a rich understanding of the ADO objects and the capabilities each brings to data access. In the next chapter, you will expand your understanding of these objects, learning about the most important properties and methods of each while you review application code that shows how to use the objects in a variety of scenarios.

Learning ADO Basics

So far, you've learned that OLE DB is the system-level interface for accessing diverse data stores. You've seen some of the OLE DB architecture. But, most important, you know that ADO is the application-level programming interface that can help you to meet the demands of all kinds of development. Whether you're programming middle-tier business objects, server-side scripting, or client applications, ADO should be used to meet your data access requirements.

You also were given a description of each ADO object and example code to show how easy it is to program COM objects (which, as mentioned, is what ADO objects are). In this and the next several chapters, you'll explore each of these objects in more detail. Along the way, you'll learn basic and advanced programming with these objects in a variety of scenarios.

What You'll Learn

In Chapter 1, you learned that OLE DB and ADO are not just a platform initiative but also a developer tool initiative. Therefore, as you read, keep in mind that this portion of the book aims primarily to teach about the practical usage of ADO objects. While tools like Visual Basic 6.0 incorporate the usage of ADO in its IDE (via data classes and the Data Environment), that is not the focus of this portion of the book. Our aim here is not to teach the details and nuances of working with specific developer tools. Our focus is to show you the details of working with ADO objects, and to enable you to master ADO itself so you can apply it to different development efforts and your work in multiple developer tools. If this is your initial foray into ADO, you'll benefit from clear, concise explanations. But even if you've used previous releases of ADO, you'll increase your understanding as well as learn about features new to ADO 2.0.

Specifically, you'll learn about each ADO object and essential features. Here, summarized, is what you can expect from this chapter:

Getting Connected. In this section, you'll learn how to open ADO Connections with and without DSNs. You'll see examples that use the Microsoft OLE DB Provider for ODBC and other providers. Further, you'll come to understand how the Connection object is useful for executing SQL statements and stored procedures. You'll explore the usage of the ADO's transaction methods, event model, and support for asynchronous operations.

Handling Errors. In this section, you'll explore the use of the Errors collection and the Error object. You'll learn the difference between ADO and provider errors and receive guidance on how to handle both types of errors in your applications.

Taking Command. In this section, you'll learn about the Command and Parameter objects, how to execute SQL statements and stored procedures, and how to use a Command to retrieve a cursor. You'll explore the use of Parameters to specify input criteria and retrieve output from stored procedures.

Using Recordsets: The Basics. In this section, you'll learn the essentials of Recordsets: how to open them and when to use specific cursor types. You'll explore how to navigate, sort, filter, and find specific records. You'll learn how to retrieve Recordset data in data pages. Finally, you'll learn how to modify Recordset data. (In Chapter 3, you'll extend your understanding of Recordsets by mastering intermediate and advanced Recordset features.)

Handling Binary Data with Recordsets. In this section, you'll learn how to store and retrieve large text and binary data using the AppendChunk and GetChunk methods of the Recordset's Field object. Essential to many different types of application development, this information will help you handle the manipulation of binary or large text data through ADO.

Getting Connected

The natural place to start in a chapter about data access is how you access a data source. Remember that the Connection object allows you to do this. Regardless of whether you're programming middle-tier business objects, scripting server-side ASP pages, or developing client applications, you must first establish a connection to a data source. In fact, whatever you're programming, you usually follow a common set of steps in your effort. Those steps start with establishing a connection.

1. *Connect to a data source.* Establish a connection to a data source using the appropriate provider.

2. *Optionally, create a command.* If appropriate, you can create a command that returns rows from the data source or updates rows with or without the use of parameters. Commands can be executed in the scope of transactions.

3. *Optionally, create a Recordset (cursor).* If the operation you're performing requires you to return rows for viewing or modification, creating a Recordset gives you robust capability.

4. *Handle errors.* Throughout the operations you perform, you can handle runtime errors via the Errors collection or the IDE's error-handling mechanism.

This list looks straightforward, but at each step, there is much to learn. Let's start with the first step, opening a connection.

Opening a Connection

The Connection object allows you to establish a physical connection to a data source by using the underlying OLE DB interfaces to establish an OLE DB session. When you use the Connection object, you always use a data provider for the data source you're trying to access. The data provider is a compiled set of interfaces that knows how to manage operations for a given data source. When ADO was first released, there were few data providers. The first available was the Microsoft OLE DB Provider for ODBC (MSDASQL). This provider uses OLE DB interfaces on top of ODBC for access to ODBC-compliant data sources. It can be used for access to SQL data sources for which no specific OLE DB provider exists (Figure 2.1). As time goes on, Microsoft and other vendors will produce more OLE DB providers for specific data sources, SQL data sources, and others. At the time of this writing, Microsoft had published a number of providers, and by the time you read this, more providers will certainly be available. Currently, some of the available providers include:

Microsoft OLE DB Provider for ODBC

Microsoft OLE DB Provider for Microsoft JET

Microsoft OLE DB Provider for Microsoft SQL Server

Microsoft OLE DB Provider for Microsoft Index Server

Microsoft OLE DB Provider for Oracle

Microsoft OLE DB Provider for Active Directory Service (ADS)

Microsoft OLE DB Text Provider

 In the following, you'll explore how to open a connection using the MSDASQL provider to access a SQL Server 6.5 database called OrderManager. The OrderManager database contains tables for Customers, Orders, OrderItems, and SalesReps. This database will be used throughout Part 1 of this book to illustrate ADO object features.

DSN-Based Connections

In the next code sample, a connection is opened using the MSDASQL provider and a physical system DSN. A system DSN, created in the ODBC Administrator, defines and

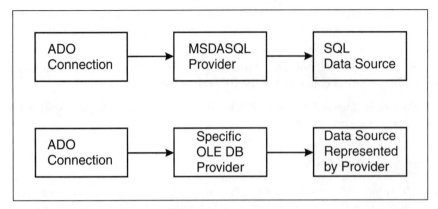

Figure 2.1   You can use the Microsoft OLE DB Provider for ODBC to access SQL data sources if no specific data provider exists.

then stores in the registry information pertinent to establishing a connection to the data source through ODBC.

```
Public Sub OpenWithDSN()

Dim objCnn As New ADODB.Connection
Dim objRst As New ADODB.Recordset

'Set Connection and Command Timeouts
'Defaults are 15 and 30 respectively

objCnn.ConnectionTimeout = 30
objCnn.CommandTimeout = 30
objCnn.Provider = "MSDASQL"

'Open the connection
objCnn.Open "DSN=ADOBook"


'Add code to create a Recordset from Execute method
Set objRst = objCnn.Execute("Select * From Customers")

'Close and destroy
objCnn.Close
Set objCnn = Nothing

End Sub
```

 Error-handling code has been omitted from the examples in this book for the sake of clarity. When the discussion involves specific error-handling techniques, error-handling code will be shown.

Declaring Object Variables

In the next sample, a connection object variable, objCnn, is declared and an instance is created.

```
'Early Binding
Dim objCnn As ADODB.Connection
Set objCnn = New ADODB.Connection
```

The ProgID of the ADO Connection type library (ADODB.Connection) is referenced to allow for *early binding* to the component. Early binding essentially means that the interfaces of a COM component can be referenced at design time. When using a developer tool such as Visual Basic that supports the use of early binding, you should use this approach to bind to objects, as opposed to *late binding*, which would mean declaring the variable not as an ADODB.Connection but, in this case, the generic Object type.

```
'Late binding
Dim objCnn as Object
Set objCnn = New ADODB.Connection
```

Or:

```
'Late binding
Dim objCnn as Object
Set objCnn = CreateObject("ADODB.Connection")
```

In other development contexts such as VBScript in an Active Server Page, a Connection object would be instanced this way.

```
'Active Server Page w/ VBScript

<% Set objCnn = Server.CreateObject("ADODB.Connection") %>
```

Setting Properties before Opening

Before you open a connection, you can set properties that control the behavior of the Connection object. These include the ConnectionTimeout, CommandTimeout, and Provider properties. You can see these in the next code sample, followed by a more detailed explanation.

```
objCnn.ConnectionTimeout = 30
objCnn.CommandTimeout = 30
objCnn.Provider = "MSDASQL"
```

ConnectionTimeout. Governs how long the application will wait trying to establish a connection to the data source once the Open method has been issued. You do not have to set this property, as it has a default value of 15 seconds. Indeed, in many cases, you may not have to set this property because the connection will be established in much less time. However, depending on the load placed on the server at the time the connection is being opened, it could take longer. Consider a Web application that uses Active Server script to open connections to a data source. Furthermore, consider that at some point in time a large number of users will access the server—all trying to establish connections. This scenario would certainly increase the time it would take to open connections, in which case setting the ConnectionTimeout to "too low" a number would adversely affect the user's experience. With this in mind, consider the demand placed on the server at peak times to determine a viable ConnectionTimeout.

CommandTimeout. Governs the time allotted for executing statements with the Connection objects' Execute method. The ADO Command object also has an Execute method and its own CommandTimeout property. Setting the CommandTimeout at the "connection level" does not mean that ADO Command objects created under the connection will inherit the connection level setting. While the CommandTimout default value is 30, consider increasing the value for commands that can take longer to execute under specific environment conditions.

Provider. You can specify the Provider property value prior to opening a connection, as shown. If you're intending to use the MSDASQL provider, then setting this property is of little value, because ADO uses this provider by default if no provider is otherwise specified. Also, the provider can be specified in the arguments for the Open method. In the following example, if you opened a connection without specifying the Provider property, ADO would still use the MSDASQL provider, and in this case, a DSN to open the connection.

```
Dim objCnn As New ADODB.Connection
Dim objRst As New ADODB.Recordset

'Set Connection and Command Timeouts
'Defaults are 15 and 30 respectively

objCnn.ConnectionTimeout = 30
objCnn.CommandTimeout = 30

'Open the connection - uses MSDASQL implicitly and
'DSN named ADOBook

objCnn.Open "DSN=ADOBook"
```

Additional properties that can be set prior to issuing the Open method include DefaultDatabase, CursorLocation, and ConnectionString. Some of these properties will be examined later.

Using the Open Method

As you know, you issue an Open method to establish the connection. The syntax of the Open method is fairly straightforward:

```
Object.Open [ConnectionString As String], [UserID As String], _
   [Password As String], [Options As Long = -1]
```

Specifying the ConnectionString. Each of the arguments the method takes is optional. Even the ConnectionString argument is optional because you could set the ConnectionString property prior to issuing the Open method, or if you like, specify it through the argument when opening the connection.

When you open a connection based on a file, user, or system DSN, the connection string must reference the DSN name, as shown here. The construction of DSNs for ODBC data sources differs. For example, a DSN for a SQL Server database will include the name of the server, whereas a DSN for a Microsoft JET database will reference the path of the .mdb file and other information pertaining only to a JET database.

```
objCnn.Open "DSN=ADOBook"
```

Specifying the UserID and Password. Often, the UserID and Password arguments are not needed because the DSN may define these, in which case they are redundant.

Specifying Options. You can use the Options argument to open the connection using an OpenOptionsEnum that, for example, would allow you to open a connection asynchronously. Later we'll explore asynchronous operations with ADO objects.

DSN-less Connections

Opening a connection based on a file, user, or system DSN can mean laborious maintenance issues for some applications. If you're developing a client application that opens connections from client workstations, the DSN that is referenced must exist on each client workstation. This means substantive maintenance overhead for the installation of the application. Even where script or business objects in a Web application open connections (on a server, not on a client workstation), a DSN-based connection means that the DSN must exist on the server.

Fortunately, ADO, like its predecessors DAO and RDO, affords you the opportunity to create DSN-less connections for an ODBC data source. In a DSN-less connection, the ConnectionString that you define incorporates all of the necessary information to open a connection without dependence on a registry entry or file. Next, you see an ADO connection that uses MSDASQL but with a DSN-less connection. The ConnectionString information is altered to provide the information that would have come from a stored DSN.

```
Public Sub OpenWithoutDSN()

Dim objCnn As ADODB.Connection
Dim strConnect As String
Set objCnn = New ADODB.Connection

'Set Connection and Command Timeouts
'Defaults are 15 and 30 respectively
```

(continues)

(Continued)

```
objCnn.ConnectionTimeout = 30
objCnn.CommandTimeout = 30

'Define connection string
strConnect = "Provider=MSDASQL;Driver={SQL " & _
    "Server};Server=DALA;UID=sa;Database=OrderManager;"

'Open the connection
objCnn.Open strConnect

End Sub
```

Using DSN-less connections for access to ODBC data sources has no real negative side affects—it does not even slow performance. In fact, it may speed performance somewhat because it bypasses the need for a registry lookup or file read. And, of course, its primary benefit is that you don't have to worry about the administration of creating DSNs on client workstations or servers.

Beyond the World of MSDASQL

Fortunately, MSDASQL is not the only provider in the world. If it were, the far-reaching vision of OLE DB would not be any grander than for ODBC. Providers for any number of ODBC and non-ODBC data sources already exist, as explained earlier. When using providers, including MSDASQL, you should understand that the overall functionality supported by the provider differs. Where one provider accepts certain features of Recordset manipulation, another may not. These peculiarities among providers are outlined in the documentation for the provider. Usually, it is at least partially documented and sometimes well documented.

Since each provider exposes somewhat different capabilities to the ADO programming model, how your application interacts with ADO objects will vary slightly between providers. The differences you need to be aware of usually fall into one of three categories:

- Connection arguments that make up the ConnectionString property
- The behavior of Command objects and their handling of Parameter objects
- The capabilities of Recordset objects

Getting Connected with the JET Provider

From a coding standpoint, opening a connection using a provider other than MSDASQL is simple. Next, a connection is opened to a Microsoft JET database called OrderManager.mdb, and a Recordset Fields collection is enumerated. This code uses the Microsoft OLE DB Provider for Microsoft JET.

```
Public Sub UseJetProvider()

Dim objCnn As New ADODB.Connection
```

```
Dim objRst As New ADODB.Recordset

With objCnn
    .CommandTimeout = 15
    .ConnectionTimeout = 15
    .Provider = "Microsoft.Jet.OLEDB.3.51"
    .Open "D:\Book\Code\OrderManager.mdb", "admin"
End With

objRst.Open "SELECT * FROM Customers", objCnn

Do While Not objRst.EOF
    Debug.Print objRst(1)
    objRst.MoveNext
Loop

objRst.Close
Set objRst = Nothing
objCnn.Close
Set objCnn = Nothing

End Sub
```

As you can see, you set the Provider property to Microsoft.Jet.OLEDB.3.51. The Open method contains the path to the .mdb file (for the ConnectionString argument) and the default JET password, "admin," for the UserID argument.

Using this provider implies that you do not need to load the resources of Microsoft DAO. Since the memory footprint of the Microsoft JET OLE DB provider is smaller than that of DAO, using this provider instead of DAO makes sense. You may also notice performance gains in some operations using ADO instead of DAO.

Getting Connected with the SQL Server Provider

You can use the MSDASQL provider to connect to a SQL Server database, but you can also use the Microsoft SQL Server OLE DB provider. When you examined the code for the JET provider, you saw that setting the Provider property referenced the provider. You can also set the provider value by setting the Provider argument of the Connection-String, as shown next. You refer to the SQL Server provider as SQLOLEDB. The Location argument specifies the name of the server; the Data Source argument supplies the name of the database.

```
Public Sub OpenWithSQLProvider()

Dim objCnn As New ADODB.Connection
Dim strConnect As String

strConnect = "Provider=SQLOLEDB;Location=DALA;" & _
    "Data Source=OrderManager;User ID=sa;Password=;"

objCnn.Open strConnect
```

(continues)

(Continued)

```
'Additional statements

'Close when finished
objCnn.Close
Set objCnn = Nothing

End Sub
```

Cleaning Up Shop

Whenever you use Connection objects, you should get in the habit of closing the connection when you are finished by using the Close method (as you've seen in the samples so far). Or you can use the Close method to reuse the same object variable for different connections. Similarly, the Recordset object has a Close method and can be used in a similar fashion. And to ensure that you release the memory overhead of ADO objects, you should also set them to Nothing when you are finished with them. (Note: Technically, you should not have to do this, since COM objects should release themselves from memory when they "go out of scope." But to be on the safe side, it's a good idea to explicitly destroy them.)

Executing Commands

The Connection object also affords you the ability to execute SQL statements or stored procedures with the Execute method. You can use the Execute method of the Command object for the same purpose, but using the Connection object's Execute method (where applicable) is more efficient. Generally speaking, you can reduce the amount of code you need to write, as well as eliminate the need for one or more Command objects that consume resources. In the following code samples, the Execute method is used to execute a SQL INSERT statement, a stored procedure, and finally, to execute a SELECT statement that returns a Recordset.

Executing a SQL Statement

Using the Connection Execute method requires using up to three arguments. The first, CommandText, specifies the SQL statement (or stored procedure name). The second argument, RecordsAffected, which is optional, provides a by-reference argument so you can know after processing the operation how many records were acted on. Finally, the Options argument, which is also optional, specifies the nature of the execution with one or more intrinsic constants. Here, a SQL INSERT statement adds a row to the SalesReps table.

```
Public Sub ExecInsert()

Dim objCnn As New ADODB.Connection
Dim strConnect As String
Dim strInsert As String
Dim intRecsAffected As Integer
```

```
'Define connection string
strConnect = "Driver={SQL " & _
    "Server};Server=DALA;UID=sa;Database=OrderManager;"

'Define SQL statement
strInsert = "INSERT INTO SalesReps (srRepID, srFName, " & _
    "srLName, srMidInit, srSSN, srCommissionRating) " & _
    "VALUES (20, 'Jon', 'Smith', 'J', '555-55-5555', 3)"

'Open the connection and execute SQL
With objCnn
    .Open strConnect
    .Execute strInsert, intRecsAffected, adCmdText
End With

Debug.Print intRecsAffected & " record(s) were processed"

objCnn.Close
Set objCnn = Nothing

End Sub
```

The Options argument can be set to a number of public Enum types, including: adCmdText for executing SQL statements; adCmdStoredProc for executing a CommandText that identifies a stored procedure name; and adAsyncExecute for executing a command asynchronously. Later, adAsyncExecute will be used to show asynchronous operations.

> **The Options argument specifies CommandType values. The CommandType and all the available Enum values will be covered later in the discussion on ADO Command objects.**

Executing a Stored Procedure

Using the Execute method to execute a stored procedure is fairly straightforward. That said, you may find that the Command object's Execute method is more capable for stored procedure execution. One of the practical values of defining stored procedures is to define parameters that can be dynamically supplied, which means the procedure can be defined once, then used with different input and/or output values repeatedly. The Connection object's Execute method has no means of handling parameters, but the Command.Execute does. Later you'll learn about using the Command object's Execute method in conjunction with parameterized stored procedures.

The next sample code illustrates executing a stored procedure that inserts a row into the Sales Rep table, as did the earlier example. Here, the CommandText argument specifies the name of the stored procedure instead of a SQL statement, and the Options argument specifies that CommandText be understood as a stored procedure name.

```
With objCnn
    .Open strConnect
    .Execute "AddSalesRep", intRecsAffected, adCmdStoredProc
End With

Debug.Print intRecsAffected & " record(s) were processed"
```

Getting a Recordset Down and Dirty

Finally, you can use the Execute method to return a "Volkswagen of a Recordset." (Actually, I own a Jetta and it's pretty nice, so maybe the metaphor doesn't apply.) The point is, the Recordset that is returned from executing a SQL Select statement is a forward-only cursor. Later, you'll learn all about the implications of cursor types, but for now understand that this cursor is "cheap" with regard to the resources it requires—but then it doesn't do a lot for you either except allow row by row navigation in a forward-only direction. As such, it is useful for retrieving rows economically and for displaying data a row at a time.

This code sample declares a Recordset object variable and uses it as the object returned by the Execute method.

```
Public Sub GetCheapRecordset()

Dim objCnn As New ADODB.Connection
Dim objRst As ADODB.Recordset
Dim strConnect As String
Dim strSQL As String

'Define connection string
strConnect = "Driver={SQL " & _
    "Server};Server=DALA;UID=sa;Database=OrderManager;"

'Define SQL statement
strSQL = "Select * From Customers Where " & _
    "cuCustomerID < " & 1050 & "Order By cuCustomerName"

'Open the connection and execute SQL
With objCnn
    .Open strConnect
    Set objRst = .Execute(strSQL, , adCmdText)
End With

'Do something intelligent with the records

'Close
objRst.Close
Set objRst = Nothing
objCnn.Close
Set objCnn = Nothing

End Sub
```

Creating Transactions

Whenever you need to make a series of changes to a data source, you may want to ensure that all, or none, of the changes take place. The classic example is the transfer of money between a saving and checking account. You would not want to allow money to be withdrawn successfully from the saving account if for some reason a failure prevents the money being added to the checking account. Or, in an order entry system, you would not want an item added to an order that somehow leaves the product's table OnHand balance unaffected.

So the Connection object also provides transaction methods: BeginTrans, Commit-Trans, and RollbackTrans. ADO's successful use of these methods depends on the provider you're using. Some providers do not allow transactions, others do; some do not allow transaction nesting, others do. You can check the "Transaction DDL" property in the Connection object's Properties collection to determine if the provider supports transactions. More on the Properties collection later.

With the transaction methods, you can ensure atomic completion or cancellation of a series of changes that you make through the following:

- Statements or stored procedures executed through the Connection object's Execute method.

- Statements or stored procedures executed through the Command object's Execute method.

- Records modified, inserted, or deleted through the Recordset object.

In the following code sample, three procedures, TransactionExample, UpdatePhone, and UpdateFax are executed within the context of a transaction. The TransactionExample procedure manages the transaction and calls the other two supporting procedures. As such, the Connection.Execute methods (in UpdatePhone and UpdateFax) are written to memory upon completion. Only when the CommitTrans method is executed are the changes written to the database. If an error happens at any point during the procedures, the code will execute the RollbackTrans method. In either case, the two procedures either consistently change the state of the database or do not change it at all.

```
Public Sub TransactionExample()

Dim objCnn As New ADODB.Connection
Dim strConnect As String
Dim blnSucceed As Boolean
Dim strAreaCodeOld As String
Dim strAreaCodeNew As String
Dim strReturnMsg As String
Dim intRecsAffected As Integer

strConnect = "Provider=MSDASQL;Driver={SQL Server};" & _
    "Server=DALA;Database=OrderManager;UID=sa;" & _
    "PWD=;"

With objCnn
```

(continues)

(Continued)

```
    .Open strConnect
    .BeginTrans

    'Execute the first command
    strAreaCodeOld = "727"
    strAreaCodeNew = "344"
    blnSucceed = UpdatePhone(objCnn, strAreaCodeOld, _
        strAreaCodeNew, intRecsAffected)

    'Check return value
    If blnSucceed = False Then
        .RollbackTrans
        strReturnMsg = "Update phone area code failed."
        GoTo Exit_TransactionExample
    Else
        're-initialize blnSucceed and execute second command
        blnSucceed = False
        strReturnMsg = "Update phone succeeded.  " & _
            intRecsAffected & " rows updated." & vbCr
        blnSucceed = UpdateFax(objCnn, strAreaCodeOld, _
            strAreaCodeNew, intRecsAffected)
    End If

    If blnSucceed = False Then
        .RollbackTrans
        strReturnMsg = "Update fax area code failed."
    Else
        .CommitTrans
        strReturnMsg = strReturnMsg & "Update fax " & _
            "succeeded. " & intRecsAffected & " rows updated."
    End If
End With

Exit_TransactionExample:
    lblStatus.Caption = strReturnMsg
    Exit Sub

End Sub
```

The supporting procedures, UpdatePhone and UpdateFax, simply execute a SQL UPDATE statement using the Connection object's Execute method. The procedures are written to return a success or fail value.

```
Private Function UpdatePhone(pobjCnn As ADODB.Connection, _
    pvntAreaCodeOld As Variant, pvntAreaCodeNew As Variant, _
    pintRecsAffected As Integer) As Boolean

    On Error GoTo Error_UpdatePhone

    Dim strSQL As String
```

```
    Dim intRecsAffected As Integer

    strSQL = "UPDATE Customers SET cuContactPhone = '" & _
        pvntAreaCodeNew & "' + {fn RIGHT(cuContactPhone, 9" & _
        ")} WHERE ({fn LEFT(cuContactPhone, 3)} = '" & _
        pvntAreaCodeOld & "')"

    pobjCnn.Execute strSQL, intRecsAffected
    UpdatePhone = True

Exit_UpdatePhone:
    pintRecsAffected = intRecsAffected
    Exit Function

Error_UpdatePhone:
    UpdatePhone = False
    GoTo Exit_UpdatePhone

End Function
```

Similarly, the UpdateFax procedure updates the cuContactFax field.

```
strSQL = "UPDATE Customers SET cuContactFax = '" & _
    pvntAreaCodeNew & "' + {fn RIGHT(cuContactFax, 9" & _
    ")} WHERE ({fn LEFT(cuContactFax, 3)} = '" & _
    pvntAreaCodeOld & "')"

    pobjCnn.Execute strSQL, intRecsAffected
    UpdateFax = True
```

 The SQL code in the UpdatePhone and UpDateFax procedures uses Transact SQL Left and Right functions. Therefore, this code will not work as written for databases other than SQL Server.

Events and Asynchronous Operations

New to ADO 2.0 is the ability to use object events and perform some operations asynchronously. Before we delve into the specifics of working with asynchronous operations, however, let's take a moment to understand why and how events are incorporated into the ADO programming model.

If you've worked with an event-driven programming tool such as Visual Basic, the idea of events will not be new to you. For example, a command button has a Click event that fires when a user clicks on an instance (command button object). The command button is defined by a class or template that governs the behavior of objects (instances) of the command button placed on a form. The command button class defines an event called Click, which is internally programmed to respond to the user clicking on the but-

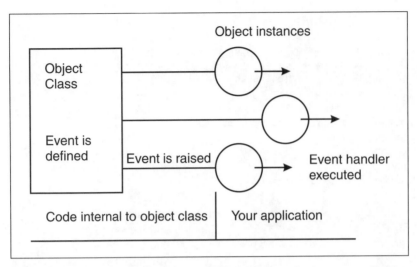

Figure 2.2   An object class defines events and raises them. Your application uses an event handler to respond appropriately.

ton. When this happens, the event is raised and an event handler, known to Visual Basic programmers as an event procedure, is executed. The programmer can then add code to the event handler or event procedure to carry out the specific operations desired. See Figure 2.2.

In the same way, some ADO 2.0 objects include events that fire in response to certain operations (usually methods). There are two categories of ADO events: Those that fire before an operation starts and those that fire after an operation completes. There is even a stray event or two that fire during the processing of an operation. For example, you could write code for the Connection object's ExecuteComplete event that fires after an Execute statement completes. ADO's incorporation of events is extremely powerful and a step beyond earlier object models. In the case of ExecuteComplete, if you did not have this event to work with, you would be forced to poll some property using a timer and/or looping structure to find out if the execution had indeed completed. With the use of the event handler, you do not have to do anything to calculate when the execution completes; ADO takes care of that by firing the event at the right time, which means all you have to do is write the desired code in the event handler (procedure).

ADO events apply to the Connection object and the Recordset object. Table 2.1 summarizes the Connection object events. Later, when discussing the Recordset object, we'll examine the use of its events.

It's important to understand that ADO events fire whether or not an operation is successful. You as the developer can use arguments that are automatically passed into the event handler to determine which action should be taken. ADO events can be used with or without asynchronous operations. Here are some examples of what you might do with some of these events. Later, you'll see code that shows the use of the Execute-Complete event.

Use the WillConnect Event. Use this event to write code that can determine if the connection that is about to be established will indeed be successful. If it is not going to be successful, then modify ConnectionString arguments to correct the problem.

Use the RollbackTransComplete Event. Use this event to determine when a transaction rollback occurs. In response, you may choose to roll back other transactions as well.

Use the ExcecuteComplete Event. Use this event to determine when the execution of a command finishes and whether it was successful, then choose to proceed or not proceed with other operations based on the results.

Asynchronous Operations

Some ADO operations can be performed asynchronously. This essentially means that the operation runs in another process. For example, if you issue an Execute method asynchronously, the method runs in another process and immediately returns control to the client application (your application) to execute subsequent lines of code. But if the operation is running in another process, how do you know when it is complete? By using the event handler. When the operation concludes, it raises the appropriate event, where you can then respond as appropriate. This feature of COM objects is known as a *callback;* it utilizes the COM event model to facilitate it.

Asynchronous operations are implemented for Open methods such as the Connection.Open method or the Recordset.Open method. They are also implemented for Exe-

Table 2.1 Connection Object Events Used to Handle Operations

EVENT NAME	DESCRIPTION
BeginTransComplete	Raised after a BeginTrans method completes.
CommitTransComplete	Raised after a CommitTrans method completes.
ConnectComplete	Raised after a connection starts.
Disconnect	The event is raised when a connection ends.
ExecuteComplete	Raised after a command (Execute method) completes.
InfoMessage	Raised whenever a ConnectionEvent warning is returned by a provider.
RollbackTransComplete	Raised after a RollbackTrans method completes.
WillConnect	Raised before a connection starts. The parameters to be used in the pending connection are supplied as input parameters and can be changed before the method returns.
WillExecute	Raised before a connection starts. The parameters to be used in the pending command are supplied as input parameters and can be changed before the method returns.

cute methods such as the Connection.Execute and Command.Execute methods. Using asynchronous execution for long-running operations can be very powerful. For example, you may allow the user to execute a stored procedure that may take more than a few moments to complete. By running the operation asynchronously, you can enable the user to go on with other tasks; he or she can then be notified when the stored procedure has completed.

Asynchronous ExecuteComplete Example

This example updates the srRepID field in the Orders table for a particular sales representative. The Orders table has more than 10,000 rows, and the rows that are updated are in the hundreds. The Execute method runs asynchronously. Let's take a look at the code.

```
Private Sub ExecuteCompleteExample()

Dim strConnect As String
Dim strSQL As String
Dim intRecordsAffected As Integer

'Start the connection
'Uses mobjCnn Connection - must be declared in class mod
'declarations

Set mobjCnn = New ADODB.Connection
```

Here, the necessary variables are declared. The Connection object variable, mobjCnn must be declared to enable event handling using the WithEvents keyword. As such, it cannot be defined in a procedure but must be declared as a Private or Public member of a class module (which includes Visual Basic form modules). The Declarations section of the class module declares mobjCnn.

```
Private WithEvents mobjCnn As ADODB.Connection
```

If you're using Visual Basic, once you've declared an object variable using the With-Events keyword, the object instance will display in the object list in the code editor, and the events will display in the procedure list. See Figure 2.3.

The ExecuteCompleteExample procedure continues by assigning the Connection-String arguments and defining a SQL UPDATE statement. Then the procedure opens the connection and executes the SQL statement using the adAsyncExecute option. Because the Execute method runs asynchronously, the code that sets the status bar text and disables the command button runs immediately.

```
strConnect = "Provider=MSDASQL;Driver={SQL Server};" & _
    "Server=DALA;Database=OrderManager;UID=sa;" & _
    "PWD=;"

strSQL = "UPDATE Orders Set orRepID = 5 Where orRepID = 4"

With mobjCnn
```

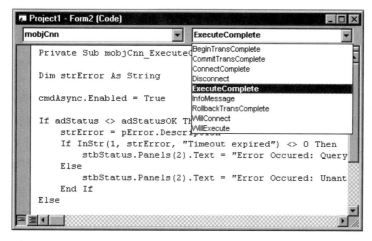

Figure 2.3 Objects declared using WithEvents display in the code editor.

```
    .CommandTimeout = 20
    .Open strConnect
    .Execute strSQL, intRecordsAffected, adAsyncExecute
    stbStatus.Panels(2).Text = "Executing Query: " & _
        "You may proceed with other tasks."
    cmdAsync.Enabled = False
End With

End Sub
```

When ADO determines that the execution has completed, whether successful or not, ADO raises the ExecuteComplete event. This in turn causes the event handler (event procedure) mobjCnn_ExecuteComplete to fire.

```
Private Sub mobjCnn_ExecuteComplete(ByVal RecordsAffected _
    As Long, ByVal pError As ADODB.Error, adStatus As _
    ADODB.EventStatusEnum, ByVal pCommand As ADODB.Command, _
    ByVal pRecordset As ADODB.Recordset, ByVal pConnection _
    As ADODB.Connection)

Dim strError As String

cmdAsync.Enabled = True

If adStatus <> adStatusOK Then
    strError = pError.Description
    If InStr(1, strError, "Timeout expired") <> 0 Then
        stbStatus.Panels(2).Text = _
        "Error Occurred: Query timeout expired. " & _
        "Please try again."
    Else
        stbStatus.Panels(2).Text = _
```

(continues)

(Continued)

```
                "Error Occurred: Unanticipated
    End If
Else
    stbStatus.Panels(2).Text = _
        "Query Completed: " & RecordsAffected & _
        " records processed."
End If

End Sub
```

ADO passes by value object references and other arguments into event handlers. The arguments that ADO passes to an event handler differ from event to event. In the case of ExecuteComplete, the adStatus argument can be examined to determine if the operation succeeded, as shown in the preceding code. If it did succeed, the code sets the text of the status bar accordingly and uses the RecordsAffected argument to display the number of rows processed.

If the adStatus parameter does not equal adStatusOK, then the code examines the Description property of the pError argument and tries to determine what went wrong. A likely possibility under heavy server burden is that the CommandTimeout property may have been artificially low, causing the operation to fail. If this occurs, the user is told that the operation failed and to try again. If any other error occurs, the example traps for it and notifies the user.

Connection Objects and Events Summary

Using events is a powerful tool, particularly in conjunction with asynchronous operations. This section only summarized the Connection object events and showed a singular example, but you'll find working with events to be straightforward. Keep in mind the following when considering events:

1. Consider how the operation you are performing might be enhanced or helped by using events.

2. Determine if ADO defines event(s) for the operation you are trying to perform.

3. Determine if the operation can or should be performed asynchronously.

4. Perform the operation.

5. Code the event handler as appropriate, taking advantage of ADO arguments that are passed in the handler, to assist your code logic.

Dynamic Properties

ADO includes both intrinsic and dynamic properties. Intrinsic properties are those that you've already seen, such as ConnectionTimeout or CommandTimeout. But ADO objects also exposed through the Properties collection dynamic properties that describe the behavior of the provider you're using. The Connection, Command, Parameter, Recordset, and Field objects all have a Properties collection that holds—you guessed it—Property objects. Each of the collections contains provider-specific attributes relative to the object that holds the collection.

Each Property object has a Name, Type, Value, and Attributes property. The Name property identifies the provider-identified name for the property. The Value property contains information helpful in determining the behavior of the property. Generally speaking, since you can reuse ADO objects, you may need to examine the dynamic properties served by the provider to determine if your application can reliably perform a certain operation or to know which behavior to expect. For example, a Connection object could be reused to access data across two or more providers. First, you could open the connection, execute whichever statements were necessary, and then close the connection. But because you want to use the same Connection object variable to access another data source, you would then reuse the same object instance and open the connection to the second data source. However, the provider now being used may not support certain operations. The following code shows that by interrogating a dynamic property, you can determine how your code should execute.

```
With objCnn
    .CommandTimeout = 15
    .ConnectionTimeout = 15
    .Provider = "Microsoft.Jet.OLEDB.3.51"
    .Open "D:\Book\Code\OrderManager.mdb", "admin"
End With

objRst.Open "SELECT * FROM Customers", objCnn

intCount = 1
For Each objPrp In objCnn.Properties
    Debug.Print intCount & ") Name: " & objPrp.Name & _
        " Value: " & objPrp.Value
    intCount = intCount + 1
Next
```

The code opens a connection with the Microsoft OLE DB Provider for JET and enumerates the Properties collection of the Connection object. Figure 2.4 shows a sampling of the output.

For Further Investigation

Before moving on from the Connection object, there are some properties and methods of the Connection object not mentioned in this section that you need to be aware of. Some will be discussed later, as they are important to successfully using other ADO objects such as the Recordset; others are of lesser importance, or find use only in specific contexts. Table 2.2 lists a number of these additional Connection object properties and methods with a brief description.

Handling Errors

Certainly, in any application you write, you want to be able to properly handle runtime errors that occur. When working with ADO, remember that the Connection object con-

Figure 2.4 Dynamic properties displayed for the JET provider.

tains an Errors collection that holds Error objects. The Error objects can be used to interrogate errors passed on to ADO by the provider. The Error object has a handful of properties (shown in Figure 2.5): Number, Description, Source, NativeError, SQLState, HelpContext, and HelpFile.

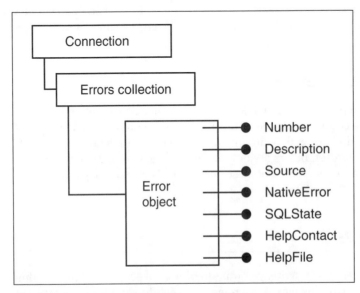

Figure 2.5 The properties of the Error object.

Table 2.2 Additional Connection Object Properties and Methods

PROPERTY OR METHOD	NAME	DESCRIPTION
Property	Attributes	Specifies XactAttributeEnum values that further define the behavior of transactions.
Method	Cancel	Used with asynchronous Execute or Open methods. Cancels a pending operation. Typically used in an event handler.
Property	CursorLocation	Defines whether server-side or client-side cursors (Recordsets) are used. Client-side cursors are required for certain Recordset operations. You will learn about these in Chapter 3.
Property	DefaultDatabase	Specifies the default database to be used by a Connection object. This property can be used in lieu of setting the database parameter in a connection string.
Property	IsolationLevel	Used in conjunction with transactions to control transaction behavior. You set the property to one of a number of IsolationLevelEnum values.
Property	Mode	Used to set access permissions for a connection.
Method	OpenSchema	Returns a Recordset that can be used to display schema information for the database.
Property	State	Returns whether the State of an object is open, in process, or closed. For example, you could query the Connection.State property to determine if a connection is open, closed, or in the process of opening.
Property	Version	Returns the version number of ADO.

When you are performing an operation with an ADO object, if a provider error occurs, the errors are passed to ADO and ADO places one or more error objects in the Errors collection. Before you examine some code that traps for errors, let's take a closer look at the information you can obtain from the properties:

Number. Use this property to identify the unique number that identifies the error condition.

Description. Use this property to extract descriptive information about the nature of the error.

Source. Returns the name of a class or ProgID that identifies the source of the error. If a provider generated the error, the Source may contain the identifier for that provider. Errors generated in ADO will return "ADODB" as part of the Source property return value.

NativeError. Use this property to retrieve the database-specific error information. For example, when using MSDASQL with a SQL Server database, native error codes that originate from SQL Server pass through ODBC and the MSDASQL provider to the ADO NativeError property.

SQLState. Use this property to read a five-character error code that the provider returns when an error occurs during the processing of a SQL statement. For example, when using MSDASQL with a SQL Server database, error codes originate from ODBC, based either on errors specific to ODBC or on errors that originate from SQL Server, and are then mapped to ODBC errors. These error codes are documented in the ANSI SQL standard but may be implemented differently by various data sources.

HelpContext. Use this property to identify a context in a help file using a Long value that is returned.

HelpFile. Use this String property to identify the path of a help file.

Error Confusion

When working with ADO code, it's important to understand that two different kinds of errors can happen: ADO errors and provider errors. ADO errors occur when you perform an illegal operation with an ADO object that has nothing to do with the provider's capabilities or use. An ADO error is raised to the error-handling mechanism that the language supplies, such as the VB and VBScript Err object. The error is not appended to the Errors collection. Hmmm. So what does this mean? Well, it means that you need to be aware of which operations cause ADO errors and which operations cause provider errors. For example, if you incorrectly reference a field in a Recordset using a faulty field name, an ADO error will result.

```
strCustomer = objrst("cuCutomer")
```

On the other hand, if you execute a Connection.Open method with a faulty ConnectionString argument, a provider error will result in one or more Error objects being placed in the Errors collection.

```
'UID argument is intentionally wrong
sConnect = "Provider=MSDASQL;Driver={SQL Server};" & _
    "Server=DALA;Database=OrderManager;UID=sd;" & _
    "PWD=;"

sSQL = "Select * from Customers Where cuCustomerID = " & 1015

With objCnn
    .Open sConnect 'This line fails because UID is wrong
    Set objRst = .Execute(sSQL)
End With
```

To make things a little more interesting, provider errors are not only returned to the Errors collection, but also, in some cases, to the language error-handling mechanism such as the Err object in Visual Basic. Depending on the language you are using, the language-specific mechanism may not report the error. Visual Basic does, but even with VB, the Err object contains information only on the most recent error. So, for provider errors that may have produced multiple error conditions, the Err object would fall short in providing a solution in some cases.

So what do you do about this relatively strange error behavior? If you're a Visual Basic or VBScript programmer, you may enjoy using VB's Err object to handle some error conditions, and in more complex scenarios, use the ADO Error object to determine an error condition, particularly if the operation produced multiple provider errors.

Error Solution

From a Visual Basic programmer's perspective, it is important to have some mechanism for handling ADO errors and provider errors. Since ADO-specific errors are not reported to the Errors collection, you must have some way of identifying ADO errors and handling them differently from how you would provider errors.

Handling ADO Errors

The next code sample shows error-handling code that identifies the Source of an error as "ADODB" and calls a supporting procedure, HandleADOErrors, to handle the error. The ADO error is generated on the line that incorrectly specifies a Recordset field name.

```
Private Sub cmdADOError_Click()

On Error GoTo Error_cmdADOError_Click

Dim objCnn As New ADODB.Connection
Dim strConnect As String
Dim strSQL As String
Dim objRst As New ADODB.Recordset
Dim strValue As String

strConnect = "Provider=MSDASQL;Driver={SQL Server};" & _
    "Server=DALA;Database=OrderManager;UID=sa;" & _
    "PWD=;"

strSQL = "Select * from Customers Where cuCustomerID = " & 1015

With objCnn
    .Open sConnect
    Set objRst = .Execute(sSQL)
End With

'Causes an ADO Error - will not be in Errors collection
'Customer field spelled wrong
strValue = objRst("cuCustomerOd")
```

(continues)

(Continued)

```
Exit_cmdADOError_Click:
    Exit Sub

Error_cmdADOError_Click:
    If InStr(1, Err.Source, "ADODB") <> 0 Then
        HandleADOErrors Err
    Else
        HandleProviderErrors
    End If
    Resume Exit_cmdADOError_Click
End Sub
```

In this sample, the Err.Source property contains the string value, ADODB.Fields, since the error was raised by incorrectly specifying a field name. Err.Number returns a long value, 3265, specifying that the object (Field object) could not be found in the Fields collection.

To handle ADO errors adequately, you ought to know the error codes and what they signify. Table 2.3 shows ADO error constants, numeric equivalents, and descriptions for each.

Handling Provider Errors

To handle provider errors, you interrogate the properties of one or more Error objects. The next example incorrectly specifies the database to be opened. This causes the MSDASQL provider to report to ADO that the OrderManagers database could not be found.

```
Private Sub cmdProviderErr_Click()

On Error Resume Next

Dim objCnn As New ADODB.Connection
Dim strConnect As String
Dim objErr As ADODB.Error

strConnect = "Provider=MSDASQL;Driver={SQL Server};" & _
    "Server=DALA;Database=OrderManagers;UID=sa;" & _
    "PWD=;"

'Open method fails because connection string has a bogus
'database (typo)

objCnn.Open strConnect

'Provider errors are reported to the runtime error handling
'mechanism

'Provider errors are also in the errors collection
```

```
For Each objErr In objCnn.Errors
    Debug.Print "Number: " & objErr.Number & ";"
    Debug.Print "Description: " & objErr.Description & ";"
    Debug.Print "Source: " & objErr.Source & ";"
    Debug.Print "NativeError: " & objErr.NativeError
Next


End Sub
```

You may have expected only one error condition to be reported, but three Error objects are appended to the Errors collection. The first contains the most useful information for discerning the problem. It yields the following results:

```
Number: -2147217843;
Description: [Microsoft][ODBC SQL Server Driver][SQL Server]Attempt to
locate entry 'OrderManagers' by name failed - no entry found under that
name. Make sure that name is entered properly.;
Source: Microsoft OLE DB Provider for ODBC Drivers;
NativeError: 911
```

As you saw in the code, interrogating the Errors collection is a matter of looping through the collection and examining the relevant Error properties such as Number, Description, Source, and NativeError. You do not have to clear the Errors collection explicitly because each time a new operation causes a provider error, the Errors collection is automatically cleared.

Taking Command

So far you've learned about the usefulness of the Connection and Error objects. Now, turning to the Command object, you'll find that the capabilities of ADO keep on growing. The Command object has a fairly narrow purpose: To execute statements that either modify a data source or return a Recordset.

You've already seen how the Connection object's Execute method can run SQL statements or stored procedures and even return a static, forward-only Recordset. The Command object also has an Execute method that allows you to do the same, with one important exception: With the Command object, you can specify parameters for queries that you want to execute, thus creating reusable, efficient operations.

Returning a Recordset

Since you've already seen the Connection.Execute method, you'll find some of this to be familiar turf. But the Command object has a number of basic properties that the Connection object does not.

The following code sample creates a Command object and runs its Execute method to return a Recordset. In so doing, a number of properties are used.

Table 2.3   ADO Error Codes

CONSTANT NAME	NUMBER	DESCRIPTION
adErrInvalidArgument	3001	The application is using arguments that are of the wrong type, are out of acceptable range, or are in conflict with one another.
adErrNoCurrentRecord	3021	Either BOF or EOF is True, or the current record has been deleted; the operation requested by the application requires a current record.
adErrIllegalOperation	3219	The operation requested by the application is not allowed in this context.
adErrInTransaction	3246	The application cannot explicitly close a Connection object while in the middle of a transaction.
adErrFeatureNotAvailable	3251	The operation requested by the application is not supported by the provider.
adErrItemNotFound	3265	ADO could not find the object in the collection corresponding to the name or ordinal reference requested by the application.
adErrObjectInCollection	3367	Can't append. Object already in collection.
adErrObjectNotSet	3420	The object referenced by the application no longer points to a valid object.
adErrDataConversion	3421	The application is using a value of the wrong type for the current operation.
adErrObjectClosed	3704	The operation requested by the application is not allowed if the object is closed.
adErrObjectOpen	3705	The operation requested by the application is not allowed if the object is open.
adErrProviderNotFound	3706	ADO could not find the specified provider.
adErrBoundToCommand	3707	The application cannot change the ActiveConnection property of a Recordset object with a Command object as its source.
adErrInvalidParamInfo	3708	The application has improperly defined a Parameter object.
adErrInvalidConnection	3709	The application requested an operation on an object with a reference to a closed or invalid Connection object.

```
Private Sub Command2_Click()

Dim objCnn As New ADODB.Connection
Dim objCmd As New ADODB.Command
Dim objRst As ADODB.Recordset
Dim objField As ADODB.Field
Dim strConnect As String
Dim strSQL As String

strConnect = "Provider=MSDASQL;Driver={SQL Server};" & _
    "Server=DALA;Database=OrderManager;UID=sa;" & _
    "PWD=;"
strSQL = "SELECT cuCustomerID, cuAcceptedDate FROM " & _
    "Customers WHERE cuAcceptedDate > '1/1/98'"

objCnn.Open strConnect

With objCmd
    .CommandTimeout = 30
    .CommandText = strSQL
    .CommandType = adCmdText
    .ActiveConnection = objCnn
    Set objRst = .Execute
End With

'Do something with the forward-only cursor

objRst.Close
Set objRst = Nothing
objCnn.Close
Set objCnn = Nothing

End Sub
```

Before executing the command, the code sets a number of important properties:

CommandTimeout Property. Earlier, you saw a property by the same name for the Connection object. Here the timeout applies to operations for this Command object. Remember, make sure that the timeout you set is not artificially low. If it is, commands may abort, causing problems with your application. Some testing of command execution under target server load conditions is warranted, especially for intensive updates.

CommandText Property. You can set the CommandText property to the value of the SQL statement, a table name, a stored procedure name, or other values. The preceding code sets the CommandText to the string strSQL.

CommandType Property. You can specify this property to define how the Command object should interpret the CommandText value. You can choose from among a number of CommandTypeEnum values, which are described in Table 2.4.

ActiveConnection Property. In order to execute, the command must be associated with an open Connection object. Since a living, breathing Command object can be instanced without first being associated with a connection, it is possible to use this property to reuse a Command object with more than one Connection object. This is important to understand. While you may be writing code that must complete three distinct update operations, it does not mean that you must create three commands. You can simply reuse the one Command object. Before associating a command with another connection, you should release it from its current connection. This is done in Visual Basic by setting the ActiveConnection property to nothing, as shown in the code that follows.

```
'Associate command with first connection
objCmd.ActiveConnection = objCnn1

'Do something at least purposeful with the command

'Release the command from the 1st connection and associate it with
'the second connection

Set objCmd.ActiveConnection = Nothing
objCmd.ActiveConnection = objCnn2
```

Execute Method. With the Execute method, you execute the statements identified by the CommandText property.

```
command.Execute RecordsAffected, Parameters, Options
```

Each argument for this method is optional. RecordsAffected returns a ByRef value that you can evaluate to determine how many rows were processed or returned. The Param-

Table 2.4 Command Object CommandTypeEnum Values Used for Setting the CommandType Property

CONSTANT	DESCRIPTION
adCmdText	Evaluates CommandText as a textual definition of a command.
adCmdTable	Evaluates CommandText as a table name in a generated SQL query returning all columns.
adCmdTableDirect	Evaluates CommandText as a table name whose columns are all returned.
adCmdStoredProc	Evaluates CommandText as a stored procedure.
adCmdUnknown	Default; the type of command in the CommandText property is not known.
adCommandFile	Evaluates CommandText as the file name of a persisted Recordset. You'll see the use of this argument in Chapter 3.

eters argument can be used to pass in a Variant array of input parameters for the SQL query. This is a somewhat useful argument, limited in that it cannot handle output parameters. You'll learn about input and output parameters in the next section. Finally, the Options argument can be used to specify some of the same options that you saw for the CommandType property, but more important, to execute the operation asynchronously using either the adAsyncExecute or adAsyncFetch values.

 The adExecuteNoRecords constant for the Options argument is useful for improving performance for queries that do not need to return data. This means that resource overhead can be reduced, because this setting tells ADO not to create a Recordset. Earlier versions of ADO always created a Recordset behind the scenes when executing a command. This setting also applies to the Connection object's Execute method.

Using Parameters

You'll find that many providers support the use of parameterized commands, commands that define a desired action, such as specifying a stored procedure name only once. However, parts of the command are treated as parameters or variables that can be supplied each time you execute the command. For example, you could write a simple stored procedure that returns a customer row, where a parameter is supplied as a variable used in the WHERE clause to restrict the returned rows to only a single row.

Executing a Stored Procedure with an Input Parameter

In this example, a Recordset is derived by executing a Command object specifying a SQL Server stored procedure for its CommandText property. The stored procedure also uses an input parameter to restrict the rows returned. The stored procedure, GetCustomerByID, looks like this:

```
Create Procedure GetCustomerByID
    (
        @CustomerID int
    )
As SELECT Customers.* FROM Customers Where cuCustomerID =
    @CustomerID
return
```

Within the parentheses, the @ symbol identifies the declaration of an input parameter, CustomerID. An input parameter is a variable whose value SQL Server will assign prior to executing the procedure. The input parameter is used to restrict the rows returned by filtering the cuCustomerID field. The Visual Basic procedure, GetCustomer, executes the stored procedure.

```
Private Sub GetCustomer()

Dim objCnn As New ADODB.Connection
Dim objCmd As New ADODB.Command
Dim objCustomer As ADODB.Parameter
Dim objRst As New ADODB.Recordset
Dim strConnect As String
```

In addition to declaring Connection, Command, and Recordset objects, you need to also declare a Parameter object, as shown in the preceding code:

```
strConnect = "Provider=MSDASQL;Driver={SQL Server};" & _
    "Server=DALA;Database=OrderManager;UID=sa;" & _
    "PWD=;"

objCnn.Open strConnect

With objCmd
    .CommandTimeout = 15
    .CommandText = "GetCustomerByID"
    .CommandType = adCmdStoredProc
    .ActiveConnection = objCnn
```

In this code, the CommandText property is set to the name of the stored procedure that will source the operation. Of course, you set the CommandType to the enum value, adCmdStoredProc. Afterward, you are ready to define the parameter.

Using the CreateParameter Method

The procedure continues by creating a parameter. Earlier, you saw how objCustomer was declared as ADODB.Parameter. You instance the parameter and assign a number of properties using the CreateParameter method of the Command object. The next code continues the GetCustomer procedure by creating the objCustomer parameter.

```
Set objCustomer = .CreateParameter("CustomerID", _
    adInteger, adParamInput, , 1015)
```

The CreateParameter method uses a bunch of arguments that help define the nature of the parameter:

Name. Simply supplies the name of the parameter.

Type. The appropriate data type for the parameter, given the provider you are using.

Direction. Specifies how the stored procedure will use the parameter as an input, output, both input and output, or a return value. For this argument, you can use any one of five ParameterDirectionEnums: adParamInput, adParamInputOutput, adParamOutput, adParamReturnValue, and adParamUnknown. In the GetCustomer example, you use the parameter as an input value.

Size. Specifies the maximum length of the parameter in characters or bytes, depending on the type.

Value. Specifies the value of the parameter.

Each of these arguments is optional. Why? Because the Parameter object has properties by the same name as each of the arguments for the CreateParameter method. So it would be possible to set all the properties as appropriate and then execute the CreateParameter method without the use of arguments. To do so, however, is somewhat less efficient than to pass the values as arguments of the method.

The Parameter object also has a couple of other properties that define its behavior but are not arguments of the CreateParameter method.

NumericScale. Use this property to set the number of decimal places to which numeric values will be resolved.

Precision. Use this property to define the total number of digits used to represent values for a parameter.

Appending Parameters

After defining a parameter, you should append it to the Parameters collection of the Command object. The GetCustomer procedure does this and then executes the command, which returns a row to the Recordset, objRst.

```
    .Parameters.Append objCustomer
    Set objRst = .Execute
End With

'Do something with the returned row

'Close down
objRst.Close
Set objRst = Nothing
objCnn.Close
Set objCnn = Nothing

End Sub
```

Executing a Stored Procedure with an Input and Output Parameter

You use parameters as input variables, but you can also use them to return values. For example, your application may need to return a specific contact name for a customer. A stored procedure takes a CustomerID as an input parameter but returns the name of the contact person as an output parameter. You might ask, "Couldn't you do the same thing with a Recordset?" The answer, of course, is yes, but for simple queries, with limited return information, such as in this example, it's a good idea to eliminate the overhead imposed by a Recordset. Numerous applications could take advantage of this type of operation. As another example, an order entry application might return a confirmation number based on an OrderID. You could make it a more efficient operation by returning the value in a parameter.

The GetContactByID stored procedure defines the operation just mentioned. The ContactName parameter is designated as an output parameter, meaning it will be used to return a value. The SELECT statement sets the ContactName parameter equal to the cuContactName field.

```
Create Procedure GetContactByID
    (
        @CustomerID int,
        @ContactName varchar(25) OUTPUT
    )

As SELECT @ContactName = cuContactName  FROM Customers
    Where cuCustomerID = @CustomerID
return
```

The GetContact procedure executes the GetContactByID stored procedure.

```
Private Sub GetContact()

Dim objCnn As New ADODB.Connection
Dim objCmd As New ADODB.Command
Dim objCustomer As ADODB.Parameter
Dim objContact As ADODB.Parameter
Dim strConnect As String
Dim vntContactName As Variant

strConnect = "Provider=MSDASQL;Driver={SQL Server};" & _
    "Server=DALA;Database=OrderManager;UID=sa;" & _
    "PWD=;"

objCnn.Open strConnect

With objCmd
    .CommandTimeout = 15
    .CommandText = "GetContactByID"
    .CommandType = adCmdStoredProc
    .ActiveConnection = objCnn
    Set objCustomer = .CreateParameter("CustomerID", _
        adInteger, adParamInput, , 1015)
    .Parameters.Append objCustomer
    Set objContact = .CreateParameter("ContactName", _
        adVarChar, adParamOutput, 25)
    .Parameters.Append objContact
    .Execute
    vntContactName = .Parameters("ContactName")
End With

End Sub
```

Notice that the Size argument of objContact is set to 25. Whenever you use a variable-length data type, as in this case, you must set the Size property to avert a runtime provider error. After executing, the sought-after contact name returns and supplies the value for vntContactName.

Prepared Execution

Sometimes you need to execute commands over and over again in the same application usage context. For example, a customer service representative may execute a query to retrieve customer information by filtering on the company name. The representative may repeatedly run the query, but each time supply different values to filter. In this case, there is room to take advantage of optimization by causing the OLE DB provider to store a compiled version of the query before the first execution. When the query is subsequently executed, the compiled version will be used, causing performance optimization.

To enable prepared execution, set the Prepared property to True before executing the command. Doing this necessarily causes more overhead the first time you execute the same command, but subsequent executions should be faster. If your provider does not support prepared execution, it may raise a runtime error or simply ignore the property setting. Next, the Command object objCmdPrep uses prepared execution.

```
strSQL = "SELECT cuCustomerID, cuContactName " & _
"FROM Customers ORDER BY cuContactName"

Set objCmdPrep = New ADODB.Command
Set objCmdPrep.ActiveConnection = objCnn
objCmdPrep.CommandText = strSQL
objCmdPrep.Prepared = True
```

More about Commands

In this section, you learned the basics about using Command objects and parameters. You've seen the most important (and nearly all) Command and Parameter properties and methods used in practical scenarios. Now, you'll take your final stop on the ADO basics tour by examining the Recordset object.

Using Recordsets: The Basics

The Recordset is the most robust of all the ADO objects. This may seem surprising since the Recordset has only two purposes:

- To provide capabilities to manipulate and present data for display

- To provide the ability to modify data

Since ADO is poised to be the data access model for all kinds of development from data-driven Web applications to desktop productivity applications, the Recordset implements many features that are useful to the kinds of applications it may be used in. This section on Recordsets is just the tip of the iceberg. In the next chapter, almost exclusively given to intermediate and advanced uses of the Recordset, you'll learn about its more extensive capabilities.

Opening Recordsets

You've already seen one way to create a Recordset: to execute a statement using a Connection or Command object. Remember, this approach produced the resource-friendly, forward-only cursor. You learned that the forward-only cursor can be used to simply navigate row by row in a forward direction. As such, the forward-only cursor is only used for displaying data.

Using the Open Method

To take advantage of more Recordset capabilities, you'll need to use the Open method to open a Recordset. The syntax of the Open method is simple, but the implications of the arguments it takes impact exactly what you can and can't do with the Recordset. In the following example, the code opens a Keyset type Recordset containing all customer rows with cuCustomerIDs less than 1,100:

```
Dim objCnn As New ADODB.Connection
Dim objRst As New ADODB.Recordset
Dim sConnect As String
Dim sSQL As String

sConnect = "Provider=MSDASQL;Driver={SQL Server};" & _
    "Server=DALA;Database=OrderManager;UID=sa;" & _
    "PWD=;"

sSQL = "SELECT cuCustomerName, cuContactName, " & _
    "cuContactPhone, cuContactFax, cuCity FROM " & _
    "Customers WHERE cuCustomerID < " & 1100

With objCnn
    .ConnectionTimeout = 15
    .Open sConnect
End With

objRst.Open sSQL, objCnn, adOpenKeyset, adLockOptimistic
```

As shown, the Open method of the Recordset takes a number of arguments:

Source. For the Source, you can specify a valid Command object name, a SQL statement, the name of a stored procedure or table name, and a file name of a persisted Recordset. (More on persisted Recordsets in Chapter 3.) In this example, a SQL SELECT statement satisfies the source.

ActiveConnection. You can set the ActiveConnection to a valid ConnectionString or a valid Connection object. Note that if you set the ActiveConnection argument to a string to open the connection, ADO implicitly creates a connection object to serve the Recordset. Therefore, if you had three Recordsets opened in this fashion, you would also have created three connections as well, which certainly is inefficient. So you should, whenever possible, set this argument to a valid, open Connection object.

CursorType. The CursorType argument defines what kind of cursor the Recordset is. The choices are:

- *adOpenForwardOnly.* A forward-only cursor, which can be used for operations that require a single pass through the Recordset. This is the default cursor if no type is specified.

- *adOpenKeyset.* A Recordset that supports changes, inserts, and deletions to rows. However, when opening, membership in a keyset cursor is fixed. This means that the cursor only knows about rows that were extracted on the basis of existing key values in the database at the time it opened. Therefore, additions other users make to base tables while your keyset is open are invisible. Use this cursor when you need an updatable Recordset, but do not care about additions other users may make to the base tables while the cursor remains open.

- *adOpenDynamic.* Like the keyset, except that membership is not fixed. This means that inserts made by other users will be visible. The dynamic cursor is the most capable of all cursors but also the most resource-intensive. Use this type of Recordset when you need to know when other users add rows to the base table(s) of the source or when otherwise required for certain operations.

- *adOpenStatic.* A cursor that represents a static copy of the data. You can use it to locate information that does not require editing or to source reports. It supports full navigation methods, so it is more useful than a forward-only cursor and only slightly more memory-consumptive.

LockType. Use the LockType argument to determine the type of concurrency locking ADO employs. You can select from four LockType Enum values:

- *adLockReadOnly.* Produces a read-only Recordset.

- *adLockPessimistic.* Produces a Recordset that uses *pessimistic locking*, where the provider locks rows at the data source when an edit is issued.

- *adLockOptimistic.* Produces a Recordset that uses *optimistic locking*, where the provider locks rows at the source when an update is issued against the data source.

- *adLockBatchOptimistic.* Used for updating rows to a cache and then later capable of updating the data source. One of the most powerful Recordset features. You'll learn all about batch mode updates in Chapter 3.

Options. With the options argument, you can open Recordsets asynchronously, for example.

Phew! As noted, the Open method is simple with regard to its syntax, but its arguments define a lot. Each of the arguments described is optional. Each argument corresponds to a Recordset property by the same name, so you could set the relevant properties prior to opening, then issue the Open method without using any arguments. Again, it is more efficient to supply the property settings through the use of the Open method's arguments, rather than making multiple property assignments before opening the Recordset.

Navigating and Finding Records

Like its forerunners DAO and RDO, ADO provides the means to navigate through Recordsets and find specific records. The ability to find specific records is actually new to ADO 2.0. Earlier versions were limited with regard to the intrinsic ability to locate rows in a Recordset based on some values.

Navigating

Whether you're using a Recordset to provide rows for a UI or using a Recordset within a middle-tier business object, you often need to be able to move the row pointer from row to row in the cursor. You can easily do this using the Move methods of the Recordset. Often the BOF and EOF properties are used in conjunction with the Move methods. They return True if the row pointer is on the beginning of file and end of file markers, respectively.

In the MoveToRecord code sample shown next, Select Case clauses execute code that moves the pointer to the desired record. In the case of the "Next" and "Previous" clauses, the BOF and/or EOF properties are tested to determine if the file marker has been reached. The MoveToRecord procedure may be used for performing record movement for a form. The "Next" and "Previous" clauses are coded to perform a rollover. In the case of the "Next" clause, the code first checks for EOF, since the pointer may be on the end of file. If so, it rolls over to the first record in the Recordset, making sure that the user cannot perform some illegal operation because the pointer was left, foolishly, on the end of file. Otherwise, the code moves the pointer to the next record. Following this, the code checks EOF again to determine if the pointer is now on the end of file. If so, the code performs a rollover.

```
Public Sub MoveToRecord(psDirection as String)

With objRst
    Select Case psDirection
        Case "First"
            .MoveFirst
        Case "Last"
            .MoveLast
        Case "Next"
            If .EOF Then
                .MoveFirst
            Else
```

```
                    .MoveNext
                If .EOF Then
                    .MoveFirst
                End If
            End If
        Case "Previous"
            If .BOF Then
                .MoveLast
            Else
                .MovePrevious
                If .BOF Then
                    .MoveLast
                End If
            End If
        Case Else
            .MoveFirst
        End Select
    End With

    End Sub
```

More about BOF and EOF

When working with the BOF and EOF properties, you should understand the behavior that makes them either True or False. Table 2.5 shows how both properties are set.

Finding Records

Once you have opened a Recordset that contains more than one row, you may want to use the Find method to locate specific records in the Recordset. This has the important

Table 2.5   Actions or Conditions That Affect the Values of the BOF and EOF Properties

ACTION OR CONDITION	BOF/EOF PROPERTY VALUES
You open a Recordset and no rows are returned.	Both BOF and EOF are True.
You open a Recordset and one or more rows are returned.	Both BOF and EOF are False.
You move the pointer onto the beginning of file or end of file marker.	BOF or EOF becomes True, depending on the marker the pointer is on.
The pointer is on the only record in the Recordset, and you delete it.	Both BOF and EOF become True.
You allow the pointer to stay on either the beginning of file marker or end of file marker and then try to do something with a field object, such as read a value.	The BOF or EOF property is True and a runtime provider error occurs.

advantage of using the in-memory cursor to find the records without requerying the data source. When you use the Find method, don't take the lazy approach. Though you could open a large set of records and then use the Find method to search for a specific record, you should not open larger than necessary Recordsets. It is better to be selective about the number of rows you'll return for a Recordset by using an appropriately crafted WHERE clause or, possibly, a stored procedure that takes parameters. With this being the case, you do not incur a huge burden. Remember, always return the least possible number of rows. Then, if necessary, use the Find method to locate specific rows.

Find Method Syntax

To use the Find method, you issue the method call using a number of arguments, as in the next example:

```
objRst.Find "cuCustomerName = '" & Trim(txtData(0)) & "'", _
    1, adSearchForward, objRst.Bookmark
```

Here, the Criteria argument of the Find method locates a record where the Customer Name equals the value of a text box. Each of the other optional arguments is explained next.

Criteria. Use this argument to supply the condition for the search. The format requires a field name, a valid comparison operator, and a value. You can use multiple criteria by concatenating conditions with the "And" or "Or" operators:

```
objRst.Find "cuCustomerName = '" & Trim(txtData(0)) & _
    "' And cuContactName = 'Shelley Storm'"
```

SkipRecords. Use this argument as an offset when starting the search. For example, you could set SkipRecords to 10 so that the search would commence 10 records from the current record.

SearchDirection. Use this argument to specify the direction of the search through the Recordset. You can set the argument to adSearchForward or adSearchBackward.

Start. Optionally, use this argument to supply a bookmark value as the starting point for the search instead of the SkipRecords argument.

After executing the Find method, the row pointer is either positioned on the found row; if the row is not found, the pointer is positioned at the end of the Recordset.

Sorting and Filtering

New to ADO 2.0 is the ability to sort and filter a Recordset. Formerly, if you wanted to sort a Recordset, you had to close an open Recordset and reopen it using the appropriate ORDER BY clause. Closing and reopening Recordsets to apply a sort order is costly. Similarly, if you wanted to exclude certain records from a Recordset, you had to apply the criteria using a WHERE clause. Once the Recordset was opened, you could not limit the number of records in memory. All this has changed in 2.0. You can sort and filter Recordset data *after* you've opened a Recordset.

Sorting

Sorting is useful for quickly changing the order of rows, as users require. For example, a Recordset containing customer data that was initially sorted by the cuCustomerID field could easily be resorted by the cuState field, as shown in this code:

```
Dim objCnn As New ADODB.Connection
Dim objRst As New ADODB.Recordset
Dim sConnect As String
Dim sSQL As String

sConnect = "Provider=MSDASQL;Driver={SQL Server};" & _
    "Server=DALA;Database=OrderManager;UID=sa;" & _
    "PWD=;"

sSQL = "SELECT cuCustomerID, cuCustomerName, " & _
    "cuContactName, cuContactPhone, cuContactFax, " & _
    "cuCity, cuState FROM Customers WHERE " & _
    "cuCustomerID < " & 1100

With objCnn
    .ConnectionTimeout = 15
    .CursorLocation = adUseClient
    .Open sConnect
End With

objRst.Open sSQL, objCnn, adOpenKeyset, adLockOptimistic
objRst.Sort = "cuState ASC"
```

As you can see, you set the Sort property to the name of a field in the Recordset, followed by the ASC or DESC descriptor to determine the direction the data is sorted. The expression can be a comma-delimited list so that you can sort on multiple columns.

Note that when using the Sort property, you must specify that the cursor library used for the Recordset is the client cursor library. You do this by setting the Recordset's CursorLocation property to adUseClient as in the preceding code. You can also set the CursorLocation for all Recordsets opened for a given connection by setting the CursorLocation property of the Connection object before opening it.

```
objRst.Sort "cuState ASC,cuPostalCode ASC"
```

To cancel the effects of the Sort property, you can set the property equal to a zero-length string. When you do this, the order the data was originally accessed will become the order in which the rows are presented.

Using the Optimize Property

When sorting, finding, or filtering records with a cursor, you can often improve performance by creating a dynamic index on the desired fields. To do this, you use the Optimize property that is contained in the Field object's Properties collection. The Optimize property is not part of the Field object's native interface, thus it is a dynamic property.

Using the previous example, you can create an index on the cuState and cuPostal-Code fields by setting their respective Optimize property values to True prior to executing the sort.

```
objRst.Fields("cuState").Properties("Optimize") = True
objRst.Fields("cuPostalCode").Properties("Optimize") = True
objRst.Sort "cuState ASC,cuPostalCode ASC"
```

To remove an index from a field, you set the Optimize property to False.

```
objRst.Fields("cuState").Properties("Optimize") = False
```

Filtering

Not only can you sort a Recordset after it is open, you can also apply a filter to an open Recordset. When you set the Filter property, you can either set it to a string that expresses one or more WHERE conditions that limit the data returned, one of a number of FilterGroupEnum values, or an array of bookmarks.

Using a Criteria String. You can construct a string that filters the Recordset, as in the next example. The code opens a Recordset, tests the record count, and then applies a filter so that the Recordset contains only those records where the cuCustomerID field is less than 1,050. The code then tests the record count again. When you apply a filter, the resulting rows are the new cursor, and the row pointer is on the first record that satisfies the filter criteria.

```
objRst.Open sSQL, objCnn, adOpenKeyset, adLockOptimistic
Debug.Print objRst.RecordCount

objRst.Filter = "cuCustomerID < " & 1050
Debug.Print objRst.RecordCount
```

You can also construct more complex filter criteria using the "And" and "Or" operators.

```
objRst.Filter = "cuCustomerID < " & 1050 & _
    " And cuState = 'IA'"
Debug.Print objRst.RecordCount

objRst.Filter = "(cuCustomerID < " & 1050 & _
    " And cuState = 'IA') Or (cuState = 'TN')"
Debug.Print objRst.RecordCount
```

FilterGroupEnums. You can use FilterGroupEnum values to specify intrinsic values that filter the Recordset. These are commonly used in conjunction with batch mode cursors, a subject discussed in the next chapter.

Bookmark Array. Here the filter criterion consists of an array of bookmark values that uniquely identify rows for the filter criteria. You'll explore the use of this when we discuss disconnected Recordsets in the next chapter.

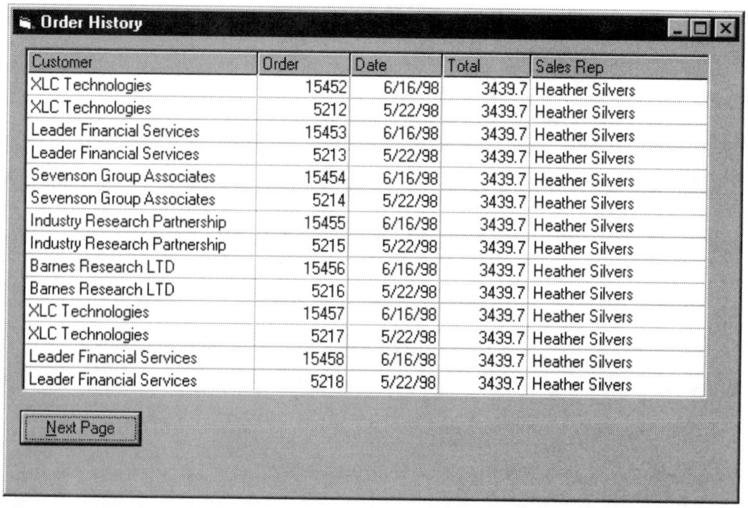

Customer	Order	Date	Total	Sales Rep
XLC Technologies	15452	6/16/98	3439.7	Heather Silvers
XLC Technologies	5212	5/22/98	3439.7	Heather Silvers
Leader Financial Services	15453	6/16/98	3439.7	Heather Silvers
Leader Financial Services	5213	5/22/98	3439.7	Heather Silvers
Sevenson Group Associates	15454	6/16/98	3439.7	Heather Silvers
Sevenson Group Associates	5214	5/22/98	3439.7	Heather Silvers
Industry Research Partnership	15455	6/16/98	3439.7	Heather Silvers
Industry Research Partnership	5215	5/22/98	3439.7	Heather Silvers
Barnes Research LTD	15456	6/16/98	3439.7	Heather Silvers
Barnes Research LTD	5216	5/22/98	3439.7	Heather Silvers
XLC Technologies	15457	6/16/98	3439.7	Heather Silvers
XLC Technologies	5217	5/22/98	3439.7	Heather Silvers
Leader Financial Services	15458	6/16/98	3439.7	Heather Silvers
Leader Financial Services	5218	5/22/98	3439.7	Heather Silvers

Figure 2.6 Recordset paging can be used to show pages of data in a form or any other user interface.

Recordset Paging

When working with Recordsets, you often want to construct a view that displays only a finite number of records at a time. Particularly, in data-driven Web applications, you may want to return, for example, only 10 rows at a time to the client for viewing. Then when the user requests more data, another 10 rows can be transmitted. ADO does this through a concept called a page, some number of records that you programmatically define. ADO allows the Recordset to be divided up into pages that allow for easy navigation from page to page in the Recordset.

For example, if you opened a Recordset containing several hundred rows, you could define a page of records as 10 rows. You define a Recordset page by setting the PageSize property. Once you set the PageSize property, ADO sets the PageCount property that determines how many pages are contained in the Recordset. To navigate from page to page in the Recordset, you set the AbsolutePage property to move the pointer to the appropriate page number.

In the next code example, code supplies data to an MS Flex Grid 14 rows at a time. The user can select the Next Page button to return the next page of data. Figure 2.6 shows the Order History form that displays Recordset data one page at a time.

```
Dim iCount As Integer
Dim sLine As String
Static iPageCount As Integer
Dim iEnd As Integer

If iPageCount = 0 Then
    iPageCount = 1
    objRst.AbsolutePage = iPageCount
Else
```

(continues)

(Continued)

```
        iPageCount = iPageCount + 1
        objRst.AbsolutePage = iPageCount
End If
```

Here, the If...End If statement initializes the AbsolutePage property to an appropriate integer value. The first time the procedure is executed, AbsolutePage is set to 1 and then incremented each time the procedure is run by using the static variable iPageCount. When the AbsolutePage property is set, the pointer is moved to the first record in the page specified.

```
flxOrders.Rows = 1

If iPageCount * objRst.PageSize > _
    objRst.RecordCount - objRst.PageSize Then
        iEnd = objRst.RecordCount - (iPageCount * _
            objRst.PageSize)
Else
    iEnd = objRst.PageSize
End If
```

A second If...End If statement determines when the last page of data is reached, by testing the PageSize and RecordCount properties. It does this so that it can derive the appropriate ending value (iEnd) for the loop following. It is important that you determine when you've reached the last page because you may find that the last page does not contain a full page of records. With this being the case, whatever looping mechanism you're using to output data must not iterate too many times.

```
For iCount = 1 To iEnd
    With objRst
        sLine = .Fields(0) & vbTab & .Fields(1) & vbTab _
            & .Fields(2) & vbTab & .Fields(3) & vbTab _
            & .Fields(4) & " " & .Fields(5)
        flxOrders.AddItem sLine, iCount
        .MoveNext
    End With
Next
```

The code inside the With...End With statement uses the MS Flex Grid AddItem method to append a row to the grid.

Data Modification

When it comes to the subject of modifying data (adding, changing, or deleting rows), you'll often find it better *not* to use a cursor to effect those changes. As you've seen earlier in this chapter, you can use the INSERT, UPDATE, and DELETE SQL commands to effect changes to data. You can also use the Command object with stored procedures that modify the data in your database.

The reason is simple: Using a SQL statement with Command objects or, possibly, a Connection object requires less overhead than creating a cursor to do the same. Even so, the Recordset provides a number of methods that allow changes to be made to a data source.

Deleting Records

To delete a record from a cursor, you can use the Delete method. First, you make sure the pointer is on the desired row, or move it there, and then delete it.

```
objRst.Delete
```

You can also specify the adAffectGroup enum value to delete all rows satisfying the current Filter property value. In this case, all rows making up the filtered cursor would be deleted.

```
objRst.Filter = "cuCustomerID < " & 1050
objRst.Delete adAffectGroup
```

As soon as the deletion takes place, it may be visible to other processes that have Recordsets open and that included the just-deleted row(s) in their source. These other processes, which must be using a keyset or dynamic cursor, will know that the deletion took place. For example, with a keyset cursor, you can issue the Resync method to refresh the data in the current Recordset before trying an operation on the row. Next, two Recordsets are opened, and a row is deleted from the first. Before testing the value of a column, the Resync method is issued on the second Recordset. The last statement in the example produces a provider error indicating that the row has been deleted—"A given HROW referred to a hard- or soft-deleted row."

With the use of dynamic cursors, after using the Resync method, the refreshed Recordset would no longer contain a reference to the deleted row.

```
objRst.Open sSQL, objCnn, adOpenKeyset, adLockOptimistic
objRst2.Open sSQL, objCnn, adOpenKeyset, adLockOptimistic

objRst.MoveNext
objRst.Delete
objRst2.Resync
objRst2.MoveNext
sValue = objRst2(0) 'Produces provider error.
```

It is more efficient, however, to execute a SQL statement without creating an ADO cursor for the operation, as shown here.

```
With objCmd
    .CommandType = adCmdText
    .CommandText = "DELETE Customers.* WHERE " & _
        "cuCustomerID < " & 1050
    .ActiveConnection = objCnn
    .Execute
End With
```

Editing Rows

To edit existing rows, you change the appropriate Recordset fields and then issue the Update method. Note: Unlike the earlier DAO model, you don't issue an Edit method.

```
With objRst
    .Fields("cuCustomerName") = "Omega Enterprises"
    .Fields("cuContactName") = "Dan Smith"
    .Fields("cuContactPhone") = "555-555-5555"
    .Update
End With
```

When using the adLockOptimistic lock type, you can trap for errors that occur upon issuing an Update. With optimistic locking, multiple users or processes can have access and can edit the same row at relatively the same time. The first user or process to issue an update is allowed to save his or her changes to the data source. Subsequent updates by other users or processes will cause a provider error. The following code simulates this with the use of two Recordset objects derived from the same source.

```
Dim objCnn As New ADODB.Connection
Dim objRst As New ADODB.Recordset
Dim objRst2 As New ADODB.Recordset
Dim sConnect As String
Dim sSQL As String

sConnect = "Provider=MSDASQL;Driver={SQL Server};" & _
    "Server=DALA;Database=OrderManager;UID=sa;" & _
    "PWD=;"

sSQL = "SELECT cuCustomerName, cuContactName, " & _
    "cuContactPhone, cuContactFax, cuCity FROM " & _
    "Customers WHERE cuCustomerID < " & 1100

With objCnn
    .ConnectionTimeout = 15
    .Open sConnect
End With

objRst.Open sSQL, objCnn, adOpenKeyset, adLockOptimistic
objRst2.Open sSQL, objCnn, adOpenKeyset, adLockOptimistic
objRst(0) = "Foo"
objRst.Update 'First to save wins
objRst2(0) = "Foo2"
objRst2.Update 'Results in provider error
If Err.Number <> 0 Then
    objrst2.CancelUpdate
End If
```

The statement objRst2.Update fails because the other cursor (objRst), representing another user or process, already succeeded with an update. And the CancelUpdate method undoes any changes to the row. Figure 2.7 shows the provider error that results.

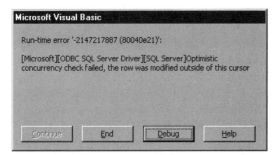

Figure 2.7 With optimistic locking, row conflicts can be managed by trapping errors resulting from the Update method.

Adding Rows

Finally, you can add new rows via the AddNew and Update methods.

```
With objRst
    .Addnew
    .Fields("cuCustomerName") = "Omega Enterprises"
    .Fields("cuContactName") = "Dan Smith"
    .Fields("cuContactPhone") = "555-555-5555"
    .Update
End With
```

In multiuser scenarios, the new record is visible with a dynamic cursor only. After refreshing the cursor, the newly added row is part of cursors that other users or processes may have had open when the addition was made.

Handling Binary Data with Recordsets

This section explains the handling of large text and binary data. In many applications, the need arises to store text data that exceeds the standards of many RDBMS standard text fields. For example, with Microsoft SQL Server, you would use the Char or Varchar data types to store text information that does not exceed more than 255 characters. However, if you needed to store alphanumeric information that exceeded that limit, you would have to use the Text data type. Similarly, to store information from a graphic file, for example, you could use SQL Server's Image, Binary, or Varbinary data types.

These data types store information in either a character or binary format. Furthermore, with SQL Server, the actual field only holds pointers to other 2K pages that actually store the information. In SQL Server, text and image data consists of character or binary data stored and managed as a linked list of 2K data pages that appear as if they were stored in a table row. A text or image column contains NULL or a pointer (assigned at initialization) to the first text page for that entry, and thus to the entire text or image value. Although text and image data type definitions do not include length, they do allow null values.

At least one 2K data page is allocated for each nonnull text or image data value. To save storage space, you can insert null values until you use the text or image column. Understand that any update (even an update that sets the value to NULL) to a text or image column initializes the column; that is, it assigns a valid text pointer and causes the first 2K data page to be allocated.

What does all this have to do with ADO? First, you cannot set the value of a field that is sourced by any of these data types simply by setting the Field object's Value property. Specifically, you must learn how to use two methods of the Field object: the Append-Chunk and GetChunk methods. In addition, some other properties of the Field object come into the mix.

Using the AppendChunk Method

Using the familiar backdrop of the OrderManager database, let's assume that each order is accompanied by order notes that describe special information for the order. In some cases, the information may not exceed 255 characters, but in most cases it does. How would the application store this information in the Orders table? The code example that follows shows how to use the AppendChunk method to do exactly that. As you'll see, the AppendChunk method is very straightforward. This code declares the necessary variables, opens a connection, and then a Recordset.

```
Dim objCnn As New ADODB.Connection
Dim objRst As New ADODB.Recordset
Dim strConnect As String
Dim strSQL As String

strConnect = "Provider=MSDASQL;Driver={SQL Server};" & _
    "Server=(local);Database=OrderManager;UID=sa;" & _
    "PWD=;"

strSQL = "SELECT orNotes FROM Orders Where orOrderID = 5131"

With objCnn
    .Open strConnect
End With

With objRst
    .Open strSQL, objCnn, adOpenKeyset, adLockOptimistic
```

After opening the Recordset, the AppendChunk method adds the contents of a text box, txtNotes, to the orNotes field. Figure 2.8 shows the Notes form with representative data that would be stored in the field. The AppendChunk takes a single argument called Data. The Data argument is a variant containing either long binary or character data.

```
    .Fields("orNotes").AppendChunk txtNotes
    .Update
End With
```

```
objRst.Close
Set objRst = Nothing
objCnn.Close
Set objCnn = Nothing
```

When working with the AppendChunk method, you should be aware of a couple of other points. First, you can determine if a Field object supports the AppendChunk method by testing the Attributes property of the Field object. If the adFldLong bit is True, then the field supports the AppendChunk method. Second, the first AppendChunk call on a Field object writes data to the field, overwriting any existing data. Subsequent AppendChunk calls add to existing data. If you are appending data to one field and then you set or read the value of another field in the current record, ADO assumes that you are done appending data to the first field. If you call the AppendChunk method on the first field again, ADO interprets the call as a new AppendChunk operation and over-writes the existing data.

Using the GetChunk Method

You've seen the mechanics of using the AppendChunk method. To retrieve data from a large text or binary field, you use the GetChunk method. Typically, you'll retrieve only a predefined amount of data at a time using this method—although it is possible to retrieve all the contents in a single operation. But for situations where the amount of data is large and the system resources are limited, retrieving the information in seg-ments is more efficient. The GetChunk method takes a Length argument (sometimes referred to as Size) that identifies how many bytes should be retrieved from the field. By setting up a looping structure, you can extract the contents into a variable. As long as the Length argument does not exceed the value of the remaining data, the loop will con-

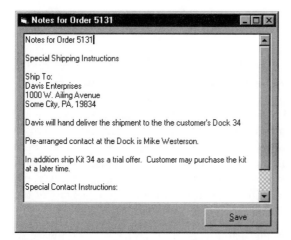

Figure 2.8 The Notes form uses the AppendChunk and GetChunk methods to store and display large text data.

tinue to retrieve the amount specified by the Length argument. When the remaining data is less than that specified by Length, then the remaining portion will be retrieved without any padding of empty spaces or null values.

The code following shows how the GetChunk method retrieves data from the orNotes field. After the code opens the Recordset, the actual size (e.g., the ActualSize property) of the field is stored to the variable lngLength to set up the condition for the looping structure that follows.

```
With objRst
    .Open strSQL, objCnn, adOpenKeyset, adLockOptimistic
    Set objNote = .Fields("orNotes")
    lngLength = objNote.ActualSize
    Do While lngLength > 1
        vntNotes = vntNotes & objNote.GetChunk(255)
        lngLength = lngLength - 255
    Loop
    txtNotes = vntNotes
End With
```

 Some RDBMS systems may not report a valid number of bytes for use with the ActualSize property. When working with the ActualSize property, SQL Server does seem to always report valid values, but other systems may not.

Each subsequent GetChunk call retrieves data starting from the point at which the previous GetChunk call left off. However, if you are retrieving data from one field and then you set or read the value of another field in the current record, ADO assumes you are done retrieving data from the first field. If you call the GetChunk method on the first field again, ADO interprets the call as a new GetChunk operation and starts reading from the beginning of the data.

From Here

In this chapter you've seen the basic operations of the Connection, Error, Command, Parameter, and Recordset objects. We've covered most of what there is to know about the Connection, Error, and Command objects, but there is more to uncover about parameters and Recordsets. In fact, you're still on the tip of the iceberg as far as the Recordset object is concerned. You'll have to go deeper to learn about the full capabilities of the Recordset, and that's what you'll do in the next chapter. Devoted almost exclusively to the more exciting features of the Recordset object (most are new to ADO 2.0), you'll round out your knowledge of working with Recordsets. Some of the highlights of the next chapter include:

- Using disconnected Recordsets and batch cursors to create efficient usage of connections and extend the capabilities of users to update data while disconnected from a data source.

- Using Recordset events.
- Persisting Recordset data to a file for use with middle-tier business objects and Web applications, which can read the file at a later time and append information to a database.
- Using Recordsets without a connection.
- Using hierarchical Recordsets for creative display of data.

Getting the Most
Out of Recordsets

Don't you like it when you get your money's worth? You make an investment and it pays off because what you bought met or exceeded your expectations. I hope that is your experience with this chapter, after you learn about the features of the Recordset. Chapter 2 just scratched the surface. Some of the most innovative and exciting enhancements to ADO 2.0 belong to the Recordset.

What You'll Learn

To "get you out of the starting gate," in Chapter 2 you examined code syntax and fairly simple examples of how to use ADO objects and their properties and methods. In this chapter, the examples become more robust and specific to different application contexts. You will see code examples that are in the context of server-side script that runs in an Active Server Page. You'll also see code that runs on a Web client, yet still uses the ADO Recordset to perform the application's tasks. You'll also see ADO code running in a Visual Basic client application and in middle-tier business objects. These diverse examples are proof positive of the Universal Data Access strategy. ADO is indeed the application-level programming model for diverse data access in many different arenas of application development.

Specifically, you'll learn about the following uses of the Recordset object:

Using Disconnected Recordsets and Batch Updating. In this section, you'll learn about using disconnected Recordsets, paying specific attention to the subject of batch-updating data. After obtaining a Recordset, you can disconnect it from the connection. While disconnected, you can manipulate and modify data and then reassociate the Recordset with a connection again. Finally, you can update the changes to the database while preserving the ability to do optimistic locking.

Persisting Recordset Data. In this section, you'll explore one of the most, if not the most, valuable assets of ADO 2.0. Discussed in both the context of a client/server application and a Web application, you'll learn how to let your users gather information from a database and easily package it to a file that can be reopened any time. The section also highlights the usage of client- and server-side scripting, DHTML Data Binding, and the DHTML Tabular Data Control.

Shaping Data. In this section, you'll learn how to create Recordsets of related information in a hierarchy using the MSDataShape Provider. For example, a single Customer Recordset can contain an Orders Recordset and subsequently an OrderItems Recordset. You can then use the hierarchy to easily display the related data in any application context. This section demonstrates a middle-tier business object that retrieves "shaped" data and supplies an order history to an Active Server Page. The section also shows a "grouped" Recordset. The Shape data manipulation language allows for the use of aggregate operations for returning order totals, for example.

Working with User-Defined Recordsets. In this section, you'll learn how to create Recordsets that are built with a user-defined structure. This type of Recordset does not rely on a connection; as such, you can use it to work with data from literally anywhere. You have the benefit of being able to manipulate the data using most of the familiar Recordset features.

Using Disconnected Recordsets and Batch Updating

Disconnecting Recordsets means that you can extend the life a Recordset beyond that of its connection. A disconnected Recordset uses ADO's client-side cursor library for all the functions you may want to perform, such as sorting, filtering, updating, and deleting. Earlier, you learned that ADO supports a number of different cursor types. Each type of Recordset can be disconnected. In this section, you'll explore how to update data in a disconnected Recordset and then reestablish a connection so that the data can be transacted to the server.

While not new to ADO 2.0, this version of ADO includes updates that make disconnecting Recordsets a viable tool for application development. The following are only some of the scenarios where having the ability to disconnect a Recordset and batch updating the data source would be of value.

Client/Server Application. In some client/server applications, one approach involves keeping database connections open for as short a time as possible. Consider a simple Customer data entry form. The form loads and displays data for the user. The form also adds, changes, or deletes information. In the past, however, building a simple form like this either meant leaving an ODBC connection open the entire time the form was open, so you could preserve the ability to enforce pessimistic locking or handle optimistic locking conflicts, or if you chose to close the ODBC connection after the form loaded data, then some other mechanism had to be used to handle concurrency issues. Beginning with RDO 2 (which shipped with Visual Basic 5), Microsoft made disconnected Recordsets and batch cursors a reality. A disconnected cursor, in simple English, is a cursor that can "live and breathe" without an active connection to a data source. A disconnected cursor depends on ADO's client-side cursor engine. A batch cursor that is disconnected allows you to make changes to multiple records while disconnected and then update the data source in a batch operation.

Returning to the Customer form scenario, you can build your form so that it preserves the capability to handle concurrency issues. In short, you can open a connection, populate the Recordset and also the controls on the form. Afterward, you can disassociate the Recordset from the connection. Disassociating the Recordset does not kill it but maintains it as a full-featured, client-side cursor. You can then close the connection, instead of leaving it open for an extended period of time. The user can then add, edit, and delete rows. When the user chooses, program code can make a new connection and reassociate the cursor with the new connection. Then the data source can be updated. When updating the data source, ADO handles the likelihood of optimistic update conflicts. You can then appropriately handle those conflicts and any others with your program code.

Client/Server Application with Remote Users. Disconnecting a Recordset from a connection and keeping it alive as a client-side cache is powerful for applications that involve remote users. Consider the following scenario. A sales representative, working out of his or her home, dials in to the corporate network. He or she then opens up the Active Contacts form. Using ADO, the application loads all of the Active Contacts that the sales representative must contact. Since the application loads the information in a disconnected cursor that supports batch updating, the sales representative does not need to remain connected to the corporate network to work with the data. The salesperson can freely disconnect from the network. He or she can then do his or her job, making contacts and updating the status of each contact. Then, at a later time, he or she can reaccess the network and update the corporate database.

To summarize, disconnecting Recordsets in conjunction with the use of batch updating provides several powerful capabilities:

- If desirable, you can minimize the time that connections to a data source must be open.

- While disconnected, users can work with a full-featured, client-side cache of data. Regardless of whether they intend to update anything, this is a powerful feature.

- Using a "batch" cursor preserves the ability to handle concurrency problems through optimistic locking when working with disconnected Recordsets.

- Disconnected Recordsets are ideal for remote users, who may not want to remain connected to a network for long periods of time.

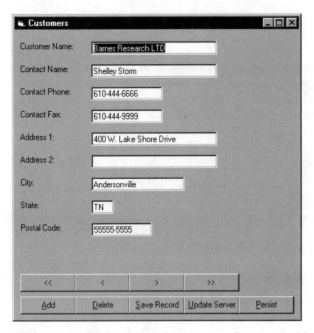

Figure 3.1 The Customers form uses a disconnected batch cursor so that data can be modified on the client without maintaining a persistent connection, and later updated to the server.

Opening a Batch Mode Cursor

Let's explore some code that shows the mechanics of how to make disconnected Recordsets work for you. In this example, we'll use the Customers form scenario, created in Visual Basic 6.0, for its relative simplicity. The form allows the user to view, add, edit, and delete records. See Figure 3.1.

In this example, the form's Load event procedure contains the code that opens the connection and establishes the batch mode cursor.

```
Private Sub Form_Load()

Dim strSQL As String

strSQL = "SELECT * FROM Customers WHERE " & _
    "cuCustomerID < " & 1250

Set mobjRst = New ADODB.Recordset
```

After initializing the appropriate variables, the Open method of the Recordset creates the batch mode cursor. You can disconnect Recordsets using ADO's other cursor types, but the batch mode cursor affords you the option of using the UpdateBatch operation to send a set of records to the server database after reconnecting. As you examine the Open method arguments, you'll see that a procedure called GetConnection is used to supply the ActiveConnection argument of the Open method. The code calls a procedure to supply a valid Connection object because the same connection attributes will be needed later. By creating a procedure that does this, some duplication of code will be avoided. Also, notice that the ADO constant, adLockBatchOptimistic, ensures that you create a batch mode cursor. Next, the MarshalOptions property is set so that only modified rows will be transmitted during an UpdateBatch operation. When setting the MarshalOptions property, you can choose between two MarshalOptionsEnum values: adMarshalAll = 0 and adMarshalModifiedOnly = 1. The default is adMarshalAll.

```
mobjRst.Open strSQL, GetConnection, adOpenKeyset, _
    adLockBatchOptimistic
mobjRst.MarshalOptions = adMarshalModifiedOnly
```

The GetConnection procedure returns an ADO Connection object. In the procedure, you'll notice that the CursorLocation property of the Connection object is set to adUseClient. When using batch mode cursors, you must set this property as such to engage the services of ADO's client-side cursor library. Indeed, any type of disconnected Recordset also uses the client-side library that supports Recordset operations on the client.

```
Public Function GetConnection() As ADODB.Connection

Dim strConnect As String
Dim objCnn As New ADODB.Connection

strConnect = "Provider=MSDASQL;Driver={SQL Server};" & _
    "Server=DALA;Database=OrderManager;UID=sa;" & _
    "PWD=;"

With objCnn
    .ConnectionTimeout = 15
    .CursorLocation = adUseClient
    .Open strConnect
End With

Set GetConnection = objCnn

End Function
```

Returning to the form's Load event procedure, the code having established a batch mode cursor, you can now disassociate the cursor from the Connection object. You do this by setting the ActiveConnection property (which was supplied a connection when the Open method executed) to Nothing. Remember that you can disassociate any cursor type from a connection, regardless of whether you use a batch cursor. The value of the batch cursor, in this example, is that you can later update all modified records to the data source.

In this example, which uses an unbound approach to supplying the form controls their data, the FillControls procedure is called. It simply supplies each control with the appropriate value from the Recordset.

```
Set mobjRst.ActiveConnection = Nothing
FillControls

End Sub
```

This example uses an unbound approach to supplying the form its data. This is not a statement of methodology, but simply makes sense given the primary purpose of this discussion, batch mode cursors. You will find that Visual Basic 6.0 has significant improvements that allow bound development to be a reality, with tools like the Data Environment and Data Classes. Those technologies are however outside the scope of this discussion.

Working with a Batch Mode Cursor

A batch mode cursor generally supports any of the features of a Recordset, including navigating, sorting, filtering, finding specific records, adding, editing, and deleting records. When working with any cursor type, including batch mode cursors, you can use the Supports method of the Recordset to determine if a particular feature of the Recordset is available. In Chapter 2, you learned that the Supports method can be tested using the following intrinsic constants: adAddNew, adApproxPosition, adBookmark, adDelete, adHoldRecords, adMovePrevious, adResync, adUpdate, and adUpdateBatch. For example, if you wanted to determine whether a cursor supports batch updates to a data source, you could test that capability this way:

```
If objRst.Supports(adUpdateBatch) Then
     'the cursor supports batch updating
Else
     'the cursor does not support batch updating
End If
```

In the Customers form example, the Add, Edit, and Delete buttons belong to a control array, cmdAction. When the user chooses to add, edit, or delete a record from the Recordset, the records in the current cache are modified. No changes are sent to the server database. Thus, the user is able to interact with the data without the need for an active connection.

```
Private Sub cmdAction_Click(Index As Integer)

Select Case Index
    Case 0 'First
        MoveToRecord "First"
    Case 1 'Prev
        MoveToRecord "Previous"
    Case 2 'Next
        MoveToRecord "Next"
    Case 3
```

```
            MoveToRecord "Last"
        Case 4 'Add
            AddRecord
        Case 5 'Delete
            DeleteRecord
        Case 6 'Save local
            SaveControls
        Case 7 'Save to Server
            UpdateServer
    End Select

    End Sub
```

Cases 4, 5, and 6 in the cmdAction Click event procedure call the AddRecord, Delete
Record, and SaveControls procedures, respectively.

Adding a Record to a Batch Cursor

Adding a record to a batch cursor is certainly not rocket science. You use the same
AddNew method that you would use with other cursor types. The only difference is that
once the record is saved (via the Recordset.Update method), the row is added to the
local cursor; the Update method does not force the changes to the server database when
using a batch cursor. The Case 4 clause executes the AddRecord procedure that simply
sets a Boolean variable to signify that a row is being added. Later, the AddNew method
will be executed.

```
Public Function AddRecord() As Boolean

    mblnAdd = True

End Function
```

Deleting a Record from a Batch Cursor

Deleting a record from a batch cursor is simply a matter of calling the Delete method of
the Recordset. Again, rows are not deleted from the data source, just the local cursor.
When the user deletes a row, the Case 5 clause executes calling the DeleteRecord procedure.

```
Public Function DeleteRecord() As Boolean

    If MsgBox("Do you want to delete '" & txtCustomer & "'?", _
        vbQuestion + vbYesNo, "Confirm Delete") = vbYes Then
        mobjRst.Delete
        MoveToRecord "Next"
    End If

End Function
```

Updating a Batch Cursor

When you want to save changes to an existing or new record, you use the Update method. The SaveControls procedure executes when the user clicks the Save Record button (Case 6). The SaveControls procedure determines if an add or edit is in progress, supplies the control values to Recordset fields, and issues the Update method.

```
Private Sub SaveControls()

Dim objCtrl As Control

If mblnAdd Then
    mobjRst.AddNew
End If

For Each objCtrl In Me
    If objCtrl.Tag <> "" Then
        mobjRst(objCtrl.Tag) = objCtrl
    End If
Next

mobjRst.Update

End Sub
```

In summary, the operations you perform on the disconnected Recordset, whether navigating, sorting, or modifying data, do not differ from the way you would perform those same operations on a connected cursor. However, at some point, it would be helpful to get all the changes that were made to the batch cursor to the database. You do this by using the UpdateBatch method of the Recordset.

Using the UpdateBatch Method

When the user is ready to update all of the local changes made to the batch cursor, he or she can update the changes in a batch using the UpdateBatch method. In the Customers form scenario, this is done when the user clicks the Update Server button. The Update-Server procedure reestablishes an active connection and then transmits the changes. The UpdateServer procedure also presents a confirmation message after the update succeeded to affirm the actual rows that were changed and which action was taken with them (remember, the user could have made changes to multiple records, and then transmitted all of them in a batch). To present this confirmation message, the procedure takes advantage of Recordset events. So, while this procedure is simple in purpose, it deals with a number of ADO Recordset capabilities.

Using the Filter Property

First, the UpdateServer procedure determines if the user actually made any changes to the local cursor by setting the Filter property to adFilterPendingRecords. This makes visible only those rows in the cursor that were modified by the AddNew, Update, or

Delete methods. After setting the Filter property, you can test the RecordCount property to determine if any changes were made. If the RecordCount is zero, then there is nothing to send to the server. The Filter can then be set to adFilterNone to return the state of the cursor to show all records that were originally retrieved.

```
Public Function UpdateServer() As Boolean

Dim strMsg As String
Dim strRowsFailed As String

'Present confirm message

'First set the filter to include only modified records
'so the message can include how many records will be updated

mobjRst.Filter = adFilterPendingRecords

'If the record count is 0 then no recs were modified
If mobjRst.RecordCount = 0 Then
    mobjRst.Filter = adFilterNone
    mobjRst.MoveFirst
    Exit Function
End If
```

Reassociating a Cursor with a Connection

Next, the code proceeds to verify whether the user wants to go ahead with the batch update. If they choose to do so, the ActiveConnection property is then set to reassociate the cursor (mobjRst) with a Connection object. Remember that the GetConnection procedure returns a Connection object. The variable, strMsg, refers to the RecordCount property to tell the user how many records were changed. Recall that, since the Filter property was earlier set to adFilterPendingRecords, the RecordCount property only yields a value for the records actually modified in some way.

```
strMsg = "Do you want to save your changes to " & _
    "the server? You changed a total of " & _
    mobjRst.RecordCount & " record(s)."

'Confirm update

If MsgBox(strMsg, vbQuestion + vbYesNo, _
    "Confirm Server Update") = vbYes Then
    Set mobjRst.ActiveConnection = GetConnection
```

Executing the UpdateBatch Method

Next, the procedure calls the UpdateBatch method passing the intrinsic constant, adAffectGroup, for the AffectRecords argument. The adAffectGroup constant tells ADO to write only those records that satisfy the current Filter property setting.

```
mobjRst.UpdateBatch adAffectGroup
```

The AffectRecords argument can be set to one of three AffectEnum constants that govern how the batch update will behave. Table 3.1 describes these constants.

When you issue an UpdateBatch method, the completion of the operation is its highest priority. Therefore, any errors that result during the operation will not cause a runtime error to be reported. The only time the operation will produce a runtime error and attempt to enter your error-handling mechanism is if all rows in the operation fail. Since an error may occur on one row, and not on others, generally, you should do some checking to determine if any of the rows that you updated did indeed fail.

 When using batch cursors that transmit data to a middle-tier business object, or when using batch cursors with Remote Data Services (RDS), you can improve performance and reduce the amount of data transmitted by setting the MarshalOptions property. You can either choose to marshal all records (adMarshalAll 0) or only the modified rows (adMarshalModifiedOnly 1). The enum adMarshalAll is the default. You may also want to use this property when middle-tier services are not in effect.

Checking for UpdateBatch Errors

The UpdateServer procedure continues to check for errors that could have occurred. It does this initially by checking the Errors collection to determine if any provider errors were returned. If so, you can use the Filter property again to make only rows that failed to update visible in the cursor. To do this, you set the Filter property to adFilterConflictingRecords. Then a loop moves through each of the conflicting records and, in this example, builds a message to present to the user. Understand that when errors occur during an UpdateBatch operation, the errors are for records that have already been modified (successfully) in the local cursor via the Delete or Update method. For example, a primary key violation or an update conflict would not be reported during an Update operation with a disconnected cursor but certainly would cause a failure during an UpdateBatch operation.

Table 3.1 AffectEnum Constants and Their Behavior during an UpdateBatch Operation

CONSTANT	BEHAVIOR
adAffectCurrent	Causes only pending changes for the current row to be written during an UpdateBatch operation.
adAffectGroup	Causes only records satisfying the current Filter property setting to be written during an UpdateBatch operation.
adAffectAll	Causes all records to be written during an update batch operation, regardless of the current Filter property setting. This is the default setting.

Figure 3.2   The Filter property can be used to determine which rows failed during an Up-dateBatch operation.

```
If mobjRst.ActiveConnection.Errors.Count <> 0 Then
    mobjRst.Filter = adFilterConflictingRecords
    Do While Not mobjRst.EOF
        strRowsFailed = mobjRst("cuCustomerName")
        mobjRst.MoveNext
    Loop
    strRowsFailed = "The following Customers did not " & _
        "update due to errors:" & vbCr & _
vbCr & strRowsFailed
        MsgBox strRowsFailed, vbCritical, _
            "Update Server Conflicts"
```

The message produced looks like Figure 3.2.

 The code in this example only uses the Errors collection to determine if errors occurred, but you could iterate through the Error objects in the collection to determine the specific nature of errors that occurred during the UpdateBatch operation. If you're unsure of how to do this, refer to the Handling Errors section in Chapter 2.

After presenting the user with the message, the Filter property is again set to adFilterNone, and the Recordset is refreshed by using the Resync method.

```
mobjRst.Filter = adFilterNone
mobjRst.Resync
```

Presenting a Confirmation Message

The Else clause (next code sample) executes when no errors were encountered. In the example, a confirmation message is supplied that enables the user to determine which Customers records where affected and which action was taken add, edit, or delete. To return the Recordset to its proper state, the Filter property is again set to adFilterNone. The record pointer is moved to the first record, and the ActiveConnection is released by setting it to Nothing.

```
Else 'present success message
        'Build up the confirm message
```

(continues)

(Continued)

```
        strMsg = "You successfully modified the " & _
            "following Customers." & vbCr & vbCr
        strMsg = strMsg & mstrRowsChanged
        MsgBox strMsg, vbInformation, "Confirm Server Changes"


        'Unset the filter
        mobjRst.Filter = adFilterNone
        mobjRst.MoveFirst
    End If
    'Shut down the connection
    Set mobjRst.ActiveConnection = Nothing
  End If

End Function
```

Figure 3.3 shows what the confirmation message looks like.

Something, however, should seem a bit odd about the preceding Else clause code. Notice the mstrRowsChanged module scope variable. It is used to show which action was taken against each customer that was changed. Okay, that's simple. But, how was it get supplied its value? It is only referred to in the Else clause; no code in the Update-Server procedure supplies mstrRowsChanged with its value. The answer lies in understanding a bit about Recordset events. In Chapter 2, you learned about Connection object events and explored the use of the ExecuteComplete event. Some Recordset operations also cause events to fire. In this example, the mstrRowsChanged variable is supplied its value in Recordset event handlers. When an AddNew, Delete, and Update-Batch method is called, a number of Recordset events fire. Let's take a short excursion into Recordset events to understand their usefulness.

Understanding Recordset Events

Remember that the key to using ADO events in Visual Basic is to declare the ADO object using the WithEvents keyword. The Recordset mobjRst used throughout this example is declared in the Declarations section of the Customers form.

```
Private WithEvents mobjRst as ADODB.Recordset
```

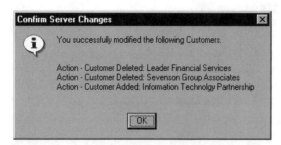

Figure 3.3   A confirmation message presented after an UpdateBatch operation.

If you're unsure about events at this point, reread the introductory material about ADO events in Events and Asynchronous Operations in Chapter 2.

ADO Recordsets support the following events that can be used for a variety of purposes. In the example code that follows, you learn specifically about the RecordChangeComplete and WillChangeRecord events. Table 3.2 lists and describes Recordset events.

Table 3.2   Recordset Events

EVENT	DESCRIPTION
EndOfRecordset	Fires when an operation attempts to move the pointer beyond the end of file marker. You may use this event to append more records to the Recordset, thus extending the end of file marker.
FetchComplete	Fires during a lengthy asynchronous operation and after all records have been retrieved. You may use this to notify the user that all rows have been returned.
FetchProgress	Fires at random during a lengthy asynchronous retrieval of data. You can use its arguments to determine how many rows of the total number have been retrieved.
WillChangeField FieldChangeComplete	WillChangeField fires before a pending operation changes the value of one or more Field objects in the Recordset. FieldChangeComplete fires after the value of one or more Field objects has changed. You can use these events to micromanage the nature of how fields are updated.
WillMove MoveComplete	WillMove fires before a pending operation changes the current position in the Recordset. MoveComplete fires after the current position in the Recordset changes. You can use these events to handle application-specific tasks that must be done anytime the pointer moves in the Recordset.
WillChangeRecord RecordChangeComplete	WillChangeRecord fires before one or more records (rows) in the Recordset change. RecordChangeComplete fires after one or more records change. Any one of the following operations can cause these events to fire: AddNew, Delete, Update, CancelUpdate, Cancel, and UpdateBatch.
WillChangeRecordset RecordsetChangeComplete	WillChangeRecordset fires before a pending operation changes the entire Recordset. RecordsetChangeComplete fires after the entire Recordset has changed. You can use these events to further handle operations that affect a set of records in the Recordset.

Using the WillChangeRecord and RecordChangeComplete Events

In the Customers form example, the reason to use these events was to allow notification when a specific action (add, edit, or delete) occurred on a record. Let's take a look at handling the delete notification first. With this in mind, code was added to the event handler for the WillChangeRecord event. The WillChangeRecord event (in this scenario) fires when an AddNew or Delete method (and some others) is issued. This event does not fire when a Recordset.Update is issued and the cursor you are using is a batch cursor. As such, it is ideal for identifying each and every time the user deletes a record from the batch Recordset. But wait a minute; why not just use the RecordChangeComplete event? We will shortly, but not for a delete operation because by the time that event has fired, the row is already gone. It's kind of hard to find out which customer got deleted if the customer is already deleted!

The following code simply polls the adReason argument to selectively identify the operation that caused the event to fire. If adReason equals the constant adRsnDelete, then the Delete operation was just executed and the event fired. The variable, mstrRowsChanged, can be updated to show the action that commenced. ADO passes a by-value Recordset (pRecordset) into the event handler so you can use it for your own specific purposes.

```
Private Sub mobjRst_WillChangeRecord(ByVal adReason As _
    ADODB.EventReasonEnum, ByVal cRecords As Long, _
    adStatus As ADODB.EventStatusEnum, ByVal pRecordset _
    As ADODB.Recordset)

'Fires when Delete method is issued
'Using this event because the row is actually deleted by the time
'RecordChangeComplete fires

If adReason = adRsnDelete Then
    mstrRowsChanged = mstrRowsChanged & vbCr _
        & "Action - Customer Deleted: " & _
        pRecordset("cuCustomerName")
End If

End Sub
```

To determine when a row is added and modified, we'll use the RecordChangeComplete event handler to selectively build up the mstrRowsChanged variable. This event fires (in this example) when an AddNew method is issued and an UpdateBatch method (and a few other times) is used. Normally, both of these events would fire also when an Update method is issued, but since a batch cursor is being used, the Update operation does not fire these events.

```
Private Sub mobjRst_RecordChangeComplete(ByVal adReason _
    As ADODB.EventReasonEnum, ByVal cRecords As Long, _
    ByVal pError As ADODB.Error, adStatus As _
    ADODB.EventStatusEnum, ByVal pRecordset As ADODB.Recordset)
```

```
Dim strAction As String

Select Case adReason
    Case adRsnAddNew 'Fires when Addnew method is called
        'Use txtCustomer because pRecSet doesn't have data yet
        mstrRowsChanged = mstrRowsChanged & vbCr _
            & "Action - Customer Added: " & txtCustomer
    Case adRsnUpdate
        strAction = "Action - Customer Changed: "

        'Avoids error when this is called from update batch
        'on a deleted row
        On Error Resume Next

        mstrRowsChanged = mstrRowsChanged & vbCr _
            & strAction & pRecordset("cuCustomerName")
End Select

End Sub
```

The adReason argument is extremely important to understand because these events fire frequently. They're even a bit unruly because they sometimes fire as a result of an operation you performed, but for which you did not expect the event to fire. Therefore, using the adReason argument to determine the operation that caused the event handler to execute is very important. Table 3.3 shows the EventReasonEnums, such as adRsnDelete, that you can use to determine why an event fired.

As you can see, Recordset events can be used for a variety of purposes. In each and every case, they allow you to write program code that responds to the specific reason for the event occurrence.

The Customers form example showed a batch cursor that could be used to allow data to be modified without a connection to a database. While this is a valuable feature, what would happen to mobjRst (the client-side cursor in the example) if the application were closed? Well, all the modifications the user made to the cursor would be lost. So, though disconnected cursors do allow data to be taken "offline," any changes to the data only occur in memory. This brings us to another useful feature of ADO 2.0, Recordset persistence. With Recordset persistence, you can truly take data offline, such that Recordset data can be persisted to a file format that can be reopened and modified again and again. In the next section, you'll explore a number of ways to persist Recordset data.

Persisting Recordset Data

Recordset persistence has the potential to be the most powerful feature of ADO 2. It implements part of the vision for Universal Data Access, one of whose goals is to allow for increased flexibility in the presentation and manipulation of data. Until now, the only way to get a Recordset was to open a connection to some data source. In many cases, the data source was a relational database system that required ODBC or OLE DB connections. Making connections to such a data source is a fairly expensive and inflexible requirement.

Table 3.3 EventReasonEnums That Determine Which Operation Caused an Event to Fire

EVENTREASONENUM	VALUE	DESCRIPTION
AdRsnAddNew	1	An AddNew method caused the event to fire.
AdRsnClose	9	The Recordset was closed with the Close method.
AdRsnDelete	2	The Delete method caused the event to fire.
AdRsnFirstChange	11	The first field in a row was changed.
AdRsnMove	10	The Move method was issued. Other operations that move the pointer also may trigger the event.
AdRsnMoveFirst	12	The MoveFirst method caused the event to fire.
AdRsnMoveLast	15	The MoveLast method caused the event to fire.
AdRsnMoveNext	13	The MoveNext method caused the event to fire.
AdRsnMovePrevious	14	The MovePrevious method caused the event to fire.
AdRsnRequery	7	An operation caused the Recordset to be requeried.
AdRsnResynch	8	The Resync method caused the event to fire.
AdRsnUndoAddNew	5	The Cancel method caused the event to fire during a pending AddNew operation.
AdRsnUndoDelete	6	The Cancel method caused the event to fire during a pending Delete operation.
AdRsnUndoUpdate	4	The Cancel or CancelUpdate method caused the event to fire during a pending AddNew operation.
AdRsnUpdate	3	The Update or UpdateBatch method caused the event to fire.

In some applications, users may only need to access data for viewing purposes or possibly to maintain information stores that need not always be completely synchronized with data in an RDBMS system. Consider these scenarios:

- A sales representative needs to have quick access to his or her contact list. The information in the contact list is fairly static; it does not change on a frequent basis. Requiring such a user to always retrieve this information from an RDBMS system may put a crimp in his or her style. Providing some means for the appropriate data to be accessed easily and efficiently while the user is offline would be of great value.

- At month's end, an executive produces a sales report. Once the sales report is generated, the executive may want to view and/or modify the data for presentation purposes. He or she may even want to do this while on a plane flying to who knows where. Providing a means for the sales data to be persisted (locally) would be of value.

■ A field technician at a client site may want to dial in to his or her corporate network and open up a service history for the client. After accessing the service history, the technician may want to keep the information around while he or she is troubleshooting the problem for later reference. Time is of the essence. Why should the technician have to dial in repeatedly to access the information from the corporate database? Or, why should he or she have to persist the information to paper? Persisting the information locally would be of value so that after it was retrieved the first time from the corporate site, he or she could open the information from a local store.

And the list goes on.

In this section, you'll look at a number of scenarios that involve Recordset persistence. First, you'll look at an extension of the Customers form example from the last section. You'll view code that allows users to persist the Customers information to a local file so they can then reopen the file at a later time and work with the data without having to requery the database. But persistence can be used in other scenarios as well. You'll see two examples of Recordset persistence in a Web application. First, you'll find out how to open a locally persisted Recordset on a Web client. Doing so allows the program to use client-side script to programmatically manipulate the Recordset data (navigate, sort, filter, etc.). Second, you'll observe another means to persist Recordset data: the GetString method. You'll see how an Active Server Page invokes the services of a COM component and persists Recordset data to a delimited text file. This delimited text file can be placed in a virtual directory of the Web server, yet opened from the client. Further, this delimited file can be accessed via the Tabular Data Control and bound to HTML objects via DHTML data binding to provide superior client-side functionality.

Saving Recordset Data to a File

In the Customers form example from the last section, a disconnected batch allowed the user to make changes to customer data without a connection being maintained. In this example, you'll explore how to save the Recordset information to a local file that can be reopened again and again and sent over the Internet.

Using the Save Method

Remember that the Customers form contained a Persist button. I know this isn't the most elegantly named button for a UI, but it works. When the user clicks the Persist button, the WriteFile procedure executes. The WriteFile procedure executes the Save method of the Recordset.

```
Public Function WriteFile() As Boolean

mobjRst.Save "d:\book\code\customer.rst", adPersistADTG

End Function
```

The Save method accepts two arguments, as shown:

```
Recordset.Save FileName, PersistFormat
```

The FileName argument supplies the path and name of the file for the persisted Recordset. The PersistFormat argument identifies the format of the file. Currently, you have two valid formats to supply. The first format is adPersistADTG and is a proprietary file format for saving the contents of a Recordset. The second format is called adPersistXML which saves the data to an XML data store. As you may already know, XML is an emerging non-proprietary, industry-standard data format that can be interpreted by many different browsers, applications, and platforms.

> **At the time of this writing, the XML format into which ADO Recordsets write their contents is very likely to change. For this reason, we will not delve deeply into the structure XML file that the Save method of the Recordset currently produces.**
>
> **Later in this chapter, we will discuss the use of ADO and XML in more detail. However, before you implement XML and ADO in an application, you should first do some research. There are some very interesting and important developments that will be happening on this front in the near future.**

So, to persist a Recordset, all you have to do is follow two simple steps:

1. Open a Recordset and supply it with data.
2. Persist the Recordset data to a file (of either proprietary or non-proprietary format) using the Save method.

That's not too difficult. Let's see how to reopen the customer information from the persisted file.

Using the Open Method to Access Persisted Data

You've already seen the Open method of the Recordset used to open a Recordset using a SQL statement, stored procedure, and other means. Here you'll use the same Open method to open the persisted Recordset file, customer.rst. The following code uses the mobjRst Recordset object variable to open the persisted file.

```
Set mobjRst = New ADODB.Recordset
With mobjRst
    .CursorLocation = adUserClient
    .Open "d:\book\code\customer.rst", , adOpenKeyset, _
        adLockOptimistic
End With
```

In this sample, the CursorLocation property is set to adUseClient to invoke the resources of ADO's client-side cursor support. If you allow the cursor to be constructed using the adUseServer argument, you'll find that some operations will fail. In most or all cases, persisted Recordsets should be opened using the client-side cursor library. Furthermore, the Source argument of the Open method is supplied by the path and file name of the .rst file. Notice that the ActiveConnection argument is omitted, since the Recordset data is not being retrieved using a Connection object.

Having opened the Customers form using the persisted data, users can navigate, sort, filter, and modify the information, just as they would with a cursor supplied by a live connection. You can then enable the users to resave the information to the file as often as needed by using the Save method again.

A persisted Recordset can also be used to update the data source at any point in time. For example, a sales representative may add information to his or her contact list (while offline), and when he or she is able to connect to the corporate database (maybe days later), update the data source. To do this, follow these simple steps:

1. Extract data from the data source into a disconnected batch cursor using the client-side cursor library or create an arbitrary Recordset structure (see Working with User-Defined Recordsets later in this chapter).

2. The user may edit the data; then your code can modify individual rows with the Update, AddNew, and Delete methods as appropriate.

3. Allow users to save their "offline"' changes by persisting the Recordset to a file.

4. Allow users to open the persisted file (Open method). Remember, open the file as a batch cursor.

5. Supply a valid connection to the "reopened"' Recordset by setting its ActiveConnection property.

6. Let the users update the server with the UpdateBatch method.

Persisting Recordset Data for a Web Client

Recordset persistence is such a flexible concept that it finds application in a number of different solutions. For example, a Web application may make use of persisted Recordset information. In some Web-based, database applications, Web servers undergo tremendous resource overhead when many users access and manipulate database information at relatively the same time. Indeed, under heavy resource burden, Web applications can experience significant delays in opening database connections and executing operations. When designing Web applications, a common practice is to share that resource burden by, for example, including a dedicated data server (on a machine other than the Web server) and offloading middle-tier business objects to additional machines on the network. These practices cannot be overlooked in the architecture and design of an enterprise Web application.

Recordset persistence also gives you the means to help reduce the burden placed on the Web server. Many applications have portions of information that remain fairly static. Depending on the application, users may be able to perform some tasks quite satisfactorily using data that is a number of days old, or perhaps a number of hours old, or even a number of minutes old. So if a user can implement data for several hours primarily for viewing purposes, without needing to requery the data source, then it makes sense to build an application that can cache that data somewhere, either on the client or server. Doing this reduces the requirement for database connections and possibly even eliminates network traffic the entire time the user is using the information. This is not a new concept. Remote Data Services (RDS), formerly called the Advanced Data Connector, is the tool that does this. Among other things, RDS allows you to access information from a server-side database and to cache that data on the Web client. We'll explore the use of RDS in Chapter 5, *Using Remote Data Services in Web Applications*. Here, you'll examine a Web application that allows customer information to be accessed from a database and then persisted on the client. Specifically, the application shows the following:

- The application code shows how to write client-side script that accesses information from a persisted Recordset file located on the Web server.

- After the data is accessed, the code shows how to persist the data on the Web client.

- The code illustrates how the persisted Recordset data can be programmatically manipulated (e.g., navigated, sorted, and filtered).

The application simply accesses and caches customer information. Before looking at the code, however, take a look at the interface of Persist.htm, shown in Figure 3.4.

 The following example is best suited for an intranet context where the browser type can be controlled. The code relies on client side components (the Tabular Data Control and the ADO Recordset) that install with Internet Explorer 4.x and later. Furthermore, the example uses Recordset persistence, a feature supported by the ADO 2.0 Recordset.

Getting Data Down to the Client

The code for this example is contained in a lengthy .htm page called Persist.htm, so for the purposes of discussion, the important parts of the code will be displayed in segments. At the end of this section, the contents of the entire HTML page will be shown.

Remember, developing something like this for your users should be for one or more of the following reasons:

- You have data that does not have to be current to be useful.

- You need to reduce server burden and/or network traffic, and an appropriate way to do so is to take some data offline.

- You would like to give your users the means to work with information that has the robust ADO Recordset behind it, and at the same time, allow them to work with the information from a local store or possibly a store that does not require an ODBC connection on the server.

And don't forget, the Web browser must be Internet Explore 4.x or newer and the client-side ADO 2.0 Recordset must be installed as a browser component.

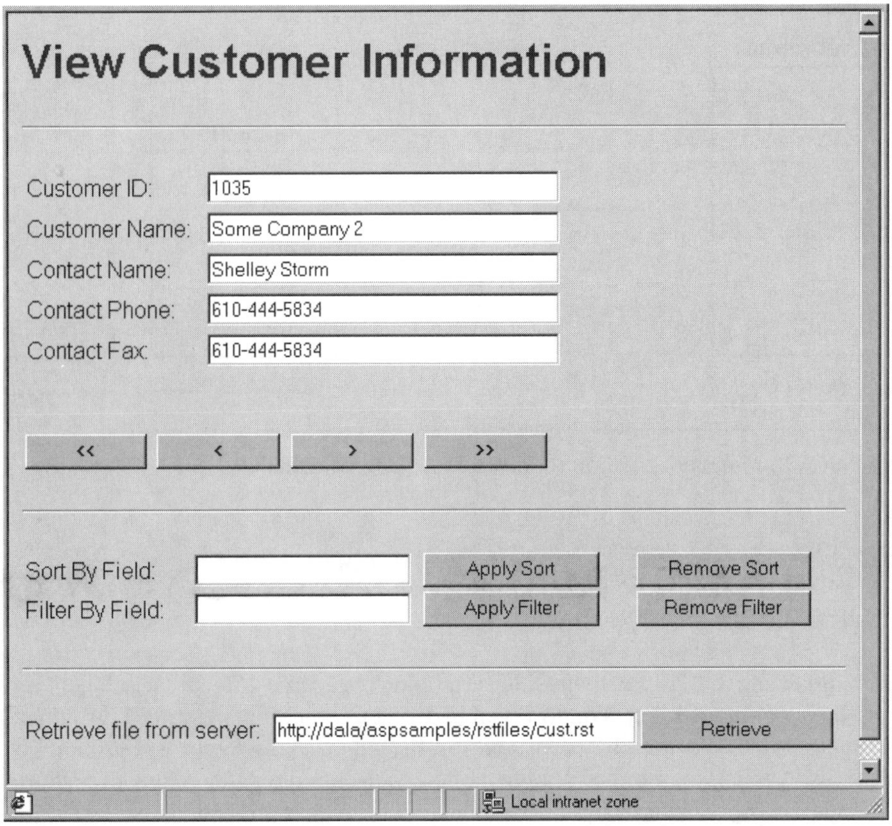

Figure 3.4   The Persist.htm web page allows for interaction with persisted customer data.

Using the Tabular Data Control

The Tabular Data Control (TDC) is an ActiveX control that installs with Internet Explorer 4.x. Typically, the TDC downloads data from a delimited text file. Extensions in Internet Explorer 4.x allow you to bind data supplied by the TDC to HTML elements on the page. The TDC also brings filtering and sorting operations to the Web client, without dependence on server-side services or data. Is this starting to sound familiar? Seems to me there is another object that can do client-side sorting and filtering. Oh yeah, that object is the ADO Recordset. Hmmm.

What's going on here is that the TDC employs the OLE DB Simple Text Provider to read data from a source and supply that data to its "invisible" consumer—yes, that's right, an ADO Recordset. You can think of the TDC as a wrapper around the ADO Recordset that is able to access data from OLE DB data sources, most often a text file (see Figure 3.5). But it doesn't stop there. Since the TDC employs the services of an ADO Recordset, you can use it to access persisted Recordset files.

To place a TDC on a Web page, you use the HTML OBJECT tag. The ClassID attribute references the unique identifier for the TDC. The ID attribute sets the name of the control.

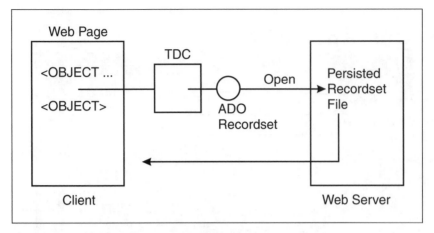

Figure 3.5   The Tabular Data Control hosts an ADO Recordset.

```
<OBJECT ClassID=clsid:333C7BC4-460F-11D0-BC04-0080C7055A83
    ID=dsoCust>
</OBJECT>
```

After initializing the TDC, a client-side script block prepares a Recordset object variable for later operations. The Window_OnLoad event, which fires as the HTML document is being sited, sets the object variable, objRst, equal to the Recordset property of the TDC (dsoCust). Because the variable, objRst, is declared outside of any procedure, it has scope for all procedures in this document and can be referenced later.

```
<SCRIPT Language=VBScript>
Dim objRst
Sub Window_OnLoad()
    On Error Resume Next
    Set objRst =dsoCust.Recordset
    If Err.Number <> 0 Then
        MsgBox "Application failed to initialize, see " & _
            "the system administrator."
    End If
End Sub
```

Retrieving a Persisted Recordset from the Web Server

Now a persisted Recordset file can be opened using the Open method of objRst. In this example, it is assumed that the persisted Recordset file has already been created and located in a virtual directory on the Web server. The script block continues with another client-side procedure named Retrieve, which declares a number of variables and defines some ADO constants. Next, the procedure determines if the user typed a value in the txtRetrieve text box.

```
Sub Retrieve()

Dim strLocalPath
Const adUseClient = 3
Const adOpenKeyset = 1
Const adLockReadOnly = 1

If txtRetrieve.Value = "" Then
    MsgBox "Type the path of the file on the Web Server."
    Exit Sub
End If
```

Now the code issues an On Error Resume Next statement, principally because some of the operations that follow could produce an error, depending on when the user runs them. Next, the code makes sure that objRst is closed because it cannot open a Recordset if it is already open. Following this, the code sets the Source property of the Recordset to a URL that identifies the file's home on the Web server. The user may type http://dala/aspsamples/RSTFiles/cust.rst to reference the .rst file on the server. Here you see that the source of a persisted Recordset does not have to be a local file path or even a network file path; the Open method will also stream a persisted file to a Web client using HTTP. Next, the code sets the CursorLocation property, as appropriate.

```
On Error Resume Next
objRst.Close
objRst.Source = txtRetrieve.Value
objRst.CursorLocation = adUseClient
```

Now you open the Recordset, caching the contents down to the client. The code then calls another procedure, MoveToRecord, that places the row pointer on the first record.

```
objRst.Open , ,adOpenKeyset, adLockReadOnly
strLocalPath = txtOpen.Value
MoveToRecord "First"

End Sub
```

Having done this, the user has extracted the desired information from the Web server and streamed it to a client-side cursor. Since the data is cached on the client, the user can freely work with it without placing more burden on the Web server and without creating additional network traffic—at least until the server file is requeried again at some point. Assuming that from time to time the persisted .rst file on the Web server is updated, the user can freely download another copy at will to refresh the client-side data set.

This approach to caching persisted data on a Web client is not the only way. One of its limitations is that manipulating the data on the client requires a fair amount of script. In the next section, you'll explore a different means of persisting Recordset data in for a Web application that takes advantage of DHTML Data Binding and so reduces the amount of client-side script. In Chapter 5, you'll learn the use of Remote Data Services to cache data on the client, and a host of other powerful features.

The preceding code samples did not show some of the client-side operations capabilities of Persist.htm. The page also uses client-side script to allow record navigation, sorting, and filtering of the information. Figure 3.6 shows the entire HTML and script for Persist.htm.

```
<HTML>
<HEAD>
">
<SCRIPT Language=VBScript>
Dim objRst
Sub Window_OnLoad()
    On Error Resume Next
    Set objRst =dsoCust.Recordset
    If Err.Number <> 0 Then
        MsgBox "Application failed to initialize, " & _
            "see the system administrator."
    End if
End Sub

Sub MoveToRecord(psDirection)
Select Case psDirection
    Case "First"
        objRst.MoveFirst
    Case "Last"
        objRst.MoveLast
    Case "Next"
        If objRst.EOF Then
            objRst.MoveFirst
        Else
            objRst.MoveNext
            If objRst.EOF Then
                objRst.MoveFirst
            End If
        End If
    Case "Previous"
        If objRst.BOF Then
            objRst.MoveLast
        Else
            objRst.MovePrevious
            If objRst.BOF Then
                objRst.MoveLast
            End If
        End If
    Case Else
        objRst.MoveFirst
```

Figure 3.6 The Persist.htm code.

```
End Select
FillControls
End Sub

Sub FillControls()

txtID.Value = objRst(0)
txtCust.Value = objRst(1)
txtContact.Value = objRst(2)
txtPhone.Value = objRst(3)
txtFax.Value = objRst(4)

End Sub

Sub Retrieve()

Const adUseClient = 3
Const adOpenKeyset = 1
Const adLockReadOnly = 1

If txtRetrieve.Value = "" Then
    MsgBox "Type the path of the file on the Web Server."
    Exit Sub
End if
On Error Resume Next
objRst.Close
objRst.Source = txtRetrieve.Value
objRst.CursorLocation = adUseClient
objRst.Open , ,adOpenKeyset, adLockReadOnly
MoveToRecord "First"

End Sub

Sub ApplySort()
Dim strSort
strSort = txtSort.value & " ASC"
objRst.Sort = strSort
MoveToRecord "First"
End Sub

Sub RemoveSort()
objRst.Sort = ""
MoveToRecord "First"
txtSort.Value = ""
End Sub

Sub ApplyFilter()
objRst.Filter = txtFilter.value
```

Figure 3.6 The Persist.htm code. (*Continued*)

```
MoveToRecord "First"
End Sub

Sub RemoveFilter()
objRst.Filter = ""
txtFilter.Value = ""
End Sub

</SCRIPT>

<!--TDC Control -->

<OBJECT CLASSID=clsid:333C7BC4-460F-11D0-BC04-0080C7055A83 ID=dsoCust
VIEWASTEXT>
</Object>

</HEAD>
<BODY bgColor=lightgrey><P><FONT face="Book Antiqua" size=6
style="COLOR: indigo; FONT-FAMILY: serif; FONT-STYLE: normal; FONT-
WEIGHT: bold"><FONT
face=Arial >View Customer
Information </FONT> </FONT></P>
<P><FONT face="Book Antiqua" size=6
style="COLOR: indigo; FONT-FAMILY: serif; FONT-STYLE: normal; FONT-
WEIGHT: bold"><FONT
face=Arial >
<HR >

<P></P>
<P></P>

<!--Define the customer controls -->

<TABLE Border=0 Width=400>
<TR><TD>Customer ID:</TD><TD><INPUT name=txtID style="WIDTH:
250px"></TD>
<TR><TD>Customer Name:</TD><TD><INPUT name=txtCust style="WIDTH:
250px"></TD>
<TR><TD>Contact Name:</TD><TD><INPUT name=txtContact style="WIDTH:
250px"></TD>
<TR><TD>Contact Phone:</TD><TD><INPUT name=txtPhone style="WIDTH:
250px"></TD>
<TR><TD>Contact Fax:</TD><TD><INPUT name=txtFax style="WIDTH:
250px"></TD></TR>
<TR><TD> </TD></TR>
</TABLE>

<!--End definition of customer controls -->
```

Figure 3.6 The Persist.htm code. (*Continued*)

```
<!--Define the navigation buttons -->

<P>
<TABLE background="" border=0 cellPadding=1 cellSpacing=1 width=380>
<TR>
<TD><INPUT name=btnFirst style="WIDTH: 87px" OnClick="MoveToRecord
'First'" type=button value=&lt;&lt;>
<TD><INPUT name=btnPrev style="WIDTH: 87px" OnClick="MoveToRecord
'Previous'" type=button value=&lt;>
<TD><INPUT name=btnNext style="WIDTH: 87px" OnClick="MoveToRecord
'Next'" type=button value=&gt;>
<TD><INPUT name=btnLast style="WIDTH: 87px" OnClick="MoveToRecord
'Last'" type=button value=&gt;&gt;></TD></TR></TABLE></P>
<HR>

<!--End definition of navigation buttons -->

<!--Define the sort and filter text boxes and buttons -->

<P>
<TABLE border=0 cellPadding=1 cellSpacing=1 id=TABLE1 >
<TR>
<TD width=100>Sort By Field:<TD width=160><INPUT name=txtSort>
<TD width=150><INPUT name=btnSort style="WIDTH: 125px"
OnClick=ApplySort() type=button value="Apply Sort">
<TD width=150><INPUT name=btnSRemove style="WIDTH: 125px"
OnClick=RemoveSort() type=button value="Remove Sort">
<TR>
<TD width=125>Filter By Field:<TD><INPUT name=txtFilter>
<TD width=150><INPUT name=btnFilter style="WIDTH: 125px"
OnClick=ApplyFilter() type=button value="Apply Filter"></TD>
<TD width=150><INPUT name=btnFRemove style="WIDTH: 125px"
OnClick=RemoveFilter() type=button value="Remove Filter"></TD>
</TR></TABLE></P>
<P>
<HR>

<!--End sort and filter text boxes and buttons -->

<!--Define the retrieve and open text boxes and buttons -->

<P></P>

<TABLE background="" border=0 cellPadding=1 cellSpacing=1 width=100%>
<TR><TD><P>Retrieve file from server:</P>
<TD width=40><INPUT name=txtRetrieve style="HEIGHT: 22px; WIDTH: 258px">
<TD><INPUT name=btnRetrieve style="HEIGHT: 26px; WIDTH: 138px"
OnClick=Retrieve() type=button value=Retrieve>
```

Figure 3.6   The Persist.htm code. (*Continued*)

```
<TR><TD width=30%>Open a local (cached) file:<TD><INPUT name=txtOpen
style="HEIGHT: 22px; WIDTH: 257px">
<TD><INPUT name=btnOpen style="HEIGHT: 24px; WIDTH: 139px" type=button
value="Open Local"></TD></TR>
</TABLE></BUTTON></FONT></FONT>
</BODY>
</HTML>
```

Figure 3.6 The Persist.htm code. (*Continued*)

Persisting Data with the GetString Method

ADO not only supports the use of the Save method for persisting data but also the Get-String method. The GetString method does not write a file as the Save method, but it retrieves the contents of a Recordset in a delimited column, row format. As such, it is ideal for persisting Recordset data to a text file for the same reasons that you would use the Save method discussed earlier. In a Web-based application, you might, for example, want to allow some users to determine what data they want to persist. You would then want to retrieve that data from a database and persist it to a delimited text file. Once the data exists in a delimited format, it could be used for a variety of purposes: It could be imported into an Access database or an Excel spreadsheet or sent in e-mail—you name it. In this example, the delimited file will be used to present the information to the user in Internet Explorer. The data will be displayed using HTML controls, the Tabular Data Control, and DHTML Data Binding.

The code shown in this section is contained in three Web pages. The pages are listed here with a description.

CreateTextFile.htm. Presents a query interface that allows the users to determine the data they want to persist. The file then uses an HTML form to transmit an HTTP request to the Web server calling the CreateTextFile.asp page. Figure 3.7 shows CreateTextFile.htm.

CreateTextFile.asp. An Active Server Page (ASP) that runs server-side script. The script calls a COM component, the RecordsetToString object created with Visual Basic 6.0. RecordsetToString receives an SQL statement from the ASP and retrieves the records from the database into a Recordset. It then uses the GetString method to prepare a delimited string of the entire contents of the Recordset. Next, it returns the string to the ASP. The ASP stores the string to a .csv file using the ASP File System Object, a prepackaged COM component that ships with Visual Interdev. Since CreateTextFile.asp doesn't present much of an interface, Figure 3.8 shows the relationship between CreateTextFile.htm, CreateTextFile.asp, and the RecordsetToString object.

TestTextFile.htm. Displays a number of HTML controls and binds them to the Tabular Data Control. The TDC gets its data from the .csv file earlier. By binding HTML controls in this fashion, some client-side script can be eliminated.

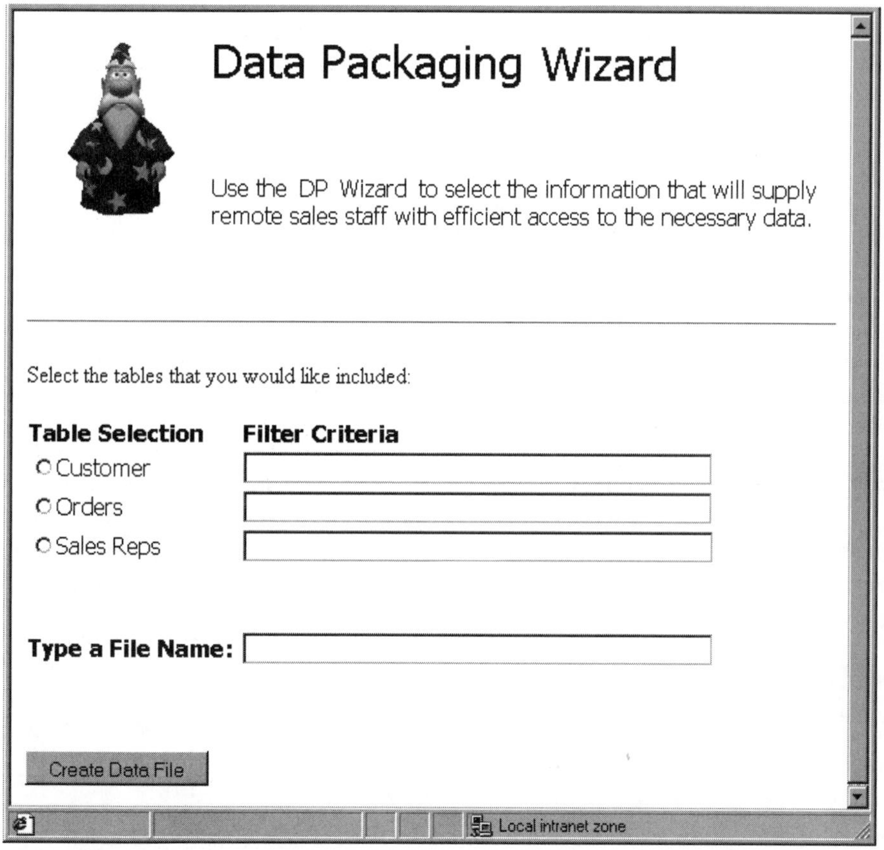

Data Packaging Wizard
Use the DP Wizard to select the information that will supply remote sales staff with efficient access to the necessary data.
Select the tables that you would like included:
Table Selection
Filter Criteria
Customer
Orders
Sales Reps
Type a File Name:
Create Data File
Local intranet zone

Figure 3.7 CreateTextFile.htm.

Internet Explorer
IIS 4.0
RecordsetToString Component
<FORM ...>
HTTP Request
</FORM>
.csv file
RDBMS
CreateTextFile.htm
CreateTextFile.asp

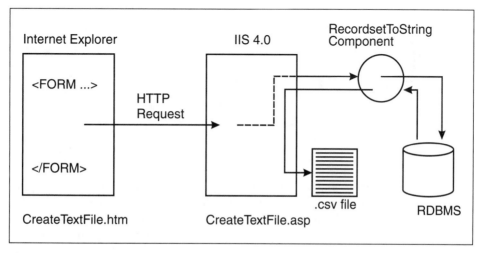

Figure 3.8 CreateTextFile.asp plays a role in creating the delimited .csv file.

Because this example uses Active Server technology, the code only operates under Internet Information Server (IIS).

The Role of the ASP

As you've seen, CreateTextFile.htm displays a simple interface that is used to determine the data to retrieve from the database. When the user clicks the CreateDataFile button, an HTML form is used to submit an HTTP request message to the Web server. The form elements transmitted contain an SQL statement and a file name for the persisted information.

When IIS receives the HTTP request, it recognizes that the request was for an ASP. IIS then passes the page on to the Active Server DLL's for processing. At this point, the script in CreateTextFile.asp executes.

The ASP first declares some variables and determines what SQL information was passed to it by using the ASP Request object to extract the information from the HTTP request server variables. Note: For sake of brevity, this example does not build the most flexible arrangement of SQL statements. The query interface does not allow the user to select fields for output. The example can be easily extended to provide increased functionality.

```
<%
Dim strSelect
Dim strWhere
Dim strData
Dim strFilePath
Dim objData
Dim objFS
Dim objTS


strWhere = ""

If Request.Form("optCustomer") = "on" Then
    strSelect = "Select * From Customers"
    strWhere = Request.Form("txtCustomer")
Elseif Request.Form("optCustomer") = "on" Then
    strSelect = "Select * From Orders"
    strWhere = Request.Form("txtOrder")
Elseif Request.Form("optSales") = "on" Then
    strSelect = "Select * From SalesReps"
    strWhere = Request.Form("txtSales")
End If
```

Next, the code invokes the services of the RecordsetToString component, which contains a CreateDataString method that returns the delimited contents of a Recordset. The CreateDataString method can be called by passing two arguments or just one. The second argument, supplying the WHERE clause, is optional. The data is returned to the ASP in the variable strData.

```
Set objData = Server.CreateObject("RecordsetToString.clsText")
If strWhere = "" Then
    strData = objData.CreateDataString (Cstr(strSelect))
Else
    strData = objData.CreateDataString (Cstr(strSelect), _
        Cstr(strWhere))
End If
Set objData = Nothing
```

The Heart of the Matter

The RecordsetToString component contains a class module, clsText, that includes the CreateDataString method. This method uses familiar ADO code and the GetString method to return the contents of a Recordset to the ASP in a delimited format. Initially, the code declares the necessary variables, opens a connection, and gets a Recordset. If the Recordset returns no records, CreateDataString is set to a zero-length string value.

```
Public Function CreateDataString(pstrSelect As String, _
    Optional pvntWhere As Variant) As Variant

Dim objCnn As New ADODB.Connection
Dim objRst As New ADODB.Recordset
Dim objFld As ADODB.Field
Dim strRows As String
Dim strHeader As String
Dim strSQL As String

strConnect = "Provider=MSDASQL;Driver={SQL Server};" & _
    "Server=DALA;Database=OrderManager;UID=sa;" & _
    "PWD=;"

strSQL = pstrSelect

If Not IsMissing(pvntWhere) Then
    strSQL = strSQL & " WHERE " & pvntWhere
End If

objCnn.Open strConnect
objRst.Open strSQL, objCnn, adOpenStatic, adLockReadOnly

If objRst.BOF Or objRst.EOF Then
    CreateDataString = ""
    GoTo Exit_CreateDataString
End If
```

The code uses a For Each…Next loop to build a delimited list of the field names. The delimiter used in this example is the tilde (~). After the loop finishes, the strHeader value is terminated with the caret (^) and a carriage return line feed.

```
For Each objField In objRst.Fields
    strHeader = strHeader & objField.Name & "~"
Next

strHeader = Left(strHeader, Len(strHeader) - 1)
strHeader = strHeader & "^" & vbCrLf
```

Next, the GetString method retrieves the contents of the Recordset. It uses the same characters for column and row delimiters. The first argument, StringFormat, is supplied by the only valid argument, adClipString. The second argument NumRows is left blank since all rows are desired in this case. Finally, the ColumnDelimiter and RowDelimiter arguments are supplied. Afterward, the value of the CreateDataString function is set to strRows.

```
strRows = objRst.GetString(adClipString, , "~", "^" & vbCrLf)
strRows = strHeader & strRows
CreateDataString = strRows

Exit_CreateDataString:
On Error Resume Next
objRst.Close
Set objRst = Nothing
objCnn.Close
Set objCnn = Nothing

End Function
```

 The RecordsetToString component could be made more reusable. You could increase the generic nature of this component by supplying more arguments to the CreateDataString method, such as ConnectionString, FieldList, ColDelim, RowDelim, and NumRows arguments.

 You may also want to investigate the GetRows method of the Recordset. This method returns the contents of a Recordset into an array.

Writing the String to a File

After the CreateDataString method returns, the ASP uses the Active Server File System Object to store the data to a file in a virtual directory on the Web server. Again, the ASP uses the ASP Request object, this time to determine the file name submitted in the HTTP request. Additionally, the code polls the Request object's ServerVariables collection to extract a relative URL for the virtual directory of the Web.

```
Set objFS = _
Server.CreateObject("Scripting.FileSystemObject") _
    strFilePath = Request.ServerVariables _
        ("APPL_PHYSICAL_PATH")  & "\CSVFiles\" & _
```

```
        Trim(Request.Form("txtFile"))
Set objTS = objFS.CreateTextFile(strFilePath, True)
objTS.WriteLine strData
objTS.Close
Set objTS = Nothing
Set objFS = Nothing
%>


The file you requested, <STRONG>
<%=strFilePath%></STRONG>has been created. Click below to view a test
page that shows the .csv data bound to DHTML fields.
<BR><BR>

<A HREF="TestTextFile.htm" border = 0><IMG SRC="barrow.gif"
border=0></IMG></A> View test page.
```

Viewing the .CSV File

Having generated the .csv file and placed it in a virtual directory on the Web server, the contents of the file can be easily viewed in Internet Explorer. In this example, the Tabular Data Control and DHTML Data Binding are used. Remember, these technologies require Internet Explorer 4.x or newer.

The TestTextFile.htm page uses the Tabular Data Control to stream the contents of the .csv file to the Web client. The RowDelim and FieldDelim attributes are set as appropriate. Since the .csv file was generated using a header row that identified the field names, the UseHeader attribute is set to True (-1). Finally, the DataUrl attribute is set to the path of the .csv file on the Web server.

```
<OBJECT CLASSID=clsid:333C7BC4-460F-11D0-BC04-0080C7055A83 ID=tdcCust>
    <PARAM NAME="RowDelim" VALUE="^">
    <PARAM NAME="FieldDelim" VALUE="~">
    <PARAM NAME="UseHeader" VALUE="-1">
    <PARAM NAME="DataURL" VALUE="/aspsamples/customer.csv">
</OBJECT>
```

HTML controls, as well as other HTML elements, can be bound to the TDC in Internet Explorer. For example, a text box can be bound to the cuCustomerName column by using the DataFld and DataSrc attributes.

```
<INPUT NAME=txtCustName DataSrc=#tdcCust DataFld=cuCustomerName>
```

As you saw in the previous section, the TDC hosts an ADO Recordset. You can use the Recordset to navigate, sort, and filter the data as necessary. You might, for example, use an HTML button to move to the next record in the Recordset.

```
<INPUT name=btnN OnClick="Move('Next')" type=button value=Next>
```

The button calls a procedure named Move and passes in a value that indicates the operation to perform. The Move procedure is contained in a client-side script block. It uses the Recordset property of the TDC to navigate. Because controls are bound to the TDC, control values are automatically refreshed whenever the pointer moves in the Recordset.

```
<SCRIPT LANGUAGE=vbscript>
<!--
Sub Move(pvntDir)
Select Case pvntDir
    Case "First"
        tdcCust.Recordset.MoveFirst
    Case "Previous"
        tdcCust.Recordset.MovePrevious
    Case "Next"
        tdcCust.Recordset.MoveNext
    Case "Last"
        tdcCust.Recordset.MoveLast
End Select
End Sub
//-->
</SCRIPT>
```

This section demonstrated how the GetString method can be a powerful means of persisting Recordset data. More than that, you've seen how Active Server technology and the use of a COM component affords you the possibility of creating a generic application that can persist data to a format of which the Tabular Data Control and DHTML can take advantage.

Converting Recordset Data to XML

Arguably, XML may be one of the most important things to happen to data since the invention of the relational database. So far in this book, we have discussed the idea of Universal Data Access from the standpoint of a proprietary client connecting to any type of data store. That is, any client that can use OLE DB (...therefore any client on a 32bit Microsoft platform) can connect to any legacy or modern data store. This approach to Universal Data Access is the reason why the earlier Web examples in this chapter required a Microsoft environment and browser.

XML approaches the idea of Universal Data Access from the standpoint of the client. What I mean by this is that any client on any platform can use XML data. This is quite different from the data access based on systems such as ODBC and OLE DB that we have discussed so far in this book. These systems provide an abstraction from the actual data store and offer a consistent interface for accessing data held in diverse stores. For example, ADO can allow a client application to communicate with a SQL Server, Oracle, or DB2 database thorough the same interfaces because the OLE DB layer translates actions executed against these interfaces into commands the "back end" database will understand.

In a way, XML is much simpler than that. When you are trying to achieve Universal Data Access to multiple types of data storage, you must depend on some sort of complex translation system that will allow you to get data from the client to and from any number of database servers. In contrast, when you are trying to achieve Universal Data Access to diverse clients, you must create data that has basic format that virtually all systems have in common. In the case of XML, what all systems have in common is the simple ability to process text. That's right, XML is just text that can be processed or parsed in a consistent, defined way.

What is XML?

For the purposes of this discussion (the topic of XML is actually much larger than what is to be discussed here), XML is a simple, text-based way to format, store, and express data. Just as HTML and the innovation of the web browser helped to de-couple format and graphical layout from any one platform, XML holds the promise to free data. The reason for this is that data that is structured in XML is usable by any system that can understand and parse text. In reality, this means that XML can be used by any type of computer, anywhere. For example, I could use XML to express a record from the Author's table in the Pubs database (distributed with SQL Server) in the following simple way:

```
<class>
<RECORD>
    <AU_ID>998-72-3567</AU_ID>
    <AU_LNAME>Ringer</AU_LNAME>
    <AU_FNAME>Albert</AU_FNAME>
    <PHONE>801 826-0752</PHONE>
    <ADDRESS>67 Seventh Av.</ADDRESS>
    <CITY>Salt Lake City</CITY>
    <STATE>UT</STATE>
    <ZIP>84152</ZIP>
    <CONTRACT>True</CONTRACT>
</RECORD>
</class>
```

In XML (Extensible Markup Language), you are able to define tags that will be used to describe certain elements of structured data. This differs from HTML or DHTML in which there is a fixed vocabulary of tags that can be used. This is why we can have tags like <AU_ID> in <PHONE> in our example. In fact, you can have any tag that you wish to create in a valid XML instance as long as the tags that you define begin (i.e., <Tag­Name>) and end (i.e., </TagName>).

You see that a record's data is enclosed in begin and end tags of different types. This record's data is structured by first enclosing the definition of a certain type of data (i.e., a record) inside a <class> tag. Then, each record in the set is enclosed in a <RECORD> tag. Finally, each field in the record is enclosed in a tag named after its field in the SQL Server database from which it came (e.g., <CITY></CITY>).

It is helpful to think of XML data as being formatted in a tree type structure. If you think about it like that, then in the earlier sample, the <class> element exists at the root of the structure, the <RECORD> element branches off of the root, and each of the field tags exist as leaves.

XML Data Islands

One of the most common and straightforward methods of making use of XML is to include XML Data Islands in the "sea" of the HTML/DHTML that makes up a web page. All that you need to do to create an XML Data Island is to take well-formed XML like the example that you saw earlier and enclose it in <XML> </XML> tags. So, using the earlier text, you could create a valid XML Data Island with an ID of "XMLTestData" in the following way:

```
<XML ID="XMLTestData">
    <class>
    <RECORD>
        <AU_ID>998-72-3567</AU_ID>
        <AU_LNAME>Ringer</AU_LNAME>
        <AU_FNAME>Albert</AU_FNAME>
        <PHONE>801 826-0752</PHONE>
        <ADDRESS>67 Seventh Av.</ADDRESS>
        <CITY>Salt Lake City</CITY>
        <STATE>UT</STATE>
        <ZIP>84152</ZIP>
        <CONTRACT>True</CONTRACT>
    </RECORD>
    </class>
</XML>
```

The DOM

The Document Object Model (DOM) is the set of objects that (among other things) allows scripting languages to access the data inside of an XML Data Island. If you have ever done client-side web scripting with VBScript of JavaScript, then you may already be aware of some of the features of this detailed object model that describe the elements on a web page through objects like Window, Document, Form, and Element. Like the earlier object structure that allows you to script interactions between the elements on a web page, the DOM allows you to programmatically access the structure and data elements of a structured data store like an XML Data Island.

As in most object models, the DOM exists as a hierarchy of objects. At the highest level is the Document itself that contains all the HTML/DHTML formatting elements and any structured data stores. When scripting, this highest level is implicit. Therefore, if you wanted to write a script that would access the "XMLTestData" XML Data Island, you could begin by simply making a call to the XMLTestData object.

The next level in this structure is called the documentElement object and it represents the *root* level of the structured data store. After this root object is established, you can navigate to the next level of the tree through the childNodes collection. Individual branches off of the documentElement can be accessed through the Items of the ChildNodes collection. Therefore, a web page that uses VBScript and the DOM to print the first record in a XML Data Island would look something like what follows.

```
<HTML>
<HEAD>
<!--Begin the XML Data Island-->
<XML ID="XMLTestData">
<class>
    <RECORD>
        <AU_ID>998-72-3567</AU_ID>
        <AU_LNAME>Ringer</AU_LNAME>
        <AU_FNAME>Albert</AU_FNAME>
        <PHONE>801 826-0752</PHONE>
        <ADDRESS>67 Seventh Av.</ADDRESS>
        <CITY>Salt Lake City</CITY>
        <STATE>UT</STATE>
        <ZIP>84152</ZIP>
        <CONTRACT>True</CONTRACT>
    </RECORD>
    </class>
</XML>
<!--End the XML Data Island-->
</HEAD>

<SCRIPT Language=VBScript>
Sub Window_OnLoad()
        'Use the Write method of the high level
        'Document object to display the data retrieved
        'by moving through the XML tree from:
        '(1)the island itself (XMLTestData),
        '(2)to the root of the store(documentElement),
        '(3)to the first node off of the root
            '(childnodes.item(0))
    document.write _
    XMLTestData.documentElement.childnodes.item(0)
End Sub
</Script>
</HTML>
```

Viewing this page would produce the following output:

998-72-3567 Ringer Albert 801 826-0752 67 Seventh Av. Salt Lake City UT 84152 True

If you wished to access the individual elements inside the accessed record, you could move deeper into the DOM by accessing the first node off of the branch's own childNodes collection (i.e., childnodes.item(0).childnodes.item(0)). Just like the higher level root childNodes collection, the individual elements of this collection can be accessed as Items. Therefore, if you wanted to print out the "fields" of this record, you could use the following code. (A With...End With block is used here to conserve space.)

```
Sub Window_OnLoad()
    With XMLTestData.documentElement.childnodes.item(0)
        document.write .childnodes.item(0)
```

(continues)

(Continued)

```
        document.write .childnodes.item(1)
        document.write .childnodes.item(2)
        document.write .childnodes.item(3)
        document.write .childnodes.item(4)
        document.write .childnodes.item(5)
        document.write .childnodes.item(6)
        document.write .childnodes.item(7)
        document.write .childnodes.item(8)
    End With
End Sub
```

As you can see, the use of XML Data Islands and accessing their structured data store is really a fairly simple (almost obvious) way to send and format data in a web browser.

ADO's Support for XML

Let me start off by saying that a lot is going to change with ADO's support for XML between the time that I write these words and the time that you read them. At the time of this writing, the ADO Recordset was able to save itself into structured XML store. However, by the time that you begin to implement this feature of ADO, the structure into which the Recordset saves itself is likely to change.

Further, at present the only way to make this conversion from ADO to XML is to use the Recordset's Save method to write a physical XML file. Although this is a more acceptable, less platform specific way of persisting structured Recordset data, it has many drawbacks. For example, it has proven to be difficult in implementation because an unnecessary amount of effort has to be made in order to provide file I/O, preserve the uniqueness of file names, and to manage the use of disk space.

 At the time of this writing, ADO was just beginning to support conversion to XML. So, although we can show you a tried, practical way of working with ADO and XML in this book, you really should do some research to learn about any added features that might be able to save you some work.

By the time that you start to implement Recordset to XML conversion, we would imagine that they have implemented a way to retrieve an XML string directly from a Recordset into a variable. Doing this at the time of this writing is not difficult (as you will see in a forthcoming example), but we would expect that when the ADO team implements it, it will be much more full featured than our humble (if working) example.

"Rolling Your Own" Recordset to XML Converter

We have created a COM component that can be used in an ASP script in order to construct an XML Data Island based on a query. In the following ReturnXMLDataIsland method, a SQL Statement and a database connection string are passed to the routine. In turn, the routine returns a well-formed XML Data Island based on the data retrieved by the query.

```
Public Function ReturnXMLDataIsland(_
    strSQLString As String,  strConn As String) As String
Dim strString As String
Dim intIterator As Integer
Dim objADORS As ADODB.Recordset
        'Open Recordset using passed SQL
        'statement and connection string
    Set objADORS = New ADODB.Recordset
    objADORS.Open strSQLString, strConn


    With objADORS
        'Add class element in which to enclose all
        'of the records
    strString = strString & "<class>" & vbCrLf
        'Iterate through RS, building a <RECORD>
        'element for each row in the Recordset
    Do Until .EOF
        strString = strString & vbTab _
            & "<RECORD>" & vbCrLf
                'Iterate through the Recordset's
                'collection of fields, creating XML
                'Elements for each one
            For intIterator = 0 To .Fields.Count - 1
                strString = strString & _
                    vbTab & "<" & _
                    UCase(.Fields(intIterator).Name) & ">"
                strString = strString & _
                      Fields(intIterator).Value
                strString = strString & "</" & _
                    UCase(.Fields(intIterator).Name) & _
                        ">" & vbCrLf
        Next
            'Close the XML <Record> element
        strString = strString & vbTab & _
        "</RECORD>" & vbCrLf
        MoveNext
    Loop
        'Close the </Class> tag
    strString = strString & "</class>"
        'Close the Recordset
    .Close
    End With


    Set objADORS = Nothing
        'Return the constructed XML data Island string
    ReturnXMLDataIsland = strString
End Function
```

The result of calling the ReturnXMLDataIsland method is a variable that contains data something like the following. Notice that (unlike the previous example of a Data Island) there can be any number of <RECORD> elements returned from the query.

```
<class>
    <RECORD>
        <AU_ID>998-72-3567</AU_ID>
        <AU_LNAME>Ringer</AU_LNAME>
        <AU_FNAME>Albert</AU_FNAME>
        <PHONE>801 826-0752</PHONE>
        <ADDRESS>67 Seventh Av.</ADDRESS>
        <CITY>Salt Lake City</CITY>
        <STATE>UT</STATE>
        <ZIP>84152</ZIP>
        <CONTRACT>True</CONTRACT>
    </RECORD>
    <RECORD>
        <AU_ID>409-56-7008</AU_ID>
        <AU_LNAME>Bennet</AU_LNAME>
        <AU_FNAME>Abraham</AU_FNAME>
        <PHONE>415 658-9932</PHONE>
        <ADDRESS>6223 Bateman St.</ADDRESS>
        <CITY>Berkeley</CITY>
        <STATE>CA</STATE>
        <ZIP>94705</ZIP>
        <CONTRACT>True</CONTRACT>
    </RECORD>
</class>
```

Using ADO, XML, and ASP

Now that we have some way (for now) to move data from a Recordset to XML, we can create a web page that displays data in very much the same way as our previous examples. The important difference here is that the web page this script produces could be viewed on *any* platform (i.e., non-Microsoft) and is not dependent on ActiveX controls, nor the client's ability to create an instance of an ADO Recordset.

This simple ASP script begins by creating an XML Data Island using the previously mentioned COM component and its ReturnXMLDataIsland method. First, the script establishes an <XML> element for the Data Island and then instances the COM component and passes it a SQL statement and connection string. The result is that the call is written into the page using a Response.Write method. After this is done, a structured XML data store is ready to be delivered to the client's browser.

```
<HTML>
<HEAD>
<XML ID="XMLIsland">
<%
Set objXML = Server.CreateObject("XMLStream.clsXML")
Response.Write objXML.ReturnXMLDataIsland( _
```

```
        "Select * from Author", _
            "Data Provider=MSDASQL;Driver={SQL Server};" & _
            "Server=(Local);Database=Pubs;UID=sa"
Set objXML = Nothing
%></XML>
```

Like the earlier examples, the data sent from the server to the client's web browser will be shown in an HTML form. Also, just like the previous examples, a client-side script is used to populate the HTML form elements. The only real difference between this version of the FillControls procedure is that in this script it uses the objects of the DOM in order to access the data held in the XML Data Island.

```
Sub FillControls(recnum)
    With XMLIsland.documentElement.childnodes.item(recnum)
        txtID.Value = .childNodes.item(0)
        txtFirst.Value = .childNodes.item(1)
        txtLast.Value = .childNodes.item(2)
        txtPhone.Value = .childNodes.item(3)
        txtCity.Value = .childNodes.item(5)
    End with
End Sub
```

Using an XML data store is different from what was seen in the previous examples because we are no longer using an ADO Recordset directly. Therefore, when the users of this page move from one record to the next, we have nothing as handy as a MoveNext or MovePrevious method. However, if we use a variable to keep track of which record we are viewing in the form, enabling the user to move forwards and backwards through the records can be achieved easily.

In the following script block, a variable named *intPos* is dimensioned and is passed to the FillControls procedure. A call is made using this variable to load the page's controls with data when the page is first shown. This variable is also used when the user clicks on the navigation buttons and triggers a call to the MoveToRecord procedure passing either a parameter of "Next" or "Previous".

```
<SCRIPT Language=VBScript>
<!-- Could be made even less platform specific by using Javascript-->

dim intPos

Sub Window_OnLoad()
    fillcontrols intpos
End Sub

Sub MoveToRecord(psDirection)
On error resume next
    Select Case psDirection
        Case "Next"
            'If the Next button was clicked, then
            'increment the variable and pass the new
```

(continues)

(Continued)

```
                    'value to the FillControls procedure
                    intpos = intpos + 1
                    fillcontrols intpos
            Case "Previous"
                    'If the Next button was clicked, then
                    'decrement the variable and pass the new
                    'value to the FillControls procedure
                    intpos = intpos - 1
                    fillcontrols intpos
        End Select
    if err.number = 424 then
            'Triggered by moving past or before the number of
            'Record elements in the XML Data Island
        msgbox "You are at the beginning or end of the file"
    end if
    End Sub
    </SCRIPT>
```

We regret that we cannot go on to explore ADO's use of XML in more detail, but at the time of this writing, this was a very new area into which ADO was moving. Although what was discussed here should remain a fine (albeit simple) approach to working with ADO and XML, remember to research (especially the book's companion Web site–www.wiley.com/compbooks/martiner) any newer developments before you implement this important new approach to working with data.

Shaping Data

One of the goals of Universal Data Access is to optimize the capability to display data for presentation purposes. The concept of *data shaping* is such a feature. In lay person's terms, data shaping means that you can return multiple, related Recordsets from a single operation. For example, if you wanted to view a customer's records, including all the customer's orders, using data shaping you could construct specialized SQL syntax that returned not one, but two Recordsets, one for the customer data and another for the orders. If you've ever worked with extracting data that can be displayed in hierarchical relationships, you've wrestled with the inefficiencies of numerous Recordset objects and creatively crafted SQL syntax. With hierarchical Recordsets, this sort of data access becomes easier.

With data shaping, there are three types of Recordset hierarchies that you can create:

Relational Hierarchy. You return a hierarchy of parent-child Recordsets, as described in the customer and orders scenario. When constructing a relational hierarchy, data for parent and children Recordsets are fetched up front.

Parameterized Hierarchy. Like a relational hierarchy, except that the child Recordset data is fetched on demand, not up front.

Group Hierarchy. Constructed using specialized data-shaping syntax that returns multiple Recordsets. Parent Recordsets contain aggregate information and children Recordsets contain the detail for the parent.

Data shaping is an ADO technology, but development tools such as Visual Basic 6.0 take advantage of the new features. For example, Visual Basic 6.0 includes a Hierarchical Flex Grid specially designed to bind to hierarchical Recordsets. This greatly reduces the amount of code you need to write to display data in this format.

Relational Hierarchies

This technology is certainly not limited to Visual Basic front ends. In this section, you'll explore a simple ASP application that uses this technology to return hierarchical data to a Web browser. Here is an overview of what you'll learn:

1. An ASP, DataShapeExample.asp, invokes a COM component that has the specialized task of creating a hierarchical Recordset of customers and orders.

2. The COM component (Orders, created in Visual Basic 6.0) uses the MSDataShape OLE DB Provider to return a hierarchical Recordset. The Orders component does this when its GetOrderHistory method is called.

3. After the Orders component derives the hierarchical Recordset, the ASP calls the GetCustomer and GetOrders methods of the component to dynamically generate the HTML that the Web client will display.

Together, the DataShapeExample ASP and the Orders component return the output shown in Figure 3.9 to the browser.

 This example uses Active Server technology and therefore requires the Web server to be Internet Information Server. Because only HTML is returned to the Web client, this solution is ideal for multiple client browser types. And though this example uses the MSDataShape Provider to produce a static, hierarchical Recordset, you can also produce hierarchical Recordsets whose data can be modified, and you can update a database as a standard Recordset.

Invoking the Orders Component

The DataShapeExample.asp page contains server-side script that invokes the services of the Orders component. The Script uses the CreateObject method of the ASP Server object to instantiate the component. Afterward, the code calls the GetOrderHistory method, passing in a delimited string of Customer ID values. Note: For sake of brevity here, the ID's have been hard-coded.

```
<%
Dim blnSucceed
Dim objOrderHistory

Set objOrderHistory = Server.CreateObject _
    ("Orders.clsOrders")
blnSucceed = objOrderHistory.GetOrderHistory _
    ("1025,1039")
```

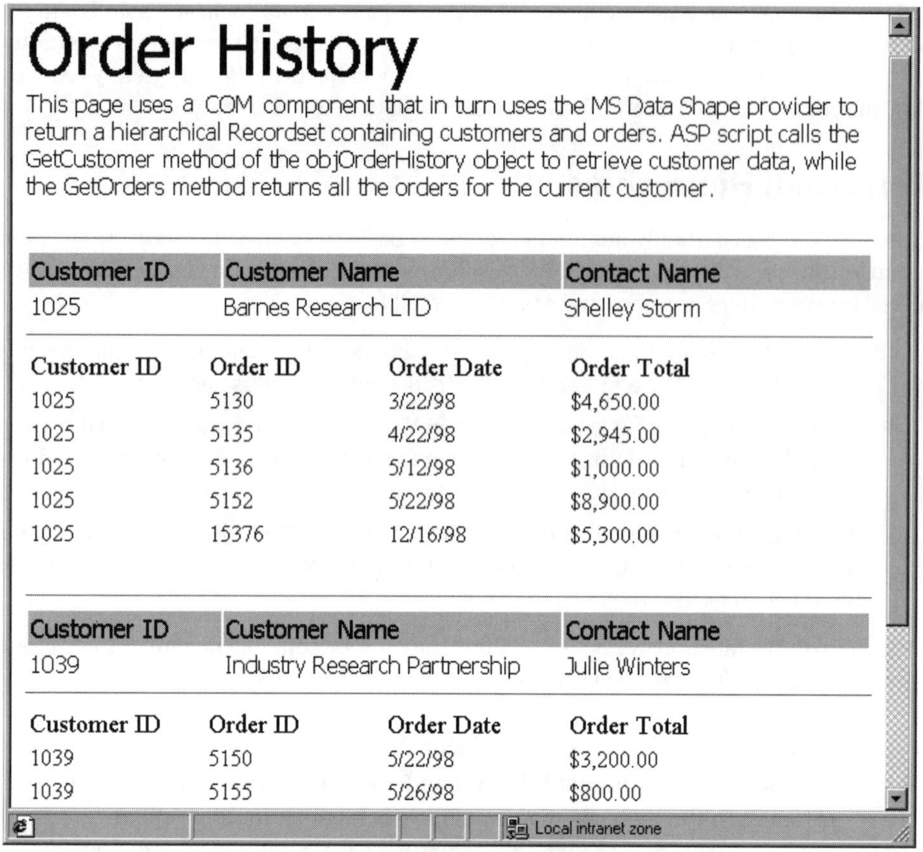

Order History

This page uses a COM component that in turn uses the MS Data Shape provider to return a hierarchical Recordset containing customers and orders. ASP script calls the GetCustomer method of the objOrderHistory object to retrieve customer data, while the GetOrders method returns all the orders for the current customer.

Customer ID	Customer Name	Contact Name
1025	Barnes Research LTD	Shelley Storm

Customer ID	Order ID	Order Date	Order Total
1025	5130	3/22/98	$4,650.00
1025	5135	4/22/98	$2,945.00
1025	5136	5/12/98	$1,000.00
1025	5152	5/22/98	$8,900.00
1025	15376	12/16/98	$5,300.00

Customer ID	Customer Name	Contact Name
1039	Industry Research Partnership	Julie Winters

Customer ID	Order ID	Order Date	Order Total
1039	5150	5/22/98	$3,200.00
1039	5155	5/26/98	$800.00

Local intranet zone

Figure 3.9   The HTML results of the DataShapeExample ASP.

The GetOrderHistory Method

The GetOrderHistory method uses the MSDataShape Provider to return a hierarchical Recordset of customers and orders. First, the code declares the necessary variables and creates a connection. To make the use of this component more generic, you may want to consider increasing the arguments this method receives, such as passing in a connection string and additional SQL arguments. Notice that the strConnect variable is set to a slightly different connection string value. The connection string information references the provider as MSDataShape and the data provider (in this example) to MSDASQL. To create hierarchical Recordsets, you must use the MSDataShape Provider.

```
Public Function GetOrderHistory _
    (pvntCustID As Variant) As Boolean

Dim objCnn As New ADODB.Connection
Dim strConnect As String
Dim strSQL As String
```

```
strConnect = "Provider=MSDataShape;" & _
    "Data Provider=MSDASQL;" & _
    "Driver={SQL Server};Server=DALA;" & _
    "Database=OrderManager;UID=sa"

With objCnn
    .Open strConnect
End With
```

Now comes a developer's dream: compact, easy-to-understand code that returns multiple Recordsets. Using the MSDataShape Provider, you can build some specialized SQL syntax to return a hierarchy of Recordsets. In the following code, the SQL statement begins with the SHAPE clause, then uses the APPEND clause to derive child sets of data and the RELATE clause to identify how the parent and child sets are related. Notice how the sets of data are referred to as Customers and Orders, respectively, by using the AS keyword. After building up the SQL code, a static, read-only Recordset is opened.

```
strSQL = "SHAPE {SELECT cuCustomerID, cuCustomerName, " & _
    "cuContactName " & _
    "FROM Customers " & _
    "WHERE cuCustomerID In (" & pvntCustID & ")} " & _
    "As Customers " & _
    "APPEND ({SELECT orCustomerID, orOrderID, " & _
    "orOrderDate, orTotal " & _
    "FROM Orders} AS Orders " & _
    "RELATE cuCustomerID TO orCustomerID) AS Orders"

Set mobjRstCust = New ADODB.Recordset
With mobjRstCust
    .Open strSQL, objCnn, adOpenStatic, adLockReadOnly, _
        adCmdText
```

When working with hierarchical Recordsets, child Recordsets are referenced as a member Field object of the parent Recordset. The data type of this field object is adChapter, to correspond to the underlying OLE DB data type DBTYPE_CHAPTER. In this example, the entire Orders Recordset is accessible by referencing a Field called Orders in the Fields collection of mobjRstCust. So mobjRstCust has a Fields collection with four fields, three that were defined in the SELECT statement and a fourth that references the Orders Recordset. See Figure 3.10.

When working with pure hierarchical Recordsets, the data in children Recordsets are fetched as the initial query executes. This means that the up-front query time can be lengthy for large quantities of data. When this is the case, the GetOrderHistory method simply returns to the ASP a value of False if no data was retrieved. If, however, there is data in the Recordset, then the CustRecordCount property is set to mobjrst.RecordCount. Similarly, the CustColumnCount property is set to the count of fields. These two properties are defined by public-property Let/Get procedures. As such, they can be used later to allow the ASP to present the data with a proper looping mechanism. See Figure 3.11 for a listing of the Property procedures just mentioned.

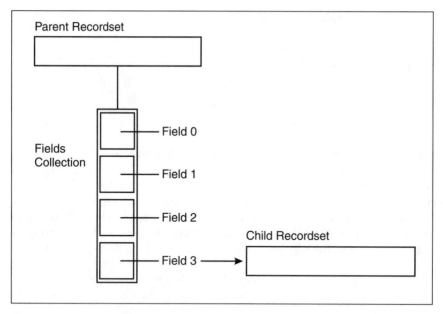

Figure 3.10   Hierarchical Recordsets are related through Field objects.

```
Public Property Get CustColumnCount() As Integer

    CustColumnCount = mintCustColumnCount

End Property

Public Property Let CustColumnCount(ByVal _
    pintCustColumnCount As Integer)

    mintCustColumnCount = pintCustColumnCount

End Property

Public Property Let CustRecordCount(ByVal _
    pintCustRecordCount As Integer)

    mintCustRecordCount = pintCustRecordCount

End Property

Public Property Get CustRecordCount() As Integer

    CustRecordCount = mintCustRecordCount

End Property
```

Figure 3.11   Property procedures used by the Orders component.

```
        If .RecordCount = 0 Then
            GetOrderHistory = False
        Else
            CustRecordCount = .RecordCount
            CustColumnCount = .Fields.Count - 1
            GetOrderHistory = True
        End If
    End With

    End Function
```

Getting the Customer Information

After the GetOrderHistory method executes, the ASP begins a loop that presents each customer column and row. The ASP code first makes sure that the GetOrderHistory method returned True, indicating that it retrieved data from the database. It then starts a For…Next loop using the Public CustRecordCount property of objOrderHistory as the ending argument for the loop. It does this so that the ASP script can dynamically produce as many table rows as there are customer rows. As you can see, the HTML tags that follow build table rows (TR) with the appropriate number of columns (TD).

```
If blnSucceed Then
    For intCnt = 1 To objOrderHistory.CustRecordCount%>
        <hr>
        <TABLE>
        <TR bgcolor=Silver>
            <TD width=150><FONT Face=Tahoma Size=4>Customer
            ID</FONT></TD>
            <TD width=275><FONT Face=Tahoma Size=4>Customer
            Name</FONT></TD>
            <TD width = 250><FONT Face=Tahoma Size=4>Contact
            Name</FONT></TD></TR>
        <TR>
```

Now the customer values are extracted from the component by calling its GetCustomer method. Each time it calls the GetCustomer method, the appropriate customer field value is returned, as indicated by intColumnCnt. The looping structure uses the Public property CustColumnCount to determine how many columns to build.

```
        <%For intColumnCnt = 1 To _
            objOrderHistory.CustColumnCount%>
                <TD><FONT Face=Tahoma Size=3>
                <%=objOrderHistory.GetCustomer(intColumnCnt)%>
            </FONT></TD>
        <%Next%>

    </TR></TABLE>
    <hr>
```

As you just saw, the GetCustomer method returns a specified field value from mobj-RstCust in the Orders component. Some logic in the method helps the procedure to know when it is time to move the row pointer to the next record (because it will be called multiple times per record, it must know when to move ahead).

```
Public Function GetCustomer(ByVal pintCol As Integer) As Variant

Static intRecsProcessed As Integer
With mobjRstCust
    If .BOF Or .EOF Then
        GetCustomer = ""
    Else
        If intRecsProcessed > 0 And (pintCol = 1) Then
            .MoveNext
        End If
    End If
    pintCol = pintCol - 1
    GetCustomer = .Fields(pintCol)
    If pintCol = .Fields.Count - 2 Then '2 orders is a column
        intRecsProcessed = intRecsProcessed + 1
    End If
End With

End Function
```

Getting Order Information

Are you starting to feel a little dizzy? Well, hang on; you only have one more step to go. As the Active Server script processes each Customer row, it proceeds to retrieve the order information. To do this, the ASP script calls the GetOrders method of the component. The GetOrders method will return a fully formatted HTML table row. The ASP Response object uses its Write method to output the response to the browser.

```
<TABLE>
    <TR>
        <TD Width=125><FONT Face=Times Size=4>Customer ID</TD>
        <TD Width=125><FONT Face=Times Size=4>Order ID</TD>
        <TD Width=125><FONT Face=Times Size=4>Order Date</TD>
        <TD Width=125><FONT Face=Times Size=4>Order Total</TD>
    </TR>
    <%Response.Write objOrderHistory.GetOrders%>
    <TR><TD> </TD></TR>
</TABLE>

<%Next

Else
    Response.Write "No information found."
End If
```

```
Set objOrderHistory = Nothing

%>
```

The code for the GetOrders method is shown in the following listing. This method is called immediately after the pointer has been moved to a new row so it can assume that the order information that should be returned is for the current row. Remember that the order information retrieved will be only those records that relate to the current row of mobjRstCust. After making sure that mobjRstCust is not on the .BOF or .EOF markers, the code creates a reference to the child Orders Recordset by referencing the Orders field value of mobjRstCust. Finally, the code starts a looping mechanism through each row and each column in objRstOrders, all the while building an HTML table that it stores in the variable sReturnRow.

As the code iterates through the Fields collection of objRstOrders, it inspects the data type of the fields by using the Type property. By doing this, it can return the data in an appropriate format. For example, the orOrderTotal data can be reported in a currency format.

```
Public Function GetOrders() As Variant

Dim sReturnRow As String
Dim objRstOrders As ADODB.Recordset
Dim intColumnCount As Integer

With mobjRstCust
    If .BOF Or .EOF Then
        GetOrders = "<TR><TD>No information for this " & _
            "customer.</TD></TR>"
    Else
        Set objRstOrders = !Orders.Value
        With objRstOrders
            Do While Not .EOF
                sReturnRow = sReturnRow & "<TR>"
                For intColumnCount = 0 To (.Fields.Count - 1)
                    If .Fields(intColumnCount).Type = _
                        adCurrency Then
                        sReturnRow = sReturnRow & "<TD>" & _
                            Format(.Fields(intColumnCount), _
                            "Currency") & "</TD>"
                    Else
                        sReturnRow = sReturnRow & "<TD>" & _
                            .Fields(intColumnCount) & "</TD>"
                    End If
                Next
                sReturnRow = sReturnRow & "</TR>"
                .MoveNext
            Loop
        End With
    End If
```

```
End With

GetOrders = sReturnRow
objRstOrders.Close
Set objRstOrders = Nothing

End Function
```

Parameterized Hierarchies

A parameterized hierarchy can be used in the same manner as a pure relational hierarchy—to return multiple parent-child Recordsets based on related field values. However, with a parameterized hierarchy, you define your SQL code such that the child rows are only fetched when asked for. For example, if you display a grid showing customer data, you might design the request for order information using a parameter so that your application does not actually retrieve the order information until the user selects a customer row in the grid.

Using the same customer order example, the data shape syntax looks a bit different.

```
Public Function GetOrdersWithParam() As Boolean

'Shape SQL to use a parameter
strSQL = "SHAPE {SELECT cuCustomerID, cuCustomerName, " & _
    "cuContactName FROM Customers} " & _
    "APPEND ({SELECT orCustomerID, orOrderID, " & _
    "orOrderDate, orTotal " & _
    "FROM Orders WHERE orCustomerID =?} AS Orders " & _
    "RELATE cuCustomerID TO Parameter 0) AS Orders"

Set objrst = New ADODB.Recordset

'Opens all customer rows, but does not fetch orders yet
With objrst
    objrst.Open strSQL, objCnn, adOpenStatic, adLockReadOnly
```

In this code, the Open method opens a Recordset containing customer data; but because of the use of a parameter in the Orders SQL statement, the actual order rows are not fetched at the outset.

After determining that some data was fetched, the code can then reference the Orders Recordset; when it does so, the child' order data is fetched.

```
    If .RecordCount = 0 Then
        GetOrdersWithParam = False
    Else
        GetOrdersWithParam = True
        'Actual data is fetched
        Set objrstOrders = objrst!Orders.Value
    End If
End With
```

Group Hierarchies

As you know, the major aim of data shaping is to help developers with the presentation of data. While relational hierarchies are powerful, so are group hierarchies. Imagine being able to extract from a data source totals of some sort (e.g., the number of customers in each postal code) and be able to contain the detail (e.g., the customer name and postal code) in a single object structure. That is exactly what group hierarchies allow you to do.

When working with relational hierarchies, you return multiple Recordsets. The same is true with group hierarchies. The difference is that the data-shipping grammar used to construct those Recordsets. In the GetCustByZipCode procedure, the shape syntax retrieves a parent Recordset that contains the CustCount, a field of type adChapter called rstDetail, and the cuPostalCode field. The Recordset rstDetail contains the cuCustomerID and cuPostalCode detail data. Thus, the code (in this case) creates a parent Recordset containing the total counts per postal code and a child Recordset (rstDetail) that contains the detail (e.g., all rows included in the calculation for CustCount).

```
Public Function GetCustByZipCode() As Boolean

Dim objCnn As New ADODB.Connection
Dim objRstCustCount As ADODB.Recordset
Dim objRstDetail As ADODB.Recordset
Dim strConnect As String
Dim strSQL As String

strConnect = "Provider=MSDataShape;" & _
    "Data Provider=MSDASQL;" & _
    "Driver={SQL Server};Server=(Local); " & _
    "Database=OrderManager;UID=sa"

With objCnn
    .Open strConnect
End With

strSQL = "SHAPE {SELECT cuCustomerID, cuPostalCode " & _
    "FROM Customers} rstDetail " & _
    "COMPUTE COUNT(rstDetail.cuCustomerID) As " & _
    "CustCount, rstDetail By cuPostalCode"

Set objRstCustCount = New ADODB.Recordset
With objRstCustCount
    .Open strSQL, objCnn, adOpenStatic, adLockReadOnly
    Set objRstDetail = objRstCustCount!rstDetail.Value
End With

End Function
```

These examples demonstrated the power and flexibility of data shaping, ASP technology, and the use of server-side COM components. By using a COM component for the shaping service, you build code reuse into your application and eliminate the need for even more ASP script. Of course, the MSDataShape Provider allows you the powerful capability to create hierarchical Recordsets.

Working with User-Defined Recordsets

Most business applications derive their data from an OLE DB data source. As you know, when you create a Recordset from such a source, the structure (e.g., fields, field data types, etc.) of the Recordset is defined by the source. Occasionally, though, you may need to work with data that comes from a non-OLE DB data source, and you may want to easily sort and filter the data or even add new information. To do so with your own application code would require a tremendous effort. Certainly it could be done, but you would probably burn the midnight oil more than once. Fortunately, ADO lets you create your own user-defined Recordsets. Thus, you can define a completely arbitrary structure and still benefit from the powerful feature set of the client-side cursor engine.

One useful scenario for implementing user-defined Recordsets is for presentation purposes. Sometimes information that you want to present to the user does not come directly from the database. In fact, your application code must calculate certain values that will be presented based on data stored in a database. For example, an application that calculates the commission payout for sales representatives may not be able to directly derive every data item from the data source. Indeed, much of the base information may be stored, such as the order totals, the date that payment was made, the sales representative's commission plan, and so on; other information may not be stored, such as the basis for calculating the commission payment. When this is the case, what would the final data items be for a report that showed the expected payout for a sales representative in a given month? The answer is that some of the data items would be derived directly from the database, while others would be calculated.

To explain the use of user-defined Recordsets, this section uses the Commission.asp page, which allows sales representatives to view their expected payout. The Commission.asp page calls upon the services of the SalesData business object to supply a user-defined Recordset that contains all of the data items necessary for display. The .asp page then enumerates the Recordset dynamically building the HTML output to send to a Web client. Figure 3.12 shows the final results of the Commission.asp page.

Calling the SalesData Component

Before presenting the information, the Commission.asp page calls the CalculateCommission method of the SalesData component. The component returns a user-defined Recordset to the asp environment. The code passes in a valid DSN, a value to filter by the representative's ID (lngRepID), an integer value for the month to report on (intMonth), and a Boolean value to tell the business component whether or not to append a summary data row at the end of the user-defined Recordset.

```
<%
Set objSales = Server.CreateObject("SalesData.clsSalesData")
```

```
Set objRst = objSales.CalculateCommission("ADOBook", _
    lngRepID, intMonth, True)
%>
```

The CalculateCommission Method

The first order of business for the CalculateCommission method is to create the structure for the final data output. It does this by appending field objects to a Recordset. When you use the Append method of the Fields collection, you specify the name and data type of the field. Optionally, you can define the size and an attribute value such as adFldIsNullable, which means that the field can be set to Null. Field objects are appended for each data item required for presentation.

Figure 3.12   The Commission.asp page displays the expected commission payout for a sales representative.

```
Public Function CalculateCommission(ByVal _
    pstrConnect As String, ByVal plngRepID As Long, _
    ByVal pintMonth As Integer, _
    ByVal pbAppendSummary As Boolean) As ADODB.Recordset

Dim objRstBase As New ADODB.Recordset
Dim objRstStats As New ADODB.Recordset
Dim objCnn As New ADODB.Connection
Dim strSQL As String
Dim curSumOrdTotal As Currency
Dim curSumBasis As Currency
Dim curSumPayout As Currency

'First, define the Stats Recordset
With objRstStats.Fields
    .Append "RepName", adChar, 20
    .Append "OrderTotal", adCurrency, 8
    .Append "Rating", adTinyInt, 1
    .Append "Basis", adCurrency, 8
    .Append "Payout", adCurrency, 8
End With
```

Table 3.5 shows the arguments of the Append method and the attribute enum values. The remainder of the code builds the necessary SQL statement and opens a base Recordset (objRstBase) from the OrderManager database. The base Recordset contains all of the necessary information that will be used to supply the user-defined Recordset

Table 3.5   Arguments of the Append Method

ARGUMENT	DESCRIPTION
Name	A valid field name for the Field object.
Type	A valid ADO DataTypeEnum value that specifies the data type for the Field object. (Refer to your ADO documentation for valid ADO DataTypeEnum constants or use your application development tool's object browser.) The default value is adEmpty (0).
DefinedSize	An optional long-integer value that specifies the field size. For fixed-length data types, this argument can be omitted; however, it is required for variable-length data types.
Attributes	A long-integer value that corresponds to an ADO FieldAttributeEnum. If you do not specify this optional argument, its default value will be derived from the Type argument. Valid FieldAttributeEnum constants include adFldCacheDeferred, adFldFixed, adFldIsNullable, adFldLong, adFldMayBeNull, adFldMayDefer, adFldRowID, adFldRowVersion, adFldUnknownUpdatable, adFldUpdatable.

(objRstStats) its data. Of importance, objRstStats is also opened. In the following, the Open method specifies only the CursorType and the LockType for the user-defined Recordset. The familiar Source and ActiveConnection arguments are omitted.

A Do…Loop structure iterates through each row of objRstBase, and either directly transfers field values to objRstStats or calculates the values that will be supplied to objRstStat fields. For example, the ModifyBasis supporting procedure processes some logic that adjusts the basis for the commission calculation. Also, the CalculatePayment supporting procedure applies a percentage based on the commission rating of the sales representative.

```
'Now, build up the SQL
strSQL = "SELECT Orders.orOrderID, Orders.orOrderDate, " & _
    "Orders.orSubTotal, Orders.orTotal, " & _
    "SalesReps.srFName, SalesReps.srLName, " & _
    "SalesReps.srRepID, SalesReps.srCommissionRating " & _
    "FROM Orders INNER JOIN SalesReps ON Orders.orRepID " & _
    "= SalesReps.srRepID WHERE " & _
    "({ fn MONTH(Orders.orOrderDate) } = " & _
    pintMonth & ") And (SalesReps.srRepID = " & _
    plngRepID & ")"


'Now, open the connection
objCnn.Open pstrConnect


'Open the base Recordset
With objRstBase
    .Open strSQL, objCnn, adOpenForwardOnly, adLockReadOnly
    'Populate the stats Recordset
    objRstStats.Open , , adOpenKeyset, adLockOptimistic
    If Not objRstBase.BOF Then
        Do While Not objRstBase.EOF
            With objRstStats
                .AddNew
                !RepName = objRstBase("srFName") & " " & _
                    objRstBase("srLName")
                !OrderTotal = objRstBase("orTotal")
                curSumOrdTotal = _
                    (curSumOrdTotal + !OrderTotal)
                !Rating = objRstBase("srCommissionRating")
                !Basis = _
                    ModifyBasis(objRstBase("orSubTotal"))
                curSumBasis = curSumBasis + !Basis
                !Payout = CalculatePayment(!Basis, !Rating)
                curSumPayout = curSumPayout + !Payout
                .Update
                objRstBase.MoveNext
            End With
        Loop
    End If
End With
```

Finally, the procedure terminates by adding a summary row at the end of the user-defined Recordset. The code then sets the value of the CalculateCommission method to refer to objRstStats so that the Recordset can be returned from the server-side business object.

```
If pbAppendSummary Then
    With objRstStats
        .AddNew
        !RepName = "Summary"
        !OrderTotal = curSumOrdTotal
        !Basis = curSumBasis
        !Payout = curSumPayout
        .Update
        'Put pointer back on first rec
        .MoveFirst
    End With
End If

Set CalculateCommission = objRstStats

End Function
```

Back to the Commission ASP

The Commission ASP can now use the user-defined Recordset to dynamically output its contents into an HTML table. A sampling of the Active Server script that does this is shown here:

```
<%Do While Not objRst.EOF
    If objRst("Rating") = "0" Then %>

<TR>
<TD><FONT face=Verdana
size=3><Strong><%=objRst(0)%></Strong></FONT></TD>
<TD><FONT face=Verdana
size=3><Strong><%=objRst("OrderTotal")%></Strong></FONT></TD>
<TD><FONT face=Verdana
size=3><Strong><%=objRst("Basis")%></Strong></FONT></TD>
<TD><FONT face=Verdana
size=3><Strong><%=objRst("Payout")%></Strong></FONT></TD>
</TR>

<%Else%>

<TR>
<TD><FONT face=Verdana size=3><%=objRst("Rating")%></FONT></TD>
<TD><FONT face=Verdana size=3><%=objRst("OrderTotal")%></FONT></TD>
<TD><FONT face=Verdana size=3><%=objRst("Basis")%></FONT></TD>
<TD><FONT face=Verdana size=3><%=objRst("Payout")%></FONT></TD>
```

```
</TR>

<%End If
    objRst.MoveNext
Loop%>
```

From Here

Talk about a powerful structure: It can be disconnected from a data source. It can be persisted to maintain its state even beyond the lifetime of an application. It can assume a hierarchical structure. It can be defined programmatically by the developer. It can be used in traditional client/server applications on the client. It can be used in server-side business components called from a number of application contexts including Active Server Pages. That's the ADO Recordset. When you were first introduced to the Recordset, you probably thought of it in light of the similar DAO and RDO cursors (if you had worked with them). Now you know the ADO Recordset is definitely the next-generation cursor.

So far in this book, we have worked with ADO in ways that were (basically) familiar to you if you have worked with the earlier DAO or RDO objects. In the next chapter, we will be exploring purely new functionality. Remember that the power of ADO is in its seamless capability to work with different providers in new ways. You'll learn about how ADO can actually be used to build the tables, indexes, and other structures in a database. Also, we'll explore the tricks of the trade for working with nontraditional providers like Microsoft Index Server.

Unusual ADO: Executing DDL with ADOX and Using ADO with Nontraditional Data Sources

So far in this book, you have seen ADO acting in its "business as usual" role. That is, as a data access structure through which you can query and update the data in a relational database. In this way, although ADO has many powerful interfaces and efficiencies, its purpose is basically the same as the earlier data access structures of DAO or RDO.

In this chapter and the next, all that is going to change. In reality, ADO is very different from its predecessors and it is its "unusual" capabilities that make it such a powerful way to deal with all sorts of data and data-related systems. In this chapter, we will discuss two such unusual capabilities: using ADO to manage the structures (tables, views, indexes, etc.) of a database and also to query non-traditional data sources like the Microsoft Index Server.

We will begin our discussion of these extensions to the traditional notion of data access objects with the ADOX API. These extensions to the ADO object model provide data definition abilities to ADO. Using ADOX, you are able to do such things as create new tables, relate tables, and create indexes, procedures, and views in a data source. If you have worked with SQL Server's Data Management Objects (DMO) in the past, then the idea of using an object structure to manipulate a database may seem familiar to you. However, in keeping with the goal of Universal Data Access, you can use the ADOX object structure to manipulate the structures in a number of data stores (for example, SQL Server, Jet, etc.).

After ADOX, the discussion will turn to ADO's (i.e., OLEDB) ability to work with a growing number of non-traditional data stores. You already know about ADO's use to query almost any database (that is, SQL Server, Oracle, Jet, DB2, FoxPro, etc.). However, ADO also allows you to work with nontraditional (and seemingly bizarre) data stores like the file system, e-mail servers, and Web pages.

Arguably, the most exciting aspect to using these extensions is the consistency they bring to your code. These OLE DB providers extend many of the same interfaces to ADO that traditional data sources do, so you can continue to work with the interfaces with which you have become familiar during the course of reading this book. That's right, using ADO you can use (basically) standard SQL syntax to return information queried from your corporate file system, intranet, or the Internet, and the data will be returned in a standard ADO Recordset.

In other words, ADO provides *abstraction* from the data store that is being used. So, just as your ADO code should work the same way when you are querying SQL Server, Oracle, or DBase data, you can expect the same interfaces and behaviors when you need to work with any other provider. Because the actual data source that is being queried is largely hidden, you can continue to concentrate on the data rather than on the technical details that enable you to access it.

What You'll Learn

In this chapter, we will examine the object structure and capabilities of the ADOX extensions to the ADO object structure. After this, we will take a short look at the power, speed, and flexibility of working with the OLE DB Provider for Microsoft Index Server. You will see how ADO can be used to query the file system or the Web with the speed and ease that you have come to expect from ADO.

 Although this chapter covers the use of the Index Server OLE DB Provider, the use and maintenance of Index Server could fill a book in itself. Therefore, this chapter should not be regarded as an exhaustive reference. Its focus is on making use of this impressive service and exploring some specific ways that this OLE DB provider can extend and empower your work with ADO.

ADOX: DDL with ADO

Basically, the ADOX API provides an object structure through which you can manipulate the definitions of a database. As was stated earlier, this is a good deal different from the uses of ADO that we have seen so far in this book. Up until now, ADO has been seen as a way to move data. However, using ADOX, you are actually able to build and then to re-define the structure of a data store.

Of course, this has some very handy and powerful implications. For example, you can use the ADOX API to move the entire structure of a database to a different location or a different data source (e.g, you could programmatically move a database from SQL Server to Oracle or a local Jet (.mdb) data store). Further, since ADOX allows for you to create database structures dynamically, a data access layer of a distributed application could be made "data access smart"; assigning and deleting indexes according to usage.

The ADOX Object Model

Since ADOX is an extension to the ADO object model, there are many elements in this model with which you are already familiar. For example, in order to begin working with a database, you use the familiar ADO Connection object. However, there are also many elements of this structure that are new. The Table 4.1 details the objects that you can use to define and maintain database structures.

Table 4.1 The objects of the ADOX API

OBJECT	PURPOSE
Connection	To provide a connection to a particular data source.
Catalog	Represents the schema of the database and contains collections of all of the tables, views, procedures, views, and users of a database.
Table	Object represents a table in the database (that is, a member of the Catalog's Tables collection). This object contains collections of Column, Index, and Key objects.
Column	Represents a column in a table or the columns that are used to create an index or key. Therefore, Table, Index, and Key objects all have collections of Column objects.
Index	The Index object represents an index on a table in the database (that is, a member of the Table's Index collection). In turn, this object contains a collection of the Column objects upon which the index is based.
Key	Represents a key on a table (that is, a member of the Table's Key collection). A Key object can have a type of primary, foreign, or unique and can reference another table in the database. Like the Index object, a Key contains a collection of Column objects upon which it is based.
View	This is the object representation of a View (that is, a filtered set of records or a virtual table) in the database. This object is found in the Catalog object's Views collection.
Procedure	The Procedure object represents a stored procedure or query in the data source (that is, a member of the Catalog object's Procedures collection).
User	Represents a user of a secured database.
Group	Represents a group account that has access to a secured database.

Getting Started: Using the Connection and Catalog Objects

Just as with the ADO interfaces that you know, to work with a database with ADOX, you must first get a connection to a data source. By this point, you should be very familiar with the creation and use of Connection objects. For example, if I wanted to get a connection to the "Pubs" database in SQL Server, I could use the following code to simply create an ADODB.Connection object and open it using a DSN-less connection string and the SQLOLEDB data provider.

```
Public Sub DBPrint()
Dim objConn as ADODB.Connection

    'Create and establish connection to data source
Set objConn = CreateObject("ADODB.Connection")
    'Use SQLOLEDB data provider
objConn.Open "Provider=SQLOLEDB;" & _
    "Server=(Local);Database=Pubs;UID=sa"

End Sub
```

Once a connection is made to the data store, the ADOX extensions to the regular ADO model can be used to modify the structure of the data. The sample code that you see above is the beginning of a routine that will print the entire structure of a SQL Server database to the VB Debug window. However, in order to accomplish this, a Catalog object must be created that will allow access to the definition of the database rather than the data held in the database.

The Catalog object represents the whole structure of the data store. It is from this object that all other objects used in ADOX are held in collections. For example, if you wanted to print out the names of the tables in the database, you could iterate through the Catalog object's Tables collection and print the Name property of each one. Also, if you want to add a Table, View, or Procedure to the database, then you will have to use the Append method of the Catalog object's Tables, Views, or Procedures collection.

You can establish a Catalog object and associate it with a particular data store by creating it and setting its ActiveConnection property to an already established ADODB.Connection object. In the following code, a Catalog object is created and a connection is established for it.

```
Public Sub DBPrint()
Dim objConn As ADODB.Connection
Dim objCat as ADOX.Catalog

    'Create and establish connection to data source
Set objConn = CreateObject("ADODB.Connection")
    'Use SQLOLEDB data provider
objConn.Open "Provider=SQLOLEDB;" & _
    "Server=(Local);Database=Pubs;UID=sa"
```

```
    'Create a Catalog object
set objCat = Createobject("ADOX.Catalog")
    'Establish a connection to the SQL Server data store
set objCat.ActiveConnection = objConn

End Sub
```

You can also use the ADOX.Catalog object to create new databases rather than to describe old ones. The Create method of the Catalog will establish a database and then can be used to add objects to the new database. In the following code, an ADOX Catalog object is used to create a new Microsoft Access Database.

```
Public Function MakeJetDB(strDBPathName As String) _
        As Boolean
Dim objCat As ADOX.Catalog

        'Create new Catalog object
    Set objCat = New ADOX.Catalog
        'Use the Create method to create a new database
    objCat.Create "Provider=Microsft.Jet.OLEDB.4.0;" & _
                "Data Source=" & strDBPathName
End Function
```

A Short Tour of the ADOX Object Structure: Reporting Database Objects with ADOX

Because all of the items in a database exist in collections of the Catalog object, a simple procedure could be written using ADOX to display the structure of a database to a user. The following DBPrint( ) procedure simply iterates through all of the members of the Tables collection and prints each of the item's name and table type (for example, System Tables, Tables, or Views). Then, to illustrate the structure of the ADOX object hierarchy further, the function continues to iterate through all of the members of the Table object's Columns collection and print each member's name and data type.

```
Public Sub DBPrint()
Dim objConn As New ADODB.Connection
Dim objCat As New ADOX.Catalog
Dim objTab As New ADOX.Table
Dim objCol As New ADOX.Column

    'Establish Connection
objConn.Open "Provider=SQLOLEDB;" & _
    "Server=(Local);Database=Pubs;UID=sa"
objCat.ActiveConnection = objConn

    'Move through collection of tables
For Each objTab In objCat.Tables
```

(continues)

(Continued)

```
        'Print each table's name and type
    '(e.g., system view, table, view)
    Debug.Print vbCrLf & "***************" & vbCrLf & _
        objTab.Name & " -Type: " & objTab.Type
    Debug.Print "Columns:"
        'Move through the table's collection of columns
    For Each objCol In objTab.Columns
            'Print each column's name and datatype
        Debug.Print vbTab & objCol.Name & " -DataType:" & objCol.Type
    Next
Next

End Sub
```

The output of this procedure to the Visual Basic Immediate window would look something like what is shown in Figure 4.1. If you look at the information displayed in this figure, you will notice that both conventional tables and virtual tables (that is,

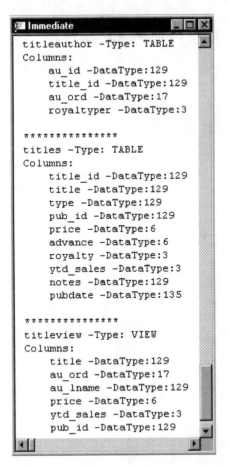

Figure 4.1   Output of tables accessed via ADOX.

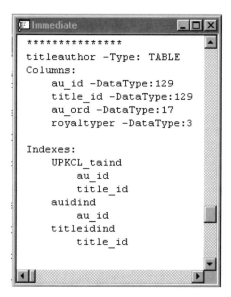

Figure 4.2 Table and index information.

Views) are reported to be members of a Catalog's Tables collection. You will also notice that the data types of the fields (that is, Columns) are reported as ADO data type constants (for example, 129 = adChar, 3 = adInt).

Although this type of information may be helpful, we can get a more in-depth view of the database if this routine also outputs the indexes that exist on each table in the Catalog. Just like interrogating and outputting then names and data types of a Table object, this is a matter of using the ADOX object structure to iterate through the Table object's collection of Indexes.

However, simply knowing the names of the indexes on a table doesn't really tell us the columns on a table that are indexed. To get this information, we must use the ADOX object structure further in order to interrogate each Index object's Columns collection. This collection is made up of the same ADOX. Column objects that were used earlier to output the fields in a table. However, in this context, this collection of Column objects are used to allow access to the column or columns (that is, in a multi-column index) that are used in a particular index on a table. Therefore, if we append the following code into the existing DBPrint( ) procedure, a fuller picture of the structure of the database can be produced.

```
For Each objIdx In objTab.Indexes
        'Print each index name
      Debug.Print vbTab & objIdx.Name
          'move through each index's
          'collection of columns
      For Each objIdxCol In objIdx.Columns
          Debug.Print vbTab & vbTab & objIdxCol.Name
      Next
    Next
```

Figure 4.3   Listing of system and user defined stored procedures.

To finish our tour through the object structure of ADOX, we'll access one of the collections of objects that are outside of the Table object structure. Until this point, most of the ADOX interfaces that have been printed in the DBPrint( ) routine have existed as members of the Table hierarchy (i.e., Columns and Indexes). Other ADOX objects include collections of Users, Groups, Views, and Procedures that exist as collections of the Catalog object. Therefore, we'll make one last change to the DBPrint( ) routine that will access and print the names of all of the stored procedures in the queried database. Just as with the previous iterations through collections of ADOX objects, the code is a simple For Each...In....Next loop.

```
For Each objProc In objCat.Procedures
    Debug.Print objProc.Name
Next
```

This will produce a listing of stored procedure names in the database that you can see in Figure 4.3. Notice that this list will contain both system and user defined stored procedures.

Creating Database Objects With ADOX

Not only are you able to report database objects with ADOX, but you are also able to define them. This can be very useful if you want to provide some way to manipulate the structure of the database (for example, create indexes, define tables) programmatically. Earlier, we had mentioned the example of implementing a "smart" middle-tier data access object that would watch for commonly queried fields and would dynamically create or drop indexes according to the most common usage. In this section, we will explore the example of allowing individual users of a system to create personal data stores.

For example, if you were writing a sales support system, you might wish to create a place in the system where a sales person could store personal information (that is, notes on contacts, etc.) that would not be accessed by any other user of the system. To do this, it would be handy if the user could create a personal table in the Database.

The following MakePersonalStore function creates this type of personal table using ADOX. This procedure accepts two arrays and a string as an argument. The first array carries the names and data types of the fields to be added to the new table. The string passed to the procedure defines the name of the table to be created. Finally, the second array is used to define the columns used on indexes on the table.

```
Public Function MakePersonalStore(aArray() As Variant, _
            strTableName As String, aIndexes() As Variant) As Boolean
'*Makes a seperate SQL Server table
'*for a sales person's contact data
Dim objConn As New ADODB.Connection
Dim objCat As New ADOX.Catalog
Dim objTab As New ADOX.Table
Dim objIndex As New ADOX.Index
Dim intIterator As Integer
```

After dimensioning all of the ADODB and ADOX objects that will be used in the procedure, the first step is to establish a connection to the database and assign that connection to the ADOX Catalog object which will be used to drive the creation of the new table.

```
'Establish Connection
objConn.Open "Provider=SQLOLEDB;" & _
    "Server=(Local);Database=Pubs;UID=sa"
objCat.ActiveConnection = objConn
```

Now that a Catalog object has been created and connected to the database, a new ADOX Table object can be created and assigned values. To start, the procedure will assign the new Table object's name to the string passed into the routine.

```
'Create Table
With objTab
        'Define table's name
    .Name = strTableName
End With
```

Then, the procedure iterates through the first array passed to the procedure and uses the Append method of the Table object's Columns collection to create a new column in the table. This Append method accepts two parameters. The first parameter will be used as the new Column's name, and the second parameter is used to define the Column's data type. Both of these parameters are assigned values from first and second dimensions of the first passed array.

```
With objTab
        'Define table's name
    .Name = strTableName
            'loop through aArray(), adding each item to the
            'table's Columns collection
    Do
        .Columns.Append aArray(intIterator, 0), aArray(intIterator, 1)
        intIterator = intIterator + 1
    Loop Until intIterator > UBound(aArray)

End With
```

Finally, the newly created Table and its collection of Column objects is added to the database by passing the object to the Append method of the Catalog object's Tables collection.

```
'Append table to Database
objCat.Tables.Append objTab
```

Once the Table has been appended to the Catalog, ADOX can be used to create indexes. If you remember, the columns to be indexed are passed to the MakePersonal-DataStore procedure in a second array. Just as we iterated though the array containing the columns to be defined, the routine iterates through the Index array. In each iteration through this array, the new ADOX Index is named and a column is added to its Column's collection. Finally, the Append method of the Table's Indexes collection is passed the newly created Index.

```
With objIndex
    'Set iterator back to 0
    intIterator = 0
        'loop through aIndexes() adding each item to
        'the the index object's columns collection
    Do
        objIndex.Name = aIndexes(intIterator)
        .Columns.Append aIndexes(intIterator)
            'Add index to the table
        objTab.Indexes.Append objIndex
        intIterator = intIterator + 1
    Loop Until intIterator > UBound(aIndexes)
End With
```

Once this procedure is written, a new table can be created with a routine like the one that follows:

```
Public Sub BuildMeATable()
Dim objExample As New clsADOX
Dim aArray(3, 1) As Variant
```

```
Dim aIndex(0) As Variant

    aArray(0, 0) = "FirstName"
    aArray(0, 1) = adVarWChar
    aArray(1, 0) = "LastName"
    aArray(1, 1) = adVarWChar
    aArray(2, 0) = "Email"
    aArray(2, 1) = adVarWChar
    aArray(3, 0) = "Phone"
    aArray(3, 1) = adVarWChar


    aIndex(0) = "FirstName"

    If objExample.MakePersonalStore(aArray, "NewTestTable", aIndex) Then
        MsgBox "Table Created"
    End If
End Sub
```

If you were to use the SQL Server 7 Enterprise manager to view the table created, you would see that the table, columns, and indexes in Figure 4.4 have been created.

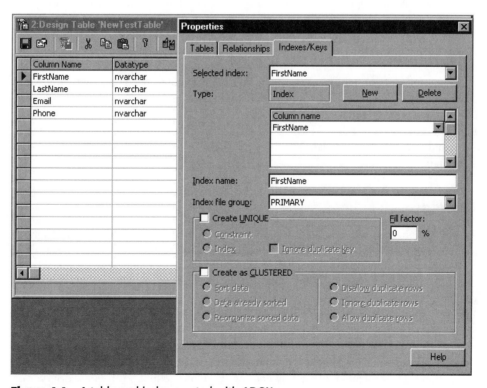

Figure 4.4 A table and index created with ADOX.

Using Index Server and Its Data Provider

As was stated earlier, one of the important ways that ADO can work to accomplish Microsoft's goal of truly universal data access is to provide some way to query file system or Web server data. The OLE DB Provider for Index Server fills this gap nicely. Using this OLE DB provider, you can use the familiar ADO interfaces to perform detailed queries on hundreds and thousands of files and return a Recordset in seconds, or even fractions of seconds. Index Server uses a background application that maintains an on-disk catalog, or index, of specified directories in a file system. Basically, this catalog is a highly optimized, super-searchable database. One way to think about the Index Server data store is as a *data warehouse* of your file system or Web site that is built and maintained on the fly.

How Index Server Works

Index Server is basically like the "crawlers" that are employed by many Internet search sites (for example, AOL's WebCrawler). Once you install Index Server, it (for the most part) looks after itself. When it senses that the server is not fully employed with some other task, it scans a specified directory structure, building and maintaining catalogs of information about the files that exist and their contents. The fundamental data store that is queried when you use the Index Server OLE DB Provider with ADO are these catalogs of information that Index Server finds during its late-night strolls around your file system.

When you query an Index Server, it uses these highly optimized catalog databases to deliver complex querying capabilities and impressive search response times. In fact, the types of queries that can be carried out with the Index Server provider are much greater in power than standard SQL 92 syntax. In fact, the most complex part of working with ADO and the Index Server data provider is learning the *additional* query syntax that you can use.

Catalogs

As mentioned, probably the best way to think about catalogs is to compare them to databases; that is, they contain tables (directories) that are indexed and then searched when you run a query. Also, like a database, you can specify which catalog you wish to use when you run a query. However, unlike most data providers, if you fail to provide a database against which to run a query, the default Index Server catalog will be used. Logically, this catalog contains some key directories, along with the root of the Web server on which the Index Server is hosted.

If you want to add or delete catalogs, or add directories to existing ones, you must use the Microsoft Management Console (Figure 4.5) and the Index Server Snap-in. Using this tool, you can create a new catalog by right-clicking on the Index Server on Local Machine heading and specifying the name of the new catalog and the physical location of where it should be stored.

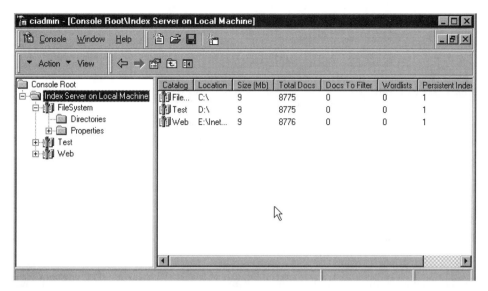

Figure 4.5 You use the Microsoft Management Console and the Index Server Snap-in to maintain catalogs.

 A word to the wise: Pay attention to where you put catalogs, as they can grow to be huge—possibly as much as 40 percent of the size of the indexed data if you have the full indexing features in use. So, if you are setting up a catalog for a number of machines on your network, make sure you have the space, or create a number of catalogs for the information that you wish to index.

After you have created a new catalog, you have to add the directories to it that need to be queried. Again, you can do this by right-clicking on the newly created catalog. When the dialog shown in Figure 4.6 is shown, simply input the path and any additional account information that is needed in order to view it. Although this is shown in Figure 4.6 as adding new directories to a new catalog, you can also use these commands to add new directories to any existing catalog on your Index Server.

The Queried Information

Once you have set up a new catalog, the information in the directories that you selected will be indexed when the system restarts. When the catalog is built, Index Server doesn't just gather simple information about the files, like their names and sizes (a simple directory search from NT Explorer will give you those results); instead, it builds information about the author of the file and when it was published; and more astonishingly, it creates an *abstract* of the file.

This abstract is the result of some fairly complex natural language processing that is built into Index Server. When the abstracting is done, Index Server "knows" what is in

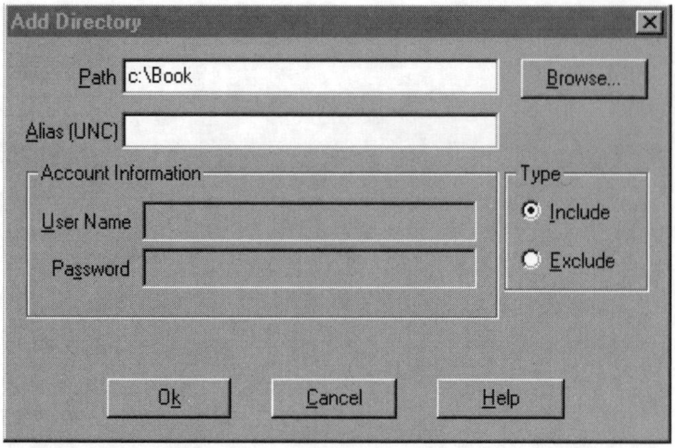

Figure 4.6 Adding directories to a catalog.

the file. That is, it can search on a word or group of words as SQL 92 can, but it can also derive natural language permutations on words so that it can derive search results that contain; for example, the word "flight" from a search on "fly**" (the double asterisk denotes a search on all grammatical variations on the word). Also, Index Server maintains a listing of "noise words" that will be excluded from a search. As a result, words like "and," "the," and "at" will not be included in the index.

These innovations are even more impressive because it is not only simple text files that are included in the index, but also files of more complex formats, including HTML files; documents created in Microsoft Word, Excel, or PowerPoint; or plain text files. Index Server even maintains a list of nondocument files in the catalog, such as executables.

Nevertheless, you will find that Index Server does not support many types of document files. In fact, only simple file structures (like text files) and Microsoft proprietary file formats (of course) are currently supported. In the future, there is hope that many more types of files will be supported as third-party software vendors adhere to the standards that enable Index Server to search their application file formats.

Scope

A catalog may be like a database, but it is definitely not a relational database. Remember that the data inside these catalogs is based on the file system, and file systems are usually created as hierarchically structured data stores. Because of this, the scope of your searches becomes very important when querying Index Server data.

It may not be appropriate that you query on every catalog, and it may not be appropriate to search through every subdirectory in the catalog's indexed directories. As you will learn later in this chapter, the syntax used to perform queries can be used to limit the folders in a catalog to be searched.

For this reason, an important concept about scope is the idea of the *traversal level*, or subdirectory depth, to which your queries will extend. If a *shallow traversal* is specified in a search, then only the highest-level folders specified in the catalog will be searched. Conversely, if a *deep traversal* is used in a search, then all of the subdirectories of the catalog's folders will be searched. Obviously, a deep traversal will be a much more time- and resource-intensive function that is likely to find much more information.

Working with the Index Server OLE DB Provider

Every time data has been queried in this book, you have seen the interaction of a COM object structure (ADO) with an OLE DB data provider. In this chapter, you will see nothing different. If you think for a minute about what "nothing different" means, you might justifiably come to the conclusion that although you might be called on to speak to multitudes of different data stores in the future, your job won't be getting much harder. Now that you have learned to work with the ADO hierarchy, any type of data store that can expose an OLE DB provider interface can be queried through techniques that you already know. This type of abstraction can make ADO a very long-term friend.

Of course, there are differences in the ways that you will be called upon to work with the ADO interfaces. In this section, you will learn about working with the Provider property of the Connection object and some funny extensions to SQL Syntax, but the ADO interfaces themselves will never change.

The important thing to remember here is that the ADO interface is the "contract" that Microsoft is making with your development efforts. What this binding contract says is that although the storage, structure, and location of your data store may change radically in the future, once ADO has been implemented, the basics of your application will continue to work. In other words, ADO and OLE DB *encapsulate* the sticky technical particulars of working with databases and allow you to concentrate on your job of building applications.

Connecting to the Provider

Let's see what it means that ADO encapsulates the particulars of the data store by comparing the code that you use to connect to a SQL Server database, running a query, connecting to an Index Server, and running a similar query. First, let's review the ADO code that executes against a SQL Server database.

To run a query against a SQL Server database, you could create a routine like the one that follows. This routine starts by dimensioning a Connection and a Recordset object and opens a connection to a database using the "LocalPubs" DSN. Then it runs a query using the LIKE keyword to find all of the records in the Titles table that contain the word "computer." Finally, the ID and title of the found records are shown in the Debug window.

```
Sub DebugRelational()

Dim objConn As ADODB.Connection
Dim objRS As ADODB.Recordset
Dim strMSGBOX As String

Set objConn = CreateObject("ADODB.Connection")
objConn.Open "LocalPubs"
```

(continues)

(Continued)

```
Set objRS = objConn.Execute("SELECT title_id, " & & _
    "title FROM Titles WHERE " & _
    "Upper(title) LIKE('%COMPUTER%')")

Do Until objRS.EOF
    strMSGBOX = strMSGBOX & objRS("title_id") & _
    ": " & objRS("title") & vbCrLf
    objRS.MoveNext
Loop

Debug.print strMSGBOX, , "Relational Search Results...."

End Sub
```

When this routine runs against a local PUBS database, it displays the records shown in Figure 4.7 in Visual Basic's Debug window.

When using the Index Server data provider, very little changes. In fact, the only thing that is different between the following code snippet and the last one is the arguments that are passed to the Connection object's Open and Execute methods. As you can see from the code in bold face in the next example, instead of using a DSN called "LocalPubs", you can connect to the Index Server provider simply by passing the string "provider=msidxs;" to the Connection's Open method. Then, in order to return useful information, a SQL statement specifying the property to return (path), the scope of the query (default), and a condition is passed to the Connection object's Execute method. Figure 4.8 shows the output from the query.

```
Sub RunIdxSvrProvider()
Dim objConn As ADODB.Connection
Dim objRS As ADODB.Recordset
Dim strMSGBOX As String

Set objConn = CreateObject("ADODB.Connection")
objConn.Open "provider=msidxs;"
Set objRS = objConn.Execute("SELECT path FROM SCOPE() " & _
"WHERE CONTAINS('ADO') > 0")

Do Until objRS.EOF
    strMSGBOX = strMSGBOX & objRS("path") & vbCrLf
    objRS.MoveNext
Loop

Debug.print strMSGBOX

End Sub
```

Index Server Query Language

Although the interfaces are very much the same, and the task of connecting to an Index Server provider is a simple task, the SQL syntax probably looks pretty strange to you

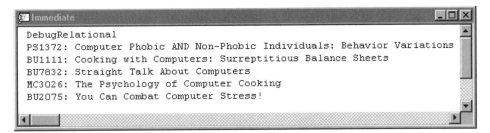

Figure 4.7   The results of a query against a SQL Server table.

right now. There are two major reasons for this, the first of which is the structure of the data store. Remember that Index Server data is built on the structure of the file system, so it is hierarchical, not relational. Therefore, you will have to specify a scope for your queries.

The second and more important reason that the SQL syntax used with the Index Server provider looks strange is because this provider allows for much more powerful queries than are possible with most other providers. In this section, you will learn about specifying the scope of a catalog to be searched and conducting a fuzzy search, along with some weird Boolean operator shorthand.

Scope

Probably the most obvious difference between conventional SQL syntax and the syntax used with Index Server is that in the place of a table list, there is a Scope() keyword. As mentioned earlier, this syntax is used to define the subset of the catalog that will be queried. In the previous example, the default setting (a deep traversal of the entire catalog) for the scope of the search was used by *not* inserting any directory names or traversal level arguments to the Scope() statement.

If you wanted to speed the query in the previous example, you could have simply limited the detail of the results by restricting the scope of the query. To do this, you would insert the keywords "SHALLOW TRAVERSAL OF," then insert the directory name to be queried between the parentheses of the Scope() argument.

```
RunIdxSvrProvider
e:\winnt\help\iis\htm\core\mtsrel.htm
e:\winnt\help\iis\htm\core\iitasks.htm
e:\winnt\help\iis\htm\core\adcrlnts.htm
e:\winnt\help\iis\htm\core\iigloss.htm
e:\winnt\help\iis\htm\core\iiinloc.htm
e:\winnt\help\iis\htm\core\iiscpb1.asp
e:\winnt\help\iis\htm\core\iiscsp1.asp
e:\winnt\help\iis\htm\core\iiscsp2.asp
e:\winnt\help\iis\htm\core\iiscsp3.asp
e:\winnt\help\iis\htm\core\iisetup.htm
e:\winnt\help\iis\htm\core\iisread.htm
e:\winnt\help\iis\htm\core\iiwlnew.asp
```

Figure 4.8   The output from the Index Server query.

In the earlier example, the Index Server query found 72 files that contained the word ADO. However, if you limited the scope of the query to search only c:\winnt\help\core by specifying a shallow traversal of that directory, the same query would return only 19 files. In the following code, you can see that changing the string passed to the Execute method of the ADO Connection object limits the scope of the query.

```
Set objRS = objConn.Execute("SELECT path FROM " & _
"SCOPE('SHALLOW TRAVERSAL OF " & """" & _
"C:\winnt\help\iis\htm\core\" & """" & "') " & _
"WHERE CONTAINS('ADO') > 0")
```

To meet the particulars of this syntax, the traversal scope argument must be enclosed in single quotes, and the name of the directory must be passed into the statement as a standalone string (enclosed in double quotes). By making this change, you are specifying that only c:\winnt\help\iis\htm\core and none of its subdirectories (shallow traversal) will be included in the query.

Columns

Of course, the most important thing that you must know about any data store is the information that it is able to return to you. In the case of querying an Index Server catalog, a defined set of fields can be returned. Table 4.2 details the names of the catalog fields and the data they contain.

Fields that are prefixed by "DOC" will only be returned by files that support these document properties. For example, if you query for DocComments, only Microsoft Office documents will respond with information for this field.

As you can see, aside from simple file information, these fields can also be used to judge the strength of a match to a query. For example, if you further wanted to limit the search results so that you only received files in which there were more than two places with the word "ADO" mentioned in the file, you could use the following Execute method.

```
Set objRS = objConn.Execute("SELECT path FROM " & _
"SCOPE('SHALLOW TRAVERSAL OF " & """" & _
"C:\winnt\help\iis\htm\core\" & """" & "') " & _
"WHERE CONTAINS('ADO') > 0 AND HitCount > 2")
```

Another way that you could limit the strength of a match of a file to the query is to only allow for the top *n*-percent of matching files to be returned. Note, however, that sometimes the HitCount is misleading because the hits are buried inside of other words (e.g., "ADO" could be found in the word "adore"). The relative ranking (or *rank* attribute) assigned to each file found is a more accurate gauge of the strength of a match. In the following Execute method, only the matches that rank above the fiftieth percentile (i.e., greater than 500 on a scale of 0 to 1,000) in strength would be returned to the Recordset.

```
Set objRS = objConn.Execute("SELECT path FROM " & _
"SCOPE('SHALLOW TRAVERSAL OF " & """" & _
"C:\winnt\help\iis\htm\core\" & """" & "') " & _
"WHERE CONTAINS('ADO') > 0 AND Rank > 500")
```

Table 4.2   Catalog Fields and Their Data

FIELD	DATA
Contents	Words or phrases in the document. When this is used to return information, it will provide an abstract of the data in the file. This field is also used as the default query field when one is not specified.
Create	The date and time the file was originally created.
DocAuthor	The author of the document.
DocComments	The Comments property for the document.
DocKeywords	The keywords specified for the document.
DocPageCount	The number of pages in the document.
DocSubject	The Subject property for the document.
DocTitle	The Title property for the document.
Filename	The name of the file.
HitCount	The number of hits for the content search in the document.
Path	The actual path and file name of the document.
Rank	The relative matching score for the query, from 0 to 1,000.
Size	The size of the file in bytes.
Vpath	The IIS virtual path and file name for the document.
Write	The date and time that the file was last updated.

Extended Syntax

As if the Scope( ) argument and fields data weren't strange enough, there are a number of small changes and extensions to normal SQL syntax that can really confuse you if you aren't aware of them.

Let's start by talking about the effect of the *noise list* that Index Server builds for itself. Recall from the earlier discussion that this is a list of commonly found but meaningless words in a search. For example, "an," "but," "is," "the," and "to" are all considered noise words. Therefore, if you were to change the example query to search on the word "is," an error would be returned indicating that the query contained "only ignored words."

Of course, this behavior is a huge advantage, but it's also strange because the matches in your queries do not have to be exact. Instead, they are something like "real language" queries. That is, in "normal" SQL syntax, the WHERE condition of "Title LIKE('%The Titanic%')" would not return a match for the title "The Making of Titanic." However, the Index Server query processor would definitely return this as a match, along with a number of other files that its query engine deemed "close enough."

The Index Server syntax also extends to *fuzzy operators* that will return matches to the "stem" of the word being searched by appending two asterisks. For example, if you wanted to search for all matches to the stem word of "swim," you would use a filter criterion of "Where CONTAINS('Swim**')." This query would return files that contained matches for the words "swim," "swam," "swum," and "swimming," among others.

One other unfamiliar syntax is the use of the tilde (~) symbol (Boolean NEAR) in a search. This is used to gauge if one word in a search is within 50 words of another. For example, the following code would return a Recordset containing information about the files in the C:\winnt\help\iis\htm\core\ directory that have the word "ADO" within 50 words of the word "IIS." When the tilde operator is used in a query, the Rank attribute of the returned files will be higher if the two phrases being sought are closer to one another. To highlight this feature, an ORDER BY clause has been added to the SQL statement to return the best matches first.

```
Set objRS = objConn.Execute("SELECT path FROM " & _
"SCOPE('SHALLOW TRAVERSAL OF " & """" & _
"C:\winnt\help\iis\htm\core\" & """" & "') " & _
"WHERE CONTAINS('ADO ~ IIS') > 0 ORDER BY Rank Desc")
```

The Search-All Application

Now that you know the basics of working with this peculiar data provider, let's advance from simple code snippets to a more practical example. As stated earlier, in the real world, much of an organization's core data is not input to a database. This unorganized distribution of information can have the effect of giving an organization "corporate amnesia." The simple search application that you see in Figure 4.9 addresses this common problem through providing one search utility for finding information in a database, contained in an intranet or somewhere on the corporate file system.

We have discussed the differences that must be noted when working with a data provider. Therefore, the goal of this application is to demonstrate how ADO allows you to work with very different data sources in very similar ways. As you can see in the previous figure, this application allows you to use ADO to query either a relational database, using the more traditional ODBC data provider, or the company intranet and the file system using the Index Server data provider.

A user can begin working with the system by entering the date that a file or record was created or edited, text, or the author's name, and then clicking on the Search button. In response to this action, the following lines of code will be run:

```
Me.MousePointer = vbHourglass
FillGrid DoSearch()
Me.MousePointer = vbNormal
```

Of course, the first line simply changes the mouse pointer into an hourglass during the search. The second line calls two procedures that perform a query and fill the grid at the bottom of the search screen. First, the DoSearch() function builds a SQL statement based on what the user has input to the form. Then, the function uses ADO to run a

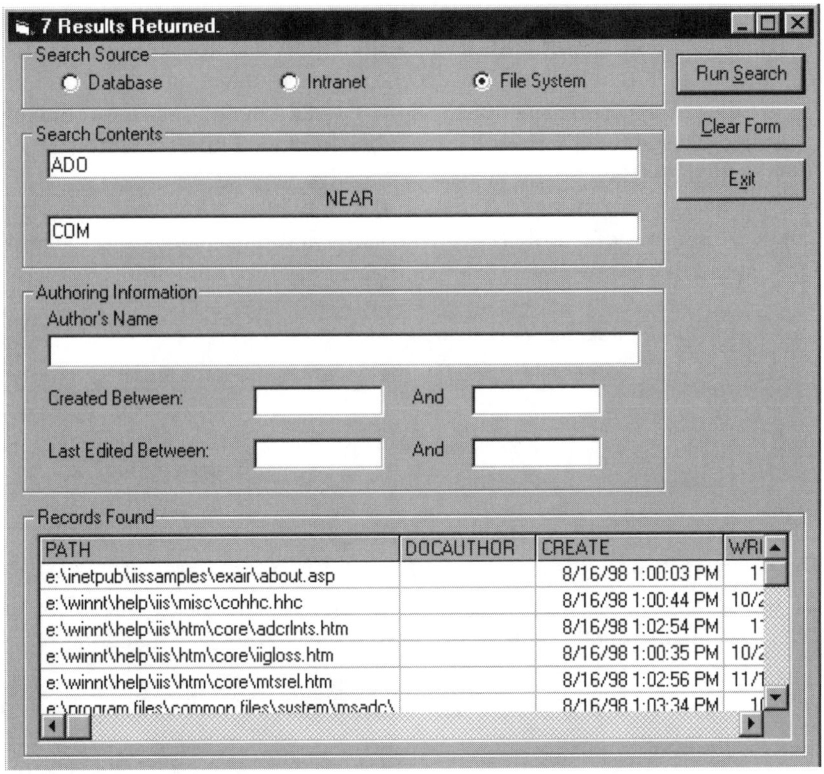

Figure 4.9   The Search-All application.

query against whichever data store was chosen by the user and passes the Recordset created by the query back to the calling procedure as its return value. Second, the Fill-Grid( ) function receives an ADO Recordset as a parameter and (as its name suggests) fills the grid.

Let's begin by looking at the DoSearch Function in detail. All that this simple function does is to make the initial decision of whether to query against an ODBC data source or an Index Server catalog. So, if the database option button has been selected (i.e., opt-Database = True), it will call the RunRelational( ) procedure and return the Recordset that it produces. If the optDatabase option button has not been selected, then this function will call the RunISCatalog( ) function that will query against the Index Server and return a Recordset.

```
Private Function DoSearch() As ADODB.Recordset
    If optDatabase = True Then
        Set DoSearch = RunRelational()
    Else
        Set DoSearch = RunISCatalog()
    End if
End Function
```

From this point, the application will continue to run queries against two different data sources. However, both the RunRelational( )and RunISCatalog( ) functions are very similar in their structures. In both, an ADO Connection object is created and its Open method is called. Then, both functions call the Execute method of their Connection objects using SQL statements returned by other functions and return the ADO Recordset created by these Execute methods.

In the following code, you can see that the RunRelational function passes the ADO Connection object the name of a DSN (i.e., "TestData") and then passes the Execute method the SQL string that is produced by the GetRelationalSQL( ) function.

```
Private Function RunRelational() As ADODB.Recordset
    Dim objConn As ADODB.Connection
    Set objConn = CreateObject("ADODB.Connection")
        'Open using ODBC DSN
    objConn.Open "testdata"
    Set RunRelational = objConn.Execute(GetRelationalSQL())
End Function
```

In contrast, the RunISCatalog( ) function passes the ADO Connection object a string that points to the Index Server data provider that it will be using (i.e., "msidxs"), and then passes the Execute method the return string from the GetISSQL( ) function.

```
Private Function RunISCatalog() As ADODB.Recordset
    Dim objConn As ADODB.Connection
    Set objConn = CreateObject("ADODB.Connection")
    objConn.Open "provider=msidxs;"
    Set RunISCatalog = objConn.Execute(GetISSQL())
End Function
```

The GetRelationalSQL( ) Function

It is in the GetISSQL( ) and GetRelationalSQL( ) functions where most of the data provider-dependent code is encapsulated. Still, the basic logic of these functions is the same: Examine the form and build a statement that can be used by the data provider. You can see that the GetRelationalSQL( ) function simply builds a conventional SQL statement that can be used by the ODBC data provider. Of course, in a real application, query by form code (like what follows) would have to handle a good deal more than just building a SQL string (e.g., dealing with single quotes entered into the form, etc.). The following code is intended to show you the essentials without boring you to death.

```
Private Function GetRelationalSQL() As String
    Dim strSQL As String
    Dim strAndFlag As String

    'Base SQL Select Statement
    strSQL = "SELECT DocumentID, DocumentAuthor, " & _
        "DocumentCreated, DocumentUpdated FROM " & _
        "ImportantDocument WHERE "
```

```
'Looks for strings to be searched & builds LIKE()
'statement(s)
If Len(Trim(txtContent1)) > 0 Then
    strSQL = strSQL & "UPPER(DocumentText) " * _
        "LIKE('%" & UCase(Trim(txtContent1)) & "%') "
    If Len(Trim(txtContent2)) > 0 Then
        strSQL = strSQL & _
            " AND UPPER(DocumentText) LIKE('%" & _
            UCase(Trim(txtContent1)) & "%') "
    End If
    'Create flag/text to
    strAndFlag = "  AND "
End If


'Builds string to search for authors
If Len(Trim(txtAuthorName)) > 0 Then
    strSQL = strSQL & strAndFlag & _
            "UPPER(DocumentAuthor) = '" & _
              UCase(Trim(txtAuthorName)) & "'"
    strAndFlag = "  AND "
End If
'Constructs Created date range
If (Len(Trim(txtCreateStart)) > 0 And _
    Len(Trim(txtCreateEnd)) = 0) Or _
        (Len(Trim(txtCreateEnd)) > 0 And _
            Len(Trim(txtCreateStart)) = 0) Then
    MsgBox "Please enter beginning and ending" & _
        " dates for your 'Created Between' Search"
ElseIf Len(Trim(txtCreateStart)) > 0 And & _
    Len(Trim(txtCreateEnd)) Then
    strSQL = strSQL & strAndFlag & _
        " DocumentCreated >= '" & _
            CDate(Trim(txtCreateStart)) & _
                "' AND Documentcreated <= '" & _
                    CDate(Trim(txtCreateEnd)) & "' "
    strAndFlag = "  AND "
End If


'Constructs Updated Date range
If (Len(Trim(txtEditStart)) > 0 And _
    Len(Trim(txtEditEnd)) = 0) Or _
        (Len(Trim(txtEditEnd)) > 0 And _
            Len(Trim(txtEditStart)) = 0) Then
    MsgBox "Please enter beginning and ending " & _
        "dates for your 'Edited Between' Search"
ElseIf Len(Trim(txtEditStart)) > 0 And _
    Len(Trim(txtEditEnd)) Then
        strSQL = strSQL & strAndFlag & _
  " DocumentUpdated >= '" & _
    CDate(Trim(txtEditStart)) & _
                "' AND DocumentUpdated <= '" & _
```

(continues)

(Continued)

```
                    CDate(Trim(txtEditEnd)) & "' "
          strAndFlag = "  AND "
    End If


    'Trims trailing AND or Where
    If Right(strSQL, 6) = "  AND " Then
        strSQL = Left(strSQL, (Len(strSQL) - 6))
    ElseIf Right(strSQL, 6) = "WHERE " Then
        strSQL = Left(strSQL, (Len(strSQL) - 6))
    End If


    GetRelationalSQL = strSQL


End Function
```

The GetISSQL Function

The GetISSQL( ) function has much of the same logic as the GetRelationalSQL( ) function. However, this function has a number of distinctly different tasks to accomplish to achieve its goal of building a query statement that the Index Server Provider can use. For example, the statement it builds must be able to return information from the fields of the Index Server catalog shown in the following code snippet:

```
strSQL = "SELECT Path , DocAuthor, " & _
    "Create, Write FROM "
```

Next, the GetISSQL( ) function must determine the scope of the query to be performed. If the user elects to search the entire file system, the FROM statement should be followed by SCOPE( ) to designate that the entire catalog should be searched. However, if the user decides only to search the company intranet, then the scope of the search should be limited to the directories that contain the intranet. The following code tests to determine if the intranet option button on the form has been selected and then builds the appropriate SCOPE( ) string.

```
If optIntra = True Then
    'Build string that contains double quotes around
    'intranet directory
    strSQL = strSQL & "SCOPE('DEEP TRAVERSAL OF " & _
  """"  & "E:\InetPub\wwwRoot" & """" & "')"
Else
    strSQL = strSQL & "SCOPE()"
End If
```

The final basic difference between the GetISSQL( ) function and the GetRelational-SQL( ) function revolves around string searching. In contrast with the GetRelational-SQL( ) function, when you use the Index Server data provider, you must use the CONTAINS( ) syntax rather than a LIKE() statement to perform string searches.

In addition to this change, when a user inputs two strings into the search form, the GetISSQL( ) doesn't simply return any file in which both strings are found. Instead, it looks for the first string appearing within 50 words of the second. Remember from earlier in the chapter that this type of search can be accomplished through the use of the tilde (~) operator.

The GetISSQL( ) function performs a test to see if any text has been entered into the Search Contents textboxes on the form. If text has been entered into the first (i.e., Len(Trim(txtContent1)) > 0), then the function will append a simple CONTAINS( ) clause to the search string. However, if a string has been entered into both textboxes, then a CONTAINS( ) clause is built that contains both strings and a tilde is inserted between them.

```
If Len(Trim(txtContent1)) > 0 Then
    strSQL = strSQL & "CONTAINS('" & txtContent1
    If Len(Trim(txtContent2)) > 0 Then
        strSQL = strSQL & " ~ " & txtContent2
    End If
    strSQL = strSQL & "') > 0 "
    strAndFlag = " AND "
End If
```

The remainder of the code in GetISSQL( ) is identical to the code found in GetRelationalSQL( ), except that Index Server catalog fields are being queried rather than database fields (e.g., DocAuthor instead of DocumentAuthor). The whole GetISSQL( ) looks like this:

```
Private Function GetISSQL() As String
Dim strSQL As String
Dim strAndFlag As String

strSQL = "SELECT Path , DocAuthor, " & _
    "Create, Write FROM "

    'Defines scope (intranet or whole catalog)
    If optIntra = True Then
        strSQL = strSQL & _
        "SCOPE('DEEP TRAVERSAL OF " & """" & _
        "E:\InetPub\wwwRoot" & """" & "')"
    Else
        strSQL = strSQL & "SCOPE()"
    End If


    strSQL = strSQL & " WHERE "

    'Build String Search
    If Len(Trim(txtContent1)) > 0 Then
        strSQL = strSQL & "CONTAINS('" & txtContent1
        If Len(Trim(txtContent2)) > 0 Then
            strSQL = strSQL & " ~ " & txtContent2
        End If
        strSQL = strSQL & "') > 0 "
```

(continues)

(Continued)

```
        strAndFlag = "  AND "
    End If


    'Build Author Search
    If Len(Trim(txtAuthorName)) > 0 Then
        strSQL = strSQL & strAndFlag & " DocAuthor = " & _
            Trim(txtAuthorName)
        strAndFlag = "  AND "
    End If


    'Build Created Between Search
    If (Len(Trim(txtCreateStart)) > 0 And _
        Len(Trim(txtCreateEnd)) = 0) Or _
            (Len(Trim(txtCreateEnd)) > 0 And _
                Len(Trim(txtCreateStart)) = 0) Then
        MsgBox "Please enter beginning and " & _
            "ending dates for your 'Created Between' " & _
                "Search"
    ElseIf Len(Trim(txtCreateStart)) > 0 And _
        Len(Trim(txtCreateEnd)) Then
            strSQL = strSQL & strAndFlag & " " & _
                "Create >= '" & _
                CDate(Trim(txtCreateStart)) & _
                    "' AND Create <= '" & _
            CDate(Trim(txtCreateEnd)) & "' "
            strAndFlag = "  AND "
    End If


    'Build Edited Search
    If (Len(Trim(txtEditStart)) > 0 _
        And Len(Trim(txtEditEnd)) = 0) Or _
            (Len(Trim(txtEditEnd)) > 0 And _
                Len(Trim(txtEditStart)) = 0) Then
        MsgBox "Please enter beginning and ending" & _
                " dates for your 'Edited Between' Search"
    ElseIf Len(Trim(txtEditStart)) > 0 And _
        Len(Trim(txtEditEnd)) Then
            strSQL = strSQL & strAndFlag & _
                " Write >= '" & _
                CDate(Trim(txtEditStart)) & _
                    "' AND Write <= '" & _
                        CDate(Trim(txtEditEnd)) & "' "
            strAndFlag = "  AND "
    End If


    'Trim Trailing AND and WHERE
    If Right(strSQL, 6) = "  AND " Then
        strSQL = Left(strSQL, (Len(strSQL) - 6))
```

```
    ElseIf Right(strSQL, 6) = "WHERE " Then
        strSQL = Left(strSQL, (Len(strSQL) - 6))
    End If

    GetISSQL = strSQL

End Function
```

Both the GetISSQL( ) and the GetRelationalSQL( ) functions return query statements that are passed to the Execute method of an ADO Connection object to create a Recordset. In turn, the resulting Recordset is ultimately passed back to the DoSearch( ) function that was called when a user clicked on the Search button on the form. Finally, the DoSearch( ) function passes the Recordset to the FillGrid( ) procedure that populates the grid on the form with data from the search, and you are back to the point at which you began exploring the search-all application.

```
Me.MousePointer = vbHourglass
FillGrid DoSearch()
Me.MousePointer = vbNormal
```

 If you want to investigate the search-all application in more detail, visit the book's Web site, www.wiley.com/compbooks/martiner shown on the cover. For more information on Index Server itself, visit www.microsoft.com.

From Here

Now that you have seen the power of ADO to create data structures and query the information on a file system or on a Web site, it's time to explore the ways ADO can be used to build robust Web applications. In the next chapter, we will continue to explore the "unusual" aspects of ADO and investigate Remote Data Services or RDS. With this technology, you'll learn how to revolutionize your Web database applications by using the RDS server-side and client-side objects.

Using Remote Data Services in Web Applications

The far-reaching tentacles of OLE DB certainly impact Web-based development, too. You've seen ADO used server-side in the context of Active Server Pages. You've learned about Microsoft Index Server. Remote Data Services (RDS) is another ADO-based technology designed for, but not limited to use in, Web-based applications. Though this chapter will focus on the use of RDS in a Web-based environment, RDS can also be used for applications that use a compiled front end on client computers.

What You'll Learn

In this chapter, you'll learn about the basic capabilities of RDS, from its architecture to its use, including the following:

Understanding How RDS Works. This section explains the purpose of RDS and the architecture that makes it work.

Appraising RDS. In this section, you will learn about the advantages and limitations of RDS. You will also come to understand when you should consider using it in your Web application development.

Using the RDS DataControl. This section details the simplest means of caching data on a Web client: the RDS DataControl. You will also see that the DataControl is a valid DHTML data source, and therefore can source data to bound DHTML controls.

Using the RDS DataSpace. In this section, you will learn how the RDS DataSpace object is used to invoke server-side components from a Web client. In this context, you will find out how to instantiate the server-side RDSServer DataFactory to return a client-side Recordset. More important, you will learn how to use the DataSpace to instantiate custom COM components that can update a database or return data to the Web client.

Creating Recordsets from an Arbitrary Structure. In this section, you'll learn how to use the CreateRecordset method of the RDSServer DataFactory to create a Recordset from a non-OLE DB source or from a completely arbitrary structure. Doing so allows you to manipulate data in the structure using all the capabilities of a client-side Recordset.

Understanding How RDS Works

One of the critical aspects of Web-based, database applications is the marshaling of data from server to client. There are numerous ways to do this, even with only Microsoft technologies. Depending on the nature of the application, the way and frequency with which you move data from a database to a Web client will vary. Some Web applications require a great amount of data currency—that is, the data displayed on the screen must be as up to date as possible. Others, as you learned when dealing with persisting Recordsets, can allow the user to work with data that is not current.

For example, an executive may want to review sales revenues for the quarter. Once the Web application initially queries the database, the information is presented on the Web client. At this point, the data is the data; in the next few minutes or hours, the sales data will not change because the quarter is over and the books are closed. However, the executive may want to filter the data by account or by business or manipulate the data in other ways. Should the data have to be fetched again from the server database and then represented on the Web client? Unless there is some vital reason for doing so, the answer is a resounding no. If the opportunity exists to manipulate cached data on the Web client (so as not to impose further network traffic, server load, and of course a longer wait for the executive), take advantage of it. This is one of the purposes behind RDS: to allow you to cache data on a Web client and then manipulate it using familiar ADO. But RDS has other purposes as well:

- As already stated, RDS provides a mechanism to cache data on a Web client for presentation and modification purposes. This involves the capability to bind data-aware DHTML and ActiveX controls to data supplied by remote servers.

- Data is cached on a Web client, thus eliminating the need for many server round-trips to fetch data; this can boost performance. Large and small sets of data can be retrieved once and then manipulated via the cache.

- RDS supports a tiered architecture, allowing you to encapsulate business logic in custom COM components and implement the components in the business tier of the application. You can call upon the services of the business components from the Web client.

- RDS affords the developer the familiar semantics of working with the ADO Recordset. Developers can also use the scripting language of their choice.

- With RDS, custom business components can be used with Microsoft Transaction Server to allow for transaction management and connection pooling.

RDS Architecture

In addition to marshaling data from server to client and client to server, RDA also handles making remote calls to server-side components via HTTP—pretty cool. But how does it do all this? To answer this question, realize that RDS implements its technology in a manner consistent with tiered or distributed architectures. Let's quickly review what a tiered architecture implies. In a tiered architecture, at least three logical categories of tasks are carried out. Put in another way, the application exists in at least three tiers, each with its unique contribution to the overall application. In a Web application, tiers may be described this way:

Client Tier. Often termed *user services*. In a Web application this tier typically consists of a client computer running a Web browser. The browser displays and allows the user to manipulate the data that is supplied from a remote source.

Middle Tier. Often called *business services*. In an RDS Web application, this tier is an NT server running Internet Information Server. This server hosts business logic in the form of Active Server scripts or compiled COM components. The scripts and components carry out the logic necessary to implement the organization's business rules.

Data Source Tier. Also called *data services*. This tier is a server-side computer that hosts a relational database management system.

Tiers are logical categories; there is no implication that a tier is analogous to a machine. For example, a three-tier application could be constructed using two types of machines: client workstations and a single server. In this scenario, the business services and the data services portions of the application would reside on the single server. A Web application that uses three tiers looks like the illustration in Figure 5.1.

How does RDS work in concert with a tiered architecture? Principally, it handles the interaction between the tiers. It facilitates the interaction between Web client and business service components by handling the communication and transfer of data between them. It also contains technology that facilitates the interaction between business service components and RDBMSs—it allows for the retrieval and storage of data. Figure 5.2 shows the role of RDS in a Web-based scenario.

You can see that RDS employs client-tier and middle-tier software. Specifically, client-tier components include the RDS DataControl, the RDS client-side Recordset, and a client cursor-engine (CE). The client-side Recordset is the means by which data is cached on a Web client. RDS uses the CE to buffer remote Recordsets in its temporary table structures. This data is exposed as an OLE DB rowset implemented on top of a static, client-side cursor. CE also maintains client updates in its cache and interacts with the OLE DB Persistence Provider to marshal the rowset across process/machine

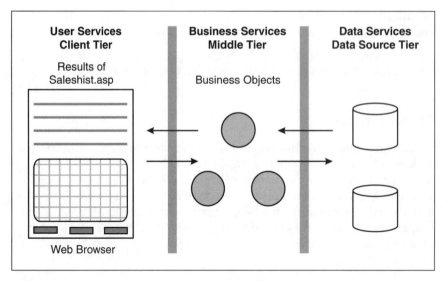

Figure 5.1   A tiered architecture implies logically partitioned application services.

boundaries. The engine's capability to update data uses a SQL query-based update mechanism and only works against SQL-based OLE DB providers.

When RDS submits a request for data to the Web server, the Web server (read Internet Information Server, IIS) receives the request and invokes the services of the managing server-side component, the ADISAPI DLL. This DLL either invokes the services of a "plain" business object, the RDSServer DataFactory for record retrieval and storage

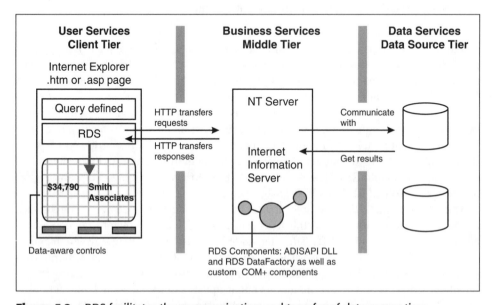

Figure 5.2   RDS facilitates the communication and transfer of data across tiers.

operations, or a custom COM component, if the request asked for one. Once data is retrieved from the database, ADISAPI formats the data in a MIME format and IIS transmits the data to the Web client. On the client, the data is repackaged as a client-side Recordset and made available to the RDS DataControl. Bound controls can display the data provided by the RDS DataControl.

 RDS Works with DCOM, too! This chapter highlights the use of RDS in Web-based applications, but RDS can also be used on a LAN to support client-side caching of data and remote access to business objects through DCOM.

Appraising RDS

Before we get into the practical nature of working with RDS in a Web application, let's stop for a moment and consider its advantages and its limitations. Perhaps the greatest advantage to RDS is its capability to cache data on a Web client. Doing so means that you can manipulate data for presentation and modification purposes without launching numerous trips to the Web server for more data. Also of extreme benefit is the capability of the RDS DataControl to act as a data source for bound ActiveX controls and even DHTML controls. This affords you considerable time-saving when building the user interface of Web applications because it decreases the amount of script you have to write. For example, you would not have to write a script that populates controls on the page.

Another advantage is the RDS capability to invoke business components from a Web client. These components reside on a remote machine, but RDS takes care of instantiating the component on the remote machine and the marshaling of data between the remote machine and the client. Since RDS allows for using your own business components, you can encapsulate the business logic of your application in a suite of server-side components instead of in thousands of lines of client-side or server-side script. These components can take advantage of transaction management and the pooling of ODBC connections with Microsoft Transaction Server. (In Part Two of this book, Windows NT Middle-Tier Services, you'll learn about using custom business components with Microsoft Transaction Server.)

Despite its advantages, you must understand that RDS is, through and through, a Microsoft technology. Obviously, if you're a Microsoft shop, this is good news. And if you're developing a Web application for a client where Microsoft technologies are mandated, this is good news. But, if you're developing a Web application where the type of Web browser and/or Web server is in question, then RDS won't do the trick. On the Web server, RDS relies on Internet Information Server. But more limiting is that RDS is implemented on the Web client as ActiveX technology, which is great, if the browser you're using is Internet Explorer. Even though other browsers support the use of ActiveX controls through plug-ins, RDS will only work with Internet Explorer. So before deciding to use RDS, make sure that, from server to desktop, Microsoft tools are being used to build and run the Web application. RDS does not, however, imply direct limitations on the RDBMS system being used.

Using the RDS DataControl

In this section, you'll examine a simple application that displays customer data using an ActiveX control, the Sheridan Data Grid, and DHTML controls. Each of these controls is bound to an RDS DataControl. In addition, a number of HTML buttons allow the user to modify data. Figure 5.3 shows the interface of the application.

Getting Data

The RDSDataControl.asp page uses the RDS DataControl to source data for the controls. The RDS DataControl is an invisible control that exists on the Web page. Using it is very simple. Let's look at the code that instantiates the control.

```
<OBJECT
    ID=RDSDC
    CLASSID=clsid:BD96C556-65A3-11D0-983A-00C04FC29E33
    CODEBASE="Cabs/msadc15.cab">
</OBJECT>
```

Using the HTML OBJECT tag, you reference the control using the CLASSID attribute. The CODEBASE attribute specifies the cab file, which can be used if the control is not

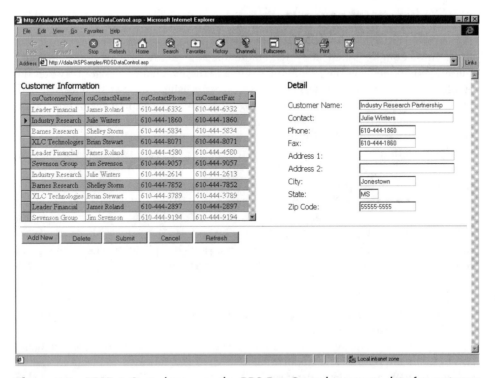

Figure 5.3 RDSDataControl.asp uses the RDS DataControl to source data for customer information.

already installed on the client desktop. As with all ActiveX controls, Internet Explorer will download the necessary files from the cab file and register them on the client computer.

The RDS DataControl has a number of other attributes that you must use to define the data it will retrieve and where to get it. These attributes could be specified using HTML PARAM tags or through script in an appropriate procedure. In this application, the data loads as the page sites in the browser, so the Window_OnLoad event procedure contains script that sets the additional attributes.

```
Sub Window_OnLoad()

RDSDC.Server = _
    "HTTP://<%=Request.ServerVariables("SERVER_NAME")%>"
RDSDC.Connect = "ADOBook"
RDSDC.SQL = "SELECT cuCustomerName, cuContactName, " & _
    "cuContactPhone, cuContactFax, cuAddress1, " & _
    "cuAddress2, cuCity, cuState, cuPostalCode, " & _
    "cuCustomerID From Customers"
RDSDC.Refresh

End Sub
```

Setting the Server, Connect, and SQL Properties

The Server attribute specifies the URL of the Web server. In this example, which is an ASP, a relative URL can be created by using Active Server script. The Request.ServerVariables ("SERVER_NAME") notation returns the name of the Web server. Doing this makes sense, since hard-coding the server name means problems if the page is hosted on another Web server at a later time.

The Connect attribute specifies the valid connection string information. Earlier, you learned about DSN-based and DSN-less connections. The Connect attribute can use either. However, understand that if you use the name of a DSN, as in this example, the DSN must exist on the Web server.

The SQL property specifies the SQL source for the request. Of course, setting the SQL in client-side script exposes the information to the users, if they select the Source command from Internet Explorer's View menu. Later, you'll learn how to use a server-side component to source data for the RDS DataControl. When you do this, you have the opportunity to hide sensitive initialization information by encapsulating it inside the server-side component.

Using the Refresh Method

To make the RDS DataControl retrieve information from the remote source, you execute the Refresh method. When you execute this method, RDS uses the attributes just specified to issue an HTTP request to the Web server. IIS receives the request and recognizes that the request originated from RDS client-side components. Therefore, it invokes the services of the core RDS server-side component, the ADISAPI DLL. This DLL creates a server-side RDSServer DataFactory object that executes the query on the data source and returns a server-side cursor. ADISAPI converts the server-side cursor into a MIME format, the contents of which is shipped via HTTP to the client by IIS. When Internet Explorer receives the MIME-encoded data, it rebuilds the data as a client-side, disconnected Recordset. This Recordset is then automatically supplied as a reference to the RDS DataControl's Recordset property.

You can use the Refresh method in client-side script anytime you want to requery the data source. Furthermore, you can reset the Server, Connect, and SQL attributes of a single RDS DataControl to return different sets of information to the client, as needed. However, a single RDS DataControl only hosts a single Recordset at a time. So, upon issuing a Refresh method, a former client-side Recordset is released and any pending changes are lost.

Pending changes? How can changes be pending? This brings up an important point about the RDS client-side Recordset. RDS uses disconnected Recordsets. Remember that a disconnected Recordset is simply a Recordset that does not have a live connection. Therefore, when modifying rows in a disconnected Recordset, the changes are made to the local cache and not immediately submitted to the server. In Chapter 3, you learned how, if you're using a batch cursor, the ADO Recordset uses the UpdateBatch method to transmit cached record changes to the server. The RDS DataControl uses a similar feature, the SubmitChanges method, which you'll learn about shortly. When retrieving data through the RDS DataControl in this fashion, the client-side Recordset is built as a Keyset cursor (adOpenKeyset) that supports optimistic locking (adLockOptimistic).

 The RDS client-side Recordset object is a somewhat slimmed-down version of the ADO Recordset, although in version 2.0, the two objects are almost identical. The programmatic ID of the RDS client-side Recordset is ADOR.Recordset, while the programmatic ID of the ADO Recordset is ADODB. Recordset. In future versions of RDS, you may find that RDS no longer requires the ADOR.Recordset but relies on ADO's Recordset object for client-side data caching and operations.

In general, the RDS client-side Recordset has these characteristics:

- It is implemented in the client-side cursor engine with static cursors (by default).

- It is a disconnected Recordset, meaning its ActiveConnection property is set to nothing.

- If the underlying provider it uses is SQL-based, then it can support batch updating.

- When updates are supported, they are based on optimistic locking semantics.

- During batch updates, either all the changes succeed or they all fail; detailed row-by-row error information is not available on the Web client.

- It supports asynchronous fetching and refreshing.

- It supports useful features like sorting, finding, and filtering.
- It can be bound to DHTML and other data-aware controls.
- Its data can be persisted.

Binding Controls to the RDS DataControl

Fortunately, ActiveX controls and DHTML controls can be bound to the RDS DataControl. This means that you will write significantly less client-side code. You do not have to write code that populates the contents of controls from the data supplied by the RDS.DataControl. Once the user modifies data in the controls, you do not have to write code that modifies the state of the client-side cache, either.

Binding an ActiveX Control

Any ActiveX control that is data-aware by today's Microsoft standards should support the capability to bind to an RDS DataControl and possibly other data source objects. In this application, the Sheridan Databound Grid displays customer information. The following code instantiates the control and binds it to the RDS DataControl.

```
<OBJECT CLASSID=clsid:AC05DC80-7DF1-11d0-839E-00A024A94B3A
    codeBase="Cabs/ssdatb32.cab"
    DataSrc=#RDSDC
    Height=275
    ID=GRID
    Width=520 VIEWASTEXT>
    <PARAM NAME="ScrollBars" VALUE="2">
</OBJECT>
```

Of interest is the DataSrc attribute. This attribute specifies the ID of the RDS DataControl with the #RDSDC notation. Since the control is bound, when the client-side Recordset is constructed, the grid fills with the data supplied by the RDS DataControl. The DataSrc property can also be set using client-side script.

Binding DHTML Controls

In Chapter 3, you learned how DHTML Controls can bind to the Tabular Data Control. There you saw how the DHTML DataSrc and DataFld attributes were set to specify the source and field for a control. The RDS DataControl is also a valid DHTML data source. Figure 5.4 shows the txtCustomer control that is bound to the RDS DataControl.

In the RDSDataControl.asp page, the binding behavior of the RDS DataControl, the grid, and the DHTML controls is exceptional. When the user clicks on a row in the grid, the grid and the RDS DataControl interact so that when the pointer moves in the grid, it also moves in the RDS DataControl's Recordset. Since the pointer moves in the Recordset, it also changes the information in the bound DHTML controls, without any coding on your part.

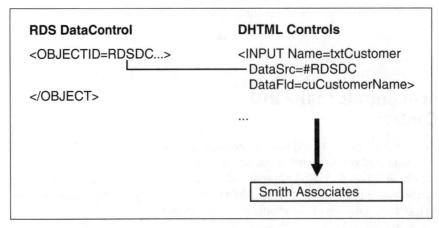

Figure 5.4   The RDS DataControl serves as a DHTML data source for binding controls.

Modifying Data

The RDS DataControl hosts an updatable, disconnected Recordset. As such, you can use it to modify records in the local cache. For example, to edit existing records, you can simply modify the data in bound controls, and the data cache is automatically updated as well. If you are working with unbound operations, you can issue an Update method on a row and it will modify the data in the cache. Each row that is modified is identified as a row that is pending update. You could then use the SubmitChanges method to send all the pending rows to the server. When you execute the SubmitChanges method, only modified rows are marshaled to the server. There, the ADIS-API DLL constructs an instance of the RDSServer.DataFactory and the rows are written to the data source. The rows that are updated on the server are written in a batch transaction. Thus, all of the rows either succeed or they all fail.

You'll find the SubmitChanges method a viable solution for nonsophisticated updates. However, any application with even modest needs may require additional code that helps to enforce business rules. Once the SubmitChanges method is issued from the client, there is no possibility of intercepting or embellishing how it performs the updates on the server. Therefore, with this method, you are not afforded the opportunity to enforce middle-tier business logic. This, of course, means that the business logic would have to be encountered prior to issuing the method on the client, which in turn would mean writing such logic in client-side script. For even modest applications, writing large amounts of business logic in client-side script is not a very elegant solution, not to mention that it breaks a tiered model substantially.

Furthermore, the number of databases supported by the native RDSServer DataFactory is limited. While theoretically RDS should be able to "talk" to any OLE DB data using an appropriate provider, you'll find that in practice, the default RDSServer DataFactory object works best with SQL Server and JET databases.

So is RDS really only a static data presentation tool? By no means! Only the SubmitChanges method may be a limited solution in some scenarios. However, RDS also allows you to invoke data modification through your own custom COM components. A little later, you'll explore how to do this. The RDSDataControl.asp adds new records and deletes records through the use of server-side COM components. For now, let's look at how the SubmitChanges method works for modifications on existing rows.

1. Data in the local cache is updated automatically through bound controls or when you issue the Update method of the Recordset object.

```
RDSDC.Recorset.Update
```

2. Changes to all pending rows are written to the server when you issue the SubmitChanges method. In the RDSDataControl.asp page, this happens when the user clicks on the btnSubmit button that calls the Submit procedure.

```
Sub Submit()
     If RDSDC.Recordset.Editmode = 2 Then 'Add
          'Call code to invoke business object (later)
     Else 'current row has been modified
          RDSDC.SubmitChanges
          End If
     End Sub
```

 The RDSServer DataFactory object also supports a SubmitChanges method. When calling its SubmitChanges method, you can supply two additional arguments for the data source connection and the Recordset that will be submitted to the server. Based on the discussion thus far, you may have thought of the RDSServer DataFactory as only a server-side object, but in fact a client-side proxy exists for this object as well.

You can also use the Recordset's Delete and Addnew methods to affect rows in the client-side cache. Having done so, the SubmitChanges method will also marshal those changes to the server when you execute it. Prior to issuing an update when a record has been edited or is in the process of being added, you can issue the CancelUpdate method to abort the operation.

A Survey of RDS DataControl Properties and Methods

The RDS DataControl hosts a number of other properties and methods. Many of these are fairly self-explanatory, but some deserve a description of what they do and when you would want to use them. Table 5.1 shows an inclusive listing of RDS DataControl properties and methods. Some pertain to asynchronous operations that you will learn about in the next section.

Table 5.1 RDS DataControl Properties and Methods

METHOD OR PROPERTY	NAME	DESCRIPTION
Method	Cancel	Use to cancel a currently running asynchronous operation. When loading data asynchronously, the user is free to do other tasks in the browser while the data is being acquired. Canceling aborts the operation and supplies an empty Recordset to the RDS DataControl.
Method	CancelUpdate	Use to abort an update operation on a row that is in the process of being added (Recordset.Addnew has been executed, but not updated yet) or a record whose fields values have been changed but not updated yet. You can test the EditMode property of the Recordset to determine if an AddNew operation is in progress (adEditAdd, 2), an edit is in progress (adEditInProgress, 1), or even a Delete operation (adEditDelete, 4). However, canceling a Delete operation is seldom of value, since there is relatively little time between the issue of the delete and the completion of the operation. If a row is not in a state of being changed, the EditMode will reflect the adEditNone value of 0.
Property	Connect	Set the Connect property to a valid DSN or DSN-less connection syntax.
Method	CreateRecordset	Use this method to create a cursor with an arbitrary structure (not created from a data source). To do this, you define an array of arrays and supply it to the method's ColumnsInfo argument. The Recordset can then be used to add and modify records. The records can then be marshaled to the server using the RDS DataControl's SubmitChanges method or the Recordset's UpdateBatch method, if the Recordset is a full-fledged ADO Recordset. This method also applies to the server-side RDSServer DataFactory object. As such, you could use it to define the structure of a Recordset for any source, such as a file listing. You could then populate it and have the benefit of working with the data in the familiar Recordset framework.
Property	DataSpace	Supplies a reference to the RDS DataSpace object (if any) that may have been used to marshal a Recordset to the client.

Table 5.1 RDS DataControl Properties and Methods (*Continued*)

METHOD OR PROPERTY	NAME	DESCRIPTION
Property	ExecuteOptions	Determines whether the next refresh will occur asynchronously. If you set the property to adcExecAsynch, the refresh will occur asynchronously, while the constant adcExecSynch produces a synchronous refresh. You should use this property in conjunction with the ReadyState property to determine if an asynchronous refresh is in progress. This is necessary because other methods will fail while it is in progress. In the next section, you will see code that uses this property.
Property	FetchOptions	Use to control how data is fetched into the client-side Recordset. The constant adcFetchUpFront means that all rows are fetched before control returns. The constant adcFetchBackground means that control returns after the first batch of records is returned. A subsequent read of a record that is not in a current fetch batch will cause the row to be fetched, after which control will return to the application. The constant adcFetchAsync causes all rows to be fetched asynchronously; control returns immediately to the application.
Property	FilterColumn	Use to set the column for which a filter should be applied.
Property	FilterCriterion	Use to specify a comparison operator for the FilterValue. Valid operators include $<$, $<=$, $>$, $>=$, $=$, $<>$.
Property	FilterValue	Use to specify a filter value for the specified FilterColumn.
Property	InternetTimeout	Use to add precision as to how long the application waits after an HTTP request has been issued. The value is expressed in milliseconds.
Property	ReadyState	Use to poll the state of the Recordset when using asynchronous refreshes. The constant adcReadyStateLoaded means that the Recordset is open, but no data has been retrieved yet. The constant adcReadyStateInteractive means that the Recordset is still in the process of retrieving data; the adcReadyStateComplete constant means that the operation is complete.

(continues)

Table 5.1 RDS DataControl Properties and Methods (*Continued*)

METHOD OR PROPERTY	NAME	DESCRIPTION
Property	Recordset	A reference to the Recordset object that is sourcing the RDS DataControl. You can use this object to exact finer control over the Recordset data, such as using its Move methods.
Method	Refresh	Use to requery the data source supplied by the Connect property.
Method	Reset	Use to invoke a sort or filter upon the client-side Recordset.
Property	Server	Use to specify the IIS server and protocol used prior to issuing a Refresh.
Property	SortColumn	Use to specify the column that should be used for sorting.
Property	SortDirection	Use to set a Boolean value to specify ascending (True) or descending (False) sort order based on the SortCoumn property value.
Property	SourceRecordset	Unlike the Recordset property, the SourceRecordset property is a write-only property. You use this property to return a Recordset supplied from a middle-tier component. You will see how to do this in the next section.
Property	SQL	Use to specify the SQL statement (in the dialect of the data source) that is executed when a Refresh is invoked.
Method	SubmitChanges	As you've already seen, use this property to submit pending records to the default RDSServer DataFactory object.

The constants referred to in Table 5.1 must be defined in the Web page where they are used. You can use the file adcvbs.inc to include the file in any Web page that might need the constants. This file is located by default in the C:\Program Files\Common Files\System\MSADC directory. You can cut and paste these constants into your Web pages, or incorporate the file as a server-side include in this manner:

```
<!--#INCLUDE FILE='[directory on Web server]/adcvbs.inc'-->.
```

If you choose to use a server-side include, then you must be using an Active Server page. The adcvbs file defines constants for use with VBScript. The constant declarations for JavaScript are in the file adcjavas.inc. Check both files to make sure that all the constants you require are defined in them.

Refreshing and Fetching Data Asynchronously

When using the RDS DataControl in a Web application, it is particularly important that the RDS DataControl refresh its data asynchronously. Depending on the means of communication and available bandwidth, the time required to return rows could take a while. Populating asynchronously means that the Refresh method call is made "out of process." Thus, the calling process is free to continue with other operations, including returning control back to the user. By default, the Refresh method executes a refresh asynchronously because the default ExecuteOptions value is adcExecAsync (2). To purposely make the RDS DataControl execute the Refresh operation on the calling thread (synchronously), you can set ExecuteOptions to adcExecSync (1).

Related to the subject of refreshing is fetching. Fetching can occur synchronously or asynchronously and refers to how the actual rows are returned to the client-side Recordset. By default, the RDS DataControl fetches records asynchronously. You can force synchronous fetching by setting the FetchOptions property to adcFetchUpFront (1). Thus, with both asynchronous refreshing and fetching, you are causing the Refresh operation to execute in another process, and individual rows are returned to the process asynchronously.

When a Refresh method is executing asynchronously, you can determine the state of the asynchronous operation by polling the ReadyState property at the appropriate time. For example, the Add New button (btnAdd) calls the AddNew procedure. This procedure initiates the adding of a new record by calling the AddNew method of the Recordset. However, if the Recordset is not open (RDSDC.ReadyState <> adcReadyStateCompleted or adcReadyStateInteractive), then the AddNew method call fails. You can avoid operation failures by including code that allows operations to be conducted only on an open Recordset. You should include code, such as the next example, for any operation that requires an open Recordset, such as the Move methods, the SubmitChanges method, the Delete method, and so on.

```
Sub AddNew()
    If RDSDC.ReadyState = adcReadyStateComplete _
        Or RDSDC.ReadyState = adcReadyStateInteractive Then
        RDSDC.Recordset.AddNew
        txtCustomer.Select
    End If
End Sub
```

Similarly, you can poll the State property of the underlying Recordset to determine if it is open. For example, the AddNew procedure in the previous code could be written this way:

```
Sub AddNew()
    If RDSDC.Recordset.State = adStateOpen Then
        RDSDC.Recordset.AddNew
        txtCustomer.Select
    End If
End Sub
```

Table 5.2   Recordset ObjectState Enums

ENUM (CONSTANT)	VALUE	DESCRIPTION
AdStateClosed	0	The Recordset is closed.
AdStateConnecting	2	A connection is in progress.
AdStateExecuting	4	The query is being executed.
AdStateFetching	8	The asynchronous fetching of records is in progress.
AdStateOpen	1	The Recordset is open.

The State property of the Recordset can be one of five values at any one time, depending on how and what progress has been made in supplying the Recordset its data. Table 5.2 shows the ObjectStateEnums and their values.

Keep in mind that once a Recordset is open, it may still be fetching records; thus, most operations will work on an open Recordset. But don't be fooled. For example, if you issue a MoveLast method on a Recordset that is open but still fetching records, the pointer will move to the "current" last record in the cache. Meanwhile, the fetching continues asynchronously. Therefore, even seconds later, a new "last" record will appear.

Using RDS DataControl Events with Asynchronous Operations

In the discussion about ADO events and asynchronous operations in Chapter 2, you found out that ADO objects (the Connection and Recordset) raise events in their client applications. The client application will then execute an event handler (procedure) that you can use to respond to the occurrence of the event. Here, the client application is Internet Explorer. IE will recognize scripted event handlers that you write for the RDS DataControl (as well as other ActiveX controls). The RDS DataControl raises a number of events that help you fine-tune how your application works in conjunction with handling these asynchronous operations. Table 5.3 lists these events and a brief description.

To help ensure that operations occur at an appropriate time, the OnReadyState-Change event handler tests the ReadyState property to determine whether some of the buttons on the page should be enabled. Certainly, you could do this without the event handler, but the handler is the more elegant solution because it will do the job every time the data set is refreshed. You can count on this because the handler fires every time the ReadyState property changes. Therefore, even if the user should click the Refresh button, the Add New, Delete, Cancel, and Submit buttons will all be disabled until the Refresh operation completes.

```
Sub RDSDC_OnReadyStateChange()
    If RDSDC.ReadyState = adcReadyStateLoaded Then
        btnAdd.Disabled = True
        btnDelete.Disabled = True
        btnCancel.Disabled = True
```

Table 5.3 RDS DataControl Events to Optimize Handling of Operations during Asynchronous Refreshing and Fetching

EVENT NAME	DESCRIPTION
OnReadyStateChange	Fires every time the ReadyState property changes. You might use this event to enable buttons on a form that should only be enabled after at least some data is fetched and the Recordset is open.
OnDataSetChanged	Fires when the asynchronous operation is complete. You might include code for its handler for operations that should only occur after all data is refreshed. Typically, if not always, this event will fire just prior to the OnDataSetComplete event.
OnDataSetComplete	Fires after the fetching is complete. You might use this event to include code for a handler that should allow an operation as soon as all records are fetched.

```
        btnUpdate.Disabled = True
    End If

    If RDSDC.ReadyState = adcReadyStateComplete Then
        btnAdd.Disabled = False
        btnDelete.Disabled = False
        btnCancel.Disabled = False
        btnUpdate.Disabled = False
    End If

End Sub
```

RDS Technology Summary

This section demonstrated how RDS technology works. You've seen how the RDS Data-Control offers an extensive client-side capability to display and manipulate data. The principle shortcoming of using the RDS DataControl to source data is that it relies on a "plain" server-side business object, the RDSServer DataFactory, to retrieve and store information in a database. Many applications require considerably more custom logic for data retrieval and writing operations. With this in mind, you'll now explore the use of the RDS DataSpace object, which you can use to instantiate custom business components on the server.

Using the RDS DataSpace

The value of the RDS DataSpace comes as a result of its role in handling the information and processing necessary to invoke middle-tier components. When a Web client calls for a middle-tier component to be created, the Web client must have an object proxy that corresponds to the actual object that is instantiated on the Web server. A proxy is an interface that handles the marshaling of data and communication requirements when a client calls an object running in another process on the same machine or a remote machine. Likewise, when a remote component is instantiated on a server, a stub is created that handles the same tasks for communicating with the client that called it. Middle-tier components are instantiated for each method call and released when the method call returns. No state is maintained between calls.

So, in fact, the role of the RDS DataSpace is fairly transparent to you the developer. You don't do much with it except use it to invoke middle-tier components. Until now, you may even have thought that the RDS DataSpace had not been used at all, but it actually had. If the RDS DataControl uses an RDSServer DataFactory (a remote automation component) behind the scenes, then object proxies and stubs are in use, and marshaling must be occurring. So when using the RDS DataControl to return data, as you saw in the last section, the code was invoking the services of the RDS DataSpace to in turn invoke the services of the RDSServer DataFactory on the IIS server. When you use the RDS DataControl's native ability to retrieve and update data sources, you don't manually (with code) instantiate the services of the RDS DataSpace; RDS takes care of that for you. However, if you want to call custom COM components located on a Web server, then you must manually instantiate an RDS DataSpace object on the Web client in order to call the business object from the client.

In this section, you'll look at several uses of the RDS DataSpace:

1. To return data from a manually created RDSServer DataFactory.

2. To return data from a custom business object located on the Web server and supply that data to an RDS DataControl.

3. To invoke a business object located on a Web server and marshal information so the business object can modify records in a database.

Instantiating the RDS DataSpace

You instantiate an RDS DataSpace object on a Web page as you would any ActiveX control: by using the HTML OBJECT tag. Once you've done this, you can use its CreateObject method that builds the client-side proxy and makes the cross process/cross machine call to instantiate a middle-tier component. The following code shows the OBJECT tag usage:

```
<OBJECT ID=RDSDS
    CLASSID=CLSID:BD96C556-65A3-11D0-983A-00C04FC29E36>
    CODEBASE="Cabs/msadc15.cab"
</OBJECT>
```

It seems as though there should be something more than that, but that's all the code that is needed to instantiate the RDS DataSpace. In the sections that follow, you'll see a number of different ways to use the CreateObject method.

Using the RDS DataSpace to Manually Create an RDSServer DataFactory Business Object

You've already seen that the RDS DataControl uses the RDS DataSpace to instantiate the "plain" RDSServer DataFactory object on the Web server. You also learned that the principal limitation of the RDSServer DataFactory is that it does not allow the inclusion of custom middle-tier logic to assist in its retrieval or writing of operations on the server. Consequently, manually invoking it has the same limitation. But the way you invoke an RDSServer DataFactory object does not differ much from the way you would invoke a custom business object. Therefore, the time spent in looking at a little code will be informative.

Using the CreateObject Method

Many objects these days have a CreateObject method, and the RDS DataSpace is one of them. The next code sample uses the CreateObject method (on the Web client) to invoke the RDSServer DataFactory object on a Web server. Following that, the GetRecordset procedure shows the code that instantiates an RDSServer DataFactory and uses it to marshal a Recordset to the Web client. Then, the code supplies the Recordset to an RDS DataControl.

```
<SCRIPT LANGUAGE="VBScript">
Option Explicit
Sub GetRecordset()
Dim RDSDF, objRst
Set RDSDF = RDSDS.CreateObject("RDSServer.DataFactory", _
    "http://<%=Request.ServerVariables("SERVER_NAME")%>")
Set objRst = RDSDF.Query("DSN=ADOBook", _
    "Select * From Customers")
RDSDC.SourceRecordset = objRst
End Sub
</SCRIPT>
```

This code assumes that an RDS DataControl and DataSpace have been instantiated using the HTML OBJECT tag, as described earlier. You'll notice that the CreateObject method takes two arguments. The first, ProgID, supplies the programmatic ID of the server-side COM component that you wish to instantiate. In this case, it is the RDSServer DataFactory. The second argument supplies the protocol used to communicate between client and Web server and the name of the Internet Information Server machine. The code also supplies this information in a relative fashion, using ASP's Request object. So, for this exact code to run, it must be contained in an .asp page.

Finally, the client-side Recordset variable, objRst, is supplied its data by calling the Query method of the RDSServer DataFactory object (RDSDF). As you might expect, the Query method requires a valid DSN or valid connection string information and a SQL statement that should be executed. After the Recordset is returned, the SourceRecordset property of an RDS DataControl (RDSDC) can be supplied the Recordset (objRst). Once you've supplied the Recordset to the RDS DataControl, you can then bind it to other controls in the same fashion as you saw earlier in this chapter.

Using the RDS DataSpace to Return Data from a Custom Business Object

In short order, your application may outgrow the generic capabilities of the RDSServer DataFactory. Fortunately, RDS does not stop there. Using the CreateObject method, you can also instantiate your own COM components that encapsulate the required, specific business logic for your application. Certainly, applications have business logic that must be enforced when modifying or deleting data. For example, a business object called Customer might include a Delete method. When the Delete method executes, a rule might require that a customer can't be deleted if the customer has orders. Still, another rule might require that a customer who has no active orders, and the date of the last order is at least one year old, be marked an inactive customer. The list goes on.

Furthermore, when you call upon business objects to retrieve data, rules may affect the way data is retrieved. Indeed, even an object that simply returns sales figures may require a number of arguments that tailor exactly what data it retrieves and how it presents the information to the client. In addition, by encapsulating any operations that access a database inside a COM component, you are inviting the possibility of significant increases in performance, as both IIS and Microsoft Transaction Server provide database connection pooling for components. In this section, you'll explore the RDS-BusObject.asp page that uses a server-side COM component to return monthly sales totals by customer. Figure 5.5 shows the results of the page.

When the user clicks the Get Sales Data button, the server-side SalesData object is instantiated with the CreateObject method of the RDS DataSpace. The CreateObject method, instead of referencing the programmatic ID for the RDSServer DataFactory, uses the programmatic ID for the SalesData object, SalesData.clsSalesData.

```
Sub GetSalesData()

Dim objSalesData
Dim objRst
Dim strConnect
Dim blnSuccess

strConnect = "Provider=MSDASQL;Driver={SQL Server};" & _
    "Server=DALA;Database=OrderManager;UID=sa;" & _
    "PWD=;"

blnSuccess = 0

Set objSalesData = RDSDS.CreateObject _
    ("SalesData.clsSalesData",
    "HTTP://<%=Request.ServerVariables("SERVER_NAME")%>")
```

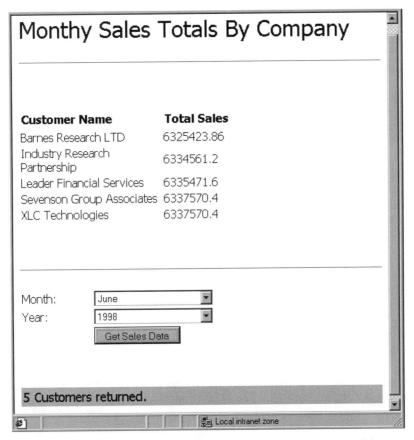

Figure 5.5   The RDSBusObject.asp page uses a custom business object to return tailored data to the browser.

Registering Custom Business Objects

When working with custom business objects, they must be registered in the system registry on the Web server. Custom business objects are typically compiled into .dll files. To do this manually, you can use the regsvr32.exe utility. If the object is not registered, the CreateObject method will fail. To use the regsvr32.exe utility, you can execute code similar to the following using the Windows Run command:

```
C:\winnt\system32\regsvr32.exe d:\book\code\Obj\SalesData.dll
```

Additionally, to allow IIS to invoke the component, another registry entry is required on the Web server. You must add the programmatic ID as a key value to the HKEY_LOCAL_MACHINE\SYSTEM\CurrentControlSet\Services\W3SVC\Parameters\ADCLaunch section. Figure 5.6 shows registry entries for custom business objects invoked through the RDS DataSpace CreateObject method. You'll see that the programmatic ID for the SalesData object is one of them.

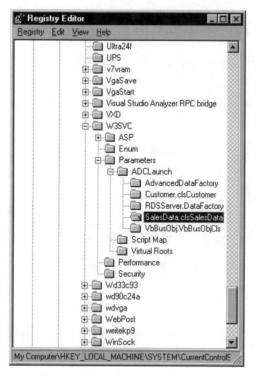

Figure 5.6 Custom business objects that are used via the CreateObject method require this registry entry.

 The registry entries shown in Figure 5.6 assume that the RDS DataSpace is being used in a Web application, with HTTP as the transport protocol. Additional registry entries are required for objects that are instantiated on a LAN environment under DCOM. Consult your RDS documentation for registry entries specific to DCOM.

 When accessing ODBC data from the middle-tier component, define all such DSNs as system DSNs (as opposed to user DSNs). This is also true for ODBC data sources accessed through RDS.DataFactory. These DSNs also must be defined as system DSNs, because when you log on to the server over an HTTP connection, the anonymous user logging on through IIS cannot view user DSNs.

The SalesData Object

After instantiating the SalesData object, the script continues by calling the GetCustomerTotals method of the object. First, the code extracts the month and year values from two HTML combo boxes. It then passes those values (e.g., vntMonth and vntYear) along with connection string information (strConnect) to the GetCustomerTotals method. The GetCustomerTotals function returns with an object reference (a Recordset) that is supplied to the local object variable, objRst.

```
vntMonth = cboMonth.value
vntYear = cboYear.value

Set objRst = objSalesData.GetCustomerTotals(strConnect, _
    vntMonth, vntYear)
```

Afterward, the SourceRecordset of an RDS DataControl (RDSDC) is supplied the Recordset object (objRst). When you set the SourceRecordset property, you are not supplying a reference but establishing a Recordset independent of its supplier (objRst). Finally, the code determines if any data was returned and sets the InnerText attribute of the HTML SPAN appearing at the bottom of the page. The code then establishes the DataSrc for a DHTML table and sets the DataFld properties for two SPAN objects located in the table columns. Binding an RDS DataControl (which contains a "set" of data) causes the DHTML table to automatically repeat enough table rows to display the whole set. Optionally, you can control how many rows are displayed at a time. Figure 5.7 shows HTML syntax that generates the table as a set. Before exiting the procedure, the object variables are set to Nothing.

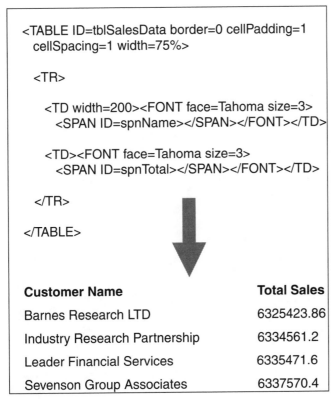

Figure 5.7 The Span element in DHTML table cells are bound to the columns of the RDS DataControl.

```
RDSDC.SourceRecordset = objRst
If RDSDC.Recordset.BOF Then
    spnStatus.InnerText = "No records returned"
Else
    spnStatus.InnerText = RDSDC.Recordset.RecordCount & _
    "Customers returned."
End If

tblSalesData.DataSrc = "#RDSDC"
spnName.dataFld = "cuCustomerName"
spnTotal.dataFld = "Total"

Set objRst = Nothing
Set objSalesData = Nothing

End Sub
```

The GetCustomerTotals Method

The GetCustomerTotals method is very straightforward, but nevertheless, handles the job of transmitting the sales data to the client. In a more robust example, the method may also perform some analysis on the data prior to returning it to the Web client.

```
Public Function GetCustomerTotals _
    (ByVal pstrConnect As String, _
    ByVal pbytMonth As Byte, _
    ByVal pintYear As Integer) As Object
Dim strSQL As String
Dim objRst As New ADODB.Recordset

'SQL Server specific SQL
strSQL = "SELECT Customers.cuCustomerName, { fn " & _
    "MONTH(Orders.orOrderDate) } " & _
    "AS Month, SUM(Orders.orTotal) AS Total, { fn " & _
    "YEAR(Orders.orOrderDate) } AS Year " & _
    "FROM Customers INNER JOIN Orders ON " & _
    "Customers.cuCustomerID = Orders.orCustomerID " & _
    "GROUP BY Customers.cuCustomerName, " & _
    "{ fn MONTH(Orders.orOrderDate) }, { fn " & _
    "YEAR(Orders.orOrderDate) } " & _
    "HAVING ({ fn MONTH(Orders.orOrderDate) } " & _
    "= " & pbytMonth & ") AND " & _
    "({ fn YEAR(Orders.orOrderDate) } = " & pintYear & ")"

With objRst
    .CursorLocation = adUseClient
    .Open strSQL, pstrConnect, adOpenStatic, adLockReadOnly
    Set GetCustomerTotals = objRst
End With

End Function
```

The SQL syntax in the preceding example is written for SQL Server in that it uses native Transact-SQL functions. This code will not work with other RDBMSs.

Using the RDS DataSpace to Invoke a Custom Business Object That Modifies Records

In the first section of this chapter, you saw how easy data modification can be with the native methods of the RDS DataControl and the client-side Recordset. However, you also learned that because those objects rely on the default RDSServer DataFactory, using them does not allow you to apply your own custom logic in the middle tier.

Marshaling Recordsets

That said, you could marshal a disconnected batch Recordset to the Web client, perform local updates, and then marshal the Recordset back to a business object. In this case, the business object could apply custom logic and then submit (UpdateBatch) the changes to the server.

Here is example code showing a business object that returns a disconnected batch cursor to a Web client. The Web client instantiates the Customer component that resides on the Web server.

```
Set objCustomer = RDSDS.CreateObject _
    ("Customer.clsCustData",
    "HTTP://<%=Request.ServerVariables("SERVER_NAME")%>")
```

The Web client calls the GetRecordset method of the business object:

```
Set objrsCust = objCustomer.GetRecordset(strConnect, strQuery)
```

Next, the GetRecordset method returns a disconnected batch cursor to the Web client.

```
Public Function ReturnRS(pstrConnect As _
    String, pstrQuery As String) As ADODB.Recordset

Dim objCnn As New ADODB.Connection
Dim objRst As New ADODB.Recordset

'Open a connection
objCnn.Open pstrConnect

'Use the client-side library
objCnn.CursorLocation = adUseClient

'Open the recordset
objRst.Open pstrQuery, objCnn, _
```

(continues)

(Continued)

```
        adOpenStatic, adLockBatchOptimistic

   'Return the recordset to the client - Returns the object,
   "not just a pointer
   Set GetRecordset = objRst

   'Disassociate
   Set objRst.ActiveConnection = Nothing

   'Close the connection
   objCnn.Close

   End Function
```

After data has been modified on the Web client, the Recordset can be marshaled back to a middle-tier component. A procedure in the component that receives the Recordset might look like this:

```
Public Function SaveRecordset(ByVal pstrConnect As String, _
    ByVal pobjRst As ADODB.Recordset) As Boolean

Dim objCnn As New ADODB.Connection

'Open the connection
objCnn.Open pstrConnect

'Set the active connection of the recordset
Set pobjRst.ActiveConnection = objCnn

'Add custom logic to validate data prior to updating

'Update all pending rows
'Assumes filter was set prior to marshaling
pobjRst.UpdateBatch adAffectGroup

'Close and set connection to nothing
objCnn.Close
Set objCnn = Nothing

End Function
```

Though this may be a fine scenario for many applications, marshaling and updating of Recordsets can prove to be too resource intensive in some circumstances. Recordsets are costly in terms of the resource burden they can impose on a server. Also, remember that RDS as an ActiveX technology requires Internet Explorer 4.x or later and may not be appropriate for some users.

Updating Data without Server-Side Recordsets

With this in mind, you can perform data modification with your own business objects that do not use ADO Recordsets on the server. Instead, the business object accepts the appropriate arguments and executes Command objects. The RDSDataControl.asp page allows the user to both delete and add new customer records. If you're a little fuzzy on what the ASP page looks like, refer to Figure 5.3. When the user clicks the Delete button (btnDelete), script calls the Delete procedure that exists in a SCRIPT block on the page. The Delete procedure then uses the CreateObject method to instantiate the Customer object on the Web server. The Customer object contains a Delete method that enforces a business rule—a customer cannot be deleted if orders exist. Similarly, when the user clicks the Add New button (btnAdd), the AddNew script procedure executes. The AddNew procedure simply enables the client-side Recordset to receive a new record. After adding the desired customer information, the user clicks the Submit button. The Submit button does the necessary work to pass information to the Customer object on the Web server. Of interest, the AddNewRec procedure in the Customer object receives a string of data that allows it to create a SQL insert statement so that a Command object can insert the new row.

Deleting a Customer Record

The Delete procedure attempts to delete the customer identified from the current row in the grid. First, the procedure does a little homework. It checks to make sure that the user has not inadvertently begun another operation and not submitted it. It does this by checking the EditMode property of the Recordset. If the EditMode property is in any state of editing, it cancels that operation with the CancelUpdate method.

```
Sub Delete()

Dim objCustomer
Dim intReturnVal
Dim vntCustID

If RDSDC.Recordset.Editmode <> 0 Then 'adEditNone
    On Error Resume Next
    RDSDC.Recordset.CancelUpdate
End If
```

Next, the Customer business object is instantiated on the server using the familiar Create object syntax. Additionally, the current Customer ID is obtained from the Recordset.

```
Set objCustomer = _
    RDSDS.CreateObject("Customer.clsCustomer", _
    "HTTP://<%=Request.ServerVariables("SERVER_NAME")%>")
vntCustID = RDSDC.Recordset("cuCustomerID")
```

The code then calls the Delete method of the business object. It passes the Customer ID (vntCustID) and a viable DSN that exists on the Web server.

```
intReturnVal = objCustomer.Delete(vntCustID, "ADOBook")
```

In a moment, we'll take a brief look at the Delete method itself. But first, let's see what happens when control returns to the Web client. Since the Customer object (objCustomer) is no longer needed, it is set to Nothing. Then a Select…Case structure evaluates an integer value (intReturnVal) that returned from the Delete method. Each Case clause reports the appropriate status to the DHTML SPAN appearing at the bottom of the page.

```
Set objCustomer = Nothing

Select Case intReturnVal
    Case 0 vorders exist
        spnStatus.InnerText = "Orders exist for this " & _
            "customer.  You cannot delete a " & _
            "customer with orders."
    Case 1 'Success
        spnStatus.InnerText = "You successfully deleted " & _
            "the customer."
        RDSDC.Recordset.MoveFirst
    Case 2 'Error occurred or not a valid customer id
        spnStatus.InnerText = "An error occurred, " & _
            "the customer was not deleted."
End Select

End Sub
```

The Delete Method

Since the Delete method imposes the modest business rule of not deleting customers with orders, it first determines if the given customer has any orders.

```
Public Function Delete(ByVal plngCustomerID, _
    ByVal pstrConnect As String) As Integer

On Error Goto Err_Delete

Dim objRst As New ADODB.Recordset
Dim objCmd As ADODB.Command
Dim strSQL As String
Dim intRecs As Integer

strSQL = "SELECT Count(orCustomerID) AS OrderCount " & _
    "FROM Orders WHERE orCustomerID = " & plngCustomerID

With objRst
    .Open strSQL, pstrConnect, adOpenForwardOnly, _
```

```
            adLockReadOnly
    If objRst("OrderCount") = 0 Then
        'No orders for the customer
```

If the Customer has no orders, then a SQL Delete statement is constructed, and a Command object is supplied the necessary property values. Finally, the Execute method executes the Delete statement and receives status on the number of rows affected. Assuming a valid Customer ID (plngCustomerID) was passed, the Execute method will delete exactly one record. On the other hand, if orders did exist, the Else clause sets the Delete method to the value of 2. When coding business objects, it is important to trap for even unanticipated errors. If a business object aborts without handling an error condition, then a vague error message will return to the client and abort any further scripts from processing.

```
        strSQL = "DELETE Customers WHERE cuCustomerID = " & _
            plngCustomerID
        Set objCmd = New ADODB.Command
        With objCmd
            .CommandText = strSQL
            .CommandType = adCmdText
            .CommandTimeout = 15
            .ActiveConnection = objRst.ActiveConnection
            .Execute intRecs
            If intRecs = 0 Then
                'Error occurred or not a valid customer id
                Delete = 2
            Else
                Delete = 1
            End If
        End With
    Else
        Delete = 0 'Orders exist
    End If
End With
Err_Delete:
    Delete = 0 'unanticipated error
    Exit Function

End Function
```

Adding a New Customer Record

The final operation supported by the RDSDataControl.asp page is to add new customers from the Web client. The page does this by calling the Customer business object that inserts a new Customer record using an ADO command. Before invoking the Customer object, the AddNew script procedure enables the addition of the new row on the Web client. The AddNew procedure executes when the user clicks the Add New button (btnAdd).

```
Sub AddNew()

If RDSDC.ReadyState = adcReadyStateComplete _
    Or RDSDC.ReadyState = adcReadyStateInteractive Then
    RDSDC.Recordset.AddNew
    txtCustomer.Select
End If

End Sub
```

After clicking the AddNew method, the user can use the bound DHTML controls to enter the customer data. Then the user clicks the Submit button (btnUpdate) to save the changes to the server. When the user clicks the Submit button, the Submit procedure is called.

```
Sub Submit()
    Dim objCustomer
    Dim strReturnVal
    Dim strFields
    Dim strValues

    If RDSDC.Recordset.EditMode = 2 Then 'Add
```

After requiring that the customer name be entered, the code updates the Recordset. Since RDS uses disconnected Recordsets, the changes are buffered locally on the client. Then, the Recordset is filtered to show only those records that are pending update to the server. Finally, a client-side script procedure, EnumFields, is called.

```
If RDSDC.Recordset("cuCustomerName") = "" Then
    MsgBox "Please enter the required " & _
        "information before submitting changes " & _
        "to the server."
        RDSDC.Recordset.CancelUpdate
        RDSDC.Recordset.MoveFirst
        Exit Sub
End If
RDSDC.Recordset.Update
RDSDC.Recordset.Filter = adFilterPendingRecords
EnumFields RDSDC.Recordset, "cuCustomerID", _
    strFields, strValues
```

The EnumFields Procedure

Since the newly added record is going to be passed to a business object that uses an ADO command to update the server, you do not have to actually marshal the Recordset to the server-side business object. By doing this, you make a somewhat more efficient business object and potentially pass less data across the wire. What the ADO command will need is a field and value list for the row that will be inserted. The RDSDataControl.asp page includes the EnumFields.htm page with a server-side include. This page contains the script that will prepare a field and value list on the client prior to invoking the business object. The EnumFields.htm page is included in RDSDataControl.asp with the following code:

```
<!-- #INCLUDE File=EnumFields.htm -->
```

The EnumFields procedure accepts a field list (pstrFields) and a value list (pstrValues) that contains only references to fields and their values for controls the user actually completed. The procedure is shown next. The pstrFields and pstrValues variables reference two procedure scope variables that can be used after the procedure finishes executing.

```
Function EnumFields(pobjRst, pstrIDField, pstrFields, _
    pstrValues)

Dim objField
Const adChar = 129
Const adVarChar = 200

pstrFields = ""
pstrValues = ""

For Each objField in pobjRst.Fields
    If Not IsNull(objField.Value) Then
        pstrFields = pstrFields & objField.Name & ","
        Select Case objField.Type
            Case adChar, adVarChar
                pstrValues = pstrValues & "'" & _
                    objField.Value & "',"
            Case Else
                pstrValues = pstrValues & _
                    objField.Value & ","
        End Select
    End If
Next

End Function
```

 The EnumFields procedure uses defined constants to identify which fields hold numeric or character data. In this example, only adChar and adVarChar represent character data. If you are going to use this procedure, you will have to add case clauses for other data types, as appropriate.

After returning from the EnumFields procedure, the code calls the Customer object. It passes in the table name, field list (strFields), and value list (strValues), as well as a valid DSN name. Afterward, the code makes sure the status (spnStatus) reflects an appropriate message.

```
strReturnVal = objCustomer.AddNewRec("Customers", _
    strFields, strValues, "ADOBook")
If Err.number <> 0 Then
    RDSDC.Refresh
    spnStatus.innerText = "An unanticipated error " & _
        "occurred the customer was not added."
Else
    spnStatus.innerText = strReturnVal
    RDSDC.Recordset.Filter = ""
    RDSDC.Recordset.MoveFirst
End If
Set objCustomer = Nothing
```

The AddNewRec Method

The AddNewRec method of the Customer object receives the arguments and immediately builds the necessary SQL INSERT statement. Business requirements dictate that the Customer ID be constructed in a specific fashion, thus the code calls a supporting procedure that constructs the Customer ID according to these requirements. While a new record could be added with just the SubmitChanges method, here you see how even a modest requirement for building an ID value necessitates a custom business object.

```
Public Function AddNewRec(ByVal pstrTable As String, _
    ByVal pstrFields As String, _
    ByVal pstrValues As String, _
    ByVal pstrConnect As String) As Variant

Dim strReturnMsg As String
Dim strSQL As String
Dim lngCustID As Long
Dim intRecsAffected As Integer
Dim objCmd As New ADODB.Command

'Begin the Insert Statement
strSQL = "INSERT INTO " & pstrTable & " ("

'Strip last comma from Fields, if there
If Right(pstrFields, 1) = "," Then
    pstrFields = Left(pstrFields, Len(pstrFields) - 1)
End If

lngCustID = GetNextID("cuCustomerID", "Customers")

'Strip the last comma from the values list
If Right(pstrValues, 1) = "," Then
    pstrValues = Left(pstrValues, Len(pstrValues) - 1)
End If
```

```
'Append the generated custid to the values list
pstrValues = pstrValues & lngCustID

'Finish the sql
strSQL = strSQL & pstrFields & ") VALUES (" & _
    pstrValues & ")"
```

Familiar ADO code prepares a Command object and executes it, being careful to determine success or failure.

```
With objCmd
    .CommandTimeout = 15
    .ActiveConnection = pstrConnect
    .CommandText = strSQL
    .CommandType = adCmdText
    .Execute intRecsAffected
End With

If intRecsAffected = 0 Then
    'errors occurred
    AddNewRec = "Errors occurred, the customer " & _
        "was not added."
Else
    AddNewRec = "The customer was added successfully."
End If
Set objCmd = Nothing
```

When RDS marshals a Recordset to the server, and vice versa, RDS converts the Recordset into a MIME string. With the EnumFields procedure, you've done a similar thing: You've marshaled the necessary information to the server; however, you were not limited by RDS's default capabilities because you marshaled the data to a custom business object. As a result, you can see how just the right client-side code and the use of business objects can extend your control over operations using RDS. For your reference, the entire client-side script block in RDSDataControl.asp is shown as Figure 5.8.

 The RDSServer DataFactory includes a ConvertToString method that exposes its capability to convert the contents of a Recordset to a MIME string. Using this method, you can return a MIME string from a Recordset.

Creating Recordsets from an Arbitrary Structure

In most business applications, you define the structure of a Recordset (i.e., fields, field data types, etc.) when you open a Recordset from a data source using an appropriate OLE DB provider. Once the Recordset is open, you can use all the properties and methods of the Recordset object to add, modify, or change the way the data is presented. Occasionally, however, you may find the need to work with data that did not come from

```
<!-- #INCLUDE File=EnumFields.htm -->

<Script Language=VBScript>

Const adcReadyStateLoaded = 2
Const adcReadyStateInteractive = 3
Const adcReadyStateComplete = 4
Const adFilterPendingRecords = 1

Sub RDSDC_OnReadyStateChange()
    If RDSDC.ReadyState = adcReadyStateLoaded Then
        btnAdd.Disabled = True
        btnDelete.Disabled = True
        btnCancel.Disabled = True
        btnUpdate.Disabled = True
    End If
    If RDSDC.ReadyState = adcReadyStateComplete Then
        btnAdd.Disabled = False
        btnDelete.Disabled = False
        btnCancel.Disabled = False
        btnUpdate.Disabled = False
    End If
End Sub

Sub Window_OnLoad()
    RDSDC.Server = _
        "HTTP://<%=Request.ServerVariables("SERVER_NAME")%>"
    RDSDC.Connect = "ADOBook"
    RDSDC.SQL = "SELECT cuCustomerName, cuContactName, " & _
        "cuContactPhone, cuContactFax, cuAddress1, " & _
        "cuAddress2, cuCity, cuState, cuPostalCode, " & _
        "cuCustomerID From Customers"
    RDSDC.Refresh
End Sub

Sub RefreshData()
    'On Error Resume Next
    If RDSDC.Recordset.EditMode = 2 Then
        RDSDC.Recordset.CancelUpdate
    End If
    RDSDC.Refresh
End Sub

Sub Cancel()
    'On Error Resume Next
    RDSDC.CancelUpdate
End Sub

Sub AddNew()
    If RDSDC.ReadyState = adcReadyStateComplete Or _
        RDSDC.ReadyState = adcReadyStateInteractive Then
```

Figure 5.8   The client-side script block in RDSDataControl.asp.

```
            RDSDC.Recordset.AddNew
            txtCustomer.Select
        End If
    End Sub


    Sub Submit()
        Dim objCustomer
        Dim strReturnVal
        Dim strFields
        Dim strValues


        If RDSDC.Recordset.EditMode = 2 Then 'Add
            If RDSDC.Recordset("cuCustomerName") = "" Then
                MsgBox "Please enter the required " & _
                    "information before submitting changes " & _
                    "to the server."
                RDSDC.Recordset.CancelUpdate
                RDSDC.Recordset.MoveFirst
                Exit Sub
            End If
            RDSDC.Recordset.Update
            RDSDC.Recordset.Filter = adFilterPendingRecords
            EnumFields RDSDC.Recordset, "cuCustomerID", _
                strFields, strValues
            Set objCustomer = _
                RDSDS.CreateObject("Customer.clsCustomer", _
              HTTP://<%=Request.ServerVariables("SERVER_NAME")%>")
            On Error Resume Next
            strReturnVal = objCustomer.AddNewRec("Customers", _
                strFields, strValues, "ADOBook")
            If Err.number <> 0 Then
                RDSDC.Refresh
                spnStatus.innerText = "An unanticipated " & _
                "error occurred, the customer was not added."
            Else
                spnStatus.innerText = strReturnVal
                RDSDC.Recordset.Filter = ""
                RDSDC.Recordset.MoveFirst
            End If
            Set objCustomer = Nothing
        Else
            RDSDC.SubmitChanges
        End If
    End Sub


    Sub Delete()
        Dim objCustomer
        Dim intReturnVal
        Dim vntCustID


        If RDSDC.Recordset.Editmode <> 0 Then 'adEditNone
```

Figure 5.8   The client-side script block in RDSDataControl.asp (*Continued*).

```
        On Error Resume Next
        RDSDC.Recordset.CancelUpdate
    End If
    Set objCustomer = _
        RDSDS.CreateObject("Customer.clsCustomer", _
        "HTTP://<%=Request.ServerVariables("SERVER_NAME")%>")
    vntCustID = RDSDC.Recordset("cuCustomerID")
    intReturnVal = objCustomer.Delete(vntCustID, "ADOBook")
    Set objCustomer = Nothing
    Select Case intReturnVal
        Case 0 'orders exist
            spnStatus.InnerText = "Orders exist for " & _
                "this customer.  You cannot delete a " & _
                "customer with orders."
        Case 1 'Success
            spnStatus.InnerText = "You successfully " & _
                "deleted the customer."
            RDSDC.Recordset.MoveFirst
        Case 2 'Error occurred or not a valid customer id
            spnStatus.InnerText = "An error occurred, " & _
            "the customer was not deleted."
    End Select
End Sub

</Script>
```

Figure 5.8   The client-side script block in RDSDataControl.asp (*Continued*).

a data source, and you may want to allow the user to manipulate the data inside some structure, because the user may want to sort or filter the data. If the data structure is arbitrary, though, how can you easily provide the user with such modest functionality as sorting or filtering?

Fortunately, RDS allows you to define a Recordset object from a completely arbitrary, user-defined structure. To do this, you use the RDSServer DataFactory's CreateRecordset method. In this example, you'll see how a custom COM component uses the CreateRecordset method to return a user-defined Recordset to the Web client. Once on the client, the Recordset can be used as the source for the RDS DataControl; and, of course, it has all the programmatic benefits of a disconnected cursor.

Script on the Client

In this example, client-side script invokes the services of the DataStructure object that resides on the Web server. Using the familiar CreateObject method, the client-side proxy and server-side stub are generated.

```
<OBJECT ID=RDSDS WIDTH=1 HEIGHT=1
    CLASSID=CLSID:BD96C556-65A3-11D0-983A-00C04FC29E36>
```

```
</OBJECT>

<OBJECT ID=RDSDC
    CLASSID=clsid:BD96C556-65A3-11D0-983A-00C04FC29E33>
</OBJECT>

<SCRIPT Language=VBSCRIPT>
Sub Window_OnLoad()
    Dim objRst
    Dim objDataStructure

    Set objDataStructure = _
        RDSDS.CreateObject("DataStructure.clsData", _
        "HTTP://<%=Request.ServerVariables("SERVER_NAME")%>")
```

Now, the BuildRecordset method of the DataStructure object is called. The method returns a Recordset and supplies that reference to objRst. If you need to manipulate the Recordset through the RDS DataControl, you can also set the SourceRecordset property. At this point, the user-defined Recordset exists on the Web client and can be manipulated as any traditionally sourced Recordset.

```
    Set objRst = objDataStructure.BuildRecordset()
    RDSDC.SourceRecordset = objRst
    Set objRst = Nothing
    Set objDataStructure = Nothing
End Sub

</SCRIPT>
```

The BuildRecordset Method

The BuildRecordset method of the DataStructure object arbitrarily defines the necessary attributes of a data structure. It then uses the CreateRecordset method of the RDSServer DataFactory to transform the data structure into a Recordset.

The RDSServer DataFactory CreateRecordset method takes an array or arrays that define the fields in the Recordset. The code creates an array, vntColInfo, that contains rows for each column in the data structure. In this example, there are two columns. Two additional arrays (one for each column) define the name, data type, size, and nullability of the column.

```
Public Function BuildRecordset() As ADOR.Recordset

Dim vntColInfo(1) As Variant
Dim vntCol0(3) As Variant
Dim vntCol1(3) As Variant
Dim objDataFactory As RDSServer.DataFactory
Dim objRst As ADOR.Recordset
```

The next code segment specifies each of the necessary column attributes. To specify the data type, a numeric equivalent of an ADO Field data type must be used.

```
vntCol0(0) = "UserName"      ' Column name.
vntCol0(1) = CInt(129)       ' Column type (129 = adChar).
vntCol0(2) = CInt(25)        ' Column size.
vntCol0(3) = False           ' Is the column nullable?


vntCol1(0) = "NumericID"     ' Column name.
vntCol1(1) = CInt(3)         ' Column type (3 = adInteger).
vntCol1(2) = CInt(-1)        ' Column size - fixed
vntCol1(3) = True            ' Is the column nullable?


'Add the columns to the recordset definition.
vntColInfo(0) = vntCol0
vntColInfo(1) = vntCol1
```

 For a listing of appropriate field data type constants and their respective values, refer to the CreateRecordset method in your RDS documentation.

After adding the two column arrays to vntColInfo, the code instantiates the RDSServer DataFactory and calls its CreateRecordset method passing in the array. The Recordset is returned to the variable objRst and is supplied as the object reference for the BuildRecordset method. Thus, the method returns a user-defined data structure as a Recordset.

```
'Instantiate the data factory
Set objDataFactory = New RDSServer.DataFactory
Set objRst = objDataFactory.CreateRecordSet(vntColInfo)
Set BuildRecordset = objRst
Set objDataFactory = Nothing

End Function
```

From Here

This part of the book described numerous scenarios that use ADO. Whether used in client-side script, server-side business objects, or ASP pages, ADO provides you with a powerful interface for manipulating data. In Part Two, Windows NT Middle-Tier Services, you'll greatly extend your understanding of building distributed applications. You'll learn how NT services give you the opportunity for scalability, transactioning of COM components, and pooling of database connections, to name just a few of the topics.

PART

Two

Windows NT
Middle Tier Services

In Part 1 of this book, you were introduced to ADO 2.0. You learned how to communicate with different data sources, the flexible object model of ADO, and the new and exciting things you can do with record sets – like passing them, disconnecting them, and even how to create them without a connection to a data store. While these are all very powerful features, ADO by itself will not satisfy your distributed application needs. To fully realize the benefits of ADO's Universal Data Access pledge, you need other tools and services to ensure that:

- Instantiating COM components is fast, efficient, scalable, and location transparent.

- Connections to data sources are fast, efficient, and scalable.

- Data access components respect the NT security model.

- All database transactions fulfill the ACID (Atomicity, Consistency, Isolation and Durability) requirements. That includes transactions across *multiple* data sources and even of *different types* of data sources.

- COM components can be transacted—not just SQL statements.

- Disconnected component communication to the server can be "recorded" for subsequent "play back" when a connection is re-established—with no additional programming.

- Sending record sets objects to another machine can be guaranteed to be delivered.

As you'll learn in the second part of this book, ADO functionality increases exponentially when coupled with Windows NT services like Microsoft Transaction Server (MTS) 2.0 and Microsoft Message Queue Server (MSMQ) 1.0. Together, these products allow the developer to deploy distributed applications easier than ever before.

And that's the goal here—simplicity. As client machines get more and more powerful and bandwidth gets wider and wider, processing across multiple machines can make a lot of sense. But to undertake such a project has always been a daunting task. The Windows NT middle tier services aim to change that thinking and bring distributed application development to the mainstream. How to accomplish that is the focus of the second part of this book.

A Roadmap for Your Journey

Here's a quick look at the different topics that will be covered in Part 2:

> **Chapter 6: Distributed Application Development—the Microsoft Way.** In this chapter, the foundation is laid for learning about Microsoft Windows NT middle tier services by examining distributed application development architecture and the benefits and drawbacks of moving from centralized systems.
>
> Then we'll take a close look at COM—the "language" in which all objects must speak to communicate with one another. COM's evolution from the Windows Clipboard to DCOM, its architecture, its presence in the Microsoft tools, and its role in distributed application development will be discussed. Next, we'll attempt to level the playing field by making sure the concepts necessary to implement technologies such as MTS, MSMQ, and ADO, are understood.
>
> Next, you'll get an overview of two of the Windows NT services that are available to you for development of distributed applications: Microsoft Transaction Server and Microsoft Message Queue Server. Lastly, we'll take a sneak peek into the future by learning about COM+—the unification of COM/DCOM and MTS, improved existing NT 4 services, as well as new runtime features that will all be part of the Windows NT 5 operating system.
>
> **Chapter 7: Microsoft Transaction Server.** Second to COM/DCOM in the Windows NT food chain is MTS—the transaction processing monitor that allows you to apply the ACID properties to *component* transactions rather than just *database* transactions. In Chapter 7, you'll learn what a TP Monitor is and what Microsoft's competition in this market, CORBA, has to offer. Then you'll find out why the concept of component development with COM, ADO, and object oriented programming principles are all required learning to develop "stateless" components in MTS. Next, you'll be guided through an in-depth look at the features of Transaction Server: Component Transactions, Object Brokering, Resource Management, Transaction Monitoring and Administration, and Security.
>
> **Chapter 8: Microsoft Message Queue Server.** In Chapter 8, you'll learn about message queuing, another valuable tool for distributed application development. We'll start with a discussion of what message queuing *really* is (hint: it's more than just e-mail) and the needs it fulfills in solving today's business problems: communication between disparate systems and connectionless communication with guaranteed delivery. Then you'll be guided through the feature set of MSMQ, Microsoft's foray into this market. You'll learn how to manage queues, send and receive messages, and trap for errors. Once again we'll incorporate COM, ADO, and MTS to build component-based, transacted messages. We'll conclude with a sample application to reinforce these concepts.

Distributed Application Development—the Microsoft Way

You can't be blamed for taking so long to delve into the world of distributed application development. No, sir. The technology just wasn't there. You didn't have the tools and services required for success. You read all the articles and you made your decision: large-scale, multitier, client/server applications had about a one in a billion chance of succeeding, let alone coming in on budget. So, who could blame you for dragging your feet?

But now the time has come. The new tools and server-side services that are now available for the Windows NT 4 and Windows 9x platform are, without a doubt, the most exciting products Microsoft has released. By now you've heard of COM, Distributed COM, Transaction Server, Microsoft Message Queue Server, Internet Information Server, SQL Server, and the other server-side goodies. In fact, we've discussed a number of those topics in the first part of this book. After a maturation process, these technologies have come of age—this stuff really works! It's ready for prime time; in fact, it's being implemented on thousands of systems worldwide. There's no reason to wait any longer to start realizing the benefits of distributed computing.

What You'll Learn

In this chapter you will gain an introduction to the concepts, advantages, disadvantages, and challenges of distributed application development. This discussion will center on the evolution and use of the Microsoft distributed computing technologies of COM, DCOM, MTS, MSMQ, and COM+. After reading this chapter, you should have gained a good basic knowledge of these ideas and technologies that will be described in more detail in the remainder of the book.

Why Distributed Client/Server Computing?

For every paradigm shift in the evolution of systems development, there were serious limitations with which to contend. On the mainframe level, we had to contend with the expense, the total reliance on one machine, the lack of GUI interfaces, and, usually, the limitation of a single, proprietary database. Minicomputers offered some relief in the area of cost, but not really anywhere else. PC file servers offered a welcome reduction in costs but were valuable only for small systems due to the lack of power, tight security, and available true relational database management systems. Large centralized systems usually interfaced with them via batch download processes for local reporting, taking some of the load off the host.

Client/server architecture was a first attempt at seamlessly integrating the power of the mainframe with the flexibility the desktop PC offered. Requests for data could be made from the client, and the server responded by sending back result sets. The client could then add, edit, and delete from the local table and then batch-commit the changes to the server. This system design had the advantages of a powerful server and some distributed computing (by offloading data entry), and perhaps business rule processing to the client. But drawbacks remained in the areas of hardware costs (mostly from maintaining the mainframe), lack of code reusability with other applications, restriction to a single, often proprietary, database, and lack of scalability.

Will distributed client/server computing solve every problem? No. Are there still issues with this paradigm as there have been in all of its predecessors? Of, course. But distributed client/server computing does answer most of the questions that IS people have been asking. When correctly implemented, it gives you the flexibility to:

- Scale up your application
- Scale down your application
- Change languages on any tier
- Employ multiple languages on any tier
- Change data sources
- Transact across multiple data sources
- Change hardware without interrupting service
- Change user interfaces without effecting other parts of the application

I'm sure you'll agree that that's a pretty impressive list, so let's get into more of the specifics as to how all this can all be accomplished.

Advantages of Distributing Computing

As the practice of procedural programming techniques declined in favor of object orientation and server-based (mainframe and file server) applications were replaced with those using a client/server design principle, distributed applications began to become commonplace—and with good reason.

- Distributed applications, which have their presentation, business object, and data repository layers physically (or sometimes just logically) separated, have many benefits over their more traditional counterparts (see Figure 6.1). As user interface standards change, entire applications do not have to be rewritten. Only the code that is responsible for presenting the data to the user needs to be rewritten. Therefore, today, had the business and data logic been separated from the user-interface, that Visual Basic 4 application you wrote in 1995 could have been rather easily updated to a Visual Basic 6 or Internet browser application just by creating new screens.

- The business object layer can be composed of components written in many different languages. This means you can write components in the tool that best fits the situation, or use time-tested, third-party components that have been created in any tool that can create COM servers (DLLs or EXEs that conform to the COM binary standard; more on this a bit later).

- The business object layer can be composed of components called by many different front ends. Imagine a scenario where different departmental systems all used the same business objects even though the systems were written in multiple languages and had disparate data stores.

- Back-end data sources can be replaced with little or no change to the other tiers of the application, thereby enabling systems to easily scale. For instance, had the data-centric business objects been separated from the user-interface, an Access 2.0 application with a JET database you wrote in 1995 could have scaled to MS SQL Server with very little change.

- The cost of developing new systems is the principal reason for the recent trend toward distributed applications. It may be much more cost-effective to maintain

Data services tier	Database Server	Stored Procedures
Business services tier	Application Server	Data-centric objects
Presentation tier	Client Workstation	UI-centric visual objects
		UI-centric business objects

Figure 6.1   A typical three-tier, physically distributed architecture.

many PCs (client workstations, application servers, and data servers) rather than a single mainframe.

- Performance is another advantage in a distributed environment. With the capability of Windows NT 4.0 to support symmetrical multiprocessing (SMP), you can have up to 32 CPUs housed in a singe machine. That's faster than most mainframes. And because it's feasible today to connect hundreds of networked PCs together, the power and scalability that can be realized is compounded. Also, by moving the UI-specific business logic of non-Web applications to the client, the load share is spread and no network traffic is necessary when it comes to presentation logic.

- Stability is another factor. Consider the mainframe application that experiences hardware problems. When trouble occurs, its users are 100 percent down. In a multiserver scenario, losing a server or two might only represent a small percentage of the total processing power, making that system a much more reliable solution.

- Scalability is also much easier in a distributed environment. You can always add more CPUs, memory, servers, and so on to enable your system(s) to grow or shrink with that of your company. You do not have to be concerned with the long-term planning necessary when purchasing a mainframe.

Challenges of Distributing Computing

The birth of distributed architectural design effectively addressed many of the most pressing IS concerns and was certainly a major step in the evolution of programming; unfortunately, it created new problems. Even today, distributed applications are faced with issues in the area of system development, deployment, and management.

Development. To include advanced functionality like transaction monitoring, resource pooling, database caching, object brokering, role-based security, dynamic load balancing, and so on, developers had to code many of these services themselves. Furthermore, they had to rely on the ODBC API, C++, or similarly complex tools to achieve these results.

Deployment. In a server-based architecture such as a mainframe application with dumb terminals, all code resides on one machine, making distribution a nonissue. However, distributed client/server applications usually have presentation-related business logic on the client with data-centric business logic residing on the server. This means that every client machine has to be updated whenever a new build is released that has UI-specific modifications—a very tedious and time-consuming task. Each client registry must also be configured for the DCOM components that will run on the server.

Management. Managing user role changes, server status and activity, transaction statistics, and so on often involved running command-line programs, going from server to server in a multiserver scenario, and even stopping the server completely. A more centralized administration tool was sorely needed.

As you will discover from this chapter, distributed client/server computing will not solve all of these issues. But this system design—coupled with the Microsoft tools and services that are available today for Windows NT—is certainly the most popular game in town.

Component-Based Development with COM

For years, IS managers have wrestled with variations of these two basic questions:

- "How do I minimize the resources required to complete an application on schedule and within budget?"
- "How can I extend the lifetime of my applications and not be forced to completely rewrite them every five to seven years?"

In the 1990s, both of these questions were answered with one word: components. To expand on the definition in the last section, a component is a reusable unit of software in binary form that can "talk" to other components with little effort. The key word here is *binary*. It's certainly not new for developers to share source code with one another or to buy a third-party utility that comes with source code. But doing so raises a shortcoming when making modifications to the code. When the source code provider releases a new version, you're left with the task of trying to determine which code to use. Reusing precompiled programs that expose nothing but an interface addresses this issue.

For years, operating systems have exposed application programming interfaces APIs (as in the Win 32 API), to programmers, but only at the operating system level. With COM components, the typical developer can write an API in one of several languages and expose its interface to other components. Once compiled, it can be used by any application that can instance COM components.

The common thread among the different tiers of a distributed application is the Component Object Model, better known as COM. The introduction of COM and Distributed COM (DCOM) enabled developers to create more powerful, maintainable, scalable applications that follow the "right tool for the job" paradigm. So let's digress for a moment to appreciate COM.

Component Object Model

Hail COM! Okay, that's enough. Though not a religion (yet) among developers, it certainly has made the life of many easier by becoming the "pipeline" through which objects can "speak" to one another. In fact, its ease of use and interoperability has resulted in the deployment of COM on some 150 million systems worldwide in an estimated $670 million market (1998).

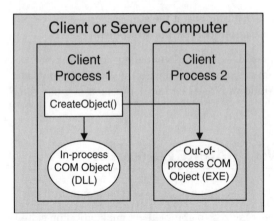

Figure 6.2 The COM runtime is built into the OS and handles requests in the same process as the client (when the component is a DLL) or in a separate process (when the component is an EXE), but the communication is always on the same machine.

If you are unfamiliar with COM technology, the Microsoft documentation defines it as follows:

> An open architecture for cross-platform development of client/server applications based on object-oriented technology. Clients have access to an object through interfaces implemented on the object. COM is language neutral, so any language that produces ActiveX components can also produce COM applications.

That's quite a mouthful, but it does highlight COM's attributes. The two keys here are language neutrality and interoperability. All of Microsoft's application development tools can instance not only COM objects for their own use but can create them as well. That means you can create classes in Visual Basic, Visual FoxPro, Visual C++, or Visual J++, compile them into DLLs (to run in-process) or executables (to run out-of-process), then register them on a local or remote machine. Doing so creates an ActiveX component or COM server (formerly known as OLE Automation Server). See Figure 6.2.

To appreciate how far component development with COM has advanced over the years, it's necessary to take a step back and examine its origins. It's actually a very interesting tale.

From DDE to COM

With COM's explosive growth in the mid-1980s, it became increasingly obvious that the Intel-based processors (80286 and 80386) were going to enable personal computers to handle a greater number of tasks—including multiple applications running simultaneously. That led to the development of desktop managers that allowed users to multitask their DOS applications by switching among multiple DOS "windows." It wasn't long thereafter that Apple's Macintosh and Microsoft's Windows multitasking, graphical user interface environments were dominating the desktop.

Armed with the ability to run multiple applications at the same time, users began to want to share data among those applications. One of the first attempts at this was Dynamic Data Exchange (DDE), a message-passing service designed for developers to give data-sharing capabilities to their users. Unfortunately, a standard was never established, and DDE was really only successfully implemented in Microsoft Excel.

Around the same time, the clipboard was becoming a popular way for end users to simply "copy" data—not only text, but bitmaps, charts, and sound clips—from one application and "paste" it into another. It was truly magical at the time, and was such a hit with users that it's still available today. The shortcoming of the clipboard was its static nature; pasting an Excel spreadsheet into a Word document was useless once the data in the spreadsheet had changed. There was a need for a way to enable a document to contain a "live" representation of the data in another application—that is, to make it a *compound document*.

After a lot of coffee and late nights, the Microsoft development team released OLE 1 as part of Windows 3.1 in 1992. Object Linking and Embedding gave Windows applications the capability to create compound documents with up-to-date data from other applications. The following year, OLE 2 was released with *in-place activation*—the capability to host one application inside another. Users could now double-click on an Excel spreadsheet embedded in a Word document to launch a scaled-down Excel session in place.

Throughout this evolution of interprocess communication standards, Microsoft developers were realizing that the architecture that seemed to resolve the issues raised by users time and time again was that of *component-based software*. Unbeknownst to them at the time, this concept would lay the foundation for what we know today as the Component Object Model (COM), which was first introduced in 1995. Binary objects were now able to communicate with one another within or across processes in a standardized fashion, exposing only to the outside world what was necessary to access its data and services.

DCOM Is Born

Following the success of COM, one goal remained: to enable objects to speak to one another across a network as they do when they are on the same machine. This would allow for centralized administration and simplified deployment—two much sought-after goals. This apparently didn't take too long to accomplish because the 1996 release of Windows NT 4.0 included Distributed COM (DCOM). And by 1997, the DCOM add-on for Windows 95 was released, making remote object communication available to the masses.

DCOM's conceptual roots actually began much earlier. Years ago, when mainframes were ruling the world of computers, software was written on a proprietary basis (IBM computers were not expected to ever speak to a Honeywell). So, in an effort to define intercomputer communication standards at the personal computer level, industry groups formed a consortium called the Open Software Foundation (OSF). Their goal was clear: to compete with the mainframe, they had to create distributed systems. But they couldn't create distributed systems unless they could all agree on a standard way to communicate with one another.

Specifications were eventually established for the Distributed Computing Environment (DCE), which established the standards that made possible the creation of distributed systems. One of the most significant of those standards defined how applications on different computers would communicate with one another across a network. This standard was called Remote Procedure Calls (RPC). DCOM uses RPCs for its cross-computer communication. To summarize: The two technologies, Component Object Model (which evolved from OLE) and Remote Procedure Calls, together defined what is now known as Distributed COM, DCOM.

How Do You Use COM?

All that background is useful, but it doesn't explain what a COM object looks like and how you create and deploy one. To delve into that, let's begin by taking a quick look at an example.

Almost every product Microsoft markets today has an object model that can expose its interface to any other product that is COM-aware. Remember, think of an interface as an object's attributes and the actions that it can perform. A *public interface* is the interface that a COM object's developer has chosen to expose to anyone wishing to use its services. (This can even be controlled via Windows NT security, which, as you'll later see, is easy using MTS.)

Usually, one function is all that is necessary for this magic to happen. For example, the CreateObject function of Visual Basic creates an instance of the class specified and returns an object reference. The client application that calls CreateObject ('COM-ServerName.ClassName') would now have a "pointer" to every property and method of the class in the COM server. This server can be something as simple as a one-function DLL or it can be an entire commercial application like Internet Explorer, Word, Excel, or Outlook.

Here's an example that you might see in a Visual Basic application. This function will programmatically launch Internet Explorer and navigate to a Web site.

Whether you realized it or not, you were seeing COM in action when you were shown how to retrieve data from a data source using ADO. The next example code snippet populates an ADO Recordset object with the contents of the Products table of the Northwind Traders database.

```
'Create an ADO Recordset
Dim objRecordSet As New ADODB.Recordset
objRecordSet.Open _
   " Select * From Products", _
   "DSN=Northwind_SS7;UID=sa;PWD=;"
```

It's that easy. The only other requirement is that the machine attempting to create the object be able to find a reference to the class and server in its registry. If that reference points to a DLL or EXE that resides on the same machine as the calling application, that's COM. However, if the client only finds on the same machine a proxy with a pointer to a stub on another machine, that's Distributed COM, or DCOM. As you might guess, it is actually DCOM that is employed most often in multitiered applications so that COM

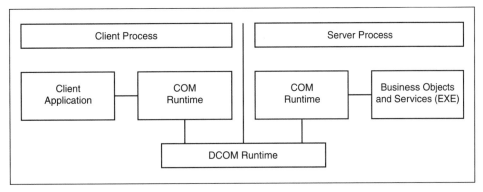

Figure 6.3 The DCOM runtime coordinates communication transparently, with the COM runtimes on the client and the server to instantiate server-side components.

objects can reside on network servers and be shared among clients. We'll come back to DCOM a little later.

Since the common language used to speak to a COM object is COM itself, you can also create GUI interfaces in any of the Microsoft Visual Studio developer tools, as well as other tools like Active Server Pages and MS Outlook, and then not have to worry about interoperability. Components of one application can be composed of COM objects written in several different languages without worrying whether they will "speak" with one another. You can even instance COM components in SQL Server-stored procedures!

Distributed Component Object Model

If you understand COM, then you already understand DCOM. The key difference is that COM implies communication between binary objects on the same machine, whereas DCOM works with standard network protocols (like TCP/IP, IPX/SPX, HTTP, and Net-BIOS) to bridge the communication between COM objects on separate machines. See Figure 6.3.

Advantages of Employing DCOM

There are several advantages to using Distributed COM over COM:

Maintenance. DCOM business objects reside on the server, so there is no client upgrade with which to contend. Any modifications to these distributed components are immediately available to all users of the application.

Single Programming Model. As far as the developer is concerned, all COM objects are created equal. No extra coding is necessary to create a DCOM component; it's only a matter of configuration and deployment. You might as well distribute the components to the server to gain the maintenance benefits if there are only limited costs to doing so.

Deployment Flexibility. Often, it makes sense to have UI-centric COM objects running in-process on the client, while the other data-centric servers run over the network. However, if the architecture of the system changes, whereby a client-side DLL needs to be distributed to the server, very little work has to be done. It's only a matter of configuration; no code needs to be changed.

Cross-Platform. DCOM is currently supported on the following platforms: Windows NT 4.0+, Windows 95, Apple Macintosh, Sun Solaris, AIX, MVS, SCO UnixWare, and Linux.

DCOM's cross-process communication across the network is made possible by the use of *stubs* and *proxies*. When a COM object is invoked on a client, it checks the machine's registry for the existence of the server and class—sometimes referred to as the *ProgID*. If that server has been configured as a DCOM component, the COM runtime would find a proxy object on the client. The *proxy object* is a component that has the *appearance* of the actual component it is representing because it has all of the same properties and methods. When it gets instantiated, it uses the DCOM runtime to look for a corresponding stub on the server. The stub then runs in the process of the COM runtime on the server, just as if it were running on the client. All of this happens transparently to the client application.

Disadvantages of DCOM

As powerful as DCOM is, it does have a couple of disadvantages:

Performance. Since DCOM components are run out of the process of the client, and must travel across the network, they are of course slower than both in-process and out-of-process COM objects.

Configuration. Deploying DCOM components can be a tedious task. It requires tools like remote automation managers and command-line utilities such as DCOM-CFG.EXE to be run on every workstation and server so that proxies, stubs, and the remote component itself can be put in their proper place.

NOT THE ONLY GAME IN TOWN

As powerful as COM is, it's not a new technology. The Object Management Group (OMG), a consortium of companies that joined forces to develop an object communication standard, defined the Common Object Request Broker Architecture (CORBA) specification many years ago. The two methodologies are very similar: Both are proponents of putting all nonuser interface logic into business objects that can be deployed anywhere that a client can communicate with a server.

CORBA, COM's chief competitor, is successfully implemented in commercial and proprietary client/server applications throughout the world. It is only in the last few years that Microsoft has decided to enter the middleware arena and look beyond its comfortable desktop foothold and compete for a share of the CORBA market.

Fortunately, MTS addresses these issues. MTS allows out-of-process servers to run within the context of an MTS transaction, thereby making it virtually in-process again. And the MTS Explorer has made deployment of DCOM components much more seamless. We'll be looking at these services and tools a lot more closely next.

 When referring to COM in the rest of the book, the technologies of COM and DCOM are implied since DCOM is just a variant of COM. From a developer standpoint, COM and DCOM look the same; it's the registry entry that makes the distinction.

A First Look at Transaction Server

Hopefully, you're beginning to appreciate the benefits of designing object-oriented systems, employing a COM-based application development paradigm and physically distributing COM components to different machines. If you have, that also means you've bought into the idea that DCOM will be the vehicle by which you'll get your objects to communicate with one another. However, though that's a great strategy, the complexity of a distributed application and the shortcomings of DCOM mean that you're going to need some additional tools to round out your developer's toolbox. You'll need a tool that will:

- Allow you to speed up the cross-computer communication of DCOM.
- Simplify the deployment of DCOM components.

If a single product could do these two things and its price were affordable (like free), you no doubt would be a satisfied customer. As luck would have it, Microsoft Transaction Server can meet these needs. In fact, these features just scratch the surface of the MTS capabilities.

What Is Transaction Server?

MTS is a middle-tier runtime service that runs under Windows NT. Its primary function is to free the developer from the tedious "plumbing" work that is necessary to build a multitier, distributed system. MTS does this by providing a COM interface to help simplify the creation and coordination of remote component transactions, as well as dramatically improve the performance of DCOM components (see Figure 6.4). Its user interface is the MTS Explorer, which provides you with ways to simplify the deployment and administration of distributed client/server applications.

MTS was created to fill the same transaction processing (TP) roles that products like CICS and Tuxedo have been filling on the mainframe platform—that is, to provide secure transactional environments for large-scale relational databases like DB/2, Informix, Sybase, and Oracle.

The fact that MTS components are just COM components means that you can create MTS components in much the same way that you have been creating COM servers. Actually, you can run the COM servers you've already created under MTS without any

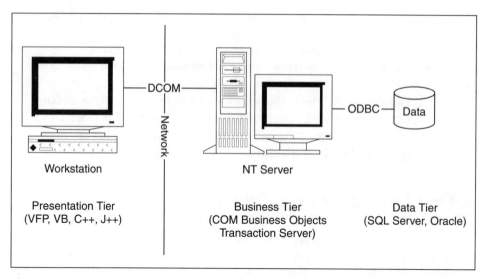

Figure 6.4   The MTS runtime resides on the business services tier of a multitier application.

changes at all. But doing so will allow you to take advantage of only the MTS capability to cache components on the server to speed up the performance of DCOM.

To take full advantage of MTS and harness its transaction coordination features, you need to add very little code to your components. However, the way you use components under MTS is contradictory to everything you've ever read or heard about managing COM servers, transactions, and database connections. As you'll learn by example in the next chapter, it's most beneficial when object references to MTS components are maintained for as long as possible, but database connections are dropped immediately after use.

That would seem to fly in the face of all logic and reason in a multiuser environment, but in fact it's another example of how MTS enables you to develop distributed components without the typical three-tier concerns. You could even write your components as if they were part of a single-user application by letting MTS handle all Begin Transaction…End Transaction/Rollback requests, database connection pooling, and multiuser contention issues on remote components.

The components of an MTS transaction are in-process COM objects. The client application can dynamically enlist these DLLs to run within the context of an MTS transaction so that they can act in unison, with each component having an equal voice in the transaction's outcome. MTS communicates with another NT service, the Distributed Transaction Coordinator (DTC), to ensure that resource managers (RM) like SQL Server reach a consistent decision on whether *database* transactions (which could even span multiple databases) should commit or abort.

Database Transactions

Before we move on to more in-depth coverage of the MTS feature set, it's essential to understand the overused term *transaction*. In this context, transaction refers to two or more units of work that are so dependent on each other that they must be treated as one. If only half of the work is successfully accomplished, the job cannot be considered complete. Just as in any exchange of products or services, a contract must be kept between both parties. For example, if you give a sales clerk your credit card to purchase a groovy new sweater, you obviously expect the sweater in return. However, if you had exceeded your credit limit, you could not expect the sweater. Right?

There are many types of transactions, but this book focuses on online transaction processing (OLTP) transactions for mission-critical applications, which have lifetimes of one to three seconds. In this world, a true transaction is defined as a unit of work that fulfills the *ACID* requirements, which stands for:

Atomic. A transaction is considered *atomic* if it executes completely or not at all. If any one portion of a transaction fails, the entire transaction must be aborted.

Consistent. A transaction is considered *consistent* if it leaves the data in a state that obeys the rules set forth in the database (i.e., referential integrity, domain integrity, and entity integrity rules). In other words, if for example, the referential integrity rules of a database prohibit orphan records (parentless children), then a consistent transaction in no way should create this situation.

Isolated. A transaction is considered *isolated* if it respects the fact that, in a multi-user environment, the same data may be accessed by several different sources simultaneously, so the database must provide safeguards against this. There are different levels of isolation, but essentially it means that, for example, debits will always equal credits in a trial balance report, even if the report is requested while a user has updated credits, but no debits yet in a transaction.

Durable. A transaction is considered *durable* if it can guarantee that data is written to disk after all of the actions performed on the database are finally committed. It must also account for media failures, power failures, and other unknown catastrophes by logging transactions before writing them to disk so that they can be restored to the last consistent state when power returns.

The Life of a Database Transaction

The typical database transaction will update a single row in a single table, multiple rows in a single table, or even one or more rows in multiple tables. Let's say a customer returns a sweater that cost $100 to a department store. To accomplish this, his or her account must be credited for the sale amount; the sales module must be debited, and the sweater must be returned to inventory. That smells like a transaction, doesn't it? What guarantees that either all updates succeed or the transaction fails is implicit or explicit code like the following pseudocode:

1. Begin a transaction. (Never fails.)
2. Increase sweater inventory by 1.
3. If step 2 was successful, credit customer's account for $100.
4. If steps 2 and 3 were successful, debit sales revenues by $100.
5. If steps 2, 3, and 4 were successful, commit the transaction. Else, if *any* step in the operation was not successful, roll back the transaction.

So, a transaction must either commit *all* updates to the database or abort *all* updates. Those are the only two choices. Any database that allows its transactions to operate any differently does not have its transactions conform to the ACID requirements.

The Life of a Distributed Transaction

Typical database transactions may appear to solve all of your transactional needs, but actually they have some shortcomings. For instance, the typical database transaction works against a *single* data source. But what if you want to transact across multiple databases, as in the case of synching the data of a remote office with that of the home office? MTS can accomplish this by being able to transact *components*, not just data sources. Thus, we can test for the success of a *component transaction* against the remote office data source and then the home office data source, without having to rely on the database itself for the transaction coordination. Not only is that very powerful, but it's greatly simplified with MTS.

Let's say that you've created an MTS component that will withdraw funds from Bank A and deposit it in Bank B. Let's also assume the available balance in Bank A has already been determined to be sufficient for the withdrawal to take place. The client application initiates this action by instantiating the Funds Processing component (DLL) on the server and calling the Transfer method, passing the appropriate parameters. The Transfer method has code to withdraw funds from Bank A's database and deposit funds into Bank B's database. When a data access call is made from an MTS component (using ADO in this case), ODBC or OLE DB first checks to see if this component requires a transaction.

If it does, it tells the DTC to tell SQL Server to start a transaction. (Did you notice how all of that was implicit? Instancing the Transfer object was all that was necessary.) Now the update of the Bank A account can occur. Then, when a data access call is made to deposit the funds into Bank B, the DTC tells Bank B's SQL Server to begin a transaction. Now there are two open transactions pending. If both updates are successful, the component can call SetComplete to request the DTC to tell the two resource managers that the transaction can be committed. Otherwise, it can call SetAbort to request that a rollback of both updates occur. This all-or-nothing contract coordinated by the DTC is known as a *two-phase commit protocol* when it occurs across multiple data sources (see Figure 6.5).

The Role of MTS in a Multitier Client/Server Application

Prior to the release of MTS, developers of distributed applications were responsible for creating system services like transaction coordination, resource management, and component security themselves. Developers also had to use cryptic utilities to configure every client workstation registry to work with DCOM. Transaction Server relieved much of this burden and freed him or her to concentrate on solving business problems. This helps to dramatically reduce the project life cycle for complicated distributed client/server systems.

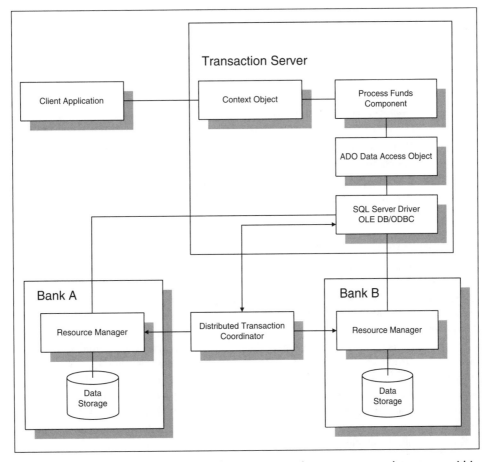

Figure 6.5   A component running under MTS can update two remote data stores within a single transaction.

The first release of MTS in 1996, however, didn't exactly stun the world, but the foundation was laid, and IT managers waited with great anticipation for MTS to fulfill the promise to simplify the management of transactions. Version 2.0, a much more stable, mature product, was released in December 1997, and the middle-tier ball was beginning to roll for Microsoft. It wasn't long before MTS was being successfully deployed in large client/server Visual Basic, Visual C++, and ASP applications. Today, MTS is a feature-rich product that can perform several roles in a multitier client/server application.

Component Transactions

You're already familiar with database transactions (like wrapping a series of SQL updates with Begin Transaction … End Transaction to ensure all updates either succeed or fail), but you've probably never given much thought to the concept of transacting components. This means that instead of transacting SQL statements, you transact COM objects, with each component having an equal "vote" in the decision to commit a transaction. MTS coordinates and monitors the transactional state of components running under its control, usually while they interact with a data source. This enables you to do things like transact across multiple databases with relative ease because MTS handles most of the work for you.

 MTS supports component transactions only when they communicate with an SQL Server or Oracle database. However, other database vendors are expected to follow suit soon. File server databases, like Visual FoxPro and Access, are *not* supported because they do not externalize distributed transactions. If you need a more portable database, SQL Server 7 might be just what you're looking for. Check out the Microsoft Web site for more details.

Object Brokering

The MTS runtime sits on the server and fields requests for COM components from multiple clients. When a request is made, MTS creates an environment called a *context* under which the component can run and maintain information about it, such as the name of the creator, transaction data, access rights, and so on. Next, MTS instantiates the object and returns a reference to the client. It will continue to maintain the instance while the client is using it, though it may deactivate the object if the client doesn't use it for a while. (Don't worry, MTS automatically creates a new instance or uses another inactive instance when the client resumes its use of the object, without the client ever losing its reference.) The great benefit of object brokering is that it doesn't matter to the client where the objects reside, or if someone else is using it; it's up to MTS to find the component, create a new instance if necessary, and run it under its control, usually within an implicit transaction.

Resource Pooling

MTS can automatically pool threads and database connections. *Thread pooling* is necessary when you allow multiple clients to access the same component. Normally, you would have to code the thread management, but MTS handles this for you. *Database connection pooling* allows your application to scale to a large number of users by enabling multiple clients to reuse a finite pool of connections to the data source. This is why it is suggested that connections be dropped as soon as possible so that other users may employ the unused connection, thereby allowing a system to have many more users than are possible with expensive connections. MTS coordinates the communication between the component and the data source automatically.

User-Definable, Role-Based Security Model

MTS encourages the use of a role-based security model, whereby collections of Windows NT users and groups are logically assembled into roles like data entry clerk, human resources, and salesperson. When a developer creates a component, he or she can do so with these roles in mind, changing the behavior of the component based on who is calling it.

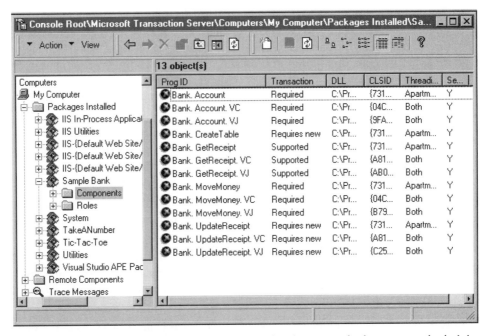

Figure 6.6 MTS Explorer: the interface to MTS development, deployment, and administration.

This makes a lot more sense from a development standpoint. Most systems today are built on the premise that an administrator will grant a user access to only the tables and other database objects that the user needs to perform his or her duties. However, making this decision is often difficult since database design is not typically done from a business logic perspective, but rather from a normalization/optimization perspective.

With role-based, component security, users are not given access to any base tables, but to business objects on a middle tier. The business server(s) are the only "users" capable of accessing database objects. Developers can then write business components from a "people-based" point of view and without any data-related restrictions.

Administration of Business-Tier Configuration

Using the Transaction Server Explorer (another snap-in to the Microsoft Management Console), you can add MTS components and set their properties, specify where components will run (on the local server or another remote server), see the status of active components, create roles for security, and much more (see Figure 6.6). Transaction Server Explorer is also fully scriptable so that all of its functionality can be implemented programmatically as well.

Benefits of Using Transaction Server

By using MTS to "wrap" your business objects into one functional unit, you accomplish many things:

Simplified Programming. MTS takes much of the complex programming out of the project life cycle. For instance, the developer does not have to be concerned with thread management, database connection pooling, table-level security, object caching, database transaction coordination (even across multiple databases or disparate databases), and more. This accomplishes the fundamental goal of MTS: allowing developers to get back to the job of solving complex *business* issues, not complex *programming* issues.

Code Reusability. Transactional components can all be written the same way and then used interchangeably. All they need to do is start an MTS transaction, perform their function, and then signify their success via the SetComplete or SetAbort methods. If written correctly, they can be called in any order, thus maximizing their reusability.

Centralized Administration. Transaction Server Explorer administers components both during development and deployment.

Scalability. MTS helps applications scale much higher due to the "statelessness" of components. Dropping database connections and reusing inactive component instances really cuts down on server resources and makes them available to other users.

Performance. MTS components execute very efficiently because they are not only in-process COM objects but are also cached on the server—even when they're inactive. That way subsequent calls will be much faster, yet at the same time allow you to keep your component stateless.

A First Look at Microsoft Message Queue Server

For all of the wonderful things Transaction Server can bring to the distributed application development table, it does make a few major assumptions that might not be acceptable in every situation.

The Need for Connectionless Communication

An MTS transaction, or any transaction for that matter, is not complete until all operations within it have either successfully completed or failed. In fact, the system usually cannot continue until you receive some sort of acknowledgment from your component that one of these two resolutions has occurred. How else could you account for multi-user contention if you didn't make this assumption?

Another assumption is that the data source to which you are committing changes is always available. While that seems like a pretty reasonable request, there are many situations—such as on-the-road salespeople entering sales orders or nightly batch file transfers—where the receiving side does not necessarily need to be immediately available. Salespeople like to save their orders locally for subsequent upload when they eventually hook up to the network. Likewise, batch file transfers are usually not time-dependent. There might be a window of 12 hours (perhaps from 6:00 P.M. to 6:00 A.M., before the next business day starts) in which a daily sales summary text file can be sent to the corporate Web server on the other side of the world, where it might then be published on the Internet. An operator should not have to keep pressing Send every five minutes just because the Web server was too busy at 6:00 P.M. due to all of the salespeople uploading their work.

Most distributed applications also make the assumption that the platform with which they are communicating is the same on both sides of the wire. This is not always the case. Take for example the monolithic COBOL mainframe application in which your company has perhaps invested millions of dollars. If you approach the MIS director (after you've finished reading this book) with this grand idea of building a distributed application, replacing the mainframe with an NT Server, and replacing all of the dumb terminals with PCs, be prepared for a fight.

But you *can* sell the concept of slowly integrating the new system by providing a way for the two disparate systems to communicate with one another—seamlessly. If you could guarantee that the Visual Basic front end you are going to build for the human resources department could update the NT Server and the IBM 3090 in a single transaction, the director would be pretty impressed.

Many companies have already developed several client/server applications, but the systems don't communicate with one another. So, usually what ends up happening is that a custom batch file transfer routine is created to bridge this communication gap.

What Is Message Queuing?

The preceding are some of the issues that face corporate IS teams today. The way many of them resolve these problems is through a technology called *message queuing*, a process in which communication between two systems can be guaranteed to be asynchronous, loosely coupled, and language-agnostic. There are a number of products available today that are categorized as *message queue middleware* (MQM). Each of them satisfy the following minimum criteria:

Guaranteed, One-Time, In-Order Delivery. Messages sent from System A are guaranteed to be delivered to System B at some point in time, even if communication problems arise. And that message will be received only once by the recipient, even if communication problems force the message to be resent several times. Last, the message will be delivered in the order in which it was queued, while respecting the message's priority.

Asynchronous Communication. Messages sent from System A do not have to wait for an acknowledgment from System B for program execution to continue. Messages are not sent directly to a data source, but rather reside in a queue indefinitely—waiting to be retrieved by the recipient application.

Loosely coupled. Since messages sent to System B are actually first sent to a queue, System A does not have to have a permanent link to System B. So System A can send all the messages it wants even if System B is unavailable. When System B is finally available, it can be responsible for downloading its pending, queued messages.

Common Message Format. Messages must be formatted in a platform-independent way so that all MQM providers can interpret them.

Kind of, Sort of Like E-mail, But Not Really

The easiest way to understand message queuing is to use the infamous e-mail analogy. Do you know how your e-mail system works? It's pretty simple but very effective (as all good systems should be). When you create an e-mail message in a mail client, like Microsoft Outlook Express, and choose Send, one of two things can happen. If you're not online with your mail server, your e-mail message will obviously sit in a queue (usually called the outbox) on your local workstation.

When you finally do connect, the message will be sent to your mail server with the address of the recipient's mail server. Your mail server will then send it to your recipient's mail server where it will wait in another queue until the recipient is online and chooses to retrieve his or her e-mail. It will then be downloaded to him or her. This is called *store-and-forward messaging* and, architecturally speaking, message queuing works in a very similar manner.

Benefits of Message Queuing Middleware

Simple concepts so far, right? Perhaps, but the e-mail analogy exemplifies several benefits that are inherent to message queuing, yet missing from typical real-time, transactional database applications:

Store-and-Forward Communication. Messages are not sent directly to recipients; they are *stored* in queues and *forwarded* to recipients when network communication is available. The roaming salesperson typifies this need for connectionless communication with guaranteed eventual delivery.

Defensive Communication. Local area networks (LANs) get more and more reliable, but are still prone to failure; wide area networks (WANs) are even more troublesome. To get around the problems that may arise in a distributed network environment, MQM applications resend messages when confirmation of delivery is not received; they can hold messages in a queue during peak periods of server activity and be a very efficient, low-overhead method of transporting data across a network.

Concurrent Execution. Short of writing very complicated multithreading software in low-level languages, sending requests to multiple recipients simultaneously is typically a very difficult task. Message queuing middleware allows for asynchronous messaging so that you can send messages to multiple recipients without having to wait for an acknowledgment from each before continuing. If an immediate acknowledgment is not necessary—such as in an Internet online order—then your application can serve many more requests by having them all reside in a queue until order processing is ready to process them.

Journaled Communication. Most MQM products offer the capability to journal all messages to serve as an audit trail of activity. This is much more easily accomplished with message queuing than in a transaction server environment because state is maintained, even after messages are processed, so they can be replayed at any time. There is also no additional overhead that audit trails cause in typical database environments because a synchronous update is not required.

What Is Microsoft Message Queue Server?

Microsoft recognized the limitations inherent to distributed applications, and to address them, it developed its version of message queue middleware and coined it Microsoft Message Queue Server (MSMQ). Competing products on the mainframe platform like IBM's MQ Series have been around for years, and have gained wide industry acceptance for the solutions it provides. But the distributed client/server application environment was sorely in need of a product that would simplify the connectionless communication need, and Microsoft was there to fill it. MSMQ can be regarded as the final piece of the distributed puzzle because it fills the gaps left by concurrent communication systems. As you might guess, MSMQ was developed to run on Windows NT and Windows 9x (clients only), but it can, of course, communicate with other platforms because the data format is standardized.

MSMQ provides the following message queuing features:

Connectionless Messaging. MSMQ implements store-and-forward message queuing, allowing users to conduct their business without the concerns inherent with unreliable LANs and WANs. If you were to solely use a COM/DCOM solution, both sides of the wire would have to be available at all times. With MSMQ, the sender and receiver do not even need to support the same protocol (one can be IP while the other is IPX) since MSMQ supports a nonsession-based, application-level model.

Guaranteed Delivery. Messages can be logged to a RAM-based (express) or disk-based (recoverable) medium. RAM-based is more efficient, but disk-based provides the ability to guarantee delivery because a physical record of the message is maintained. So even in the case of a power outage, messages can be recovered for subsequent resending until they are finally delivered.

Network Traffic Prioritization. Just as you can indicate the priority of an e-mail message, you can use MSMQ's message prioritization feature to send the more important messages to recipients in order of priority. For example, credit checks may get a higher priority than, say, return requests.

Transactions. Although it might seem contrary to the spirit of message queuing, you can wrap your message in a transaction and reap all of the benefits a transaction provides. Transactions might be used if your application is dependent on a message confirmation before continuing. MSMQ integrates completely with MTS to provide COM-based component transactions.

Smart Routing. MSMQ supports the capability to route messages via the most efficient way available at the time. It can detect high activity and slow links to reroute messages accordingly.

Security. MSMQ is tightly integrated with Windows NT security. Senders must identify themselves with digital signatures so that receivers can decide if they are a trusted source before accepting their messages. Encryption and authentication are also supported using public and private keys.

Disparate System Integration. At this time, MSMQ can communicate natively only with other Windows-based systems. However, Microsoft has partnered with a firm called Level 8 Systems, which develops connectivity products that allow MSMQ to run on several other platforms, including MVS, MQ CICS, OS/2, and AS/400 from IBM; and Sun's Solaris, HP-Unix, and AIX-Unix. The MSMQ Software Development Kit (SDK) is available to help integrate MSMQ with these other platforms. For more information on Level 8 Systems products and product availability, contact Level 8 Systems, or see the Level 8 Systems Web page at www .level8.com.

What Sets MSMQ Apart

MSMQ applications communicate with one another through *messages*, which are defined as units of information or data. Every message contains information about the sender and receiver, as well as its textual or binary content. The fact that MSMQ messages can pass binary content opens up a world of opportunity. Can you guess how precisely? Here's a hint: What's the single most useful piece of binary data you'll encounter using COM-based programming? If you recall from Chapter 1, it's the ADO Recordset object.

If you haven't just said to yourself, "Whoa," you need to go directly back to Chapter 1 (do not pass Go and do not collect $200). An ADO Recordset object is a binary representation of a temporary table or array, if you will. However, since it's a COM component, we can obtain an object variable reference to it and use it for good—not evil. For example, instead of passing a simple text file from system to system, passing a Recordset object would enable the receiving side to simply call its UpdateBatch method to generate the SQL statements that will send its contents to a data source. That's a perfect solution to the salesperson-on-the-road scenario. (You'll be looking at a detailed example like this later in the book.)

Other than passing ADO Recordsets, the fact that MSMQ is fully COM-aware (exposing 10 objects in its ActiveX object model) and can run as a Windows NT service means that MSMQ integrates quite easily into your Microsoft tool-based, distributed client/server application. It also means that all of the Visual Studio tools can be used to develop MSMQ-based solutions. ASP-based Web applications and MTS transactions can also be seamlessly integrated. So, as you can see, MSMQ is not glorified e-mail; it really has some very powerful benefits.

MSMQ Architecture

Now that you see the void that MSMQ can fill in a distributed client/server application, it's time to look at the topology of the message-based portion of your application.

The MSMQ Enterprise

An MSMQ application is composed of a number of computers that can, in some way, communicate with one another—sometimes referred to a *connected network* (CN). When you define a CN, you are simply defining a label. When you install an MSMQ server, you associate each network address on the computer with the appropriate CNs. These CNs form logical groupings of computers that can communicate directly.

This collection of computers, connected networks, sites, site links, and systems that intend to participate in message queuing is known as the *MSMQ Enterprise*. At the pinnacle of the MSMQ Enterprise is a server called the *primary enterprise controller (PEC)*. Normally, you would only have one PEC in an organization.

The PEC supplies information that's contained in a distributed database called the *MSMQ Information Store (MQIS)* to each computer in the enterprise. The MQIS is *not* used to store messages. Only queue and routing information, as well as the certification keys used in authenticating messages, are published by the MQIS. The contents of the queues (the messages themselves) reside in memory-mapped files on MSMQ-independent clients and servers.

> **Under Windows NT 4, MSMQ requires that the MQ Information Store be an SQL Server database. In NT 5, this will not be necessary, as this data will be stored in the Windows Active Directory Service.**

Sites and Controllers

When you install MSMQ, you will be asked to provide the name and location of the machine that will serve as the primary enterprise controller. Once that has been done, you can add one or more *sites* to the enterprise (see Figure 6.7). A site is exactly what you'd expect it to be: the location of another system with which you would like to communicate.

Sites are typically defined by physical boundaries, like offices, and can have their own network or multiple networks. However, one machine normally serves as the *primary site controller (PSC)*. A PSC is similar to a PEC, but it contains queue and routing information specific to that site. In fact, the PEC is actually a PSC as well because it not only maintains information pertinent to the entire enterprise but also information specific to the primary site.

> **A PSC is not *required* at any site other than the PEC. But without it, you lose many of the benefits of MSMQ, including the ability to persist the routing of messages at a site. If the site is disconnected from the PEC, all messages sent will fail without this intermediary queue layer.**

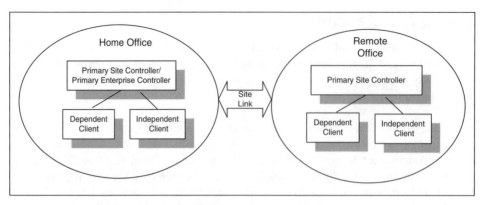

Figure 6.7   A typical MSMQ Enterprise topology.

In addition to a PSC, it's a good idea for a site to have one or more *backup site controllers* (BSC) installed to provide load balancing and failure recovery, should the PSC or PEC fail. The BSC holds a read-only copy of the primary site controller or primary enterprise controller's MQIS database. It also functions as an MSMQ routing server, as primary site controller's do. In addition to the PEC, both the PSC and the BSC get their site data from the MQ Information Store (which is currently stored in an SQL Server database).

Sites can also contain one or more *MSMQ routing servers*. These contain no site information and are used to dynamically route messages between queues. They are especially useful when networks based on disparate protocols need to communicate with one another. This can occur within a single site or across sites. Sites are connected to one another with communication links called *site links*. Once these links are made via the MSMQ Explorer, a user-defined *site link cost* can be set to help the routing server to choose the least expensive interlink path (see Figure 6.8).

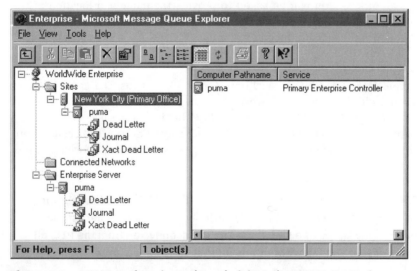

Figure 6.8   MSMQ Explorer is used to administer the MSMQ Enterprise.

Messages and Queues

Like e-mail, messages are stored in either local or server queues, depending on server availability. They reside in local queues until a client is connected to an MSMQ server. Once messages have been sent to the server, they can reside in either a *public* or *private* queue.

Public queues are replicated throughout the enterprise by publishing in the MQIS, and can, therefore, be located by any client or server within the enterprise. Private queues, on the other hand, are not published in the MQIS, and therefore do not add to the MQIS replication load.

Messages can be stored in one of two ways: memory-based or disk-based. Memory based, also known as *express*, offers better performance, but does not provide an audit trail of activity. Disk-based messages, also known as *recoverable*, are most often used in production because messages will not be lost in case of computer failure. For this reason, and the fact that communication within sites is normally very efficient due to 10MB–100MB Ethernet network lines, the performance hit can be tolerated in most situations.

Independent and Dependent Clients

Once the site servers are established, client workstations can be added to the MSMQ Enterprise. Clients fall into two categories: independent and dependent.

An *independent client* can send and receive messages to private or public network queues, as well as create and modify local queues. And this can all be done *without* the need for synchronous communication with an MSMQ server—a tremendous advantage for the roaming salesperson. However, a primary site controller must be available at installation time so that the client can gather information from the MQIS and use it to package the message with the appropriate site data.

The primary differences between MSMQ-independent clients and MSMQ servers are that independent clients do not have the intermediate store-and-forward capability of MSMQ servers, nor do they store information from the distributed MSMQ database.

Dependent clients, on the other hand, cannot store information locally. They utilize DCOM to communicate with the site controller and utilize the server's functions to store all messages on queues. In other words, dependent clients can only send and receive messages synchronously—a connection to the server must be established before a message can be sent or received. MSMQ servers can support up to 15 dependent clients.

As you might expect, the independent client is most often used so that the connectionless communication functionality we're looking to add to our distributed applications can be realized. This connection to the server can be made via the typical IP or IPX protocols, or through RAS to support remote clients.

 While the site controller machines must be running Windows NT Server, Enterprise Edition, the clients may be running either Windows 9x, Windows NT Workstation 4.0 or later, or Windows NT Server 4.0 or later.

You can also install the MSMQ Explorer on MSMQ-independent clients running under Windows NT Workstation or Server so that you can administer your MSMQ Enterprise remotely from computers running Windows NT Workstation.

To summarize, MSMQ can enhance our distributed applications by providing connectionless messaging for disconnected sites, support for transactional messages via integration with MTS, and a standardized way for disparate systems to communicate.

A Peek into the Crystal Ball: COM+

To accomplish Microsoft's goal of simplifying distributed application development, there was still work to be done. COM, DCOM, MTS, and MSMQ are great services, but deploying them together necessitated managing too many pieces of the puzzle at the same time. Configuration and deployment of clients, middle-tier servers, and data sources could be an administrative nightmare in some environments because COM, MTS, IIS, IE, Windows NT, and so on were each introduced into the marketplace as separate functional products and services. The versioning alone could accelerate the aging process.

Recognizing this, Microsoft developed the COM+ Services. COM+ is the *unification* of these technologies, the embedding of them into the Windows NT 5.0 operating system, the addition of new language runtime features, and the provision of a single point of administration: the COM+ Explorer. This is a breath of fresh air from Microsoft—long known for introducing new products faster than anyone can possibly absorb them. So don't look at COM+ as something new, but rather as a simplification of existing products, with some additional goodies as well.

COM+ is not a single entity or product. Rather, it is a collection of operating system-level, middle-tier, runtime services that include:

- The merging of the COM/DCOM and MTS programming models to alleviate the difficulties encountered when trying to deploy a multitier application using several independent technologies.

- Enhancements to the existing features of MTS 2.0: component transaction monitoring, object brokering, resource pooling, role-based security, and central administration.

- New runtimes services for queuing components, dynamic load balancing, caching databases in memory, and an event class service that allows subscribers' components to receive notification whenever a publisher has fired an event.

- The embedding of all of these services into the Window NT 5.0 operating system for tighter integration, simpler deployment, and more efficient processing. Unlike COM and MTS, the COM+ services are part of the Windows NT 5.0 operating system core. So, instead of managing the installation and deployment of several APIs, just installing NT will do much of the work for you. As you would expect, these services now operate much more efficiently, operating as a whole instead of as disparate parts. This also means that COM+ is now more tightly integrated with Internet Information Server, making Web development a more seamless process.

- The COM+ Explorer makes deployment easier by virtue of its central administration, scriptable catalog interface, and import and export wizards.

- The same reasons you have chosen to follow a three-tier model apply to COM+ as well: code encapsulation and reusability, scalability, thinner (read cheaper) clients, resource pooling, interchangeable front ends, and business object-based security.

From Here

In this opening chapter of Part 2 of the book, we covered a lot of ground. But hopefully you are enjoying the process of learning how to make the transition from file server or mainframe application development using these exciting client/server technologies from Microsoft. By now, you have enough background into COM-based client/server distributed application development to begin getting your hands dirty with the NT tools and services we've briefly overviewed: MTS and MSMQ. Our next step will be to take an in-depth look at Microsoft Transaction Server in Chapter 7, the transaction processing service that is bringing distributed application development to the masses. Then in Chapter 8, we'll do the same for Microsoft Message Queue Server. Let's move on to the fun stuff!

Microsoft Transaction Server

In the introduction to Microsoft Transaction Server in Chapter 6, you learned that MTS is a rather complex product, reflecting its rich and sophisticated functionality. Fortunately, as with all good products, much of this complexity has been shielded from the user. This is in keeping with the goals of Microsoft Transaction Server, which include:

To provide today's, modern object–orientated developer a way to use existing tools to make distributed client/server application development a reality on the PC level. And while doing so, to keep in mind the Microsoft philosophy of making tools easier to use by having consistent user and component interfaces, enabling developers to leverage what they already know, and allowing them to concentrate on the task of solving business problems rather than a system's low-level internals.

With those goals in mind, MTS enters the marketplace at a time when its features are much sought after. As traditional client/server and Internet application development expands, more mainframe systems are being downsized for economic reasons. Consequently, the PC arena needed more tools to help its applications scale to mainframe proportions. MTS was born to fill the gaps that prevented applications created with desktop tools to technically compete with the "big iron."

What You'll Learn

At the time of this writing, the subject of how to use MTS has been covered extensively in several other publications. And as you'll soon learn, administering packages, components, user roles, and so on are actually pretty trivial tasks in MTS. So, rather than reiterate the user documentation and provide a reference of every property, method, and feature of MTS and the Transaction Explorer, this chapter attempts to take a slightly different approach.

The intent of this chapter is to teach you how to write successful MTS component applications. We make no assumptions of prior MTS knowledge, thus you will be guided through every step you need to take to follow the examples. And conceptually speaking, every part of MTS will be covered. What's most important is that you leave this chapter understanding how to create and deploy MTS-enabled components in your applications. This approach should give you the most "bang for your buck" because it recognizes that technical developers like yourself already have certain skills and experience, which just need to be pointed in a new direction. We make the preceding statement because although MTS allows you to harness any object-oriented or component-based development experience you have, it also changes a lot of the rules. These new concepts focus on the areas of how "stateful" a business component should be, how long to maintain database connections, how long to maintain object references, and how to write components with user roles in mind.

All the while, the ADO thread will continue to run through this chapter. Specifically, you'll learn how MTS helps ADO complete the goal of transacting—even across multiple, disparate data sources. To reinforce theses principles, typical Visual Basic business-related classes are included to illustrate how a component looks before and after it is MTS-enabled.

But before you begin learning the new component creation concepts, how to create MTS packages and components, how to set their properties, how to create and assign user roles, and how to use the MTS Explorer, a little more groundwork needs to be laid. Specifically, you need to clearly understand what exactly a transaction server is and how it differs from a transaction monitor.

Transaction Monitors and Servers

Microsoft Transaction Server, in conjunction with the Distributed Transaction Coordinator, fills a very important void that exists on the PC level: the ability to monitor database transactions as they interact with Transactional Resource Managers like MS SQL Server and component transactions as they consume server resources. On the mainframe level, transaction processing (TP) monitors for years have been an essential part of most OLTP systems, with IBM's CICS and IMS and BEA's Tuxedo on the Unix platform leading the way. The PC client/server world, however, has had no such animal.

Without a TP monitor, you have to rely on the API of the RDBMS itself to enforce ACID requirements on database transactions. While that may be fine for small- to medium-sized, nondistributed applications, these types of transactions usually cannot cross multiple resource managers, and consequently, the application tends not to scale very well. TP monitors also allow you to track the success or failure of transactions, the speed at which they execute, and other statistical information.

What's a TP Monitor?

A TP monitor is sometimes referred to as an operating system for database transactions, which acts on top of the existing operating system, and typically performs these two roles:

Process Management. This includes the starting and stopping of server processes, funneling work to them, monitoring their execution, and balancing their workloads.

Transaction Management. The ACID properties are guaranteed to be enforced on all transactions that run under its control.

On the PC level, a TP monitor—more often referred to as a transaction manager (TM)—sits on an application server and accepts requests for the services of a function within a DLL. The TP monitor routes the execution of the DLL function to server classes—groups of processes or threads that have been prestarted and are waiting to be used. Each process or thread in the class is capable of doing the work, and the TP monitor balances the work among them.

The process flow goes something like this: When a request is made for a DLL, the TP monitor gives the work to an available process in the server class pool. The server process dynamically links to the DLL function called by the client, invokes it, oversees its execution, and returns a message to the client. At this point, even though the client application may still have a reference to the object that it requested the server to create, the server process is free to be used by another client. The OS keeps the DLL loaded in memory, where it can be shared across processes.

TP monitors enable client requests to be shared among running server processes, thereby eliminating the one-process-per-client requirement. Requests for data connections are "juggled" in the same manner. Shared database connections, processes, memory requirements, and open files can all be dramatically reduced on the server, enabling your application to handle a much higher volume of users (Figure 7.1). With the aid of transaction managers, your server's operating system will respond in kind with snappier performance, and your user license requirements will not necessarily have to grow as your user base does.

Enter Microsoft Transaction Server

MTS, first introduced to the marketplace as a standalone package and now bundled with the Windows NT 4.0 Option Pack (and eventually integrated with COM+ on Windows NT 5.0), sought to give PC client/server applications the same capabilities that TP monitors were giving mainframe applications—and then some. With MTS, the components (classes of ActiveX DLLs) already built can run under a transaction-monitoring environment and capitalize on many advanced features without your having to code them.

The MTS feature set can be broken down into five major areas. These areas were briefly discussed in Chapter 6, but they will be examined in greater detail in this chapter.

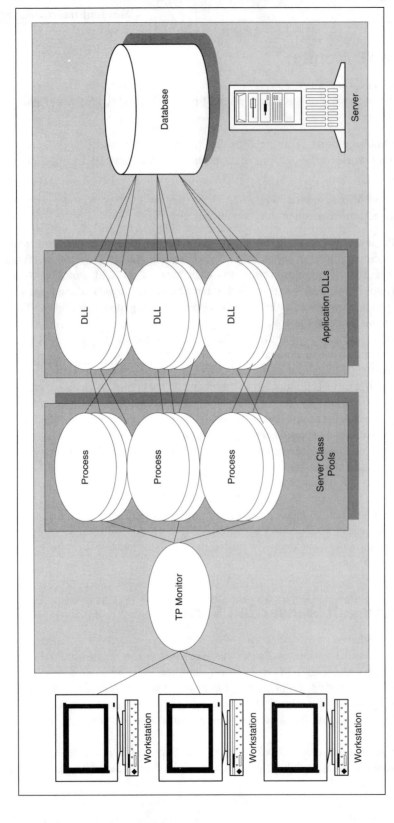

Figure 7.1   Transaction managers can dramatically reduce the resources required of a server, thereby enabling your application to service many more users.

- Component transactions
- Object brokering
- Server resource management
- Transaction monitoring and administration
- Security

Component transactions, object brokering, and server resource management will be discussed together because it's difficult to separate them; because when you write "proper" component transactions, MTS will take care of the object brokering and server resource management for you. These three features are implicit, and enable your applications to scale without writing any additional thread management or resource pooling code. They really go hand in hand.

How MTS Changes the Way to Write Components

In Chapter 6, you learned that components run under MTS control can capitalize on the MTS capability to reuse resources in a way that helps your application scale. For this to happen, though, MTS needs a little cooperation from the component developer. As you'll see, it's actually quite simple to MTS-enable a component. Where this chapter will attempt to really offer advice is in the restructuring of your components to best utilize the benefits MTS can bring to your COM components.

The Northwind Project DLL (NWProject.DLL) depicts a group of typical Visual Basic classes. These classes create sales orders on the Northwind Traders sample database that ships with SQL Server 7.0. Although simplified for illustration purposes, the NWProject DLL has good examples of the type of memory-efficient classes most commonly used in business.

The approach this chapter takes is to first look at the classes (in pseudo-code) written in a manner typical of a two-tier application, where the DLL is on the client workstation. This is to level the playing field; that is, to ensure that whatever your VB experience, you will be able to understand the concepts presented here. With this foundation in place, a discussion of the key concepts involved in creating server-side MTS-enabled components will follow. Lastly, the NWProject2.DLL code will be shown. This is the NWProject.DLL code after it has been MTS-enabled.

Examining Stateful VB Classes

The infamous Sales Order process will be used to analyze how the creation of Visual Basic data access components differs from that of a component that was created to run under MTS control. Keep in mind that this is *not* the way to write MTS components; but sometimes it's as helpful to understand what not to do as it is to understand what to do.

The areas of concentration that these classes exemplify are:

- Methods that create ADO connections and Recordsets.
- Methods that instantiate a number of business components.
- Methods that query, insert, and update data in a database.

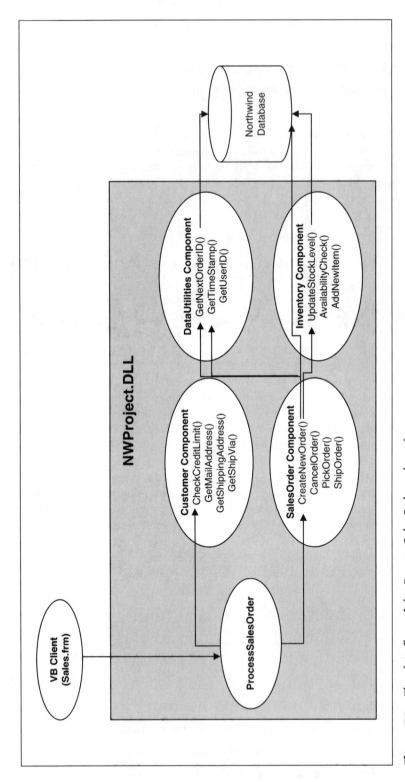

Figure 7.2   The data flow of the ProcessSalesOrder subroutine.

Database Connections

The first thing we notice from the pseudocode is that, in typical client/server fashion, a connection to the data source has been established on application startup, held in a global variable, and not released until the session has ended.

```
Create global ADO connection handle to the database in Sub Main()
```

Since establishing and storing database connections has historically been the slowest, most resource-intensive single operation your application performs, it makes perfect sense to want to do it only once. Typically, a logon screen is provided, requesting the user for a user ID and password. This information is then passed as parameters to the database in an effort to create a user-specific connection. Once stored in a global object variable, the ADO connection handle can then be reused in all subsequent methods without having to incur this overhead again.

Creating a connection to a database through ODBC can at times take up to two or three seconds, depending on configuration and available resources.

Component References

When the services of a business object are requested, the duration of the object's lifetime is normally dependent on the given circumstance. Assuming a three-tier model, whereby all non-UI-related business objects reside on an application or data server and are accessed via DCOM, one of two choices must be made. If an object's services are only required for a very short period (like a single function call), the reference to it is normally destroyed immediately after use. Such is the fate of the Customer object, which gets its object reference released from memory as soon as the credit check is completed. To wait any longer would consume unnecessary server resources, as well as interfere with other users attempting to access the same component (VB cannot create multithreaded objects, but as you'll see, MTS really helps make this a nonissue).

```
Instantiate the Customer business class
Call CheckCreditLimit() of Customer class
Create an ADO Recordset object for credit check
Get credit limit from customer table
Compare the credit limit to the value of the order
Free the Recordset object
Free the Customer object
```

On the other hand, if a business object's services are required for multiple calls within a single function, or even across multiple functions, then the object reference is maintained for as long as is reasonably necessary. Bear in mind that doing so would tie up server resources, so it is wise to perform short tasks during its lifetime. The life of the Data Utilities class is a perfect example because the functions that are called, GetNextOrderID() and GetTimeStamp(), each have minimal work to do.

```
Instantiate the Data Utilities class
Call GetNextOrderID() of the Data Utilities class
Call GetTimeStamp() of the Data Utilities class
Free the Data Utilities class
Execute the SQL Insert of the new order header and detail
If successful commit the transaction, else roll it back
Free the SalesOrder object
```

Transactional Database Updates

The duration of the SalesOrder class is something of concern. A lot of work is done between the time CreateNewOrder( ) is called and the time the class is freed. This block of pseudo-code is a perfect candidate for a component transaction; each step in this process must succeed in order for the sales order to be committed.

```
If customer is creditworthy, instantiate the SalesOrder class
Call CreateNewOrder() of SalesOrder Class
Begin a database transaction
Instantiate the Inventory class
Call UpdateStockLevel() of Inventory class
Create an ADO Recordset object for availability check
Perform stock availability check
If stock available, update inventory table
Free the Recordset object
Free the Inventory object
Instantiate the Data Utilities class
Call GetNextOrderID() of the Data Utilities class
Call GetTimeStamp() of the Data Utilities class
Free the Data Utilities class
Execute the SQL Insert of the new order header and detail
If successful commit the transaction, else roll it back
Free the SalesOrder object
```

It would not be unrealistic to say that in a real-world scenario, much more work might have to be done before the Sales Order class could be released, including getting a surrogate primary key from a table, performing several record-level business rule validations, adding the new sales figures to a summary table (perhaps aggregated by year and month or by salesperson), inserting records into an audit trail table for historical purposes, and others. All this activity would certainly lengthen the time the SalesOrder class was in use by this user, creating contention for it on the server and chewing up valuable server-side memory.

MTS Component Basics

Now you've seen why typical VB classes are considered stateful and unable to efficiently scale an application. If this is the way you currently write your applications, you're in good company. But the reason you're reading this book is because your goal is to maximize the resources available to you in an effort to make your applications support more users and a higher transaction volume, but at PC prices. And now it's time to learn exactly how to go about integrating MTS into your applications.

In its simplest form, an MTS-enabled component has the following structure:

```
Public Function MyFunction(ByVal strParameter As String) As Boolean
On Error GoTo Err_MyMethod
Dim objContext As ObjectContext      'Member of MTS Type Library
Dim objClassName As MyClassName
Set objContext = GetObjectContext()
Set objClassName = objContext.CreateInstance("MyServerName.MyClassName")
If objClassName.MyClassName() = True Then
  objContext.SetComplete
Else
  objContext.SetAbort
End If
Exit Function

Err_MyMethod:
objContext.SetAbort

End Function
```

As you can see, MTS communicates with an object through an *object context* (see Figure 7.3). Let's take a more in-depth look at what an object context is and how MTS uses it to fulfill component transacting. After that, we'll reexamine this MTS-enabled component, pointing out its many subtleties and the implicit action that MTS is quietly performing.

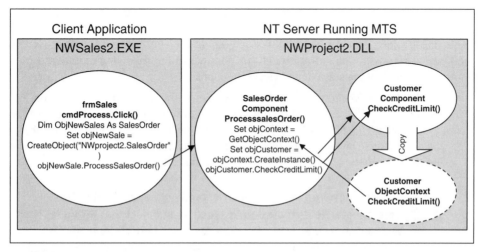

Figure 7.3 The relationship between a client, a remote component, and the object context through which they communicate.

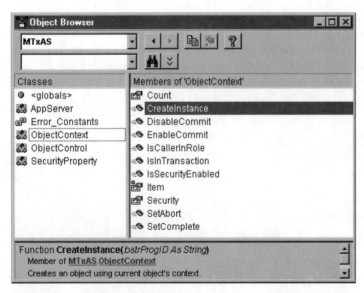

Figure 7.4 The MTS Application Server runtime, MTxAS.DLL, and the interfaces it exposes. The global method, GetObjectContext(), and the members of the IObjectContext interface are the most significant.

The ObjectContext Interface

When you instantiate a component, regardless whether it's running under MTS control, that component maintains state, or data specific to an instance of an object. An object context is state that is implicitly associated with a given MTS object. It holds information like the object's creator, transaction-related data, and any other details that have to do with the environment in which this object is being executed.

The MTS runtime (MtxAS.DLL) contains two interface objects: IObjectControl and IObjectContext (see Figure 7.4). IObjectControl will be discussed shortly. The global method GetObjectContext is your hook to accessing IObjectContext's methods. GetObjectContext returns an object reference (or pointer) to the following methods, which allow you to control the state of an MTS component.

CreateInstance. Creates an MTS object using the *current* object's context, enabling you to instantiate child objects that can run within the same transaction of the caller. This differs from CreateObject because even though CreateObject will also create a new instance of an object, it will do so with a *new* object context, and thus cannot be enlisted into an existing transaction.

 The New keyword in Visual Basic should *not* be used with MTS objects because it creates an instance of an object that MTS does not have access to. MTS, therefore, does not know how to give it a context, so it cannot be run within a transaction. See the Visual Basic documentation for more details.

SetComplete. Tells MTS that the object running under this context has successfully completed its work and would like to register its *affirmative* vote on whether the transaction should be committed. SetComplete also signals to MTS that the resources for the object context can be freed and its state destroyed, making more resources available to other users.

SetAbort. Tells MTS that the object running under this context has *not* successfully completed its work and would like to register its *negative* vote on whether the transaction should be committed. SetAbort, like Complete, also signals to MTS that the resources for the object context can be freed and its state destroyed, making more resources available to other users.

Other ObjectContext Methods

The ObjectContext class also exposes the following methods:

IsInTransaction. Tells you whether or not the object is executing within a transaction.

DisableCommit. Allows you to disable (either temporarily or permanently) a transaction from committing, usually because the data is in an inconsistent state. This is most often used in situations where the same method is called repeatedly from a client, but not until that method has put the database in a consistent state (e.g., debits = credits) should the client allow a SetComplete.

DisableCommit. Prevents an object from losing its state between invocation calls, which would happen automatically in the case of an ASP when SetComplete is implicitly fired at the end of a page. This allows a client to maintain data about a child object even though control has returned from the called object.

EnableCommit. Like DisableCommit, EnableCommit does not destroy an object's state, but it does tell MTS that the transactional updates are consistent and that any *subsequent* call to SetComplete or SetAbort will officially end the transaction. EnableCommit is the default setting when an object is created. This is why an object should always call SetComplete or SetAbort before returning from a method, unless you want the object to maintain its internal state for the next call from a client.

IsCallerInRole and IsSecurityEnabled. Discussed later in the section on security.

The ObjectControl Interface

Another MTS COM interface, IObjectControl, can optionally be implemented in Visual Basic by using the Implements keyword:

```
Implements ObjectControl
```

Doing so will give your class a secondary interface with the following three methods:

- Activate
- Deactivate
- CanBePooled

These methods provide placeholders for you to put code that you would want to fire when a class is activated or deactivated, and another that allows you to specify whether that object can be pooled. You would typically implement IObjectControl when you want your object to take part in MTS object pooling. This code would be put in the general declarations:

```
Implements ObjectControl
Private Function ObjectControl_CanBePooled()
  ObjectControl_CanBePooled = True
End Function
```

However, you can also use its other two methods when you want to create a public variable (which is actually private to this class) to hold a reference to the object context so that you don't have to call GetObjectContext in every method. When an object is activated or deactivated in an MTS-enabled component implementing IObjectControl, the Activate and Deactivate methods are implicitly called, respectively.

```
Implements ObjectControl
Private objContext

'Call GetObjectContext() whenever class is instantiated
'Now can use this global variable in all methods
Private Function ObjectControl_Activate()
  Set gobjContext = GetObjectContext()
End Function

'Clean up global variable when the component is destroyed
Private Function ObjectControl_Deactivate()
  Set gobjContext = Nothing
End Function
```

 The current version of MTS 2.0, does not support object pooling. However, the hook to use this feature has been provided by MTS so that when it is finally implemented, your components will enjoy that functionality without your having to change any code. No adverse effects will occur with this code in place even with object pooling support.

A Closer Look at an MTS-Enabled Component

Now that you understand a bit more about what's going on "under the hood," what follows is a more detailed examination of that skeletal component function.

Functions whose interface is intended to be exposed cannot be privately scoped; they must be public so that their interface is properly published. And if arguments are passed, they should be by value so that the client memory address does not have to be updated remotely with any changes to this parameter's value.

```
Public Function MyFunction(ByVal strParameter As String) As Boolean
```

Errors are handled inline, just like in any other VB code.

```
On Error GoTo Err_MyMethod
```

The ObjectContext is a class of the Transaction Server Type Library. You set a reference to it under Project | References. Thereafter, the now-global GetObjectContext method can be called to attain an object context reference. All communication with your component will be done through the object context.

```
Dim objContext As ObjectContext
Set objContext = GetObjectContext()
```

Next, allocate memory to the class you wish to instantiate, the same as you would do for any other VB class.

```
Dim objClassName As MyClassName
```

Instead of using the CreateObject or New Visual Basic functions to instantiate MyClassName, use the CreateInstance method of the ObjectContext class so that, among other things, this component is capable of running within the context of a transaction that has already begun. This is called *automatic enlistment* because CreateInstance does all of the transaction determination work for you. Of course, this all depends on the transaction support level; it could even signal that a new implicit transaction should begin.

```
Set objClassName = objContext.CreateInstance("MyServerName.MyClassName")
```

Next, perform some work. If all goes well, call the SetComplete method of the ObjectContext to signal to MTS that you're happy with the results of this method. The Transaction Support Level property setting will now be evaluated to determine if a transaction should be committed yet. If not, SetComplete or SetAbort will serve as votes in determining if a potential calling component's transaction should commit. SetComplete or SetAbort also tell MTS to destroy any state created by this function so that others have more server resources.

```
If objClassName.MyClassName() = True Then
   objContext.SetComplete
Else
   objContext.SetAbort
End If

Exit Function
```

If an error occurs, be sure to abort a transaction and cast a negative vote. You would typically raise an error here, but be sure not to use a message box in a DLL; that could halt the server for all clients.

```
Err_MyMethod:
objContext.SetAbort


End Function
```

The Good News

As you can see, the good news is that there really isn't much work to MTS-enabling a component. Also important is that MTS does not force you to completely abandon everything you've learned about component development. It just requires a slight restructuring of thinking to integrate a new tool into the core of your application.

That said, if you don't attempt to remove any unnecessary state, your COM servers will unnecessarily supply resources to clients that don't really need them. Remember that the point of using MTS is to enable your client/server LAN applications to scale to a level akin to mainframe applications. With just a little help from you, MTS can get you there.

MTS Component Rules to Live By

To take advantage of the MTS pooling, caching, and brokering features, you need to keep three very important things in mind, rules component developers need to adhere to in order to maximize the impact MTS will have on their application. Ignoring these rules will leave you disappointed with MTS, for without your cooperation, it cannot fulfill its promise of scalability. After becoming familiar with these rules, you'll be introduced to the VB sample classes to illustrate the concepts.

Stateless Components

Traditional client-side COM components are written as *stateful* objects; they maintain data in the form of variables and properties for their entire lifetime. So, what's so wrong with that? Isn't that what object-orientation development gurus have always preached? In fact, the definition of an object as *a collection of data and methods that act upon that data* reenforces this design decision.

Actually, there's nothing wrong with that logic as long as the component resides on the *client*. Moving to a distributed architecture and deploying COM servers on an application server to achieve scalability, maintenance, and performance changes the way developers need to write those components.

Here are the problems with server-side stateful components:

Poor Performance. If a component resides on an application server, and its role is, for example, to provide data to a Visual Basic form on a client, the typical VB technique of using Property Let and Get can make performance really suffer. Each property of the component that the client requests (Get) would translate to a separate Remote Procedure Call. On a complicated form, that model can cause a lot of network traffic, slowing the initialization of the form.

High Resources. Stateful components that hold on to information for a long time—like connections and object references—consume valuable server resources because the server has to maintain data in memory for *every* object instantiated by *any* client.

Resource Contention. Another resource problem has to do with the one-to-one relationship that exists between a component and the client that instantiates it. While a server-side component is maintaining state, another user cannot reuse that same component because the data would most likely be different. So, either the server needs to spawn another instance of the component and run it in a separate memory space to avoid conflict, or (worse) the server must deny the request to create a new instance until the first one is freed.

For these reasons, systems that deploy business objects on an application server via DCOM have not exactly proliferated the marketplace. This has historically been CORBA territory.

Pass Arguments by Value

The default in VB is to pass arguments by reference (ByRef). By specifying that you want to pass your arguments to MTS component methods ByValue, you will reduce the amount of Remote Procedure Calls your clients would need to otherwise make.

Reduce Network Calls

It may be necessary to create client methods that are a little larger than you would normally want. This would be the case when you need to make multiple calls to the server in succession. By combining the calls, you eliminate producing state when you leave the method.

Use Forward-Only Cursors

The default ADO Recordset cursor type is ForwardOnly (CursorTypeEnum = adOpen-ForwardOnly). It's best to use this read-only cursor type whenever possible since it's the "lightest" available.

Disconnect from the Data Source Early and Often

Surprised? The typical two-tier design of maintaining a global connection handle for the life of an application session is about the *worst* thing you can do when you're trying to scale it utilizing MTS components. Since MTS caches connections to data sources (even after you've closed and released an ADO connection object), reattaining one is a very quick, efficient process.

By not establishing a connection until the last possible moment, and then dropping the connection as soon as possible, you free from the server most of the approximately 50K of memory required to maintain each connection. In fact, it's optimal to drop the connection between the time that you've already populated an ADO Recordset but have not yet committed the changes to the server.

You'll also reduce the number of available connections (and expensive user licenses) necessary to run the application because there will no longer be the one-connection-per-user requirement that existed with the global connection handle design. MTS will make the connection you just dropped immediately available to another user.

Maintain References to Components for as Long as Necessary

Yes, you read that correctly. Though this rule appears to go against the spirit of MTS, and directly contradicts the rule for database connections, it actually makes perfect sense. Remember, when you execute the GetObjectContext method inside an MTS-hosted component and then call the CreateInstance method of the ObjectContext class, MTS returns to the calling application a handle to an *object context*, not a handle to the actual object. This intermediary object (essentially a blueprint of the actual object) maintains information about the transaction, the thread, the caller, and of course, the state of the original object requested.

When you have an outstanding reference to an MTS component, but are not actually using it, MTS—after a specified period of time (or on demand)—deactivates the component, freeing up server resources and allowing other users to access the same component unimpeded. Since there is very little overhead in maintaining the context object, it makes sense to hold on to it for as long as you think you might use it again, without consequence.

This also has the advantage of making your components simpler to program because you don't have to constantly destroy no-longer-needed object references.

SetComplete or SetAbort as Soon as Possible

The SetComplete and SetAbort object context methods both signal to MTS that, for the time being, the services of the component in question are no longer needed, and its state (data) can be destroyed. So it makes sense to call one of them as soon as the fate of your component has been logically determined (e.g., a credit check has been completed). For the most part, you'll want to call them at the end of every MTS-enabled component method as long as you don't plan on retaining any of the object's state.

Furthermore, even though you may call *another method* of the *same component* further down in the current method, in a high-volume environment, it still might be more efficient to call SetComplete or SetAbort so that MTS can let some other client freely use that component.

Of course, you would only call SetComplete or SetAbort when you are no longer interested in the state (the data represented by component variables and properties) the object is in. Once you've done that, you've told MTS that you don't need to maintain that data anymore and to free the memory for others to use.

MTS does have a way to handle properties that you feel must have a scope that is longer than what has been recommended as a suitable lifetime; it's called the Shared Property Manager. Since we will not be discussing the usage of the Shared Property Manager, please see the MTS documentation for further details.

In Visual Basic, *apartment-model* threading is used to provide thread safety. In apartment-model threading, each thread is like an apartment: All objects created on the thread live in this apartment, and are unaware of objects in other apartments.

Visual Basic's implementation of apartment-model threading eliminates conflicts in accessing global data from multiple threads by giving each apartment its own copy of global data. Currently, all components used in MTS run under the apartment-threading model, regardless of whether the ActiveX DLL was created with multithreading capabilities.

Setting Up Shop

MTS ships with both Visual Studio 9x and the Windows NT 4.0 Option Pack. It is also available for download at www.microsoft.com/ntserver/basics/appservices/transsvcs/. When you install MTS, be sure to check the option to include all of the samples (which might not be the default) so that you have the Sample Bank application. This application is essentially an ATM form that uses the Pubs database and includes the same components written in VB, C++, or J++. We won't be covering those samples here, but they are another good source of reference for you.

The MTS example components presented in this chapter are written in Visual Basic. Certainly, any language or product that can create COM servers could have been used, but VB seems to be the language most widely used and easiest to understand—even if you don't already know it. (Actually, the way things are going with Microsoft, Visual Basic may supplant Spanish as the United States' second most widely used language!) These components must be ActiveX DLLs, their Instancing property must be set to MultiUse, and their threading model must be set to Apartment.

The Northwind Traders sample database that ships with Microsoft SQL Server 7.0 will be used for the data source of the following examples. This database contains the sales data for a fictitious company called Northwind Traders, which imports and exports specialty foods from around the world.

Note that two structural modifications have been made to the database to support the examples that follow. A field, CreditLimit (of money type), has been added to the Customers table, and a default value of $10,000 has been generously given to all customers. Also, the Identity attribute of the OrderID field in the Orders table has been removed; the sample uses a class to get the next order number. Both modifications were made purely for illustrative purposes. To make these modifications, run NWSetup.EXE (see Figure 7.5). You can always revert the changes via the Installation Wizard.

The goal of the Sales Order Process is to, of course, commit a sales order. To do so, it must check if this order's value would exceed the customer's credit limit. If not, the stock level for the product on order must next be verified to be sure it is sufficient to ful-

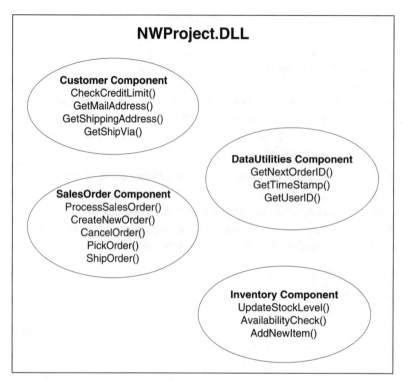

Figure 7.5 The components of the NWProject.DLL.

fill the order. If there is enough inventory, the stock level is decremented and the order record is then inserted into the Orders and Order Details tables.

The client is a Visual Basic form, frmSales (frmSales.frm of NWSales.vbp), which will kick things off by instantiating the SalesOrder class via DCOM and calling the Process-SalesOrder function. This is where our analysis of the Sales Order Process will begin.

 These examples have been greatly simplified. In other words, we don't condone many of the techniques we've used, but felt they worked best for illustration purposes. In Chapter 11, you will be shown the *correct* way to build MTS component applications based on the knowledge you will derive from this chapter. So, throughout this chapter, keep in mind the MTS-related concepts being explained, not necessarily the implementation.

Transaction Server Integration with Visual Basic 6.0

In Visual Basic, you must set a reference to Microsoft Transaction Server Type Library in the Project in order to expose the interface of MTXAS.DLL. This makes the GetObjectContext method of the COM interface IObjectContext global and available to any method in the project.

After doing so, it's a good idea to launch the Object Browser (press F2) and choose MTxAS from the drop-down list of DLLs referenced to peruse its classes' members.

Also, if you set a reference to the MtxAddIn Type Library, the Add-Ins menu pad will be populated with two additional options: AutoRefresh after compile of current project, and Refresh all components. These are helpful in that you won't have to go into Transaction Explorer and choose Refresh all components every time you recompile components after making changing to them.

ActiveX DLL in Visual Basic 6.0 has a new property, MTSTransactionMode, to allow you to set the transaction support level from the VB side. However, you will need Service Pack 4 of NT 4.0 for it to function properly. Setting this property in VB will automatically set the Transaction Support Level property when you install the component in MTS.

In general, it's a good idea to create and debug your components in Visual Basic *before* installing them in MTS. As long as you have a Project Reference to the MTSAX DLL, your code will run fine—unaffected by the fact that you have not created a package and installed your components as yet.

Putting It All Together

It's finally time to examine the Sales Order Process after it has been MTS-enabled. The new code will show how to make components start a transaction implicitly, how to enlist a component into an existing transaction, and how to commit or abort a transaction. Doing so will exemplify three important features of MTS:

Component Transactions. Allow you to wrap groups of method invocations into transactions, where each method has an equal vote in the success or failure of the transaction.

Resource Pooling. Allows your application to reuse a finite set of server resources, like database connections, for all users. MTS will coordinate the communication between a business object and the data source so that it is possible for there to be many more users than there are available database connections.

Object Brokering. Allows your application to reuse idle component instances even though the client has not released its reference to it. MTS is smart enough not to lose your state, or data, until you have explicitly said you don't need it anymore with SetComplete/SetAbort.

Again, the main goals of MTS components are to have no state across methods (unless absolutely necessary), to drop unused database connections immediately, and to maintain object references for a long as necessary in a single method. These rules will be strictly adhered to in the MTS-enabled Sales Order Process.

The Sales Order Process

The client application is a Visual Basic form (frmSales of NWSales.vbp). This code is called in the Click event of the Process Sale command button. After attaining a reference to the SalesOrder component of the NWProject2.DLL via DCOM, the ProcessSales-

Figure 7.6 The Sales Order Entry Visual Basic client.

Order method is passed the form's textbox values. (Note: For clarity, the code is *not* shown in its entirety.) See Figure 7.6.

```
'Remote call to MTS component on server
Dim objNewSale As NWProject2.SalesOrder
Set objNewSale = CreateObject("NWProject2.SalesOrder", "PUMA")
objNewSale.ProcessSalesOrder txtProductID, _
                             txtQuantity, _
                             txtUnitPrice, _
                             txtCustomer
```

The SalesOrder Component:
The Broker Object

ProcessSalesOrder serves as the broker, or parent, or root MTS object. It will start the transaction, call the subordinate objects, and then commit or abort the transaction. Note that it is a public function residing on the server so that it is within the scope of MTS.

```
Public Function ProcessSalesOrder(intProductID As Integer, _
intQty As Integer, curUnitPrice As Currency, strCustomer As String) _
As Boolean

On Error GoTo Err_ProcessSalesOrder    'Set Error Trap
Dim boolSuccess As Boolean             'Return value
```

Before we can process the order, we must first do a credit check on this customer. (We can't just give the stuff away!) That of course means instantiating the customer object. To do that, we *could* use the CreateObject function; however, since we want to group all of the steps necessary to process an order, we need to create a component transaction. And only objects created with CreateInstance can join a component transaction.

Thus we need to allocate memory to the necessary object variables and then get an object context for the customer object. We'll use this object context's methods to communicate with MTS. Since we set the transaction support level on the customer object to Requires a Transaction, CreateInstance will begin a new transaction because one has not already been launched.

```
Dim objCustomer As Customer

Dim objContext As ObjectContext
Set objContext = GetObjectContext()
Set objCustomer = objContext.CreateInstance("NWProject2.Customer")
```

Once instantiated, we can perform the customer credit check using the parameters passed from the Sales Order Entry form.

```
    boolSuccess = objCustomer.CheckCreditLimit _
(strCustomer, curUnitPrice * intQty)
```

If the credit check succeeded, it's okay to create the new order.

```
If boolSuccess = True Then
  'OK to create new order
        boolSuccess = CreateNewOrder(intProductID, intQty, _
curUnitPrice, strCustomer)
End If
```

If the new order was created successfully, we can return True to the calling form so that a success message can be displayed. But more important, we can now decide whether to commit this transaction. Issuing SetComplete at this point will finally commit the data updates that have been made since we first instantiated the customer object using CreateInstance. It will destroy this object's state, freeing up server resources. If something failed along the way, we just issue SetAbort and the entire transaction is rolled back.

Object Brokering

You really no longer need to worry about methods being very short and concise. If MTS needed your idle component instance, it would deactivate it on the server (maintaining the object context so as not to lose your state) and then branch off to field another request for its services. When you needed it again, it would instantly activate it—perhaps stealing it from some other idle component instance.

```
If boolSuccess = True Then
  ProcessSalesOrder = True
  objContext.SetComplete
Else
  ProcessSalesOrder = False
  objContext.SetAbort
End If
```

And if we encounter any errors, we can easily abort the transaction.

```
    Err_ProcessSalesOrder:
ProcessSalesOrder = False
objContext.SetAbort
Err.Raise Err.Number, "ProcessSalesOrder", Err.Description
```

The Customer Component:
Performing the Credit Check

The Customer component is now hosted in an MTS component transaction. Let's look at how the CheckCreditLimit function also uses an object context in order to register its vote in the overall success of the transaction.

```
Public Function CheckCreditLimit (strCustomerID As String, _
  curOrderValue As Currency) As Boolean

Dim objRecordSet As New ADODB.Recordset
Dim boolCreditWorthy As Boolean
```

Even though we don't need to use the CreateInstance function in this method, we still need to get an object context so that we can call its SetComplete or SetAbort method.

```
Dim objContext As ObjectContext
Set objContext = GetObjectContext()
```

This code does the actual credit check by querying the CreditLimit field of the Northwind database's Customer table. (In production, we probably would have used a stored procedure for this operation instead of inline SQL; that topic is discussed in Chapter 11.)

```
objRecordSet.Open _
  "Select CreditLimit From Customers " & _
  " Where CustomerID = '" & strCustomerID & "'", _
  "DSN=Northwind_SS7;UID=sa;PWD=;"

If Not objRecordSet.EOF = True Then
  If objRecordSet("CreditLimit") > curOrderValue Then
    boolCreditWorthy = True
  Else
        boolCreditWorthy = False
  End If
Else
  'Customer not found
  boolCreditWorthy = False
End If
```

Time to vote. Issuing SetComplete here will do two things: Tell MTS that this component did its job successfully, and that if we are not in a nested transaction, commit this transaction. But since we are in a nested transaction, just free the server resources for this object and register an affirmative vote. You can figure out SetAbort.

```
If boolCreditWorthy = True Then
  objContext.SetComplete
Else
  objContext.SetAbort
End If
```

While it has always been important to clean up after yourself (both at home and in programming), it becomes crucial when you deploy your objects on a shared application server. Dangling object references often result in unexpected behavior, so it's good practice to write your cleanup code immediately after creating an object in order not to forget to do it later.

```
objRecordSet.Close
Set objRecordSet = Nothing
```

The SalesOrder Component: Creating the Order

If the credit check succeeded, it's okay to call the CreateNewOrder function of the SalesOrder component. Of course, we'd like this method to be automatically enlisted in the current transaction. And it will be because it's a member of the same SalesOrder class.

```
Public Function CreateNewOrder(intProductID As Integer, _
   intQty As Integer, curUnitPrice As Currency, _
   strCustomerID As String) As Boolean

'Set error trap
On Error GoTo Err_CreateNewOrder

Dim boolSuccess As Boolean
```

Component Transactions

Again, it's time to get an object context so that a stock level check and update can be made. The Inventory class is a good example of where you would want to use the Requires a Transaction support level. The process of checking the inventory and then updating it should, of course, reside in a transaction so that some other user doesn't update the stock level *after* you queried it but *before* you've updated it.

So, if this component requires a transaction, it will be automatically enlisted in the current transaction—the desired behavior of this example. But if it were called in some other scenario, a transaction might not yet already have been started, so it would begin a new one. That makes this component very reusable.

```
'Allocate memory for context object and get object context
Dim objContext As ObjectContext
Set objContext = GetObjectContext()

'Decrement (Qty * -1) the stock level of this product in inventory
```

(continues)

(Continued)

```
Dim objInventory As Inventory
Set objInventory = objContext.CreateInstance("NWProject2.Inventory")
boolSuccess = objInventory.UpdateStockLevel(intProductID, intQty*-1)
```

The DataUtilities class component then joins the transaction. This component should run in a transaction as well because the Order ID is a document number that would typically come from a system table, so you would not want to lose a consecutive number in cases where the update failed. It isn't very exciting, so it isn't shown; it's more or less the same drill as the Update Inventory class.

The Inventory Component: Updating the Stock Level

ADO Connection and Recordset objects are used to query and update the inventory.

```
Function UpdateStockLevel(intProductID As Integer, _
  intQty As Integer) As Boolean

'Create an ADO Recordset
Dim objRecordSet As New ADODB.Recordset
Dim objConnection As New ADODB.Connection
objConnection.Open "DSN=Northwind_SS7;UID=sa;PWD=;"
```

An object context is used to enlist this component in the current transaction.

```
Dim objContext As ObjectContext
Set objContext = GetObjectContext()

'Set error trap
On Error GoTo Err_UpdateStockLevel

'Do stock availability check first
objRecordSet.Open _
  " Select UnitsInStock From Products" & _
  " Where ProductID = " & CStr(intProductID), _
  objConnection

Dim boolAvailableStock As Boolean

'If sufficient stock, update stock levels
If objRecordSet("UnitsInStock") > intQty Then
  'Decrement the stock level in the inventory table
  'intQty is already negative, so just need to add it

  Dim strSQLUpdate As String
  strSQLUpdate = "Update Products" & _
    " Set UnitsInStock = UnitsInStock + " & CStr(intQty) & _
    " Where ProductID = " & CStr(intProductID)
  objConnection.Execute strSQLUpdate
  boolAvailableStock = True
```

```
Else
  MsgBox "Insufficient stock to process this order!", _
    vbExclamation
  boolAvailableStock = False
End If
```

Again, it's time to vote on the success of this method.

```
If boolAvailableStock = True Then
   objContext.SetComplete
Else
   objContext.SetAbort
End If
```

Resource Pooling

Notice that we no longer use a global Connection object. Rather, we create and destroy one in every method in which we have a need to access the data source. MTS will get you another very quickly if you need one because it pools and caches connections. So it makes sense to drop the connection as soon as possible so that someone else can utilize it and to free up the memory allocated to it.

```
'Clean up
objRecordSet.Close
Set objRecordSet = Nothing
Set objConnection = Nothing
```

The SalesOrder Component: Saving the Order

Assuming everything was successful this far, it's finally time to insert the new order header and detail records. Again, in order to keep connections open for as short a time as possible, we open a new ADO connection in this function and use it to send the inline SQL statements to the Northwind database.

```
Dim objConnection As New ADODB.Connection
  objConnection.Open "Northwind_SS7", "sa", ""

  'Updated stock, so it's OK to create the new order header
  Dim strSQLInsert As String
  strSQLInsert = "Insert Into Orders " & _
    "(OrderID, CustomerID, EmployeeID, OrderDate, RequiredDate)" & _
    " Values " & _
    "(" & CStr(intOrderID) & ",'" & strCustomerID & _
    "',1, '" & CStr(dateTimeStamp) & "'," & _
    "'" & CStr(dateTimeStamp) & "')"

  objConnection.Execute strSQLInsert

  ' Now create the order detail record
  strSQLInsert = "Insert Into [Order Details] " & _
```

(continues)

(Continued)

```
    "(OrderID, ProductID, UnitPrice, " & _
    "Quantity, Discount)" & _
    " Values " & _
    "(" & CStr(intOrderID) & "," & _
    CStr(intProductID) & _
    "," & CStr(curUnitPrice) & "," & _
    CStr(intQty) & "," & _
    "0)"
    objConnection.Execute strSQLInsert

    'Free connection resources
    objConnection.Close

  If boolSuccess = True Then
    objContext.SetComplete
  Else
    objContext.SetAbort
  End If

CreateNewOrder = boolSuccess

End Function
```

Transaction Monitoring and Administration

When working with MTS, the Transaction Server Explorer window is the only user interface. But a lot of functionality is built into this hierarchical tree view of computers, packages, components, roles, and other goodies. If you have used the Microsoft Management Console (MMC) or any of the other snap-ins to the MMC (like SQL Server 7 Enterprise Manager or the IIS Internet Service Manager), you'll feel right at home with Transaction Server Explorer.

As a developer, however, you probably won't spend a ton of time using the interface because you can develop and test MTS components in tools like Visual Basic *without even installing them* into the Transaction Explorer. This is really only necessary to create a package and install components into it when you're satisfied that the code is bug-free (if there is such a thing) and is ready to be deployed. This will most likely occur on build day.

You can navigate the Explorer very quickly because of its intuitive and familiar interface, so expect this learning curve to be short. Your business object administrator (who might also be the DBA since DBAs are running out of things to do in the new SQL Server) will be the person who takes your brilliantly developed-with-MTS-rules-in-mind DLLs and:

- Builds packages, installs components, and sets their respective properties.
- Creates user-defined roles and assigns NT users or groups of users to them.
- Monitors the success/failure and response time of component transactions.

Packages

To run under MTS, all components must first be installed into a package. A package is nothing more than a set of functionally related components. For instance, the components created in this chapter to create a sales order all have a logical relationship with each other, so it makes sense to group them together. You create packages with the Transaction Server Explorer, then add components and roles, and finally, set their properties. MTS supports packages with two different types of activation: library and server.

Library Package. A Library package runs in the process of the client that creates it. Library packages do not support many of the benefits for which you are using MTS in the first place: component tracking, role checking, or process isolation. The Utilities package that ships with MTS is a Library package. For performance reasons, its components will run in the creator's process because security and component tracking are unnecessary. Choosing this option, though, would put the creator object as risk if this component were to crash.

Server Package. For the most part, you will be creating Server packages—the default (see Figure 7.7). A Server package runs in its own process on the computer in which it was installed. This is akin to the concept of a VB executable (which runs out-of-process) except that with MTS, server packages must be ActiveX DLLs. Server packages support role-based security, resource sharing, process isolation, and process management—essentially the feature set you expect from MTS.

This property can be set in the Transaction Explorer by right-clicking on the Northwind Package, choosing Properties from the Shortcut menu, and selecting a package activation type from the Activation tab.

Benefits of Packages

Creating packages is a simple process; it takes only seconds. However, to achieve the most from MTS, you will need to spend some time designing what your packages will

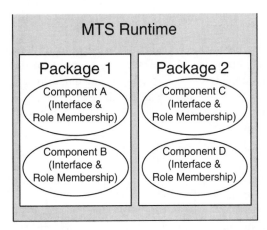

Figure 7.7 Packages consist of MTS components.
Components contain interfaces and role memberships.

look like before actually building them. This process is similar to designing your class libraries in the OOP world. In terms of developer time, it's much "cheaper" to thoroughly analyze which packages your components belong to *before you've built the components*, so that they can be written by the developer with performance (logically grouping related components) and security (MTS user roles) in mind.

By defining a package, you will be rewarded with the following benefits:

Performance. All components within an MTS package execute in the same server process. So, for example, if every time you create a new order you need to do a credit check, it makes sense to put those components in a position to run most efficiently. Adding them to the same package will provide the desired performance gains.

Security. User-defined security is established at the package level. Developers can write components with business logic, not database schema, in mind. For example, a user role called Order Entry Clerk could be configured to have access rights to a sales order-related package, even though a DBA might not normally give any of the Order Entry personnel access to the Customer table. Security will be explored in more detail later.

Deployment. There's an Export Package Wizard that can be used to create a PAK file with information about all of the components and their property settings. The PAK file can be easily created on a development machine and then just as easily imported on the production machine using the Import Wizard.

Building a Package

Okay, enough gibberish. Let's create an MTS package and add the components of the NWProject2.DLL.

The first thing you need to do is to click on Packages Installed in Transaction Server Explorer. Then right-click and choose New to add a new package. Doing so will launch the Package Wizard where you are given two options: Install prebuilt packages or Create an empty package. Choose the button to create an empty package; later I'll show you how to export a package for subsequent import. (Installing a prebuilt package is the same as importing a PAK file.)

You will then be prompted for a name for the package. Call yours Northwind Traders. When you choose Next, you'll be requested to select the NT security account for the package to run under. You can use the default, interactive user, or you can click Browse to choose an NT user or group. For now, leave the default as is; it will be covered again in the section on security. Click Finish, and you should see the new package in the right pane of Transaction Server Explorer (Figure 7.8).

Server Process Shutdown Property

Now that you have a new package, there are a few properties that you should be aware of. Right-click on the Northwind Traders package and choose Properties. Click on the Advanced tab to examine the Server Process Shutdown property. This gives you the option to leave the server running while no one is accessing it or force it to time out

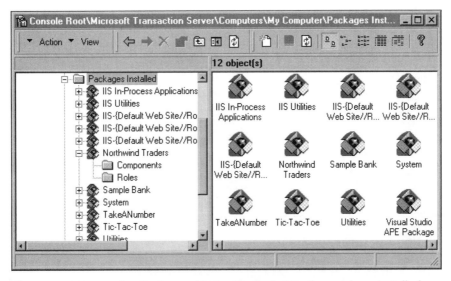

Figure 7.8 Transaction Explorer with the Northwind Traders package installed.

after a specified period of inactivity. The default, Shut Down after being idle for three minutes, is fine for our test but could be changed to another value (up to 1,440 minutes, or one day), depending on your configuration and needs.

While we're on this subject, note that it's good practice to shut down any server processes that are running *before* attempting to add or remove components or delete an entire package. You can do so either at the package level or at the computer level by right-clicking on the appropriate package or computer icon and choosing Shut Down.

Remember that MTS wants to deactivate your component as soon as possible to free resources on the application server. This setting allows you to tell MTS how long it should let the server process run idle before shutting it down.

 A server process is considered idle after its creator has explicitly or implicitly called SetComplete or SetAbort. This can occur even if the object reference of the calling client has not yet been destroyed.

Permissions Property

It is here that you can also set permissions for the editing of this package. For instance, to prevent an accidental deletion of this package, you can choose Disable Deletion. Likewise, you can choose to disable changes to prevent other developers from accidentally changing your well-thought-out settings. Of course, they can just deselect these permission settings and have free rein over the other properties, so you would have to handle that level of security through Windows NT.

 These permissions have nothing to do with user privileges. They are administrative settings for your internal use.

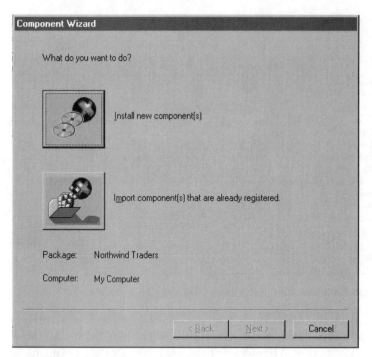

Figure 7.9 The Component Wizard guides you through the Northwind Traders component installation.

Installing Components

As already stated, a component (in the COM world) is nothing more than a COM object or a group of COM objects that can be instantiated. The SalesOrder, Customer, Inventory, and DataUtilities sample classes that were created in Visual Basic are the components that will be added to the Northwind Traders package. Once that's done, the registry entry for these components will change so that they can be routed through MTS. MTS will then manage that component for its lifetime. You add components to packages by performing the following steps:

1. In the left-hand pane of Transaction Explorer, right-click on the Component folder under the Northwind Traders package and choose New.

2. In the Component Wizard (see Figure 7.9), choose Install New Component(s) and press the Add Files button. Navigate to the location of the NWProject.DLL and choose Open. You should now see the NWProject.DLL in the Files to Install window and its classes in the Components Found window (see Figure 7.10).

3. Choose Finish to add the components to the Northwind Traders package (see Figure 7.11). Of course, you can add multiple DLLs if you wish; MTS will install them into the same package. This can be done either all at the same time or consecutively.

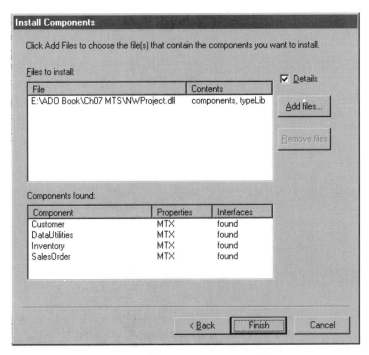

Figure 7.10   The Install Components dialog after adding the DLL; NWProject displays its components.

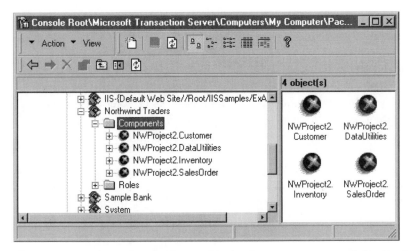

Figure 7.11   Transaction Explorer with the four components of the Northwind Traders package installed.

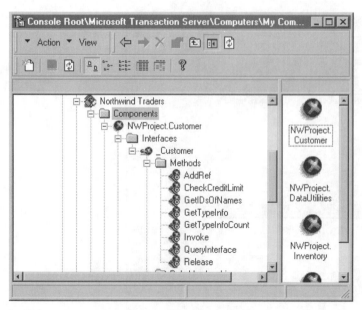

Figure 7.12 The Customer component exposes an interface with the user-defined method, CheckCreditLimit(), as well as the IUnknown and IDispatch methods, which are requirements of COM.

 Because Visual FoxPro type libraries have a slightly different structure from other libraries, after you choose a DLL to install, if there are no classes displayed in the Components Found pane, you will need to add the library type (in addition to the DLL) to the Files to Install.

 For drag-and-drop lovers, there's another way to install components: Shut down all servers in the package, delete the components you've just installed, open the Windows Explorer, and navigate to the NWProject.DLL. Next, click on the Components folder on the Transaction Explorer tree control. Finally, if you drag the NWProject2.DLL from Windows Explorer to the right pane of the Transaction Explorer, the components will install themselves without the wizard. This might not be any faster, but it sure is more fun!

If you expand the branches of the hierarchical tree control beginning from the Customer component, you will see the members of its interface. Some of them are user-defined, like the CheckCreditLimit method, while others are requirements of all COM objects, like the AddRef and GetTypeInfo methods (see Figure 7.12).

Component Properties

Aside from security and general descriptions, there is really only one property to set at the component level: Transaction Support. After you have installed your components, you must tell MTS which transactional level each of your components will support. This is, without a doubt, the most important property setting in MTS. It tells MTS what to do when this component is activated, such as whether or not to start a new transaction. To set this property, right-click on the Customer component and choose Properties.

The Transaction tab shows these four transaction-level support options:

Requires a Transaction. Tells MTS that the component should always run under a transaction but that it should not necessarily *start* one. If the calling object that instantiated this component already started a transaction, this component will run *within the context* of that transaction. If no transaction was under way when this component was instanced, a *new* transaction will begin.

Requires a New Transaction. MTS will begin a new transaction when this component is created, even if the calling component has already started one. You choose this level of support when you do not want the success or failure of a child component to affect the success or failure of the calling transaction.

Supports Transactions. MTS will run this component under a transaction only if its creator has already started one. If no transaction is under way, this component will run without one.

Does Not Support Transactions. MTS will not run this component within a transaction. You might use this if you're using this component for a purpose that's not at all related to the function of other components.

Choosing the Right Transaction Support Level

The most obvious question right now is, "Well, which setting do I use and why?" There's no one right answer here; it really depends on your design. Essentially, there are two design choices, which I'll term Broker Object Design and Independent Object Design:

Broker Object Design. With this architecture, one object will always serve as the Broker in every transaction. The Broker is at the top of the calling tree and is responsible for beginning a transaction, thus its Transaction Support level should always be set at Requires a New Transaction. Since all other subordinate objects are called *from* the Broker, they can all be set at Supports Transactions, relieving them of the burden of determining whether or not to start a transaction.

Independent Object Design. If you really want to get the maximum mileage out of your components and cut down on the design time, you could set the Transaction Support level for all of your components that may participate in a transaction to Requires a Transaction. In this design, every component can be a broker or a subordinate so they can all be designed exactly the same way.

Often, a combination of both techniques is used; it really depends on your system's overall design.

Deploying Packages

After you have created and tested your components in your language of choice, installed them into MTS packages, and further tested them, you're ready to deploy them. Typically, you'll work on a development machine with MTS installed to prototype the production environment. At deployment time, you need to get your packages installed on the production server. That's a simple process with MTS Export Package Wizard.

All you need to do is right-click on the package you want to deploy and choose Export. The wizard will then ask you where you want to create the PAK file. That's it. Now all you have to do is go to the production machine and follow the same steps you did to create a new package, except this time choose Install a prebuilt package. Navigate to the PAK file you exported, click Open, and a new package will be created with all of the components and their properties set.

DCOM Configuration

Creating a PAK file via the Export Wizard also does one other thing: It creates a directory, client, beneath the directory where the PAK file was created. There you will find an executable with the same name as the PAK file. This is your DCOM configuration file. Call this EXE as part of your workstation installation to register the DLLs you installed into MTS. When your client application issues CreateObject, the registry will tell Windows that this component is not actually on the local workstation but on the server, and will be accessed via DCOM. That's a very simple DCOM configuration process.

Monitoring Transactions

The Transaction Explorer gives you three different windows of information pertaining to transactions that are managed by the MS Distributed Transaction Coordinator (MS DTC): Trace Message, Transaction Statistics, and Transaction List.

To understand the value of these windows (or views), it's important to know the lifetime of a transaction. A transaction that for some reason cannot commit will continue to remain active until it times out. The length of that period can be set in the Options tab of the computer properties. The default is 60 seconds. After that period, transactions that remain active are automatically aborted by the system. A setting of 0 will keep the transaction active indefinitely, which is helpful for debugging.

Transaction Statistics. This window (Figure 7.13) gives you a graphical snapshot of the state of every transaction that was executed under MTS since the last time the DTC was started. In it, you can see how many are currently active (have not issued a SetComplete/SetAbort), the most that have been active at one time, and how many are in doubt of succeeding.

You also can see aggregate information about the successfully committed or aborted transactions. Since SetComplete is issued four times within the sample nested transaction, the Committed total increments by four for each successful sales order created.

Transaction List. This view is for troubleshooting transactions that have not committed or aborted for a period of time, which is set in the Advanced tab on the computer level; for some reason, they remain in an Active status. Right-clicking in the right pane when Transaction List is selected will reveal a shortcut menu with options to manually Resolve Commit or Resolve Abort. After manually resolving a transaction in trouble, it is often necessary to Forget the transaction; delete a forced committed or aborted transaction from the DTC log.

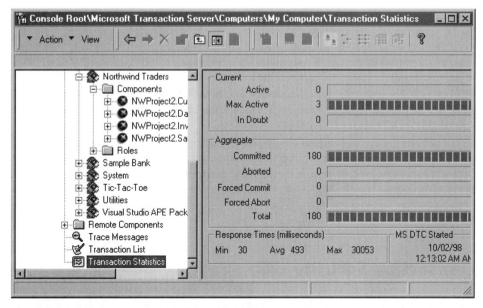

Figure 7.13 The Transaction Statistics window gives you a graphical snapshot of the state of every transaction that was executed under MTS since the last time the DTC was started.

The Transaction List also shows transactions In Doubt, where one of the coordinating DTCs is inaccessible.

Trace Messages. Similar in look and function to the Windows NT Event Viewer, the Trace Messages view (Figure 7.14) displays trace messages issued by the DTC. This enables you to track the things such as the DTC startup and shutdown, and any other issues that might affect the DTC's performance.

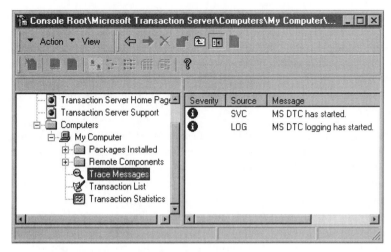

Figure 7.14 The Trace Messages view shows current DTC log activity, which is helpful for debugging unresolved transactions.

Programmatic Administration

Although beyond the scope of this book, it is important to mention that MTS administrators can use scriptable COM-based administration objects to automate MTS application deployment and administration. These objects, which can be written in Visual Basic or Microsoft C++, allow you to do things like add and remove packages and components, install remote components, set role security, and more—pretty much everything you can do with Transaction Explorer.

There's an entire scriptable hierarchy that includes the following objects: CatalogObject Object, CatalogCollection Object, PackageUtil Object, ComponentUtil Object, RemoteComponentUtil Object, and the RoleAssociationUtil Object. A catalog is an internal data store kept by MTS that contains information pertaining to packages, components, and roles. The catalog object is at the top of the hierarchy and aids in reading and setting properties at all levels.

Transaction Security

The MTS implementation of security differs from the traditional ways we have protected client/server data and objects in the past. Typically, our applications would notify the server as to the identity of the caller, and the UserID was captured from an application table or through the Widows OS. The UserID was then often mapped to valid users on the server to grant or deny access to database objects like tables, views, and stored procedures. There are two main areas of concern with this implementation of security.

Administration. As employees come and go, user maintenance can be an administrative nightmare. Each personnel change (termination, resignation, promotion, demotion, or other change in duties) causes an ensuing action by a database administrator. In a large company, just managing attrition can be a full-time position.

Programming. Developers hate security. They just want to write code that solves the specified business problem and be done with it. But usually developers are forced to write code with specific users, groups, and database objects in mind because the DBA typically restricts access to a personnel-related table by someone in Sales Order Data Entry, for example. This severely hamstrings a developer because he or she has to constantly keep in mind which tables he or she is accessing as he or she codes.

MTS, on the other hand, implements two kinds of *component-based security*. As you might guess, security is established at different component levels. Users and groups are given or denied rights to access these components. By setting the security at the business object, instead of at a database object, you can write components with functional groups of people in mind rather than tables and stored procedures.

For example, a component that does a customer credit check can be used by any user or group that requires this knowledge. Hidden from the user is that encapsulated within this business object is data access code to confidential tables, to which someone in Order Entry would typically be denied.

How can someone with minimal rights have access to highly secure data? Because no matter which user (client) calls an MTS component, it is always MTS that calls the data source. If a user has rights to a component, the user will have rights to the data source no matter which tables are actually accessed. The MTS component does not take on the identity of the caller; the caller, if it has rights to the component, takes on the identity of the MTS component.

Using this model, the DBA does not have to create access rights to database objects for each user/group. The only clients are the secured MTS components. MTS implements two types of component-based security: *declarative* and *programmatic*.

Creating User-Defined Roles

Like the previously mentioned Transaction Explorer tasks, creating user-defined roles is a very simple process. Roles allow you to customize your components for a desired audience. You can use the IsCallerInRole and IsSecurityEnabled methods of IObject-Context to conditionally run component code, further extending the reach of your code. The steps to accomplish creating roles will be discussed here, but its integration with components will be covered in the following subsection on security.

Creating a user role is just a matter of right-clicking on the Roles folder beneath the Northwind Package and choosing New | Role. You are then prompted to supply a useful name, so add Human Resources, Sales Order Data Entry, and Accounting. Now you can add NT users and/or groups to each of these roles to associate a person (or group of people) to a user-defined role in the application. To do so, right-click on Users beneath the Sales Order Data Entry role and add one of more appropriate Windows NT users or groups for a Sales Order Data Entry role.

Declarative Security

In this security model, users are granted or denied access to an entire package, an entire component, or certain methods within those components. This can be done through Transaction Explorer in the Role and Role Membership folders (see Figure 7.15). You first create roles at the package level and then add Windows NT users and/or groups to each role. These roles then become available for the next level, component-level role membership. The roles are also available to be set as the role membership at the interface (a group of one or more methods) level. You've already seen how to create these roles in the Transaction Monitoring and Administration section.

Programmatic Security

For an even finer grain of security, MTS provides a way to conditionally execute code based on the caller. The IsCallerInRole method of the IObjectContext interface accepts an argument role, so that you can write code like the following:

```
boolBeanCounter = objContext.IsCallerInRole("Accounting")
If boolBeanCounter = True Then
    'Let them see financials
```

(continues)

(Continued)

```
    Else
        'Deny them access to this information
End If
```

However, this technique will not give you the desired behavior if you have a nested transaction. What if you need to know the *original* caller? The Security property of the IObjectContext interface returns a reference to the SecurityProperty class of the MTXAS.DLL. You can use a combination of the following four methods that it exposes to determine exactly who it was that started the ball rolling:

GetDirectCallerName. Determines the name of the user who called the currently executing method.

GetDirectCreatorName. Determines the name of the user who called this method from another process.

GetOriginalCallerName. Determines the name of the user who originated the sequence of calls from which the call into the current object originated.

GetOriginalCreatorName. Determines the name of the user who initiated the activity in which the current object is executing.

By default, security is enabled for all Server packages. However, if you are either executing a component in a Library package or have deselected the option to Enable Authorization Checking at the package or component level, you might want to utilize the other security-related object context method, IsSecurityEnabled.

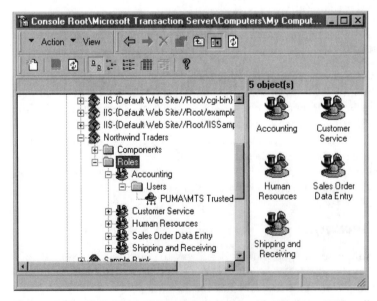

Figure 7.15 Transaction Explorer integrates with Windows NT by allowing you to add NT users and groups to MTS user-defined roles.

```
If IsSecurityEnabled = True Then
  boolBeanCounter = objContext.IsCallerInRole("Accounting")
  If boolBeanCounter = True Then
            'Let them see financials
        ShowFinancials
      Else
        'Deny them access to this information
  End If
Else
      'Let them see financials
        ShowFinancials
End If
```

From Here

At this point in your journey to building distributed client/server applications, you're already familiar with how to use ADO and MTS. That's a good start, but there's another tool that you should have in your toolbox: Microsoft Message Queue Server. This product is much more than just fancy e-mail; it's a way to integrate your ADO and MTS knowledge to create highly scalable applications. Where MTS solves concurrency issues, MSMQ takes the exact opposite approach by providing a solution for situations when not all data updates need to be immediate, transacted, and real-time. In Chapter 8, we'll examine some scenarios where guaranteed, eventual delivery of data actually makes more sense, along with the services MSMQ provides.

Microsoft Message Queue Server

Chapter 7 presented an overview of Microsoft Message Queue Server (MSMQ), where we introduced the technology of message queuing. The topics covered were: the assumptions that typical online applications make, the core functionality of a message queuing system and how it compares to e-mail, the need for this technology in business, and the benefits it brings to today's networked systems. We then examined the feature set of Microsoft Message Queue Server, how its integration with MTS and use of ActiveX technology set it apart from its competition, and the topology of an MSMQ Enterprise.

What You'll Learn

With that knowledge under your belt, it's time to learn how to work with MSMQ from both a developer and an administrator standpoint. First, some common business scenarios will be presented to illustrate where typical online systems fall short of providing a complete enterprise solution. Next, we'll get you up and running with MSMQ and use the MSMQ Explorer to create queues and send sample messages to test your installation. MSMQ ships with a few sample applications, one of which, the API Test, will be used to demonstrate the steps you would take to create, open, and set the appropriate properties for queues, as well as to send and receive messages from them.

At that point, you will have a conceptual picture of how message queuing works and how using MSMQ can enhance your applications. You'll then be introduced to the MSMQ ActiveX object model to learn how to interact with MSMQ through development languages like Visual Basic. Though you can also program MSMQ through its C API, the COM interface offers a simplified programming model and opens the door for applications that cannot access an API, like Active Server Pages. The performance penalties for programming MSMQ through COM (versus the API) are negligible—especially if your components are hosted under MTS.

Finally, we put all of your newfound knowledge into practice by creating a sample application. The salesperson on the roaming laptop (a nomad if there ever was one) will be the focus of this discussion. You'll learn how to write an MSMQ-enabled application that will work the same whether the user is at the home office connected to the network or on a plane to Topeka, Kansas, to land the big widget deal. To be realistic, this app would not work *exactly* the same in both locations; with no access to the network, there would be no way to query the database for validations or lookups. But in terms of entering batches of orders, a salesperson could populate an order entry screen, save it without failure, and continue to enter additional orders. The orders would be stored in a local queue and automatically sent to the server upon connection to the network. At that point they could be validated and either committed or aborted. The server—via return messages—could acknowledge failed messages.

You'll also learn how the ADO Recordset can be an integral part of your MSMQ-enabled application. Since MSMQ messages can contain binary attachments, an ADO Recordset object can be appended to an MSMQ message and sent over the wire just as any other message. That opens up a world of opportunity if both sides of the wire know how to work with ADO. In fact, it would actually eliminate the need to format data into text files, send them as the body of a message, and then parse them out again on the receiving side to create SQL Insert statements.

As if that weren't enough, the entire process of sending a message with an ADO Recordset, inserting it into the database on the receiving side, and getting an acknowledgment of its success or failure can all be *transacted* through the integration of MTS with MSMQ. Very exciting stuff, indeed. So, let's get to it.

A Quick Review

Before moving on to the business scenarios, here's a quick review of the MSMQ basic concepts. (Refer to Chapter 7 for a more detailed discussion.) Patterned after the success of IBM's MQ Series on the mainframe level, MSMQ is Microsoft's attempt to bring message queuing to the PC client/server arena. Message queuing is a process whereby communication between two systems can be guaranteed, asynchronous, loosely coupled, and language-agnostic. The concept is similar to e-mail in that messages are sent to temporary holding places called queues before being routed to the addressee when requested. But message queuing, specifically MSMQ, can do much, much more.

MSMQ applications communicate with one another through messages, which are defined as units of information or data. Every message contains information about the sender and receiver, as well as its textual or binary content. The fact that MSMQ messages can pass binary content allows you to attach, among other things, ADO Recordset objects. This provides you with an excellent structure for passing data from system to system, as opposed to passing text files, strings, and arrays.

Other than passing ADO Recordsets, the fact that MSMQ is fully COM-aware (exposing 10 objects in its own ActiveX object model) and can run as a Windows NT service means that MSMQ integrates quite easily into your Microsoft tool-based, distributed client/server application. It also means that all of the Visual Studio tools can be used to develop MSMQ-based solutions. ASP-based Web applications and MTS transactions can also be seamlessly integrated. As mentioned in Chapter 7, MSMQ is not glorified e-mail; it has some very powerful benefits.

The MSMQ Enterprise

An MSMQ application is composed of a number of computers that can, in some way, communicate with one another—sometimes referred to a connected network (CN). When you define a CN, you are simply defining a label. When you install an MSMQ server, you associate each network address on the computer with the appropriate CNs. These CNs form logical groupings of computers that can communicate directly.

This collection of computers, connected networks, sites, site links, and systems that intend to participate in message queuing is known as the MSMQ Enterprise. At the pinnacle of the MSMQ Enterprise is a server called the primary enterprise controller (PEC). Normally, you would only have one PEC in an organization.

The PEC supplies information that's contained in a distributed database called the MSMQ Information Store (MQIS) to each computer in the enterprise. The MQIS is *not* used to store messages. Only queue and routing information, as well as the certification keys used in authenticating messages are published by the MQIS. The contents of the queues (the messages themselves) reside in memory-mapped files on MSMQ-independent clients and servers.

Under Windows NT 4, MSMQ requires that the MQ Information Store be a SQL Server database. In NT 5, this will not be necessary as this data will be stored in the Windows Active Directory Service.

Sites and Controllers

When you install MSMQ, you will be asked to provide the name and location of the machine that will serve as the Primary Enterprise Controller. Once that has been done, you can add one or more *sites* to the enterprise. A site is exactly what you'd expect it to be: the location of another system with which you would like to communicate.

Sites are typically defined by physical boundaries like offices and can have their own network, or multiple networks. However, one machine normally serves as the primary site controller (PSC). A PSC is similar to a PEC, but it contains queue and routing information specific to that site. In fact, the PEC is actually a PSC as well because it not only maintains information pertinent to the entire enterprise, but also information specific to the primary site.

In addition to a PSC, it's a good idea for a site to have one or more backup site controllers (BSC) installed to provide load balancing and failure recovery should the PSC or PEC fail. The BSC holds a read-only copy of the Primary Site Controller or Primary Enterprise Controller's MQIS database. It also functions as an MSMQ routing server, as Primary Site Controller's do. In addition to the PEC, both the PSC and the BSC get their site data from the MQ Information Store (which is currently stored in a SQL Server database).

Sites can also contain one or more MSMQ routing servers. These contain no site information and are used to dynamically route messages between queues. They are especially useful when networks based on disparate protocols need to communicate with one another. This can occur within a single site or across sites. Sites are connected to one another with communication links called site links. Once these links are made via the MSMQ Explorer, a user-defined *site link cost* can be set to help the routing server choose the least expensive interlink path.

Messages and Queues

Like e-mail, messages are stored in either local or server queues, depending on server availability. They reside in local queues until a client is connected to an MSMQ server. Once messages have been sent to the server, they can reside in either a public or private queue.

Public queues are replicated throughout the enterprise by publishing in the MQIS and can therefore be located by any client or server within the enterprise. Private queues, on the other hand, are not published in the MQIS, and therefore do not add to the MQIS replication load.

Messages can be stored in one of two ways: memory-based or disk-based. Memory-based, also known as express, offers better performance but does not provide an audit trail of activity. Disk-based, also known as recoverable, are most often used in production because messages will not be lost in case of computer failure. For this reason, and the fact that communication within sites is normally very efficient due to 10MB–100MB Ethernet network lines, the performance hit can be tolerated in most situations.

Independent and Dependent Clients

Once the site servers are established, client workstations can be added to the MSMQ Enterprise. Clients fall into two categories: independent and dependent.

An independent client can send and receive messages to private or public network queues, as well as create and modify local queues. And this can all be done *without* the need for synchronous communication with an MSMQ server—a tremendous advantage for the roaming salesperson. However, a primary site controller must be available at installation time so that the client can gather information from the MQIS and use it to package the message with the appropriate site data.

The primary differences between MSMQ-independent clients and MSMQ servers are that independent clients do not have the intermediate store-and-forward capability of MSMQ servers, nor do they store information from the distributed MSMQ database.

Dependent clients, on the other hand, cannot store information locally. They utilize DCOM to communicate with the Site Controller and utilize the server's functions to store all messages on queues. In other words, dependent clients can only send and receive messages synchronously; a connection to the server must be established before a message can be sent or received. MSMQ servers can support up to 15 dependent clients.

As you might expect, the independent client is most often used so that the connectionless communication functionality we're looking to add to our distributed applications can be realized. This connection to the server can be made via the typical IP or IPX protocols, or through RAS to support remote clients.

Okay, that's the recap. What follows are a couple of business scenarios that should get you thinking about where you might best utilize message queuing software.

Business Scenarios

We are all creatures of habit; that's human nature. Consequently, we don't always know about all the tools available to accomplish a task because we already know how to do so in another, more familiar way. Take someone—let's call him Drew—who has been running a small advertising firm for the past 30 years without the aid of computers. Manual systems may have sufficed for so long that even the *thought* of automating sends cold shivers down Drew's spine.

Drew's a smart guy, but like most people he's reluctant to change his ways when he knows what he currently does works. Even the inefficiency of manually recording every lead, every campaign strategy, all of the customer profiles, and the tedious tasks of billing, payroll, and posting don't induce Drew to enter a new realm. How do we liken this to message queuing?

It's safe to say that more people would utilize message queuing if they understood the technology. Perhaps that's unfair to the mainframe proponents because many of them have for years been using products like IBM's MQ Series. Maybe it's safer to say that the technology has come so far at the PC level and now integrates so seamlessly with existing tools, that it would be almost inexcusable not to research this technology and see if it has a place in your business.

Where can you use message queuing? If you've ever been involved in a scenario where, as part of an application, a message or file had to get from System A to System B, message queuing could have helped. The key in the last statement is *"as part of an application."* There are less sophisticated technologies, like MAPI, RPC, FTP scripts, and the like, that can handle the simple task of transferring messages or files. But MSMQ can *integrate* into a distributed client/server application and provide not only connectionless messaging, but also guaranteed delivery, network traffic prioritization, transaction support, smart routing, security, and disparate system integration. Thus, you receive the benefits of the store-and-forward architecture of today's mail servers with the COM-aware feature set of MSMQ.

To take this point further, if an existing application were written using a true, multi-tier, OOP model, MSMQ might be able to be integrated without harming any of the previously written business objects. You'll see an example of this as the Sales Order Process is enhanced to add message queuing capabilities.

Let's examine a couple of business scenarios in which message queuing technology could be implemented. Perhaps it will get your mental wheels spinning as to how best to apply MSMQ in your world.

ATM Machine Scenario

Have you ever been in the situation where finding an ATM machine is akin to discovering the Holy Grail? And isn't it frustrating when, after you finally find one and approach the machine, the screen reads, "Sorry, cash withdrawals not available at this time"? As

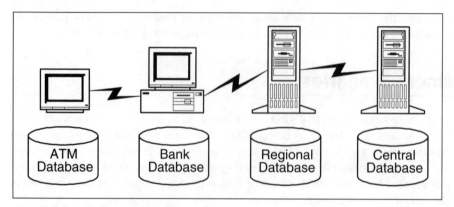

Figure 8.1 The typical ATM banking system architecture.

annoying as that can be, aside from occasionally being out of cash, ATMs are actually very reliable because of their architecture.

Typically, each bank ATM is itself a personal computer with its own database. Those databases communicate with local data centers, which may communicate with regional data centers, which may communicate with the central database at the bank's financial headquarters (see Figure 8.1). If the ATM loses communication with any of the data centers, it can continue to dispense cash, take deposits, and give account information (although not necessarily the *latest* information). The transactions (bank transactions, that is) that take place during this period will be held in a local database, or queue.

When the communication link is reestablished, the ATM will detect that and begin to send messages (the offline transactions it has been holding) from its queue to a queue at the local data center. That's *connectionless communication*; essentially, the system operates the same way whether connected or disconnected from the central database.

It is also critical for the send operation to be completed in its entirety to ensure that balances are kept intact; debits must of course always equal credits. MSMQ transactional messaging can be used to not only guarantee that messages will be delivered but delivered only once, and in the order they were placed.

Last, MSMQ security can be implemented to ensure that messages are digitally signed and encrypted to prevent unauthorized interception of and tampering with the content as they move from system to system.

Roaming Salesperson's Laptop Scenario

Think back to the Sales Order Process application in Chapter 7. The client in that situation was a Visual Basic executable that did nothing more than provide a simple form to gather enough data to process an order: Product ID, Quantity, Unit Price, and Customer ID. The Click event of the Submit button instantiated the server-side, MTS-hosted SalesOrder component, which in turn called several subcomponents to support the creation of the order. Let's see if the inclusion of MSMQ could have made this one application suitable for not just a salesperson entering orders (batch orders) on his or her laptop while on the road, but also for the data entry clerk at the home office in New York (online orders).

If we've created our distributed application correctly—as discussed in Chapter 7—the client portion, like any portion of the three-tier model, should be replaceable. Well, there certainly is very little code necessary on the client-side to process an order, so it shouldn't be too hard to tweak it in order to extend its functionality. In fact, this client could just as easily have been an HTML form (fed by an ASP) with nary a difference in code.

```
Dim objNewSale As NWProject2.SalesOrder
Set objNewSale = CreateObject("NWProject2.SalesOrder", "PUMA")
objNewSale.ProcessSalesOrder txtProductID, _
                             txtQuantity, _
                             txtUnitPrice, _
                             txtCustomer
```

The obvious problem with this code is that it instantiates a server-side component via DCOM. A traveling salesperson obviously will not have this luxury. What this client needs is a mediator class to take the data entered by the salesperson, perhaps perform minimal validation, and then store it locally to some persistent file structure. These file structures can be attached to the body of messages and sent to their destination on the server. (This extra repository is necessary so that a holding place exists for offline data entry.)

If there is no connection to the network at the time an attempt was made to send each message, it will remain in the queue until a connection is available. To the salesperson, the application appears to work the same whether online at the corporate office or offline at the motel bar enjoying a well-deserved draft beer after a successful day of booking orders. It sounds a lot like the store-and-forward behavior of e-mail, doesn't it? And by setting properties like acknowledgment flags, delivery timeout, transaction status, and so on, connectionless communication with guaranteed delivery and failure acknowledgment is a reality.

Now you don't *need* MSMQ to accomplish something as simplistic as this; you could have just taken the field contents, written them out to a delimited text file, and provided a batch upload program for when the salesperson connects to the server. But that would involve, at minimum, the following tasks:

- Coding the upload procedure for the client application and trapping for all of the complicated network-related issues.

- Coding the parsing of the data into parameters while accounting for data type conversions, apostrophes, and the like. A table-based structure would surely be easier.

- Sending an acknowledgment to the client that everything either performed correctly or somehow failed.

- Ensuring that multiple messages (like header and detail) are included in a transaction.

Using ADO, MTS, and MSMQ together can make almost all of this code (and certainly more complicated variations of it) unnecessary. All we need is a slight variation of the original VB Sales Order Entry form used in Chapter 7 and another routine on the server to preprocess the order to make our client application reusable, scalable, and fault-tolerant.

The key is ADO. You learned in the first part of the book how ADO can create not only *disconnected Recordsets* (Recordsets populated from the server that can remain intact even after disconnecting), but also *constructed Recordsets* (Recordsets created from an arbitrary structure, without the need for a connection to the server). Using an ADO-constructed Recordset, we can make the following modifications to the *client-side* of our application:

- Install an MSMQ-independent client on every salesperson's laptop. (Microsoft will love this idea!) Remember that independent clients can store messages in a local queue for subsequent synchronization to a central queue when a connection is established. A dependent client must have a constant link to the server.

- When a salesperson saves an order, take the data entered and insert it into an ADO Recordset that will be created on the fly.

- Create an MSMQ message using the COM interface that MSMQ exposes. (Here's the fun part.) Attach the ADO Recordset to the body of the message and set the other appropriate properties, like the name of the computer at the New York site.

- Attempt to send the MSMQ message to New York. MSMQ will recognize when the target queue is unavailable and leave the message in the local queue until it is back online. *No error will be reported to the user even when offline.* Remember that the application should work the same whether on- or offline.

On the server-side, MSMQ will be installed as a primary enterprise controller. The MSMQ Server will be waiting for messages from computers like the salespersons'. One additional routine on the New York office side will also have to be written. It needs to retrieve the messages from appropriate queue(s), take the ADO Recordsets attached to the body of the messages it finds, extract the order parameters, and pass them to the SalesOrderProcess class.

Remember that if the SalesOrderProcess class cannot create an order from the parameters it was passed, it will return False. We can use that information to create another MSMQ message and route it back to the salesperson, advising him or her of the failure. Of course, that message will be queued on the server if the salesperson has already logged off by the time his or her orders were processed.

That's really all there is to it. We'll be examining exactly how to do this after covering the basic concepts of working with queues, messages, and the topology of the MSMQ Enterprise.

Installing MSMQ

Microsoft Message Queue Server currently ships with both Visual Studio 9x and as part of the Windows NT 4.0 Option Pack—the same place you found Microsoft Transaction

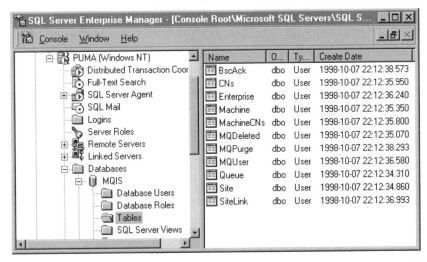

Figure 8.2 The MQ Information Store database resides on SQL Server and feeds data about the Enterprise to site controllers.

Server. If you don't have the CD, you can download it from the Microsoft Web site, www.microsoft.com/ntserver/basics/appservices/transsvcs/.

Like MTS, MSMQ will ship as an integral part of the much-anticipated Windows NT 5.0 operating system when it becomes available. In fact, MSMQ, MTS, COM, and Internet Information Server (IIS) will, together, form the foundation of NT 5.0's operating system-level services called COM+.

If you have not already installed MSMQ, it's a good time to do so now. Here are a few things you need to keep in mind before and during the installation:

- SQL Server version 6.5 or later must first be installed. This chapter, like Chapter 7 on MTS, uses the Northwind database that ships with SQL Server 7.0 for its examples. If you don't have SQL Server 7.0, you can get information on how to acquire it at www.microsoft.com/sql. If you're coming from a Visual FoxPro or Access background, you'll feel right at home with the intuitive user interface of SQL Server 7.0. It's now much simpler to do just about anything in this product.

- You may be asking, "Why do I need SQL Server at all to install MSMQ?" The current version of MSMQ Server requires the use of SQL Server because the installation creates a database called MQIS that contains queue and routing information about the MSMQ Enterprise. The primary enterprise controller, the primary site controllers, and the backup site controllers all get their site data from the Message Queue Information Store (see Figure 8.2). So be sure that SQL Server's services are running when you install MSMQ.

- You do not need multiple computers to develop and test an MSMQ-enabled application. You can prototype the creation of a PEC (which is also the PSC for the Enterprise site), a connected network, and multiple queues that can send and receive messages to and from one another—even on a single machine.

- The installation will ask you for the name of the MSMQ Enterprise. We called ours Headquarters.

- The installation will ask you for the name of the connected network, which is just a label for a group of sites. We called ours Local CN.

- The installation will ask you to name the site on the Local CN. We called this site New York.

- The installation will ask you for the size of the MQIS database and log. Since you can always change this at a later point, and we're just testing, we've made ours pretty small: 10MB for the database and 2MB for the log.

That's all of the information you need to supply to get up and running with MSMQ. When the installation is complete, launch the MSMQ Explorer, which should be an available menu item on the Windows NT 4.0 Option Pack program group, or by executing the program, C:\Program Files\MSMQ\MQXPLORE.EXE.

Testing the Installation

MSMQ provides no fewer than five ways to test that your installation is indeed running properly.

Visual Basic

We could write a simple program in Visual Basic that creates two queues and send messages among them, but we'll save that technique for later because there are faster, simpler ways.

MSMQTest.TXT

MSMQ ships with a file, MSMQTest.TXT, that contains instructions for testing computer-to-computer (or really, queue-to-queue) message sending and receiving via command-line statements. MSMQTest.C is a C program that is installed with the other samples and makes calls to the MSMQ API. This works, but it is a little cryptic in lieu of a better option.

MQPing

To test the communication link to the other computers on your network, you can use a form of Ping called MQPing. To execute MQPing, right-click on any machine and choose the MQPing option. If successful, a green arrow will appear on the computer icon.

MSMQ Explorer

The MSMQ Explorer menu has an option called Send Test Messages under the Tools menu pad (see Figure 8.3).

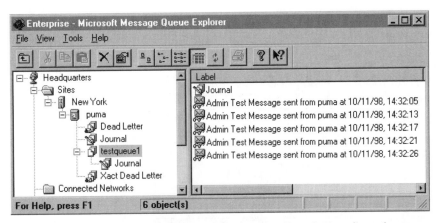

Figure 8.3 The MSMQ Explorer provides a tool to test the sending of messages to test queues. These messages have a predefined label, but no body.

  The Send Test Messages option is enabled *only* after you have selected a computer in the tree view. In our example, the PEC, PUMA, was selected to enable the Send Test Messages option.

Finally, we have found a quick and easy way to test our installation. Let's give it a try.

1. Click a computer, click Tools, and then click Send Test Message. The computer you select is the computer that will send the test message.

2. Create a new Destination Queue by clicking on New Queue, and specify the full path name for the target queue (for example, PUMA\TestQueue1).

3. Click Send; you should see the 0 Messages Sent label increment accordingly. Send a couple more messages if you'd like...have a ball!

It's very important to take note of the following points:

- After closing the Send Test Messages window, you may need to refresh the MSMQ Explorer window to see the new queue. You can do so by pressing F5, the Refresh button on the toolbar, or the Refresh option on the View menu pad.

- Even if you have already created a queue on your own, the drop-down list of Destinations will be empty in the Send Test Messages dialog because this tool only allows you to send messages to test queues that it creates.

- You can use MSMQ Explorer to create test queues or change the ID type of existing queues so you can send test messages to the queues.

- Only transactional messages can be sent to transactional queues.

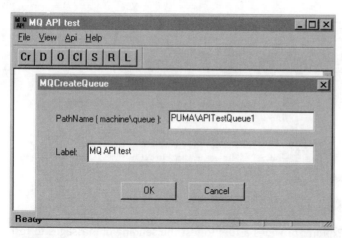

Figure 8.4   The MQCreateQueue dialog of the API Test application.

API Test Sample Application

The last way to test the sending of messages is to use the API Test sample application that ships with MSMQ. Similar to the MSMQTest program, this application provides a form and options to create, delete, locate, open, and close queues, as well as send and receive messages using the MSMQ API.

Since we'll be using COM in our application, we'll actually be insulated from direct API calls. But the API menu pad option displays the objects that the MSMQ API exposes, so we can get a general idea what the MSMQ ActiveX objects will be called.

This program, Mqapitst.exe, can be found in C:\ProgramFiles\MSMQ\sdk\samples\bin\ or under the Microsoft Message Queue program group. So for one more test, invoke the following actions from the API menu pad (or feel free to use the tool bar):

1. Choose MQCreateQueue (Figure 8.4) and create a new queue, PUMA\APITest Queue1.

2. Choose MQOpenQueue to open the APITestQueue1 queue (Figure 8.5). Set the Access privilege property to MQ_SEND_ACCESS to gain the rights to send messages to this queue.

3. Choose MQSendMessage to launch the MQSendMessage dialog (Figure 8.6). For now, just fill in the Label and Body properties as shown in the figure. The other properties will be examined in detail later. Then refresh your MSMQ Explorer tree view to see the new queue and the message inside it.

4. To receive the message, this queue must be closed and then reopened with receive access privileges. So choose MQCloseQueue to close the APITestQueue1.

5. Choose MQOpenQueue and set the Access privilege property to MQ_RECEIVE_ ACCESS on the APITestQueue1 queue to gain the rights to receive messages from this queue.

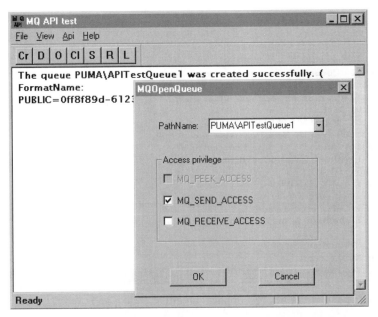

Figure 8.5 The MQOpenQueue dialog of the API Test application.

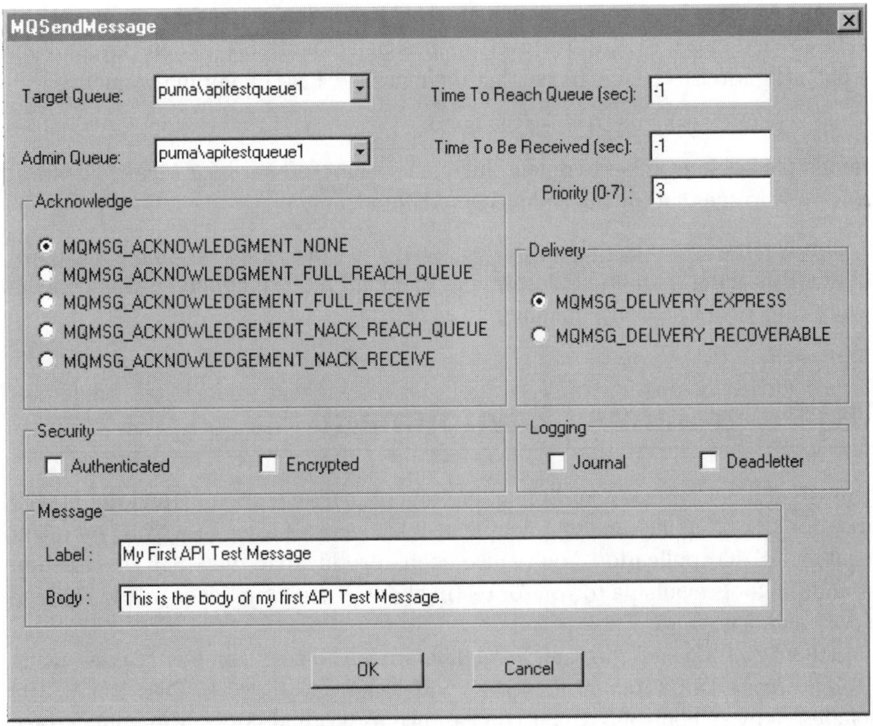

Figure 8.6 The MQSendMessage dialog of the API Test application is another valuable tool to enable you to test your MSMQ Enterprise.

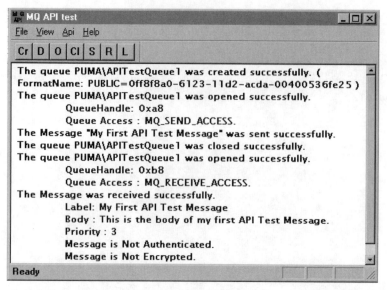

Figure 8.7 The results pane of the API Test application after sending and receiving a message.

6. Choose MQReceiveMessage to launch the MQSendMessage dialog. Accept the defaults and choose OK to receive the message (Figure 8.7). Then refresh your MSMQ Explorer tree view to see that the message is no longer in the queue.

7. Choose MQCloseQueue to close the queue

8. Choose MQDeleteQueue to delete the queue. Then refresh your MSMQ Explorer tree view to see that the queue has been deleted.

This exercise may seem trivial, but it does give you your first hands-on experience with MSMQ. If nothing else, it should provide you with a more concrete, less conceptual, idea of the flow of message queuing.

MSMQ Programming Environment

You've now had a quick review of the technology of message queuing and the MSMQ Enterprise topology, highlighted by a couple of business scenarios in which you might implement an MSMQ application. You've also been introduced to the MSMQ installation process and the tools available to you for testing how to send messages to and retrieve messages from queues.

The MSMQ API, on which the sample application was based, can be accessed using the MSMQ Software Development Kit (SDK) with languages like C or C++. But MSMQ also includes ActiveX controls, which you can use to write MSMQ-based applications with any of the development tools in Microsoft Visual Studio, including Visual Basic, Visual FoxPro, Visual J++, and Visual C++. By using COM, not only will your application development effort be reduced dramatically, but you will also gain all of the other benefits of ActiveX development, which was discussed in Chapter 6.

 The MSMQ SDK and related documentation are installed when you select Development Workstation or Development Server during setup. The use of the SDK is beyond the scope of this book.

The performance penalty imposed by the added overhead of COM is insignificant in most situations. If you haven't found this to be the case, be sure to try again with NT 5.0, as the MSMQ, MTS, IIS, and COM runtime services become one with the operating system. COM is also the only way ASP can work with MSMQ. This is due to the fact that, for security reasons, the scripting languages ASP can use (natively, VBScript, JavaScript, Perl, and others via extensions) cannot access APIs.

Besides, COM is a simple, intuitive way to develop object-oriented software. APIs, on the other hand, have been known to make your head hurt. But if you're a low-level kind of person, feel free to enjoy the API. For our purposes, the ActiveX objects will suffice.

The MSMQ Object Model

The MSMQ ActiveX object library contains 10 objects (Figure 8.8). Working with them can be a little confusing for a couple of reasons. First, as you'll see, the names of the objects so closely resemble each other that it's easy to mix them up. Second, some MSMQ objects actually create other MSMQ objects. For instance, the Open method of a MSMQQueueInfo object returns a reference to an MSMQQueue object. You then use the new queue object to interrogate a queue. This should remind you of ADO, in that objects

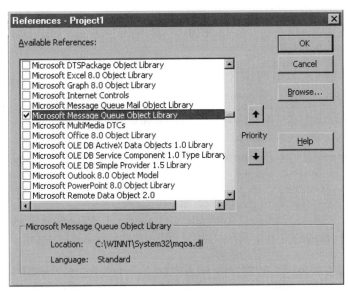

Figure 8.8 The classes of the MSMQ ActiveX object interface.

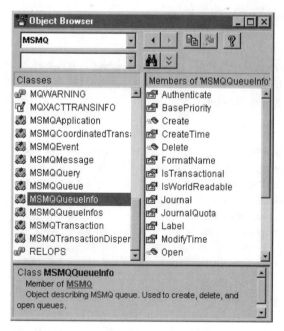

Figure 8.9   A project reference must be made to the Microsoft Message Queue Object Library (mqoa.dll) to expose its interface.

do not have to be instantiated in any particular sequence. You could create a queue through the MSMQQueue reference that MSMQQueueInfo returned or directly through the MSMQQueue object. It's a little tricky in the beginning, but it gets clear pretty quickly.

Each of the MSMQ objects will now be briefly defined and illustrated through Visual Basic examples. They will be listed in approximate order of importance and usage. To try these examples, do the following:

1. Create a new Standard EXE Project in Visual Basic.

2. Add a command button to the default form, Form1.

3. Add the project reference Microsoft Message Queue Object Library (mqoa.dll) to expose its interface (Figure 8.9).

4. Add the project reference Microsoft ActiveX Data Objects Recordset 2.0 Library (msador15.dll) to expose its interface.

5. Paste the code snippets provided to the button's Click event.

MSMQQueueInfo Object

This MSMQQueueInfo object contains methods that allow you to create a new queue, open an existing queue, update a queue's properties, delete a queue, and refresh a queue. Its member objects are either returned by a query or created by you. One of its most significant properties is PathName, without which you cannot create a queue. You normally use this object on queues that have not already been opened. Once open, the MSMQQueue object is typically used to set properties and close or read messages in a queue.

Create Method

To create a queue, you must first instantiate an MSMQQueueInfo object. Based on the properties you set, the Create method will produce a queue accordingly. The Create method has two optional arguments:

```
objQueueInfo.Create ([IsTransactional][,IsWorldReadable])
```

When IsTransactional is true, it indicates that the queue is a transaction type queue. All messages sent to a transaction queue or read from a transaction queue must be done as part of a transaction. Its default is false. We'll discuss transactional queues later. When IsWorldReadable is true, anyone can read the messages in the queue and its queue journal. When false, the default, only the owner can read the messages.

PathName and Label Properties

The PathName specifies the physical location of the queue; it must be set before executing the Create method. Here's all you need to do to create a queue on the local computer:

```
Dim objQueueInfo As New MSMQQueueInfo
objQueueInfo.PathName = ".\NYSalesOrders"
objQueueInfo.Create
```

You can create a queue on a foreign computer (or be more explicit in creating a local queue) by specifying the machine name in the PathName: "PUMA\NYSalesOrders".

While we're at it, let's add a label as well, or else the default will be the queue name. The label is a string of up to 124 characters that help identify the queue. It's actually more than just a friendly name because the label can be used as a parameter to query the enterprise for queues. So, a logical naming convention can help in querying queues of a particular context. For instance, a <Site>-<Status>-<Context> convention (i.e., "New York-Pending-SalesOrders") would help in querying a site, or sites, for their salesperson's unprocessed sales orders.

You can create multiple queues at a site with the same label without consequence; only the PathName has to be unique. How you would query them will be discussed in the subsection on MSMQQuery object.

If the queue is already open, the Update method should be called so that the queue label can be refreshed. If it's not already open, the queue will have the correct label when it is opened.

```
Dim objQueueInfo As New MSMQQueueInfo
objQueueInfo.PathName = "PUMA\NYSalesOrders"
objQueueInfo.Label    = "New York-Pending-SalesOrders"
objQueueInfo.Create
```

Public and Private Queues

The queue is by default public. A public queue has its information maintained in the MQIS database on the primary enterprise controller so that it can be queried by other MSMQ applications. Private queues, on the other hand, are registered on the local computer and usually cannot be seen by other MSMQ applications. Private queues are faster to work with because they are not stored in the MQIS, but neither do they have the persistence of public queues. You might use them when you need a temporary, local data store for messages that you intend to discard or send elsewhere. You'll work most often with public queues.

A word of caution: Don't confuse local queues with private queues. Local queues are where independent clients temporarily store messages that cannot reach their destinations because of server unavailability. The messages of private queues never leave the machine on which they were created.

 By default, private queues are not displayed in the MSMQ Explorer. To see them, you can right-click on the site controller icon (PUMA, in our case) and choose Show Private Queues.

To make a private queue, all you need to do is add \PRIVATE$\ after the machine name and before the queue name. This will put the private queue information into a local directory that can be accessed via its FormatName property. We'll discuss the FormatName later, but for now just know that it is used to do things like open a queue, as shown in this code snippet:

```
Dim objQueueInfo As New MSMQQueueInfo
objQueueInfo.PathName = "PUMA\PRIVATE$\NYSalesOrders "
objQueueInfo.Label    = "New York-Pending-SalesOrders"
objQueueInfo.Create
```

FormatName Property

The FormatName property is a unique name for the queue that is generated by MSMQ when the queue is created. Format names can be either public or private. ActiveX applications can obtain the queue's format name from the MSMQQueueInfo object used to create the queue.

Public format names are used to specify queues registered in the MQIS. A queue's public format name is a string that looks like this:

```
PUBLIC=68438fb6-617a-11d2-acdb-00400536fe25
```

The long string following PUBLIC= is the queue's global unique identifier (GUID) generated by MSMQ when the queue is created.

Private format names look similar. Here's an example:

```
PRIVATE=2c1dd5e7-5e53-11d2-acd4-00400536fe25\00000020
Dim objQueueInfo As New MSMQQueueInfo
objQueueInfo.PathName = "PUMA\NYSalesOrders"
```

```
objQueueInfo.Label    = "New York-Pending-SalesOrders"
objQueueInfo.Create
MsgBox objQueueInfo.FormatName
```

A *direct format name* tells MSMQ not to use MQIS (for public queues) or the local computer (for private queues) to get routing information. When a direct format name is used, all routing information is taken from the format name, and MSMQ sends the messages to the queue in a single hop.

```
ObjQueueInfo.FormatName = _
  "DIRECT=<Protocol>:<MachineAddress>\<QueueName>"
```

This also allows you to create a queue using an IP address or an Internet URL.

```
ObjQueueInfo.FormatName = _
  "DIRECT=TCP:111.11.11.111\NYSalesOrders"
```

Update and Refresh Methods

When a queue is already open, changing the value of some of the MSQueueInfo properties is a two-stage process. After you assign a new value to the property (or properties) of an open queue, you then call the Update method to commit the change. Finally, you use the Refresh method so that other applications can see the new settings.

```
objQueueInfo.Label    = "New York-Confirmed-SalesOrders"
objQueueInfo.Update
objQueueInfo.Refresh
```

Delete Method

It's a trivial matter to delete a queue: Just execute the Delete method of the MSQueueInfo object. The good news is that MSMQ is kind of about open queues; it closes them before deleting. However, MSMQ does not warn you prior to deleting a queue with messages still to be retrieved in them, so you'll have to perform that error trapping yourself, first by looking at the queue, which will be talked about with the MSMQQuery object. Also, it may take some time for the MQIS to send this enterprise-level information to all sites. Consequently, it is possible to send a message to a deleted queue.

```
'Find queue to delete
Set objQueueInfos = objQuery.LookupQueue _
                    (Label:="PUMA\NYSalesOrders")
'Move to first record in queue set
Set objQueueInfo = objQueueInfos.Next
If Len(objQueueInfo.PathName) > 0 Then
   'Found the one to delete
   objQueueInfo.Delete
End If
```

Open Method

When you use the Open method of the MSMQQueueInfo object, it returns a reference to a MSMQQueue object. You then use the interface of the MSMQQueue object to work with the now-open queue.

```
Set objQueue = objQueueInfo.Open(Access, ShareMode)
```

The Open method accepts two required parameters: Access and ShareMode. Access determines how the calling application accesses the queue (with rights to peek, send, or receive). The following MSMQ constants are typically used for the Access level:

MQ_PEEK_ACCESS (32). Messages can only be read, not added to or removed from the queue.

MQ_SEND_ACCESS (2). Messages can only be sent to the queue.

MQ_RECEIVE_ACCESS (1). Messages can be either retrieved from the queue or peeked at.

This setting cannot be changed while the queue is open.

The ShareMode parameter can contain the following optional values (again, in MSMQ constants):

MQ_DENY_NONE (0). Specifies that the queue is available to anyone and must be used if Access is set to MQ_PEEK_ACCESS or MQ_SEND_ACCESS.

MQ_DENY_RECEIVE_SHARE (1). Restricts those who can retrieve messages from the queue during the current process. The queue would first have to be closed by the calling application before it would be available to others. If you attempt to set this when the queue is already open for retrieving messages by another process, this call fails and returns an error. This setting is applicable only when Access is set to MQ_RECEIVE_ACCESS.

This code attempts to create a queue, open it, and then test for its open status (using the IsOpen method) before informing the user of its success or failure.

```
Dim objQueueInfo As New MSMQQueueInfo
Dim objQueue As New MSMQQueue
objQueueInfo.PathName = "PUMA\NYSalesOrders "
objQueueInfo.Label    = "New York-Pending-SalesOrders"
objQueueInfo.Create
Set objQueue = objQueueInfo.Open(MQ_SEND_ACCESS, _
                                 MQ_DENY_NONE)
If objQueue.IsOpen Then
  MsgBox objQueueInfo.PathName & " is now open for business!"
Else
  MsgBox "Could not open queue " & objQueueInfo.PathName
End If
```

MSMQQueue Object

Each instance of a queue is represented by an MSMQQueue object. Picture a queue as you would a table or cursor; you can move through the messages in a queue as you would an ADO Recordset or similar structure. When a queue is open, the MSMQQueue properties refer to the message in the queue in which you are currently positioned, if there even is one.

It's important to understand the relationship between the MSMQQueueInfo and the MSMQQueue object. The MSMQQueueInfo object itself represents a queue, thus you can fully manage the queue through its interface. In other words, there is a one-to-one relationship between each MSMQQueueInfo object and the queue it represents. An MSMQQueue object represents an open instance of a queue, so there can be many MSMQQueue instances because many applications can be open instances simultaneously. So, you can say that there is a one-to-many relationship between the queue's MSMQQueueInfo object and each open instance of the queue.

Peek Methods

As stated, once you open a queue and you have a reference to an MSMQQueue object, you can interrogate the messages inside the cursorlike queue. You can do so with three related Peek methods: Peek, PeekCurrent, and PeekNext. The Peek method returns an object reference to the first message in the queue or waits for a message to arrive if the queue is empty. It does not remove the message from the queue. The syntax is as follows:

```
Set objMessage = objQueue.Peek ([ReceiveTimeout]_
    [,WantDestinationQueue][,WantBody])
```

ReceiveTimeout. Specifies how long (in milliseconds) MSMQ waits for the message to arrive. The default is INFINITE, so you will always want to change this so that your application does not wait forever when you attempt to peek into a queue. A setting of 1,000 to 2,000 milliseconds, or 1 to 2 seconds, should be more than sufficient in normal circumstances.

WantDestinationQueue. If set to true, the DestinationQueueInfo property of the MSMQMessage object is updated when the message is read from the queue. Since this incurs additional overhead, its default is false. You would only need this when peeking to learn where the outgoing message was bound for.

WantBody. The default is true because if a message has a body, typically you want to see it. But if you don't need to see the body at a particular time, it's more efficient to set this property to false.

You would then use the reference to the MSMQMessage object to examine the contents of the message itself. In this example, we use the MSMQQueueInfo and MSMSQueue objects to open a queue based on a path name. We could then synchronously peek at the first message in the open instance of the queue via the MSMSQueue object. (A discussion of asynchronous retrieval will be presented later.)

```
Dim objQueue As MSMQQueue
Dim objQueueInfo As New MSMQQueueInfo
Dim objMessage As New MSMQMessage
objQueueInfo.PathName = "PUMA\NYSalesOrders"
objQueueInfo.Label    = "New York-Pending-SalesOrders"
Set objQueue = objQueueInfo.Open(MQ_PEEK_ACCESS,MQ_DENY_NONE)
Set objMessage = oObjQueue.Peek
```

Receive, ReceiveCurrent, and Reset Methods

The Receive and ReceiveCurrent methods of the MSMQQueue object work just like the Peek and PeekCurrent methods; however, the Receive methods *remove* the messages from the queue after they have been peeked at. The syntax is as follows:

```
Set objMessage = objQueue.Receive ([pTransaction] _
    [,WantDestinationQueue] [,WantBody] [,ReceiveTimeout])
```

The only new parameter is Transaction, where you can begin to see MSMQ's tight integration with MTS. This optional parameter has three possible values:

MQ_MTS_TRANSACTION (1). Specifies that the call *is* part of the current MTS transaction. This is the default setting.

MQ_NO_TRANSACTION (0). Specifies that the call is *not* part of a transaction

MQ_XA_TRANSACTION (2). Specifies that the call is part of an externally coordinated, XA-compliant transaction.

The Reset method must be called to reposition the cursor to the beginning of the stack of messages in the queue. You would use this after one or more calls to PeekNext to restore the pointer.

You can receive or peek a message either synchronously or asynchronously. Synchronous retrieval means that after issuing objMessage.Receive, for example, all subsequent calls will be blocked until the next message is available or a timeout occurs. Unfortunately, you would have to use the MSMQ API function MQReceiveMessage to be able to read messages asynchronously. When reading messages asynchronously, the application is notified if a message is available or if a timeout has occurred. The message is then typically retrieved via a Win32 callback function.

MSMQMessage

The MSMQMessage object is used to create messages and send them to a particular queue. There are two main attributes of a message: the Label and the Body; and one main method, Send.

These is no explicit Create method of the message object; rather, you create messages by instantiating an MSMQMessage object, setting the appropriate properties and then sending it to an open destination queue. It's pretty darn simple.

```
Dim objQueue As MSMQQueue
Dim objMessage As New MSMQMessage
Dim objQueueInfo As New MSMQQueueInfo
objQueueInfo.PathName = "PUMA\NYSalesOrders"

Set objQueue = objQueueInfo.Open(MQ_SEND_ACCESS, _
                                 MQ_DENY_NONE)
objMessage.Body = "Test Message Body"
```

Send Method

Messages are sent asynchronously in MSMQ. After you open a queue, you can send as many messages as you like without having to wait for an acknowledgment.

The Send method has two parameters: a reference to the destination queue, as specified by the MSMQQueue object, and whether the message will participate in an MTS transaction. The constants are the same as for the Receive method, with one addition: MQ_SINGLE_MESSAGE. This setting specifies that you want to send a single message as a transaction.

```
objMessage.Send (DestinationQueue, [pTransaction])
```

That destination queue parameter has all of the necessary site, queue, and access information wrapped up into a tight little ball, thanks to the object returned from the Open method of the MSMQQueueInfo object.

```
objMessage.Send objQueue
```

You can also use the Handle property of the MSMQQueue object as the Destination-Queue parameter. You obtain it from the queue once it has been opened. Perhaps it is already held in a variable from earlier in the program.

```
longHandle = objQueue.Handle
.
.  'More code here
.
objQueue.Send longHandle
```

Label, Body, and BodyLength Properties

A label is a string of up to 250 characters that helps to identify the message. It's actually more than just a friendly name, though, because the label can be used as a parameter to query the contents of a queue or queues, so a logical naming convention can help in retrieving messages of a particular context. The same goes for a queue label.

```
objMessage.Label = "Test Message Label"
```

The body of an MSMQ message can be a string, an array of bytes, or any numeric, date, and currency type that a variant can contain. It also can contain any persistent ActiveX object that supports IDispatch and IPersist (IPersistStream or IPersistStorage). Excel and Word documents are good examples of these.

The ADO Recordset object *does not* support IPersist, so at first glance it does not look like attaching an ADO Recordset to the body is possible. However, if you create a reference to Microsoft Remote Data Services Server, you will be able to create an advanced type of data rowset using the DataFactory class of the RDSServer object.

Typically, you would use a function like TypeOf within a Case or If...Then...Else structure to determine the data type of the body so that your program can deal with whatever the sender has populated it with. This will be demonstrated later in a discussion about how to attach a Recordset to messages.

The BodyLength property is a read-only property of the MSMQMessage object that indicates (in bytes) the size of the message body. It can be used by the receiving application to determine how big the message is before actually pulling it across the wire. Likewise, sending applications can read the BodyLength *after* the Body property has been set to determine if it is an acceptable size to send. The maximum length of a body is 4MB.

Delivery-Related Message Properties

The Delivery property enables you to set whether messages are to be physically stored on the disks of the machines in which the message passes through on the way to its destination queue, or just reside in memory. As discussed earlier, memory-based messages are called express, while their more secure counterparts are called recoverable. Express messages are of course faster, but cannot be recovered in the event of a power failure or other abnormal machine shutdown.

MSMQ can only guarantee the delivery of recoverable messages. So even though the default setting is MQMSG_DELIVERY_EXPRESS, for the most part, you'll want to use MQMSG_DELIVERY_RECOVERABLE in your applications.

```
objMessage.Delivery = MQMSG_DELIVERY_RECOVERABLE
```

The MaxTimeToReachQueue and MaxTimeToReceive properties can be set to force a message to end its quest for a queue. They both default to an indefinite trek across the wire, so if you'd like to change that behavior, you can specify it in seconds. If a message does time out before it reaches its destination, it will end up in the DeadLetter queue of the machine where time expired.

```
objMessage.MaxTimeToReachQueue = INFINITE 'default
objMessage.MaxTimeToReceive = INFINITE    'default
```

A message's Priority tells MSMQ what to do with messages both while en route and when they are to be placed in a queue. Obviously, higher-priority messages are moved to the top of the stack during routing and placed at the top of the queue, regardless of what order they entered the queue. Messages with the same priority are placed in the queue according to their arrival time.

```
objMessage.Priority = 3 ' 3(default),0(lowest),7(highest)
```

The last message property this section covers is Ack. This property tells MSMQ whether and how to inform the sender as to the success or failure of the delivery of the message. The following five constants are used to indicate the desired behavior:

MSMSQ_ACKNOWLEDGMENT (0). No message should be returned to the sender. This is the default.

MSMSQ_ACKNOWLEDGMENT_FULL_REACH_QUEUE (5). Whether a message reaches its destination or not, an acknowledgment of success or failure will be sent to the sender.

MSMSQ_ACKNOWLEDGMENT_NACK_REACH_QUEUE (4). Only if the message fails to reach its destination will an acknowledgment be sent back to the sender.

MSMSQ_ACKNOWLEDGMENT_FULL_RECEIVE (14). Depending on whether a message times out or expires before it is received by the destination queue, a positive or negative acknowledgment will be sent back to the sender.

MSMSQ_ACKNOWLEDGMENT_NACK_RECEIVE (12). If a message times out or expires before it is received by the destination queue, a negative acknowledgment will be sent back to the sender. No acknowledgment is sent if the message reaches its destination queue.

Class Property

MSMQ automatically sets the Class property to indicate the type of message it is. A message can be a normal MSMQ message, a positive or negative (arrival and read) acknowledgment message, or a report message. After you send a message, you can determine if it has reached its queue by checking its class, rather than having to peek for it.

```
objMessage.Send objQueue
If objMessage.Class = MQMSG_CLASS_ACK_REACH_QUEUE Then
  MsgBox "The message reached the queue."
Else
  MsgBox "The message did not reach the queue."
End If
```

MSMQQuery

The MSQuery object is at the top of the MSMQ object hierarchy because it can query the entire MSMQ Enterprise, take the resultant set of queues, and store it in an object structure. Its one and only member, the LookupQueue method, is used to return this collection of queues. Once the results are returned, you then traverse the MSMQQueueInfos object to work with the queues. MSMQQueueInfos will be defined next.

LookupQueue

The LookupQueue method has several parameters, all optional, that help you to narrow the scope of your search for queues.

```
objQuery.LookupQueue(  [QueueGuid]
[, ServiceTypeGuid]
[, Label]
[, CreateTime]
[, ModifyTime]
[, RelServiceType]
[, RelLabel]
[, RelCreateTime]
[, RelModifyTime])
```

We'll first take a look at a couple of the fastest ways: Label and QueueGuid. They are the fastest ways to find queues because the Queue table of the MQIS database is indexed on those fields.

Label. Can be used to help find queues that are exactly or similarly named.

```
'Use the queue label as search criteria
Set objQueueInfos = _
objQuery.LookupQueue _
(Label:= "New York-Pending-SalesOrders")
```

Relationship Parameters. If you're not looking for an exact match, or have a compound condition you'd like to apply to the query, you can use the combination of relationship parameters with comparison operators to create a more complex query string.

The relationship parameters. RelServiceType, RelLabel, RelCreateTime, and RelModifyTime provide simple Boolean comparison operators that can be used in conjunction with their respective lookup parameter. These comparison operators include:

CONSTANT	MEANING
REL_EQ	equal to
REL_NEQ	not equal to
REL_LT	less than
REL_GT	greater than
REL_LE	less than or equal to
REL_GE	greater than or equal to
REL_NOP	ignore lookup parameter

To find all of the queues at the New York site, for example, you could have used this query, which will return all queues with a label that begins with the string "New York".

```
Set objQueueInfos = _
objQuery.LookupQueue _
(Label:= "New York", RelLabel:=REL_GE)
```

QueueGUID. When a queue is created, a global unique identifier (GUID) is assigned to it. If you examine the properties of any queue, on the General tab you'll see an ID under the PathName that looks something like this: {672C9804-6223-11D2-ACDE-00400536FE25}. GUIDs are supposed to be unique throughout the world because of the algorithm used to generate them. (It's some machination of a date/time stamp, the serial number of your network card, your high school locker combination, and the hex representation of your mother's maiden name...or something like that.)

Regardless, the GUID guarantees that every queue in our enterprise will have a unique address. So when you need to find a single queue, what better way than to use the GUID. And since multiple queues can have the same label, the GUID ensures that you find the queue you're interested in.

```
'Grab the GUID from the queue's property sheet for this test
Set objQueueInfos = objQuery.LookupQueue _
(QueueGuid:="{672C9804-6223-11D2-ACDE-00400536FE25}")
```

MSMQQueueInfos Object

It's difficult to demonstrate the usage of the LookupQueue method of the MSMQQuery without discussing the MSMQQueueInfos object because they are so tightly coupled. The MSMQQueueInfos object allows you to select a specific public queue from a collection of queues that are returned by a call to the LookupQueue method. Unfortunately, this collection is not exactly like the collection you might be accustomed to, so you cannot iterate through it the way you would a Visual Basic collection.

The reason this is so is because of the dynamic nature of the queues. Queues might be added or deleted at any time, so there is no queue count property available for moving through the collection. Instead, the MSMQQueueInfos object provides an end-of-list (EOL) mechanism to indicate when you have completely moved through the collection. As a result, here's how the LookupQueue method shakes out in Visual Basic:

```
Private Function LookupQueue() As Boolean
  Dim objQuery As New MSMQQuery
  Dim objQueueInfos As New MSMQQueueInfos
  Dim objQueueInfo As New MSMQQueueInfo
  Dim objQueue As MSMQQueue

  'Use the queue label as search criteria
  Set objQueueInfos = _
  objQuery.LookupQueue(_
    Label:= New York-Pending-SalesOrders, _
    RelLabel:=REL_GE )

  'Move to the top of queue set
  objQueueInfos.Reset

  'Gets the next queue
  Set objQueueInfo = objQueueInfos.Next
  Do While Len(objQueueInfo.PathName) > 0
    MsgBox "Found Queue: " + objQueueInfo.PathName
    'Open each queue in the result set
    Set objQueue = objQueueInfo.Open( _
      MQ_SEND_ACCESS, MQ_DENY_NONE)
    Set objQueueInfo = objQueueInfos.Next
  Loop
End Function
```

Journals

Journals are used to maintain an audit trail of the activity of a computer and its queues. They come in three varieties: machine queue, queue, and message. When a computer is added to the MSMQ Enterprise, an associated *machine journal queue* is automatically created. It is here that MSMQ will automatically place an audit trail of the messages sent from the computer and MSMQ-generated report messages.

When a queue is added to a computer that has its Journal property set to the constant MQ_JOURNAL, MSMQ creates a *queue journal* where the queue is located. The queue journal is used to store copies of messages *after* they have been removed from a queue. (Remember that you remove messages from a queue by retrieving them. Peeking a message would not add the message to a journal.)

The default is MQ_JOURNAL_NONE, meaning that messages are not stored in a journal queue when they are removed from the queue. MSMQ will not automatically remove messages from a journal queue. They must be either retrieved or purged (programmatically or through the MSMQ Explorer).

The maximum size (in kilobytes) for a queue journal can be established by setting the JournalQuota property. If you are going to journal your queues, it's generally a good idea to maintain the default, INFINITE, so that messages will not unexpectedly cease from being logged. Again, you can always manually purge them after a network backup and as part of the system's maintenance.

```
Dim objQueueInfo As New MSMQQueueInfo
Dim objQueue As New MSMQQueue
objQueueInfo.PathName = "PUMA\NYSalesOrders"
objQueueInfo.Label    = "New York-Pending-SalesOrders"
objQueueInfo.Journal = MQ_JOURNAL
objQueueInfo.JournalQuota = INFINITE 'the default anyway _
objQueueInfo.Create
```

Messages also have the Journal property. When set to MQMSG_JOURNAL, a message sent from one machine to another will be kept in the machine journal on the originating machine.

```
objMessage.Label = txtMessageLabel
objMessage.Body = txtMessageBody.Text
objMessage.Journal = MQMSG_JOURNAL
objMessage.Send objQueue
```

Dead Letter Queues

Dead letter queues are similar to journals in that they record an audit trail of activity. But whereas journals store messages after they have been retrieved, *dead letter queues* hold messages that could not be delivered. A message that is not delivered before it times out, or when the queue name is incorrect, would end up in the dead letter queue.

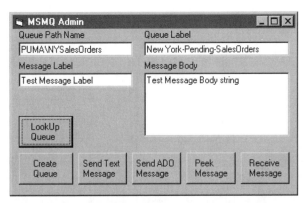

Figure 8.10 The MSMQ Admin application is a VB form containing the code samples of managing queues and messages.

You cannot add messages to this queue yourself; MSMQ must do that for you. But you can read the dead letter queue through the MSMQ API. When a message is placed in a dead letter queue, MSMQ sets the message's class property to the appropriate negative acknowledgment.

Alas, the End of the MSMQ Objects

Well, that's a sizable percentage of the MSMQ objects and their members, and that should at least provide a solid foundation on which you can begin to build an MSMQ application or MSMQ-enable an existing one. For gutting your way through these objects, you've been rewarded with a VB application that will look up and create queues, as well as peek, send, and receive messages (see Figure 8.10).

Now let's see if we can apply your newfound knowledge to the MTS sample application. As mentioned in the Business Scenarios discussion, the goal is to MSMQ-enable the Sales Order Processing application developed in Chapter 7. If you skipped Chapter 7, you may want to go back and read it now, unless you are already familiar with Visual Basic and MTS.

Wouldn't it be great if we could make the VB client application from Chapter 7 work for a salesperson on the road? And being lazy, as most of us programmers tend to be, wouldn't it be even greater if we didn't have to break any of the existing code to do so?

MSMQ-Enabling the Sales Order Process

The Sales Order Process created in Chapter 7 will now be MSMQ-enabled. The goal is to have one set of code work for both a roaming salesperson and an in-house data entry operator. The code should be written in such a way that does not introduce unnecessary complexity into a rather simple process. Figure 8.11 shows what the new process will look like.

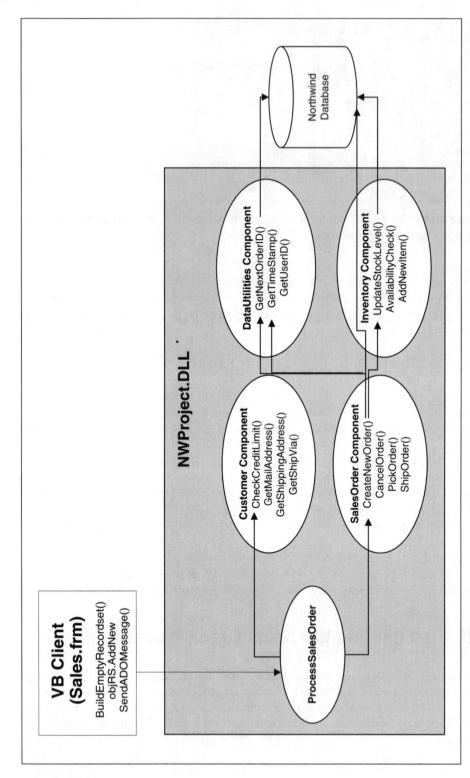

Figure 8.11 The Sales Order Process now preprocesses the order by attaching an ADO Recordset to a message.

Submitting the Order

The cmdProcess.Click method starts the ball rolling. This is fired after the user has entered a CustomerID, ProductID, Unit Price, and a Quantity, and elects to submit the order.

```
Public Sub cmdProcess_Click()

On Error GoTo Err_CmdProcess
```

Use your imagination to picture more fields on the form, and perhaps some validations right about here.

Next, we need to build an empty ADO Recordset structure to store our form fields.

```
Dim objRS As New ADOR.Recordset
BuildEmptyRecordset objRS
```

Then we add a new record to the Recordset and populate its field values with contents of the form.

```
objRS.AddNew
objRS.Fields("UserID") = "JFALINO"
objRS.Fields("ProductID") = txtProductID
objRS.Fields("CustomerID") = txtCustomer
objRS.Fields("UnitPrice") = txtUnitPrice
objRS.Fields("Quantity") = txtQuantity
```

Now we create a message, attach the Recordset object to the body, and send it to the SalesOrder Queue.

```
SendADOMessage objRS
```

If all went well, don't be shy, let the user know it.

```
MsgBox "The new sales order has been successfully created.", _
  vbInformation, "MTS Sales Order"

Exit Sub

Err_CmdProcess:
 MsgBox Err.Description, vbExclamation, _
  "Error creating sales order"
End Sub
```

Building the Constructed Recordset

This is a very interesting method because it brings together several key concepts. In the BuildEmptyRecordset method, an ADO Recordset is created without the support of a result set, or even a connection to a data store. This technique of using the RDSServer.DataFactory class was covered in Chapter 4.

It utilizes several arrays to build the structure of the Recordset before eventually using the vntColumnInfo array as a parameter for the CreateRecordset method.

```
Function BuildEmptyRecordset(ByRef objRS As ADOR.Recordset) As Boolean
    Dim vntColumnInfo(4) As Variant
    Dim vntColumn0(3) As Variant
    Dim vntColumn1(3) As Variant
    Dim vntColumn2(3) As Variant
    Dim vntColumn3(3) As Variant
    Dim vntColumn4(3) As Variant
```

In VB, be sure to set a project reference to the RDS DataFactory Server.

```
Dim objDataFactory As New RDSServer.DataFactory
```

We're just defining the structure of each column here.

```
vntColumn0(0) = "UserID"        'Column name
vntColumn0(1) = CInt(129)       'Column type
vntColumn0(2) = CInt(25)        'Column width
vntColumn0(3) = True            'Column accept null?

vntColumn1(0) = "ProductID"     'Column name
vntColumn1(1) = CInt(4)         'Column type
vntColumn1(2) = CInt(10)        'Column width
vntColumn1(3) = True            'Column accept null?

vntColumn2(0) = "CustomerID"    'Column name
vntColumn2(1) = CInt(129)       'Column type
vntColumn2(2) = CInt(5)         'Column width
vntColumn2(3) = True            'Column accept null?

vntColumn3(0) = "UnitPrice"     'Column name
vntColumn3(1) = CInt(3)         'Column type
vntColumn3(2) = CInt(19)        'Column width
vntColumn3(3) = True            'Column accept null?

vntColumn4(0) = "Quantity"      'Column name
vntColumn4(1) = CInt(4)         'Column type
vntColumn4(2) = CInt(10)        'Column width
vntColumn4(3) = True            'Column accept null?
```

Then we add the columns to the Recordset definition.

```
vntColumnInfo(0) = vntColumn0
vntColumnInfo(1) = vntColumn1
vntColumnInfo(2) = vntColumn2
vntColumnInfo(3) = vntColumn3
vntColumnInfo(4) = vntColumn4
```

Next, we use the CreateRecordset method to populate the objRS object.

```
   Set objRS = objdataFactory.CreateRecordSet(vntColumnInfo)
   Set objDataFactory = Nothing
End Function
```

Sending the Message

At this point, we have the constructed Recordset and have populated its columns with data from the form. Now we just need to create an MSMQ message and attach the Recordset to its body.

```
Private Function SendADOMessage(ByVal objRS As Object) As Boolean

  On Error GoTo Err_SendMessage

  Dim objQueue As MSMQQueue
  Dim objMessage As New MSMQMessage
  Dim objQueueInfo As New MSMQQueueInfo
```

Then it's time to open a reference to the SalesOrder queue in New York. We create a message with a label "Batch Sales Order", attach the Recordset to the body, and then send it. The Ack property has been changed from its default of not sending acknowledgment under any circumstance, so that a failed message will fire a system-generated acknowledgment message. We really only need to know if something went wrong; no news is good news, in this case.

The Delivery property was also changed to Recoverable, from its default, Express. The security of recoverable messages will make you sleep better.

```
   objQueueInfo.PathName = "PUMA\NYSalesOrders"
   Set objQueue = objQueueInfo.Open(MQ_SEND_ACCESS, MQ_DENY_NONE)
   If objQueue.IsOpen Then
     objMessage.Label = "Batch Sales Order"
     objMessage.Body = objRS
     objMessage.Ack = MSMSQ_ACKNOWLEDGMENT_NACK_REACH_QUEUE
     objMessage.Delivery = MQMSG_DELIVERY_RECOVERABLE

     objMessage.Send objQueue
   Else
     MsgBox "Could not open queue" & objQueueInfo.PathName
   End If

Exit Function

Err_SendMessage:
    MsgBox "Can't send message." & _
    Err.Description
End Function
```

If the user running this VB application is online and can see the PUMA computer on the network, the order should make it to the appropriate queue. If offline, this message will sit in a queue on the sending machine—as long as that machine serves as an MSMQ independent client. Upon connection to the network, like e-mail, the messages will be automatically routed to their intended destinations.

Receiving the Message

At this point, the orders have been sent to the NYSalesOrder queue and await retrieval. Since peeking and retrieving requires almost the same code, this routine has been written to either peek or retrieve, depending on the boolPeekOnly parameter. (Again, Retrieve removes a message from a queue, Peek does not.)

```
Function ReceiveBatchOrderMessages(ByVal boolPeekOnly As Boolean) _
As Boolean

  On Error GoTo Err_ReceiveMessage

  Dim objQueue As MSMQQueue
  Dim objMessage As New MSMQMessage
  Dim objQueueInfo As New MSMQQueueInfo
  objQueueInfo.PathName = "PUMA\NYSalesOrders"
  If boolPeekOnly = True Then
    'Could use receive access as well for peeking
    'But all we need is peek access
    Set objQueue = objQueueInfo.Open(MQ_PEEK_ACCESS, _
                                     MQ_DENY_NONE)
  Else
    'Can't use peek access to receive, must have receive access
    Set objQueue = objQueueInfo.Open(MQ_RECEIVE_ACCESS, _
                                     MQ_DENY_NONE)
  End If
```

After attempting to open the queue, let's be sure it worked.

```
  If objQueue.IsOpen Then
    'If you don't set the timeout, could lock your application!
    'Wait 3 seconds before giving up on looking for messages.
    If boolPeekOnly = True Then
      'Let's only wait 1 second to peek
      Set objMessage = objQueue.Peek(ReceiveTimeout:=1000)
```

With the queue now open, we can retrieve its messages. We'll get them one at a time, and then interrogate the body—if there is one. Assuming so, we can now use the Fields collection of the body because it has taken on the attributes of an ADO Recordset.

```
  Else
    Set objMessage = objQueue.Receive(ReceiveTimeout:=3000)
  End If
```

```
      'Close the queue
      objQueue.Close
```

This sample code just displays a message box with the customer ID, proving that the proper message was received. But what you would do in the live code is take the four parameters in Recordset and pass them to the SalesOrderProcess method of the MTS-hosted NWProject DLL. All of the rest of the code works just as it used to. You just need to set a reference to that project in the VB client project so that it can be instantiated in this method. It's as simple as that!

```
      If TypeOf objMessage.Body Is Object  Then
        MsgBox "Received sales order for customer:" & _
          objMessage.Body.Fields("CustomerID"), vbExclamation, _
          "MSMQ Application"
      Else
        MsgBox objMessage.Body
      End If
    Else
      MsgBox "Could not open queue" & objQueueInfo.PathName & _
      Err.Description
    End If

Exit Function

Err_ReceiveMessage:
    MsgBox "Can't receive message." & _
    vbCrLf & Err.Description
End Function
```

From Here

Message queuing is a technology that you're going to see a lot of in the years to come, especially as the growth of the Internet continues to bring businesses around the world closer together. Products like Microsoft Message Queue Server only compound this issue because it brings the historically mainframe-level, cryptic technology of message queuing to the masses. Microsoft has accomplished this by creating a product that not only serves the Windows platform but can also communicate with other operating systems. And with the inclusion of ActiveX support, MSMQ greatly simplifies application development and can seamlessly integrate with an existing COM-based system.

Hopefully, you'll leave this chapter a little wiser about the concepts of message queuing and how MSMQ Server can fit into the distributed client/server application picture. That concludes this section of the book on the distributed application development with Windows NT services. From here on, the book presents a hard-core programming approach, to reinforce the concepts we've covered in the first eight chapters. First up is a how-to approach to building an ADO application. Enjoy.

PART

Three

Developing a Distributed Application with ADO

I bet I can guess why you are reading this. You're looking for code or techniques to steal for your own use, aren't you? You are looking to cheat at your job—trying to find some way get more done while exerting less effort. I even bet that you are looking to get far enough ahead with your work to re-introduce yourself to your family, take some time off, catch up on some reading, write a book, or just take it easy, right?

Well, congratulations, you've come to the right place. The remainder of this book deals with techniques and technologies that can help you attain these lofty goals.

In the first part of this book, you learned about how ADO makes connecting to and working with a database more powerful much easier than was previously possible. Then, in Part Two, you learned how the Windows NT middle tier services (MTS and MSMQ) can be used to provide scalability and robustness to your distributed applications while removing many of the headaches that were associated with *n*-tiered development. This last part puts what you have already learned together into a *reusable framework* (read: something that you can steal to make your life easier) for distributed application development.

What's So Different About this Book's Example Application?

To start with, I'm not going to drag you through what so many other books have done in their code examples. You are not required to learn about some bogus (yet illustrative) little application that was written to solve the business problems of some fictional organization. Instead, I'm going to use the most generic type of application (an order entry system) to describe some of the robust, generic, reusable structures that are used in almost all business applications. As such, this framework will show you the basic, reusable patterns for:

- Moving information from the database to a user's desktop.

- Saving changes back to the database.

- Enforcing business rules.

- Implementing both pessimistic and optimistic record locking in a distributed system.

- Handling parent/child relationships in your data. (e.g., an order would be a parent data and the line items that make up and order would be child data).

- Creating, committing, and rolling-back transactions.

You see, although the following example code is written about an order entry application, the framework that you are about to read about has not been created just for one application. Instead, this framework is the product of analyzing several existing distributed applications that we have worked on over the last couple of years. This analysis consisted of recognizing the most common functional and architectural components and abstracting them into set of recognizable and reusable entities (objects).

In other words, the example code that you will read about in this last part has not really been written about a specific application. Rather, it is the digest of several (successful) development experiences. As such, the goal of the framework code that you are about to read about is to provide proven, basic architectural elements that can easily be added into broad range distributed applications written for the Windows NT environment.

A Roadmap for Your Journey

Chapter 9: The first chapter of this part of the book deals with an overall description of the application framework that will be explored in the later chapters. Aside from this simple architectural overview of the framework, some basic methodology (*n*-tiered, object oriented development) and the general rules of distributed application development will be covered.

Chapter 10: This second chapter covers the most basic common elements of distributed application design and implementation. Here, you will learn about using ADO and MTS to retrieve, add, update, and delete data. This chapter also covers a description of how optimistic and pessimistic locking can be implemented.

Chapter 11: This last chapter covers the common implementation of complex issues such as parent-child object relationships and transaction processing.

Methodology, Assumptions, and Architecture of a Distributed ADO Application

Although you have seen the capabilities of ADO, MTS, and MSMQ, you may not realize their greater impact on the way you do your job. Therefore, we'll begin this chapter by telling you that if you have done any sort of distributed application development in the past, you will be pleasantly surprised by how easy it is to develop advanced, scalable applications using these new technologies—that is, if you play by the rules.

However, this ease in development can be achieved only if you adhere to certain methodologies. So, the remainder of the book is primarily concerned with looking past the details of building a specific application and toward the generic features that are essential to this type of application development. We believe that the essence of any client/server application is a generic *framework*, or template, that can be applied to almost any application built using ADO and the distributed application services of Windows NT.

What You'll Learn

If you are not already familiar with the idea of *patterns*, *idioms*, and *frameworks*, then let us introduce you to one of the more useful developments in programming to emerge in the last several years. Basically, a pattern is a description of objects and relationships between objects, and is used to solve a generic design problem. Typically, patterns are approaches to problems that prove themselves or emerge from multiple applications over time.

The nature of design patterns is necessarily abstract; that is, they're not code libraries, but descriptions of proven approaches to problems. One classic example of a simple design pattern is the Momento pattern, which describes how a program can capture and externalize an object's internal state (data) so that the object can be restored at some later time. ADO makes use of this pattern when a Save method is called on a Recordset object, causing it to write its contents to a file that can be used later as the source of a new Recordset. Although the ADO Recordset uses this pattern, many less sophisticated objects also use it. If you think about it, programs that write to INI files also often play out this pattern. As these two simple examples of a very simple pattern describe, if you're looking for widescale reuse, creating or identifying the pattern is the best thing that can happen to you. Since a pattern is so abstract, it can be applied in many different situations, in many different languages, and can make use of any appropriate technology.

An idiom is different from a pattern in that it is an expression of a solution peculiar to a certain programming language. A pattern describes a solution that does not use any particular type of technology, whereas an idiom mandates the use of a certain technology or language. Therefore, when we are talking about patterns specifically using ADO, MTS, and MSMQ, any generic approach to a design problem should be considered an idiom for developing distributed applications under Windows NT.

The most specific type of pattern is called a framework. Probably the best way to think about a framework is as a template for development. Frameworks can be specific (e.g., built as a template for creating health care industry applications) or domain-neutral like the one in the following chapters that details a template that can be used in many types of Windows NT-distributed business applications.

Why should you care about all this? Well, if an idiom or framework can be found in NT client/server application development, then the ideas that it embodies have a better chance for reuse and real value than any sample application we can give you. As stated earlier, the reason why the application in the forthcoming chapters is so general is because we're not particularly interested in building some "play" example application. What we are after is essential logic in using the technologies of NT's distributed application services, SQL Server and ADO to create large-scale client/server applications.

What Does This Application Look Like?

Let's get one thing straight here: We're not going to describe how to build a GUI. The structure and code described in the following chapters form the core business logic of an application. As you will see, this part of the book focuses on the construction of *business objects*. Business objects are used to represent the core entities involved in an application. For example, Chapter 10 is about a Customer business object, which has properties that expose the data that the system has about a customer (e.g., a Name property); it also has methods (i.e., publicly accessible procedures) that perform behaviors such as saving changed customer data to the database.

In other words, business objects describe a programmatic interface of an application, not a user interface. Creating an invisible structure like this has the advantage of not being tied to any one GUI. In fact, the code described here could be used in conjunction with any GUI building tool that is able to use COM objects. Just as easily as you could create a Visual Basic form to display the data associated with the Customer object, you could do the same thing on a Web page, in a COM-aware Java applet, or even on an Excel spreadsheet.

An Object-Oriented, Distributed, MTS and ADO Development Framework

Wow, that's quite a heading for something that is supposed to make your life simpler. Really, it's not as complex as it sounds. And remember, the earlier parts of this book covered the use of MTS and ADO, so you've already got those covered. Furthermore, the framework is distributed; that is, it is built in pieces, which can be placed on:

- A client NT workstation or a Web server

- One or more MTS servers

- One or more SQL servers

The object-oriented piece is, however, going to take some explaining if you are unfamiliar with object orientation. Although this chapter will explore the concept of object orientation in much greater detail, for now familiarize yourself with the basic idea behind this methodology, which is that the core logic of any system is broken down into objects. In the upcoming example, all of the Customer data is governed by a Customer object, all of the Order data is governed by an Order object, all of the Product data is governed by a Product object...get the idea?

Order Entry System

The advantage of working with a framework is that it is abstract (and therefore reusable), but it is also this abstraction that makes a framework difficult to understand. For this reason, the generic framework described in the remainder of this book is shown in the context of an order entry system to make it easier to understand.

As you go through this chapter, keep in mind that the goal of this part of the book is not simply to teach you how to write a system that takes orders from customers, adjusts stock levels, and processes orders. Look beyond the particulars to the broader core functionality of retrieving data, saving data, handling multiuser concerns, dealing with parent-child data relationships, and transaction processing.

The best way to start describing how to use this application development idiom is to address the basic questions of why, what, and how. The discussion begins by explaining why object orientation and an n-tiered approach to development should be considered, and why Visual Basic (not a *truly* object-oriented tool) is being used to describe an object-oriented framework.

After we've answered the whys, we move onto the whats; in particular, this section will answer the questions "What is an object-oriented approach?" and "What is an n-tiered application?"

But the answer to the major question—"How do I build this type of application?"—begins to be addressed near the end of this chapter and continues in the following two chapters. To answer this question in detail, we cover object modeling in this chapter, followed by a lengthy code example in Chapters 10 and 11.

Why Use Object Orientation, Distributed Components, and Visual Basic?

It's always best to know why you are going somewhere before you begin the journey.

This sounds obvious, but too often IT professionals begin something new with only the faintest ideas of why they want to do so. They start to learn some new whiz-bang technology because someone in some magazine wrote a glowing review about it. This is the danger of media "buzz."

The goal of this section is to break away from that lemming mentality. We will try to give you practical reasons that you should set off on this journey to learn the approaches presented in the framework. After all, object orientation and *n*-tiered development will force you up a somewhat steep learning curve before they make you more productive, so it's better to know the whys and wherefores before you go through the trouble of learning this new stuff.

Why Object Orientation?

If you have started to work with COM and MTS without any formal design principles, then you already know that the creation of components to be used in MTS or COM will only add overhead to your development process. Worse, developing components outside of the object-oriented approach leads to components that are artificially imposed over a nonobject-oriented structure and often fall far short of being robust, complete, and reusable logical entities.

Simply put, distributed application development without an object-oriented approach is like trying to force a square peg into a round hole: It will make your job harder, your programs weaker, and the logical architecture of your application clumsy. In contrast, using an object-oriented approach will guide you naturally and logically into the creation of powerful, meaningful, and reusable components.

Marriage of Technology and Methodology

In Grady Booch's watershed book on object-oriented design, *Object-Oriented Analysis and Design with Applications* (Benjamin/Cummings Publishing Company, 1994), he makes the statement that object orientation was born of "programming-in-the-large." This means that object-oriented ideas came about in order to deal with the creation of huge, complex, enterprise-level applications that drive a business for long periods of time.

From reading the previous sections of this book it should also be obvious to you that this "programming-in-the-large" is the direct target of the COM and ADO technologies. Therefore, the marriage between these technologies and the methodology of object orientation is both obvious and necessary.

In the most practical terms, if you don't use the features of MTS and MSMQ with your business objects, then a large system's goals of performance and scalability are unlikely to be met. And if you don't use an object-oriented approach in your work with MTS and

MSMQ, then the integration of your software with other software and the larger system of COM components will be artificially imposed, less maintainable, less reusable, logically unstructured, and ugly.

In its proper context, these new NT distributed application services force your hand into developing applications using object-oriented design principles. If you have already made the leap into object orientation, you may be enthusiastic about the fact that it is such a necessary element in developing distributed applications. However, there are many people who have yet to discover object orientation or to fully explore its impact on application development.

Not Just for the Large Application Developer

Although many of the driving ideas behind MTS, MSMQ, ADO, and object orientation come from the large application development arena, a good argument could be made for the fact that object orientation using these technologies is actually more beneficial to the small application developer. In large application development, an object-oriented approach can ease the process of designing the application and enable the application to take advantage of the enhanced performance and load-handling features of MTS and MSMQ.

However, the opportunities for reuse in large applications are generally fewer than they are for small application development, because a well-designed component can be reused in a large number of different small applications. For example, if a business object is created in a large application to handle information about the employees of a company, it may only be used in a couple of places in the large application. But once this employee object has been created, it can be reused and shared by the organization in a much larger number of small applications that deal with things like employee bonus plans, employee attendance, requisitions management, payroll, and resource allocation.

So, although object orientation, MTS, MSMQ, and ADO were created with the large application developer in mind, if your work typically involves the creation of smaller applications, you may actually benefit more from these technologies and techniques.

A Natural Evolution

If the apparent benefits of an object-oriented approach are not enough to sway you into trying this method of development, consider that the evolution toward object orientation is natural; that is, most people who work in a language that supports some level of object-oriented or object-based development start off using objects gradually, finding useful tasks for which combining code and data is an advantage. For example, one of the first object-oriented tasks you might have undertaken is to create a class that manages data displayed in a form. While doing this, you may have discovered how to create objects and to call properties and methods.

After working with objects in this way for a while, most people begin to add more objects to their programs and to see relationships among them. Subsequently, they begin to make programming decisions that are more dependent on business objects and their relationships. As a by-product of this, more robust techniques, such as hiding complexity behind easy-to-use interfaces, begin to emerge.

The last step in this evolution is to realize how business objects and their relationships change the nature of programming. In this last stage, there is an awareness that business objects are the core of application development and that any program can be understood through its objects and the relationships in which they exist. At this level, the use of objects is not a handy trick or an optimization technique; it is a way of seeing.

With that in mind, the last part of this book focuses on how the object-oriented approach is magnified and made even more powerful through its new association with ADO, MTS, and MSMQ.

Only the Disciplined Can Be Lazy

Finally (and maybe most important), object orientation can give you the discipline to be lazy. If you have the discipline to create applications from the ground up, concentrating on reuse and extensibility, you will become a more efficient programmer because you will have to rewrite less code. It follows that if you have to rewrite less code, then you have to write less overall code. To the lazy person, the programmer who writes the least code and still produces excellent work is nothing short of a hero.

The creation of this generic framework would be impossible without the use of object-oriented design principles. It is only by abstracting an application into its basic entities (i.e., objects) that common architectural patterns can begin to emerge. In other words, when you break up an application into its parts, reusable entities become more apparent.

This is the case not only in software, but also in many different engineering situations. For example, the world would be a cheaper, less complicated place if all electrical engines were of a standardized size and voltage. Imagine that you were trimming your lawn with a Weed Whacker on a hot summer day and you got the urge for a nice cold milkshake. Well, if appliances were designed the same way as software *should* be, then you would be able to pop the electric engine out of your garden trimmer, walk inside, pop the engine into your blender, and make yourself that milkshake.

Why Use Distributed Components?

This topic was covered in some depth in Chapter 7, but before we dive into the specifics of the methodology and implementation of n-tiered development, let's review the reasons for separating an application's core functionality into either physically (in different components, on different machines) or logically (different objects).

- As user interface standards change, entire applications do not have to be rewritten. Only the code that is responsible for presenting the data to the user needs to be rewritten.

- The business object layer can be composed of components written in many different languages. The business object layer can be composed of components called by many different front ends. Back-end data sources can be replaced with little or no change to the other tiers of the application, thereby enabling systems to easily scale. The cost of developing new systems is the principal reason for the recent trend toward distributed applications. Performance is another advantage in a distributed environment. Stability is another factor. Consider the mainframe application that experiences hardware problems.

■ Scalability is also much easier to administer in a distributed environment.

Why Visual Basic?

The reason we coded the sample application in Visual Basic is because the language itself can be used to strengthen the message of how COM objects (like ADO) interact. If you routinely code in Visual Basic, it might be comforting to you to see that your understanding of the object model has been extended into COM. If you routinely code with a "true" object-oriented language, it may bother your sensibilities when you see how Visual Basic works with objects. Everyone knows that Visual Basic is not strictly an object-oriented language.

The Microsoft Corporation, which sells a number of object-oriented development environments (VC++, VJ++, and Visual FoxPro), has refused for a couple of years to add "real" object-oriented features to the language. Typically, Microsoft is neither strategically stupid or particularly slow to capture a market. So it leads us to wonder why one of their flagship development products has no traditional support for such a powerful and popular feature as object-orientation. There must be some reason.

It seems an odd coincidence that the object model of Visual Basic is a direct match to the COM object model. Just like COM+, Visual Basic supports the principles of abstraction, encapsulation, modularity, and "part-of" hierarchy, and falls just short of the machinations of conventional "is a" hierarchy. In other words, the Visual Basic programming environment is made to work in a direct parallel to the object paradigms of the operating system. Since Visual Basic was designed as "the" environment in which to create Windows applications (remember the early Microsoft marketing pitch "Visual Basic gives you the power to crack Windows"?), it would follow that its take on the object model is a direct match with COM.

What Is Object Orientation and Distributed Application Development?

The next questions to answer are the "whats" of the application. If you have worked with an object-oriented system or a distributed system in the past, then you might want to flip ahead to the next section of this chapter. But if you are unfamiliar with either of these approaches to development, or if you have not dealt with the COM or Visual Basic "flavor" of object orientation, read on.

What Is Object Orientation?

The term "business object" has been around for a while and has consequently come to mean different things to different people. At the most basic level, business objects are "objects" that reflect or represent your "business." What that means is that your programs can be viewed as models of the real world. Using business objects, programs are created to simulate aspects of the world, to record what is happening, and to make predictions about what might happen.

If you are new to objects, all of this may be a little confusing. But being confused is fine for now. As anyone who has made the jump to using objects will tell you, you need to take some time to process the information before the fog begins to clear. If, however, you have been working in an object-oriented language, you certainly won't be confused by the terminology, but you may be surprised by the changes that COM makes to programming with objects.

 Whatever your level of knowledge on this topic, be aware that the rest of this chapter focuses on object-oriented ideas and the basic impact of COM on these ideas. But also be aware that these topics are huge—indeed, entire books have been written on many of the subjects covered here—so this discussion should not be considered comprehensive. Further, object-oriented ideas initially are often abstract and difficult to understand, so be patient. All of the concepts presented in this chapter are reinforced with examples in the following chapters and in the construction of a sample application at the end of the book.

Object Basics

According to Booch, an object is simply "something you can do things to." That is, as mentioned earlier, an object is a code-based abstraction of something in the real world. Booch's definition goes on to state that "an object has state, behavior, and identity." This means that any object has data (state information), a set of methods or routines (behav-

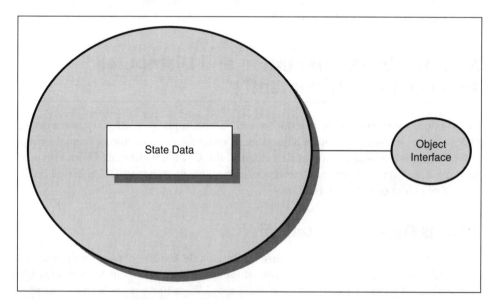

Figure 9.1   The basic nature of an object is that it has state, behavior, and an interface.

ior), which pass *messages* (interact with other objects) or alter the objects data; finally, an object has a nature that distinguishes it from all other objects. We extend this simple definition by adding that an object has an interface (or multiple interfaces) with which other objects can interact. It may be helpful to picture an object as a structure like the one shown in Figure 9.1.

Later in the book, we will begin building a sample application that uses a Customer object that models a customer of a company. This object would have *state* information, such as the customer's name and address; *behavior*, such as routines that could place and cancel an order by communicating with other objects in the application; its *identity* would be established with a Customer ID; finally, this object would expose an *interface* with which other objects could interact.

Interface

For the purposes of COM, we are primarily interested in the interface that objects expose to other objects. An object's interface is composed of *properties*, *methods*, and *events* that work together to expose an object's state, behavior, and identity to other objects in a system.

- *Properties are attributes that describe an object.* For example, the simple application described in the last section of this book contains a Customer object. As its name suggests, this object represents, or models, a customer of a company. Therefore, any instance of this object would have state data, like the name and address of the customer, which might be accessible to other objects through a property.

- *Methods are services that objects provide.* Using either their own data, or parameters passed to them, methods manipulate information and produce some sort of result. For example, the Customer object has a CreateOrder method that produces a new instance of an Order object and prepares it to place a new sales order for the Customer object that created it. In other words, this method of the Customer object passes a message to the Order object to get it ready to place a new order.

- *Events can be viewed as another sort of message, but one that is triggered when something happens to an object.* In some object-oriented circles, everything that happens to an object is an event, from setting a property to destroying the object. Under COM, you can think of an event as a message that is sent to anyone that happens to be listening as a result to an action against an object.

Classes

Booch's definition further describes an object as something that has its structure and behavior defined by a common class. A class is essentially a template from which an instance of an object is created. This means that many different instances (or objects) can be created from a single class (see Figure 9.2). This is not to say that these instances are just copies of the same thing. Remember, a class has state, behavior, and identity, so each instance of a class is its own "thing." If you were viewing three different instances

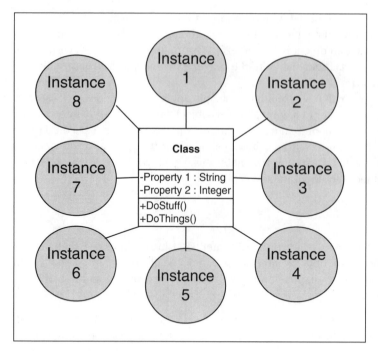

Figure 9.2   Many objects (or instances) can be created from the same class.

of the Employee object, they would all have the same behavior but would represent three different employees because their identity and state data would be different. Therefore, when you accessed each instance of the Employee object and retrieved its Name property, you would be given different information.

Components

One of the problems with object-oriented design is that until relatively recently it was tied to the programming languages in which it was implemented. If you program in Java, C++, Visual FoxPro, or some other object-oriented programming language, you probably have come to enjoy the powerful features of object-oriented programming. However, without the use of some bridging mechanism like COM, these languages provide no real way of working with objects that were created with some other language (or sometimes even in earlier versions of the same language).

As you can imagine, the language-dependent use of objects was limiting in many ways; it also ran counter to some of the practical and labor-saving features of object orientation. First, the fact that object orientation was purely language-based tied the use of objects to a specific development tool. Although language-specific implementations might not sound like such a bad approach in the short term, this type of implementation is obviously less attractive when examined with an eye toward the technology changes and staff turnover over the lifetime of an application.

Second, a huge benefit of the object-oriented approach to development is the level of code reuse that it affords. However, cross-application reuse is severely restricted by language-dependency. For example, in the sample application code that will be examined later in the book, the Customer business object described is definitely a candidate for reuse. Once this object is created for one program (e.g., order entry), it can be reused in the company's commission tracking system, its Web page, and any other place where information about the company's customers are needed. However, under language-dependent object orientation, if the Customer object were used in several different compiled programs and then a basic change was made to the object, you would have to find, change, and recompile each copy of the object in all of the applications where it was in use.

For these reasons and others, the use of components has become very popular in application development. Although the formal definition of a component is a matter of debate, for purposes here, we define a component as a precompiled, language-independent object or group of objects; that is, components are programs (i.e., groups of objects) that communicate with other programs without regard to the language in which they were created, through the mechanism of COM. Components offer a number of elegant opportunities for code reuse, enable on-the-fly software maintenance, and provide a powerful way to extend applications throughout their lifetime.

The COM or Visual Basic Way of Object Orientation

Since the atomic unit of COM is the component, COM's view of the use of objects is distinctly different from what you may be familiar with in object-oriented programming. Even though components are based on object technologies, they also extend and change the way that you must view objects and their interactions. Probably the best way to approach the differences between COM's use of objects and "pure" object orientation is to explore how the basic principles of object orientation, or the *object model*, exist in both. Once again turning to Booch's definitions, the object model is:

> The collection of principles that form the foundation of object-oriented design; a software engineering paradigm emphasizing the principle of abstraction, encapsulation, modularity, hierarchy, typing, concurrency, and persistence.

Since the object model is the basis of the principles of object orientation, we use its main principles (abstraction, encapsulation, modularity, and hierarchy) to guide our discussion of where the COM way of object orientation meets the traditional definition and where the impact of COM programming can be seen.

Abstraction

Booch states that:

> An abstraction denotes the essential characteristics of an object that distinguish it from all other kinds of objects and thus provide crisply defined conceptual boundaries relative to the perspective of the viewer.

Abstraction is one of the basic ways with which our minds deal with complexity. For example, the complexities of the American system of government would be overwhelming if we were to try to understand it by getting to know about all of the people who take part in it and what each person's job is. Instead, we are taught about the three branches of government and the generalized roles of the people who work in them (e.g., a senator proposes and votes on the enactment of laws). Therefore, schools teach civics first by "abstracting" the U.S. government into three branches and then the people who work in these branches by recognizing what is similar about them and ignoring the differences between them. Using this basic strategy for understanding complexity, the "Senator object" is defined by its "essential characteristics" of writing and voting on laws; and it has "crisply defined conceptual boundaries" between it and the "President object" from our "perspective" as a citizen of the country.

What abstraction means to application development is that we can ease the analysis of a complex system by creating objects that are based on abstractions of real-world things. By doing this, we focus the creation of software to solve a business problem before getting bogged down in the technical details involved in the implementation. In other words, the principle of abstraction leads us to create the business objects that make up the entities involved in an application. For example, in the application built later in this section, everyone who buys products from a company is abstracted into a Customer object that has the "essential characteristics" of being a consumer of the company products.

As far as the concept of abstraction goes, there is no difference between object-oriented development and COM component-based development except that abstractions must exist within the context of a component, and the object's interfaces are accessible from there. Really, this impact of the COM on abstractions is an example of the modularity principle of the object model that is described later.

Encapsulation

Booch describes encapsulation as:

> . . .the process of compartmentalizing the elements of an abstraction that constitute its structure and behavior; encapsulation serves to separate the contractual interface of an abstraction and its implementation.

Imagine for a minute what driving a car would be like if the engineer had not adhered to the principle of encapsulation. Without encapsulation, you would have to manually monitor the temperature of the engine, constantly be mindful of the way that the gasoline was getting from the tank to the engine, and come up with some way of changing the angle of the tires if you wanted to turn.

Luckily, cars are built on the basis of abstraction and encapsulation. Remember, our definition of an object requires that an object have an interface. *Encapsulation is the rule that objects should expose an interface that keeps the inner workings of what it does secret from any other object.* Another way of putting this is that an object's interface is a *black box* because it should be totally independent of its implementation. Going back to the car example: You have encapsulation to thank whenever you turn the steering wheel and don't have to worry about (or even understand) how the action of twisting the steering wheel makes the car change direction.

Since an object is to hide its inner workings and still be useful, it must expose an *interface* to the rest of the system. To use the earlier example, the steering wheel is the interface to a car's turning mechanism. An object's interface is the foundation of its "contract" with the rest of the system. That is, its interface is what the rest of the system can trust that the object will supply. As a general rule, once an interface is made known to the system, it should always be supported. For example, when you depress the "brake" interface in a car, you trust your life to the "contract" between the "brake" interface and the "brake pad" interface to stop the car, not to recline the seats.

This separation between interface and implementation is essential to the sample application in the last section of this book. The Customer object uses the principle of encapsulation to hide the implementation details: how it saves the changes made to it in the database. It does this because it would be inappropriate for any other object that changes the Customer object to have to know the database tables to which it saved. If this were not the case, and customer information was ever moved to a different table or was stored in a different way (perhaps in the system registry), not only would the code in the Customer object have to change, but any code that dealt with customer data throughout the entire system would have to change. Therefore, the fact that the Customer object encapsulates its implementation not only makes the system more logically structured and understandable, it also makes it incredibly maintainable.

From the standpoint of encapsulation, there is really no difference between object-oriented encapsulation and the encapsulation that is available through COM components. However, the idea of an object's interface as its *immutable contract with the rest of the system* must be emphasized when coding for COM.

Think about it: If an object shifts its interface inside of an object-oriented language, then it will only affect one program; however, if an object does not honor its interface "contract" under COM, it has the possibility of grinding your entire enterprise to a halt, as other objects call out to methods and properties of the object that may no longer be supported.

Modularity

Booch defines modularity as:

> . . .the property of a system that has been decomposed into a set of cohesive and loosely coupled modules.

More than any other principle of the object model, the idea of modularity is what so closely ties COM to the object orientation. Basically, when we speak of COM components, we are just using another way to express the principle of modularity. Under COM, we place the objects that make up the logical structure of the system into components that form the system's physical architecture. This use of components is necessary not only from the standpoint of physical architecture, but when it is used correctly, it allows us to provide a meaningful way to group and couple the objects that make up an application.

Aside from this benefit, the use of components also enables us to reduce the cost of software by making it possible for each to be built and revised independently. As long as the individual object interfaces that the component exposes honor their interface "contracts" with the rest of the system, the modularity that COM components provide is a huge advantage.

Modularity, however, is also the principle most greatly impacted by the behavior of COM because the reasoning behind the partitioning of objects into components has to account not only for the logical and strategic reasons for grouping but for the technical issues introduced by COM, MTS, and MSMQ, as well. Therefore, when a group of objects is partitioned, you must weigh the technical reasons for the partition against the logical ones. Very often, this is difficult to do.

As you will see, COM has a major role to play in the modularization of the sample application in the last section of this book. For example, in order to encapsulate the functionality of saving each business object to the database, there are three different implementation objects: Presentation, Messaging, and Persistence; these three objects act together to change data stored in the database (see Figure 9.3):

- The *Presentation* object exposes the business object's interface to other business objects and any other components that may interact with the object. In order to do this, the Presentation object must maintain its state data for relatively long periods of time.

- The *Messaging* object reads the presentation business object's state data and messages it to the persistence object. Since this object is simply reading and messaging, it does not have to maintain any state data.

- The *Persistence* object decomposes the state data into SQL commands and commits the changes to a database. Like the Messaging object, this object does not need to maintain its state.

So, if another business object were to call the Customer object's Commit method, it would call a method of the Messaging object to read its changed state data and message the data to the Persistence object, which would make the changes to a database table.

In the discussion of encapsulation, we established that it was appropriate to hide the implementation details of saving a business object from other business objects. In turn, it is appropriate to hide the implementation of marshaling data to and from a remote server from the business object since the method of marshaling on the remote server may change during the lifetime of the application. Finally, it is appropriate to hide the physical structure (i.e., SQL commands) of the database because the table structure of the database may be changed (denormalized) for optimization reasons, or another vendor's database may be used.

Using the strategy of encapsulation, any business object would be able to change where it stored its information to any format (e.g., SQL Server, Oracle, DB2, Text File…) or any location (e.g., local system, a network server, or across the Internet) without causing any change to an application that uses the business object. In other words, where the object stores its data is kept "secret". Consequently, we are able to build a logical system that will be durable enough to weather significant physical and technical changes to the system.

Though the reason for encapsulating this functionality is logical, the question of how to group these objects into components is more difficult to achieve. As you will see in the following chapter, there are a number of seemingly correct ways to partition the objects in an application into components.

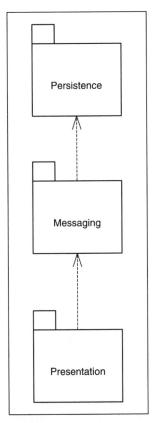

Figure 9.3 The interactions between three different objects are used to encapsulate the actions that save an object's data to a database. There are logical and technical arguments for a number of ways to group them into components.

- *Place all three objects in the same component.* This would make logical sense from the standpoint that their physical implementation would be based on their logical entity (the business object being saved would be represented wholly in one component). This solution would probably be pretty fast on an individual computer since everything would be in the same component, thereby cutting down on the amount of cross-process messaging. However, this partition would probably not scale to meet the demands of a large number of users because business objects would need to hold onto their state data for such a long period of time that this solution could not take advantage of the object pooling, connection pooling, or transactions available in MTS.

- *Put each object into its own component and deploy them all on different physical machines.* This makes the most logical sense and would be the most durable to changes in the system, but it may be slow because it has to message so frequently between processes and over the network.

- *Group the Messaging object and the Presentation object in one component and the Persistence object in another.* This would have the advantage of cutting down on the amount of messaging, and it would take advantage of the object-brokering services of MTS. However, it would degrade the level of modularity in the application because this partition would require us to recompile and redistribute the presentation/messaging component if it were ever made to communicate with a different persistence layer.

As you can see, creating the correct COM components for your application is no trivial undertaking. Later in this section, we will deal in some detail with the guiding principles of partitioning objects into components and pick one of the modularization scenarios just described to use in the sample application.

Hierarchy

Booch writes, simply:

Hierarchy is a ranking or ordering of abstractions.

It is in the subject of hierarchy where COM is the most different from pure object orientation. Once again, since the atomic unit of COM is the component, the object model is impacted. Recall that we defined components as a precompiled, language-independent object or group of objects. Because of the "language-independent" feature of COM components, it is impossible to use the ideas of inheritance and polymorphism as in object-oriented languages.

Before we look at how COM uses the hierarchy principle of the object model, it's important to discuss the idea of hierarchy. The basic idea behind hierarchy is that *objects not only exist in relationships with one another and send messages to one another, but they can be built from one another and can collect one another.*

Hierarchies are often referred to in terms of objects existing in either an *"is a"* structure, in which objects are based on other objects (true inheritance), or as a *"part of"* structure, in which objects collect by or are aggregated by other classes. An example of a "part of" structure is the hierarchy in the last section's sample application. The Customer object has a collection of Order objects that represent the orders that a customer has made. In other words, orders are "part of" the object that models a customer. As you may have already realized, this "part of" hierarchy is largely language-independent. As such, aggregation relationships are largely unimpacted by development under COM.

In contrast, the "is a" structure that exists in many programming languages describes the fact that a new class can be based on an existing class, inheriting its interface and functionality from the original class. In an object-oriented language, a class can gain all the properties and methods that make up the interface of the base class and then extend the interface by adding properties and methods of its own. For example, the Employee object may be (but is not in the sample application) based on a more generic Person class. The Person class may have a Name property and a Commit method that the Employee object inherits. After inheriting these generic behaviors from the Person object, the Employee object may go on to add a JobTitle property and a Requisition method in order to specialize its interface to model the behavior of an employee.

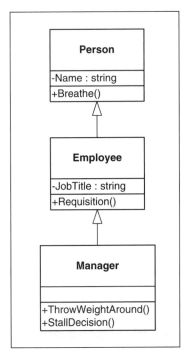

Figure 9.4   Inheritance between the Employee object and the (fictional) Manager object.

In turn, the Employee object may be used as a base class for the Manager class, which would have the Name property and Commit method inherited from the Person class and the JobTitle and Requisition method inherited from the Employee object, and may further specialize by adding a StallDecision method (see Figure 9.4). This type of behavior is called inheritance (really multiple inheritance in the previous example) and is largely viewed as a requisite of an object-oriented language; it is usually supported by the language itself, via some method like the Extends syntax used in Java.

Often, this idea of inheritance is coupled with the idea of polymorphism, or the capability of classes having different implementations, but extending the same interface. Returning to the example used in the preceding paragraph, the Manager object may extend the Requisition method inherited from the Employee object, but the method may be implemented much faster than the same method in the Employee object. Therefore, objects have common interfaces, but their implementations can differ.

As stated at the beginning of this section, since COM is language-independent, the way that it meets the hierarchy principle of the object model is different from "pure" object orientation. To be more exact, COM components cannot perform language-specific implementations of inheritance and polymorphism.

Does this mean that the use of objects in COM is actually an object-based paradigm, not an object-oriented one? That distinction is up to you because there are ways to force a type of both single inheritance and polymorphism through the techniques of *interface inheritance, containment,* and *delegation* concepts described next.

Interface Inheritance

Interface inheritance is the technique of copying every property and method that makes up a base class into the child class. By doing this, you can affect something such as the single inheritance found in object-oriented languages like Java. For example, if you were to implement interface inheritance from the base Person class to the Employee class, you would make sure that every property, method, and event that the Person class exposes is also exposed by the Employee class. Notice that this is just the interface and not the implementation code that is used in interface inheritance. Through this process, any child objects honor the "interface contract" that was made between the parent object (base class) and the system.

Containment and Delegation

Though interface inheritance may extend the "interface contract" to the children of a base class, it does nothing to aid in coding and the economy of expression that "real" inheritance offers to the development process. In fact, these benefits of object orientation can only be realized between COM components through the principles of containment and delegation. Containment is the idea that an object can have a private instance of another object hidden inside it.

So, if an Employee object were performing COM inheritance from the Person object, it would first implement the interface of the Person object, then it would create a private instance of the Person object with which no object outside of the Employee object could interact. Then, in order to reuse the code in the base class, the Employee object would *delegate* any call to one of the inherited properties or methods of Person class to the private instance of the class (see Figure 9.5). In other words, if the Name property of the Employee object were requested, it would simply turn around and request the Name property of the contained Person object.

Under this scheme, polymorphism could be achieved under COM simply by adding implementation code in any inherited method before or after the delegation call to the

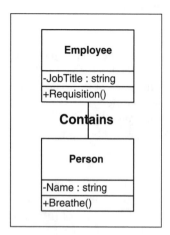

Figure 9.5 The Employee object contains the Person object and delegates operations to it.

contained object. Under this construct, if COM inheritance were to be implemented between the Employee object and the Manager object, then the implementation of the Manager object's Requisition method might do something such as execute its ThrowWeightAround method before calling the contained Employee object's Requisition method. By doing this, the Manager object would expose the same method as the Employee object, but when it was called, different actions would take place.

The way COM allows you to implement inheritance and polymorphism may not be perfect object orientation, but in practice, this is not a problem, because in practice, the "is a" hierarchies that require "true" object-oriented inheritance and polymorphism occur most often *within* components, and "part of" hierarchies occur most often *between* components.

This means that if you are used to working with the "true" inheritance supported by your language, you can continue using it in the construction of components. Remember that COM is only used when objects contained in separate components are made to interact. So it is only in "is a" hierarchies between COM components that the principles of inheritance and polymorphism are impacted by COM. In practice, this type of hierarchy between COM components is rare.

What Is Distributed Application Development?

We're not going to go into great detail here about what distributed application development is because this topic was covered in detail in Chapter 6. To recap, developing an application in multiple tiers is the process of decomposing an application into self-contained components that are distributed on a network. Distributed development is conceptually very similar to object orientation. The real difference is that rather than simply partitioning the logic of your applications into code-based entities either in one application or on one machine, you spread out these entities over any number of machines for the sake of maintainability and performance.

This is why understanding of object orientation is so crucial to your mastery of distributed application development. To repeat, these two methodologies are intricately entwined. Object orientation is a methodology that calls for the partitioning of an application in the *conceptual world*, whereas distributed development is a methodology that calls for the partitioning of an application in the *physical world*. Therefore, really robust distributed application development can only be possible when the partitions of an application are made both on the basis of correct concept *and* optimal physicality. In other words, you have to use both an object-oriented view and a physical view in your distributed application development.

How Do You Do This Stuff?

If at this point either your head is spinning with new ideas or you are bored with all the conceptual stuff, rest assured, we're about to launch into a more practical discussion of distributed application development. The remainder of this chapter (indeed, of this book) focuses on the construction of the sample distributed application framework.

We begin here with some general rules to follow when creating a distributed application; then we move into a discussion of object modeling the framework in the context of an order entry system. This discussion continues through Chapters 10 and 11, as it shows you the underlying code of this chapter's models.

Rules of Distributed Application Development

As with any type of development, there are some general rules you must be aware of whenever you are creating a distributed application. Although there may be many other rules that your organization or client might impose, the two rules (really one rule) that follow are probably the most important.

Rule 1: Get Off of the Wire!

This is important. If you remember only one thing in distributed application development, make it that traveling over the network is probably the most expensive thing that you will do in terms of the performance of your application. The wire between computers is slow, making connecting to another computer slow.

Here are a number of things that you can do to avoid the evil wire.

Avoid chatter at all costs. Chatter is when one component sends a lot of messages to another component. *Avoiding chatter is the cardinal rule of distributed application development.* For example, using an updateable ADO Recordset to perform a number of updates is a fairly chatty construct between the client and the database server because every time an Update method is issued, another message goes out to the server. If you wanted to reduce chatter with a Recordset, you could require it to operate in batch update mode. This way, after making many changes, all of them could travel to the server in one trip.

Know the object to which your message is going. When you use ADO command objects against a stored procedure, you have the choice to either build and send the parameters that you know about to the stored procedure or populate the Command object's collection of Parameter objects with the values that you wish to send. In this instance, it pays to know where your message is going because when ADO populates a Command object's Parameters collection, it is forced to make a trip to the database server.

Use big parameter lists or send arrays as parameters. Another way that you can avoid the wire is to send long lists of parameters or arrays into remote method calls. The idea is to get all of the communication between two components done in one shot. The expensive part of cross-process or cross-network communication is establishing the initial link. Once the lines of communication are open, the amount of information that is made to pass is relatively meaningless.

Send parameters by value rather than by reference. The advantage gained in passing long lists of parameters or an array to a remote object can be undone, *unless* these parameters are passed by value. When a parameter is passed by value,

> **THE POWER OF VARIANT ARRAYS**
>
> If you are thinking that you cannot send arrays to a procedure by value, you are absolutely correct. However, a nicety of the Visual Basic variant data type provides a great means by which to transport a large and variable (i.e., the number elements can be added to or changed) set of data across the wire. When an array is sent to a remote object as a by-value Variant data type, the Variant type dutifully moves through the entire structure of the array and copies all of the values and the structure of the array into its own internal structure. In other words, a by-value Variant array will travel as a stream across the network. Sure, the Variant data type might be more memory-consumptive than strong types, but we bet you'll be willing to trade that minor memory inefficiency any day for the power to pass so many values over the wire in such a structured and efficient package.

a copy of it is made and sent across the wire. In contrast, when a parameter is passed by reference, the receiving object must message back to the sending object in order to gain the referenced value. This is especially damaging when passing arrays, because so many messages would have to be sent to the sending object.

Rule 2: Keep Your Rules Close

By "keeping your rules close," we mean, make every effort to implement business rules in the physical partition that also contains the rules that they govern. One of the worst architectural decisions that you can make is to enforce a business rule on a physical partition that is different from the matter that it governs. For example, can you imagine anything more annoying than enforcing a required attribute rule on an object on a middle (nonpresentation) tier? Doing this would prevent a user from knowing if he or she had missed a required field until a message was sent across the network to a middle tier, the rule was checked, and a message was sent back to the client. Another painful example of a *rule partition mismatch* would be an attempt to enforce referential integrity on a database from a middle tier. Implementing this rule anywhere but on the database would require you to query and query and query to ensure that parent-child data relationships were maintained correctly.

To follow this rule, simple common sense demands that you:

- Implement rules that deal with data input and that don't require database access in the client component.

- Implement rules that deal with data input and that require database access or rules that govern appropriate user access to data in a middle-tier component.

- Implement rules that deal with the structure and relationships of the database in the database itself.

Using the Database as a Logical/Physical Tier

In Chapter 10 and 11, you will see the frequent use of stored procedures. In some academic, object-oriented circles, the use of stored procedures is discouraged because they do not fit neatly into the object-oriented conception of how to build applications. But if you have ever implemented an application using stored procedures, then you know the logical and performance advantages they can offer.

Furthermore, we would maintain that database stored procedures are the correct physical partition for dealing with such purely database-focused rules as:

- Referential integrity
- Record locking
- The adjustment of values in one table based on the values inserted into another.

Object Modeling

When you begin to develop using these techniques a good habit to get into is modeling your application *before* you code. This enables you to *visualize* the application that you are about to build and, therefore, think in detail about the pieces and interactions that make up the system.

As noted by Booch, experiments by psychologists suggest that the maximum number of chunks of information that most people can simultaneously comprehend is around nine. This is a real handicap when dealing with large, complex systems. However, one trick for getting around this limit is to decompose complexity into logical entities and then represent these entities visually. Modeling can help you think more clearly about complex systems and/or in ways that you could not without modeling.

In addition to that remarkable advantage, modeling allows you to communicate with others about your ideas much more easily. In any physical engineering pursuit, it would be unthinkable to begin work without some type of drawing or blueprint of what was to be built. Just as you would never agree to build a house without first drafting blueprints, you should never begin building software without modeling.

Modeling Tools

There are several tools that you can use to model an application (including a napkin and a pencil). However, using a tool like Rational Rose or the Visual Modeler application, which is included with the Enterprise Edition of Microsoft Visual Studio, has marked advantages over manual methods of modeling. First, the diagrams you produce will be easy to read; and because these tools use standardized notation, you can easily use the files produced to communicate with others.

Second, once analysis is finished using one of these tools, you can automatically generate code to define your interfaces. This is especially important when using development tools like Visual Basic in which you can set *version compatibility* with some prebuilt components. This feature will not allow a project to be compiled unless it presents an identical COM interface to a specified, preexisting .exe or .dll. Therefore, when you use either of these tools and the version compatibility features of your design environment, not only can you easily define modeled interfaces, but you can also actually enforce that they do not change without approval during the coding process.

What's With All the Boxes and Lines?

The scope of this book prevents an in-depth discussion on the Unified Modeling Language (UML) that is used in the following diagrams. Therefore, we're only going to cover the most basic level of using UML to create object models. Nevertheless, taking this step (even at its most basic level) is one of the wisest things that you can do for your application.

 To learn more about object modeling (and we encourage you to), there are several excellent books (e.g., *Instant UML* by Pierre–Alan Muller or *UML ToolKit* by Hans-Erik Eriksson and Magnus Penker) and Web sites (e.g. www.rational.com) available on the topic of UML. Do some research into this method of modeling and you will be amazed at the level of detail that can be expressed with these simple boxes, lines, and labels. In just a couple of minutes, you should be able to catch on to the basics of UML, which are used in the following chapters.

So, without further ado (pun intended), here are the basics of UML: *The boxes are objects, the file-folder looking things are groups of objects (i.e., packages), and the lines represent types of relationships between objects or packages.*

Got it? Obviously, there is more to it than that, a lot more. However, for the purposes of this chapter, this simple definition is a pretty good starting place. As we continue through this chapter and Chapters 10 and 11, more UML will be presented and described in the course of exploring the sample framework. For now, just understand the meaning of the boxes and the lines. By the end of the book, you should have a pretty good understanding of the basics of Unified Modeling Language.

Packages (Big Chunks of App)

At the highest level of modeling are the *packages*. As you can see in Figure 9.6, packages are expressed in UML by a folder shape; the dotted, pointed lines that run between them are used to express that these packages have dependencies on one another.

In an application, packages are groups of classes gathered together to address some portion of the system's functionality. In our sample, we will be examining three basic packages: BusinessServices, Transport, and DataServices. Each of these packages will be responsible for some part of the flow of information out of the database to the client and from the client back into the database.

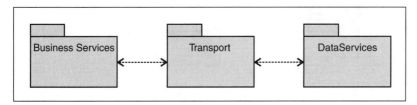

Figure 9.6 The packages used in the framework.

BusinessServices Package/Component

The modularization of the sample framework breaks down pretty cleanly along the lines of the packages that were just described. But this is not always the case. In fact, the only reason we are not describing more packages at this point is because the concentration of this framework is necessarily on the physical model; we are not so concerned with *what* the application does (the logical model), but with *how* it does it (the physical model).

The first such package/component is the BusinessServices component. This component is physically placed on a client's machine or a Web server and is used as the first stage in building a bridge between user (i.e., GUI) and the database. The objects in this component respond to requests from a client application in order to execute a business task (e.g., create a new order for a customer or return a Recordset as the result of a query). When it is necessary to return data from the database, the objects in the BusinessServices component send and receive messages from the Messenger object shown at the left corner of Figure 9.7.

As explained earlier, all of the boxes that you see in this figure represent objects, and the lines between them represent relationships. Notice that there are two different types of lines used in the model: solid lines and dotted lines that end with an arrow.

The solid lines represent the linked objects that have some type of association with one another (e.g., every LineItem object is linked to a Product). The dotted lines ending with an arrow represent that one object is instantiating another (e.g., the Factory object instantiates the Customer, Order, LineItem, and Product objects). Keep in mind that we are only using a small portion of the UML notation in this model, but the distinction between these two types of object relationships is important to note.

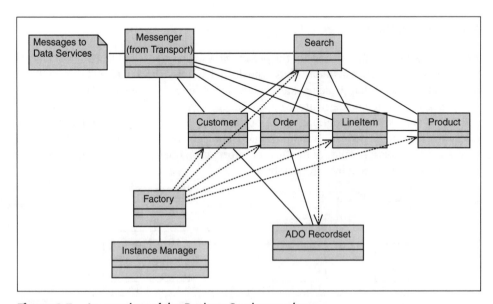

Figure 9.7   An overview of the BusinessServices package.

The Factory Object

The Factory object is the object that instances all of the other objects that will be used by a client of the BusinessServices component. To populate requested objects with property values from the database, it makes use of the Messenger object to contact the objects in the DataServices component.

The InstanceManager Object

You will notice in the model that the Factory object has a relationship with the Instance-Manager object. As its name would suggest, this object pools and manages instances of other objects. Before the Factory object retrieves data from the database in response to a request, it first checks to see if there is a current instance of the object being managed by the InstanceManager object. As you will see in the implementation in the last chapter of the book, this object plays an important role in dealing with the referencing problems inherent to parent-child object relationships.

The Search Object

The Search object is used to return objects and Recordsets (which should be seen as mixed-object attribute cursors in the context of this framework) from the database. Other objects in the system specify the query that they wish to run and pass an array of parameters to one of this object's methods; it returns a Recordset (with field names aliased to object attribute names to preserve the encapsulation of the database). When one of the core business objects (i.e., Customer, Order, LineItem, and Product) receive a Recordset from the Search object, it uses it in conjunction with the Factory object to instance child objects (e.g., an Order object's LineItem child objects).

Clients of the BusinessServices component can also use this object to run a query and return a disconnected Recordset to the client machine. As you already know from the earlier chapters, having a client-side Recordset is extremely useful and fast for populating a GUI with data from the database. Without the ADO Recordset returned from this component, a GUI could only be populated by enduring the processing overhead of "walking" the relationships between objects. (e.g., To fill a combo box on a form with a customer's name and order date, two queries would have to be run to instance two entire Customer and Order objects for each line.)

The Customer Object

As you would expect, the Customer object is responsible for exposing the data (e.g., name) and behavior (e.g., saving changed data to the database) of the customers of a company. As you can see in the model, this object is created by the Factory object; it saves its data through its association with the Messenger object and is associated with the Order object (i.e., customers place orders). It also has an association with the Search object, which it uses to return its associated Order objects, which in turn, save their data into a local ADO Recordset.

The Order Object

All of the core business objects (Customer, Order, LineItem, and Product) have many of the same relationships with the supporting or creating objects (i.e., Factory, Search,

Messenger, and the ADO Recordset). So, like the Customer object, the Order object is created by the Factory object. It saves its data using the Messenger object and is associated with its own collection of LineItem objects, which it returns using the Search object and manages in a local ADO Recordset.

The LineItem Object

The LineItem object is responsible for managing the data and behavior in the system related to the individual line items listed in an order. Its relationships with the supporting objects are identical to the previous objects, except that it has an association to one (and only one) Product object. Therefore, it does not use a Recordset object to manage a collection because it has no collection to manage.

The Product Object

The Product object represents the products that can be ordered by the customers of the system. As such, it keeps track of the number of units that are currently available in stock, along with simple descriptions of the products. It is instanced and persists itself using the same Factory and Messenger objects as the other objects; but it is associated with no lower-order object. This is the end of the line of parent-child object relationships in the application.

Transport Package/Component

The Transport package exists only to carry messages between the client-side BusinessServices component and the MTS-sited DataServices component. This component exists so that the client-side BusinessServices component can be made to communicate with a different DataServices tier simply by swapping one Transport component for another (see Figure 9.8). For example, if this application were to be placed on a salesperson's laptop so that he or she could enter new orders while disconnected from the network, all you would have to do would be to disable or remove the Transport component that communicates directly to the DataServices component and replace it with one that communicates with MSMQ.

Therefore, this Transport component encapsulates (i.e., hides) the connection to the server-side component. The application framework benefits from this construct because a change-of-server application would have no impact on the BusinessServices component or on any GUI application that derived its information from the BusinessServices component. In other words, things on your network could change radically and the application's client-side code would be protected.

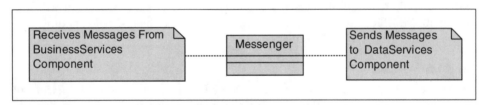

Figure 9.8 An overview of the Transport package.

The Messenger Object

The only object in the Transport component is the lonely Messenger object, whose many methods are called by the BusinessServices component's object; in turn, the Messenger object makes calls to the DataServices component's objects. Basically, the Messenger object is just a relay between the BusinessServices component and the DataServices component.

DataServices Package/Component

Finally, the DataServices component is responsible for all direct interactions with the database (see Figure 9.9). In most instances, the objects in the client-side BusinessServices component map directly to a matching object in the DataServices component. Also, in most cases, the objects contained in this component use ADO Command objects to pass parameters and execute stored procedures that will add, update, delete, or return data from the database. Complex business rules, or business rules that require interaction with the database, can also be implemented in this component.

Perhaps the most important aspect of the DataServices component is that it is sited in MTS. To take advantage of this unique environment, the objects in this tier of the application framework are completely stateless; that is, no data is persisted between method calls originating from the Transport component.

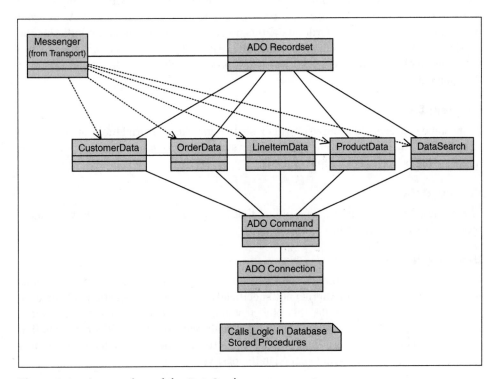

Figure 9.9 An overview of the DataServices component.

ADO Command Object

Because almost every interaction with the database is done through a stored procedure, every DataServices object makes use of the ADO Command object and its collection of Parameter objects.

ADO Connection Object

Recordsets created by Command objects typically cannot be disconnected from their connection to the database. However, you can still achieve a disconnected Recordset by setting a number of properties on the Connection object, which the Command object uses to establish its database connection. Since one of the most efficient and structured ways to pass data from the MTS server to the client is through disconnected ADO Recordsets, the ADO Connection object plays an important role in this framework.

CustomerData

Like the client-side Customer object, the server-side CustomerData object is responsible for information and behavior pertaining to the customers of a company. On the server, the responsibilities of this object include returning customer-specific sets of records, saving customer information to the database, and initiating the persistence of child objects (i.e., orders) when it is directed to process a transaction.

OrderData Object

Just like the CustomerData object, this object interacts directly with the database in order to respond from messages sent to it from the Transport component. Aside from managing the persistence of Order data, this object is also responsible for initiating the persistence of its associated LineItem data. In the last chapter of this book, you will see the code involved in the iterative, transacted process that saves Order and LineItem data in a batch.

LineItem Data

As its name suggests, this simple object exists to persist and return LineItem data. Since this object's data is the endpoint of the system's transactions, it has no responsibility for initiating the persistence of child objects.

Product Data

This is another simple persistence object that manages all interactions with the database, specifically data related to products.

DataSearch Object

Like the client-side Search object, the DataSearch object is responsible for interactions with the database that run queries not specifically tied to the interactions of the core business objects. For example, this object would handle queries that return filtered result sets (e.g., all companies whose names begin with the letter B) or queries that would return data from more than one object's attributes (e.g., the name of customers and the dates of the orders they placed in the past year).

Basically, this object uses the ADO Command object and the ADO Connection object to return disconnected ADO Recordsets to the Transport component. The Transport component, in turn, passes the Recordset on to the BusinessServices component and, finally, to the client application that issued the request.

From Here

By now, you have a background in the concepts and basic structure of the framework described in the last part of the book. The final two chapters explore the particulars of this framework and show you example code that is used to make the structure work.

Developing an Enterprise-Level Application with ADO: Adding, Updating, and Deleting

Our first look into the code of the sample application deals with the basics: Adding new records, finding existing records, updating records, and deleting records. Talk about your generic application behavior—anyone who has ever written an application that deals with a database has had to confront these basic problems.

These basics have been played out in countless applications and have probably been implemented in countless ways. If you have been programming for any length of time, no doubt you have seen this type of basic implementation change many, many times. Doing *n*-tiered, object-oriented, ADO-based development will be no different: You will need to address these basic problems once again.

The good news is that there are many more advantages to developing applications using these technologies and this methodology. We know you have probably heard that before, but trust us, because this methodology is based upon COM components, you can develop your core in whichever language you feel is most appropriate for the job, then show it to the user through any COM-capable interface. For example, we could develop our core logic in Visual Basic, Visual C++, or Visual FoxPro, and then choose to display the application to the user through conventional forms, any COM-capable application (like Microsoft Excel), or even over the Web.

What You'll Learn

This coding methodology and technology is all about taking shortcuts, and in this chapter you will learn how to cheat on the basics of database application development (we proudly consider ourselves to be sneaky, no-good cheats). The focus here is on the creation of the sample application's Customer object; the basic logic that handles adding, searching, editing, and deleting customers is ostensibly the same as that which exists in all other core data-handling objects in the application. In other words, this is our basic reusable framework for creating core business objects. In brief then, this chapter explores:

- Factory objects that are used (of all things) for the manufacture of objects.
- Messaging components that move data between the client and server (so that the application server can change radically and all you have to do is install a new build of this component).
- Handling state data in objects.
- Setting object properties that will be stored in the database.
- Sending an object's data to the server to be saved.
- Working with basic MTS components that marshal disconnected ADO Recordsets.
- The magic of stored procedures.
- Searching the database.
- Handling optimistic and pessimistic record locking without a persistent connection to the database.

 It's all the same from here. By design, all of the other objects in this application work in much the same way. Consequently, once you know the basic mechanics of the Customer object, you also know the basics of all of the other objects. This might make for boring coding, but it also makes for quick-to-develop, fast-to-mature, easy-to-maintain, stable programs.

Lie, Steal, and Cheat!

If the freedom from a mandated language or interface isn't enough to convince you of the value of these technologies and approach to coding, consider this: Using them allows you to take (almost immoral) shortcuts. It is a truism that good programmers are basically lazy sandbaggers who spend most of their time lying (that is, making application performance *appear* faster), stealing (usually code—like the code that you are about to see), and most important, cheating (good programmers design applications that allow for them to cheat on later programming efforts by reusing large sections of code). Cheating is what this type of development is all about.

- ADO gives you a chance to cheat by allowing you to write reusable, data source, nonspecific code.
- An object-oriented approach encourages coding specifically built for reuse and extensibility.
- MTS, MSMQ, and COM allow you to create components that serve the purpose of the application that you are coding yet can be used by other applications. What's more is that components shared in this way can be updated (or fixed) in one spot,

and the improvements can be seen on many machines and in many different applications. What a good, effective way to dodge work!

Creating a New Customer

The most logical place to begin the exploration of the sample application is with the creation of a new Customer object. In many object-oriented frameworks, a generic pattern called a *Factory method* is used to create instances of classes. The application framework in this book is no different. In the BusinessServices component (the client-side business objects), there is a publicly createable object named Factory. It follows, then, that to create a new Customer object, you must call that Factory object's CreateCustomer( ) method.

The Factory Object

The reason for employing a Factory object in this application is that it gives a central, encapsulated point in the application for creating instances of any class (Figure 10.1). Then, if classes were added to the application in the future, there would already be a Factory object in place to handle the things common to the creation of all classes. Also, it is the only object that knows anything about the creation of individual objects. Therefore,

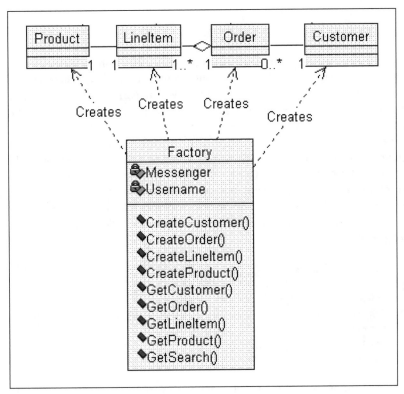

Figure 10.1 The Factory object creates new objects and gets existing ones.

if you use a Factory object, you are making your job easier (there's only one point of change) when it's time to add classes to the application or change those already there.

Not only does the Factory create all of the components in the application, it is also the only publicly visible class; in other words, it is the key to the whole application. Providing a single point of entry into business objects is especially important from the standpoint of reuse. By implementing a Factory object, external applications do not need to know the names of individual classes to instance them. Instead, any external application simply has to know how to create the Factory object and that it has a CreateCustomer( ) method. If you are familiar with the idea of design patterns, then you might recognize this area of the application as an implementation of the Abstract Factory Pattern. If you want to learn more about design patterns, we recommend the book *Design Patterns, Elements of Reusable Object-Oriented Design*, Addison-Wesley, 1995

The Messaging Component

As programs go, the Messaging component is almost embarrassingly simple (see Figure 10.2). It has only two functions in life: to establish a pointer to objects sited in MTS, and to relay messages between the client application (i.e., the BusinessServices component) and the MTS Server objects (i.e., the DataServices component). As simple as this component is, however, it is a requirement that it be created and passed to the Factory object *before* any work begins.

Gaining Early References to MTS Objects

You may well ask why you would want to create such a simple component. The answers lie in the way you should reference MTS components from your client applications and in creating an easy path to extending the system. First, as you learned in Chapter 7, you should establish references to MTS components as soon as possible in an application and maintain them as long as you can.

Since MTS manages and reuses objects, maintaining pointers to these objects costs you nothing in terms of system resources and the overall scalability of the system. In fact, the only time that references to MTS objects impact the speed of your system is when you first reference to them. That said, our sample application uses the Messaging object to gain references to MTS server components as soon as it is instanced. So, in the Messaging component's one Messenger class, you will find the following code in the Class_Initialize( ) event procedure:

```
Private Sub Class_Initialize()
    Set mobjSearch = CreateObject("DataServices.DataSearch")
    Set mobjCustomer = CreateObject("DataServices.CustomerData")
    Set mobjOrder = CreateObject("DataServices.OrderData")
    Set mobjLineItem = CreateObject("DataServices.LineItemData")
    Set mobjProduct = CreateObject("DataServices.ProductData")
End Sub
```

In the sample application, we could probably get away with instancing these objects as soon as the Messaging object is created. However, if we were gaining references to a

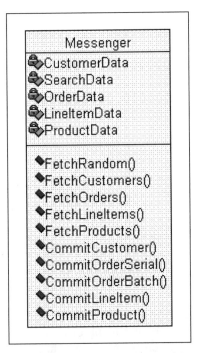

Figure 10.2   The Messenger object.

larger number of MTS objects, it might be wise to come up with a scheme to gain references only when we need them. Anyway, the point here is to try to get our MTS references early and hold on to them as long as we can.

Extensibility

The other great thing about having a Messaging component is that it can be easily replaced in order to replace the server application that will be used by the client-side business objects. For example, the Messaging object in this application is built to handle a connection to MTS objects, but it could easily be rewritten to communicate with a middle-tier application hosted on a Web server.

Imagine if some remote workers wanted to run an application that you had created to run on a LAN. If you wrote that application with connections to the server established directly in the client-side business objects, you would be forced to rewrite the entire client-side BusinessServices component to accommodate the change. But if you made use of a Messaging component, you could just tweak the existing Messenger so that it made use of the RDS components (which you learned about in Chapter 5), install this new Messenger on the remote worker's systems, and your job would be done.

Passing the Messenger to the Factory

The extensibility features of using a Messenger become more pronounced when client applications that make use of the client-side BusinessServices component can assign their own Messengers to the Factory object as they see fit. For example, if a number of different Messengers were installed on a system, a client application could assign a different Messenger for different processes (e.g., to update the sales database, you pass an Internet Messenger, and to update a stock database, you pass a local Messaging component). This could even be useful for load balancing. For example, if an application were coded so that it timed all interactions with MTS objects, it could be made to pass a Messenger to the Factory object that communicated with a back-up MTS server if the wait ever got too long.

For these reasons, the sample application requires that client applications instance and pass a Messenger object to the Factory object before it does any work. So, if the Factory object was to be instanced and used when a Visual Basic form was loaded, the following code could be used:

```
Private Sub Form_Load()
Dim objCourier as New Transport.Messenger
Dim objFactory As New BusinessServices.Factory
    Set mobjFactory.Messenger = objCourier
End Sub
```

Since the sample application requires that a Messenger be established for the Factory object, the Factory object calls its Ready() function at the beginning of each of its method calls. This simple function checks to see if the Factory's Messenger has been established; if not, it raises an error.

```
Private Function Ready() As Boolean
    If mobjMessenger Is Nothing Then
        ERR.Raise vbObjectError + 1, "Business Services",
            "Messenger must be set before creating or " & _
                "getting any object"
        Ready = False
    Else
        Ready = True
    End If
End Function
```

The Factory's CreateCustomer() Method

The Factory object method that creates new Customer objects is very simple. In fact, it only has to accomplish five things:

- Check that the Factory object has been assigned a Messenger.

- Create a Customer object.

- Assign a reference to the Factory's Messenger for the new Customer object.

- Mark the Customer object as new.

- Assign the Customer object a unique value that the program and the database will use to identify it.

Following is the complete code found in the Factory's CreateCustomer() method:

```
Public Function CreateCustomer() As Customer
Dim objCustomer As Customer
If Ready() then
    Set objCustomer = New Customer
    Set objCustomer.Messenger = Me.Messenger
    objCustomer.EditState = objectadd
    objCustomer.Moniker = GetMoniker()
    Set CreateCustomer = objCustomer
End Function
```

Although the dimensioning and creation of the Customer object is rather straightforward, the assignment of the Customer object's Messenger, EditState, and Moniker properties beg more detail. First, the Factory assigns a pointer to the same Messenger component to which the Factory was assigned so that the new Customer object has pointers to MTS components when it is time to save the Customer's data.

Second, the Customer object's EditState value is set. The EditState property is simply a value that defines whether a business object is new, edited, marked for deletion, or has not been changed since it was retrieved from the database. Internally, the Customer object stores the number 1 for a new object, the number 2 for an object that has been edited, the number 3 for an object marked for deletion, and the number 4 for an existing object that has not been edited. However, in the CreateCustomer() method, you see it being assigned with an enumerated value so that the code is more readable. The EditState enumerator is defined as follows.

```
Public Enum EditState
    ObjectAdd = 0
    ObjectEdit = 1
    ObjectDelete = 2
    ObjectNoChange = 3
End Enum
```

The assignment of the Moniker attribute is a somewhat more complicated issue. This moniker is the value that will be used to identify the object while it is on the user's machine; it will also be used as the unique identifier (primary key) in the Customer table in the database. For those reasons, it must be unique.

The GetMoniker() Function

As you might already know, the traditional way to get a unique value in an application like this one is to query against some table in the database that returns and then increments a numeric value. Of course, there are a million ways of doing this, but they all run along pretty much same lines, as in the following pseudocode:

```
'Retrieve CurrentNumber Value in SystemPrimaryKeyTable
'Update SystemPrimaryKeyTable and
'    Set CurrentNumber = CurrentNumber + 1
```

This is for generating unique values for many systems, as it definitely creates unique numeric values. Also, if these values are used as primary/foreign keys in a database, they are the most efficient type of value to index, and therefore create the most quickly "query-able" database.

However, there are also disadvantages to this method. First, the conventional method requires an extra trip to the database for every object created. Second, if a lot of new records are being created, this one section (sector) of your database could become a bottleneck for your application. So, if your system is primarily used for entering and managing data (like our sample application), you might want to turn to the operating system to generate a unique value.

The way to do this is to use the Win32 API to generate a GUID. Windows uses GUIDs to generate unerringly unique values for any COM object registered on the system. A GUID value is derived from a number of unique sources (like time and network card ID) and is guaranteed to be unique in the world. In fact, if these values were not unique, Windows would not be able to keep track of the multitude of COM components that are typically registered on a system. So, since there is already a function like this built in the OS, you might as well take advantage of it to generate unique values for your application.

Keep in mind that using the Win32 API will also help you to prevent unnecessary traffic on systems where the bulk of the activity is data manipulation and not querying. This method generates a fixed-length string guaranteed to be unique. But because it is a fixed-length string and not a numeric, it will create a (minutely) slower index to use in your queries. A word of caution: Keep your head with this; it's not magic to be used everywhere. Use it only if it is appropriate for your application (more data manipulation than queries), and benchmark to see how indexing on strings will affect your database query speed.

The Win32 API function that produces this call is WinCoCreateGuid(). It returns a peculiar structure that should (for readability's sake) be converted into a string before it is used. The WinCoCreateGuid declaration and the UDT that must be declared to hold the data that it produces are as follows:

```
Private Declare Function WinCoCreateGuid Lib _
"OLE32.DLL" Alias "CoCreateGuid" (g As GUID) As Long

Private Type GUID
    D1          As Long
    D2          As Integer
    D3          As Integer
    D4(8)       As Byte
End Type
```

As you can see, this API call will return a structure. We could elect to store this in the database, but it would be unreadable and, therefore, very hard to debug in the database. So, we use the two functions below to return the GUID from Windows and then convert it into a string.

```
Public Function GetMoniker() As String
    Dim udtGuid As GUID
    Dim sBuffer As String

    WinCoCreateGuid(udtGuid)
```

(continues)

(Continued)

```
    sBuffer = PadRight0(sBuffer, Hex$(udtGuid.D1), 8, True)
    sBuffer = PadRight0(sBuffer, Hex$(udtGuid.D2), 4, True)
    sBuffer = PadRight0(sBuffer, Hex$(udtGuid.D3), 4, True)
    sBuffer = PadRight0(sBuffer, Hex$(udtGuid.D4(0)), 2)
    sBuffer = PadRight0(sBuffer, Hex$(udtGuid.D4(1)), 2, True)
    sBuffer = PadRight0(sBuffer, Hex$(udtGuid.D4(2)), 2)
    sBuffer = PadRight0(sBuffer, Hex$(udtGuid.D4(3)), 2)
    sBuffer = PadRight0(sBuffer, Hex$(udtGuid.D4(4)), 2)
    sBuffer = PadRight0(sBuffer, Hex$(udtGuid.D4(5)), 2)
    sBuffer = PadRight0(sBuffer, Hex$(udtGuid.D4(6)), 2)
    GetMoniker = sBuffer
End Function
Private Function PadRight0(ByVal sBuffer As String _
                , ByVal sBit As String _
                , ByVal nLenRequired As Integer _
                , Optional bHyp As Boolean _
                ) As String


    PadRight0 = sBuffer & _
            sBit & _
            String$(Abs(nLenRequired - Len(sBit)), "0") & _
            IIf(bHyp = True, "-", "")

End Function
```

What's great about taking care of all of this in the Factory object is that when it is called from some client application, it knows nothing about it. Nor should it know. In fact, to instance a new Customer object on the load of a Visual Basic form, this is all the code you need to write:

```
Private Sub Form_Load()
Dim objCourier as new Transport.Messenger
Dim objFactory As New BusinessServices.Factory
    Set mobjFactory.Messenger = objCourier
Set mobjCustomer = objFactory.CreateCustomer()
End Sub
```

Setting Properties and Managing Data

Part of the definition of an object is that it has state; that is, data that it manages. The smallest amount of state data that the Customer object ever has is the pointer to the Messenger object, its Moniker value, and EditState information. This information will be present whenever the Factory creates a new object. All of the data in these objects is either stored in an array or (as we will see in the following chapter) as a reference to a row in an ADO Recordset.

If you look at the General Declarations section of the Customer class, you will see the following declarations that will be used to store all of the object's data.

```
Private CustState(CustState(14)) As Variant
Private mobjHomeCursor As ADOR.Recordset
Private mobjMessenger As Object
Private mobjRSOrders As ADOR.Recordset
Private mboolBatched As Boolean
Private mboolLocked As Boolean
```

The most important declaration for this chapter is the variant array called Cust-State( ), which will carry the bulk of the object's state. Whenever a property of the Customer object is changed, its property's let procedure changes a value in the CustState( ) array. For example, when the Customer object's CreditLimit property is changed (e.g., objCustomer.Creditlimit = 4500), then the following property's let procedure will be run:

```
Public Property Let CreditLimit(curCreditLimit As Currency)
    ProcessChange
    CustState(11) = curCreditLimit
End Property
```

The basic action of this property's let procedure is apparent: It simply takes the value passed in the property assignment and places it in the eleventh element of the CustState array.

The CustData Enum

Although the action of the property's let procedures is simple, sometimes code that references the *n*-th element of an array is hard to read. For this reason, in the Customer object's general declaration section, the following enumerated type is declared:

```
Private Enum CustData
    MonikerValue = 0
    NameValue = 1
    ContactNameValue = 2
    PhoneValue = 3
    FaxValue = 4
    Address1Value = 5
    Address2Value = 6
    CityValue = 7
    StateValue = 8
    PostalCodeValue = 9
    LastUpdatedValue = 10
    CreditLimitValue = 11
    ObjectEditValue = 12
    GotLockValue = 13
    UpdateIDValue = 14
End Enum
```

Once this enumerated type is in place, we can rewrite the CreditLimit property's let procedure so that it is more readable but still puts the passed value into the eleventh element of the CustState array.

```
Public Property Let CreditLimit(curCreditLimit As Currency)
    ProcessChange
    'CreditLimitValue is more readable, but still equals 11
    CustState(CreditLimitValue) = curCreditLimit
End Property
```

The ProcessChange Procedure

But before it does this, the ProcessChange procedure is run to change the EditState of
the object. As you can see in the following code, the ProcessChange() procedure itself
writes the change of state into the CustState array. By doing this, when this array is sent
to the server, it can determine if the customer record is to be added, deleted, or updated
in the database.

```
Function ProcessChange() As Boolean
    If Not CustState(ObjectEditValue ) = ObjectAdd Then
        CustState(ObjectEditValue ) = ObjectEdit
    End If
End Function
```

The one case in which the ProcessChange() procedure will not change this value in
the array is when the object is marked as a newly added record. The reason for this is
that if a record is to be added, it must maintain its AddedRecord value so that the server
knows to send a SQL INSERT statement rather than a SQL UPDATE statement to the
database.

Why All the Arrays?

Through the use of variant arrays, the application is made much more extensible. For
example, if the Customer's data were changed to include some new element, then the
array going to and from the server could simply be redimensioned to carry the new element. This would allow the data passed to methods to change but for the method signatures (i.e., the parameters that they take) to stay the same. Since several objects may be
using the same method, but sending a different number of parameters, maintaining a
business object's interface is crucial to building this type of application.

Experience shows that this type of flexibility is often more valuable than the more
academic correctness of an unwavering adherence to strong data types. Sure, the Visual
Basic Variant data type is more memory-consumptive than strong types, but for the
overall good of the system over its lifetime of maintenance and use, using arrays can be
a good choice. As with anything else, making this decision is a trade-off between different goods. In the end, you must analyze your application and make up your own mind.

Saving the Object's Data

All of a business object's "persistable" data is stored in a variant array. Therefore, it is a
simple matter to send the data to the MTS component in one call. In any business object,
the name of the method used to save an object's data is Commit().

From the client-side business object's perspective, this is a trivial procedure that calls the CommitCustomer( ) method of the Messaging object and passes the CustState( ) array. By doing this, it is passing all of the Customer object's attributes along with instructions (EditState) about what to do with the data when it gets to the server.

```
Public Function Commit() as Boolean
Commit = mobjMessenger.CommitCustomer(CustState())
End Function
```

Although the client-side Commit( ) method is simple, it is important because this is the point at which the server-side component (called the DataServices component) really begins its work.

Getting the Object's Data to the Database

The first step in sending the Customer object's data to the database is taken with the Messenger component. In this case, the Messenger is acting as a relay to whichever server-side component it has been implemented to use. So, when the client-side Customer object calls the Messenger's CommitCustomer( ) method, the Messenger turns around and calls the AddUpdateDelete( ) method of the MTS CustomerData object, to which the Messenger object established a connection when it was initialized (see Figure 10.3).

```
Public Function CommitCustomer(aParams() As Variant) As Boolean
    CommitCustomer = mobjCustomer.AddUpdateDelete(aParams())
End Function
```

The DataServices Component

The DataServices component is that part of the application sited in MTS and in charge of making all changes to the database and enforcing database knowledge-dependent business rules. Because it is sited in MTS, all objects of the DataServices component are stateless and support transactions. The one object that we will concentrate on in this

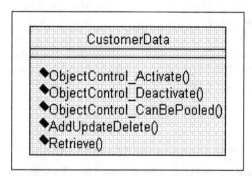

Figure 10.3   The server-side CustomerData object.

discussion is the CustomerData component. This object manages all interactions with the database concerning the addition, deletion, and alteration of customer data.

Playing by MTS Rules

All DataServices objects are very careful to "play by the rules" set by MTS. By this we mean, for example, that the server-side CustomerData object implements the MTS ObjectControl interface. As you learned in Chapter 8, when this interface is implemented, it adds the ObjectControl_Activate() method to the class that is run whenever an MTS component springs to life. The CustomerData object uses this event procedure to capture the MTS ObjectContext of the call and saves a pointer to that instance as a module-level variable.

```
'in the class general declarations area
Implements MTxAS.ObjectControl
Private mObjCtxt As ObjectContext


Private Sub ObjectControl_Activate()
    Set mObjCtxt = GetObjectContext()
End Sub
```

By making use of this event procedure, the CustomerData object can avoid having to call GetObjectContext() in every method. Instead, it can simply call the temporary module-level variable mObjCtxt's SetComplete() or SetAbort() as the last action of any method. Another thing to remember about all objects in the DataServices component is that they are all stateless, so you can expect there to be no persistent data between calls to any object.

The CustomerData Object's AddUpdateDelete() Method

After the CustomerData object establishes a new module-level ObjectContext variable in its Activate event procedure, the call coming from the Messaging object passes the client-side CustState() array to the CustomerData object's AddUpdateDelete() method. This method works with a SQL Server-stored procedure and an ADO Command object to commit changes to the database.

 Put the logic where it makes the most sense for your application. Using stored procedures disrupts the reusability of the logic in the stored procedure to database platforms, except for the one for which the procedure was written (e.g., SQL Server-stored procedures will not work without significant reworking on an Oracle server), so you will probably want to rewrite the logic that you see in the stored procedures in this chapter and the next into MTS server components if there is a change of database platform looming in the future of your application. That said, there are some compelling reasons for using stored procedures when it makes sense to do so.

Arguments for Using Stored Procedures

A general guideline of tiered development is that you should implement business rules in the layer closest to the matter being governed by the rule. For example, it makes the most sense to implement a business rule such as requiring a field to be entered directly in the client-side business object. Obviously, by doing this, you avoid a lot of needless network traffic and superfluous calls. Likewise, you could enforce referential integrity among tables, or record locking in a MTS component, but it would be slow (as you would have to be constantly querying) and it would be painful to implement in comparison with the referential integrity constraints that most modern databases offer.

Keep the Rules Close to the Matter

As we just said, it's best to keep business rules as close to the matter they govern. Therefore, it makes the most sense to implement actions (including the particulars of adding, editing, and deleting records, record locking, and referential integrity) in the database itself. Even though this is backend-specific code, rewriting a small number of these most basic data-handling procedures in another vendor-specific language is not an insurmountable task, especially when you consider the speed advantages gained in any server database when you use precompiled stored procedures rather than inline SQL.

Use the Level of Encapsulation That Will Protect Against the Most Likely Changes

Another argument for using stored procedures comes from the problem of object-to-relational mapping; that is, in any object-oriented system, an object may persist its data in any number of tables. Also, it is generally considered appropriate for business objects to be encapsulated from the physical structure of the database. By providing this encapsulation, the structure of tables could change, fields could be added and deleted, and it should not matter to your program.

The problem with using stored procedures to provide this encapsulation is that, although they protect against changes to the structure of the database impacting your objects, they do not protect against the impact to your objects if the database platform shifts (e.g., SQL Server to Oracle).

This encapsulation is often the heart of the argument against using stored procedures in an object-oriented system. Certainly, this concern is valid, but to make a decision about where your core data-handling logic should be placed, you have to weigh your options. The basic question that you have to ask yourself is: "What level of encapsulation do I want to provide for my application, and what am I willing to pay for it in terms of development time and application performance?"

Over time, any database will go through both small and cataclysmic changes. (A cataclysmic change would be a movement of the data from one platform to another. For example, most people who have worked in Y2K-driven client/server application development efforts would consider the movement from DB2 to a modern relational database a cataclysmic event.) Unless your organization is suffering from some sort of driving masochism, cataclysmic database events will be rare. More common events are denormalization of tables for the sake of speed, the addition and removal of database tables, and the addition and removal of database table attributes. For these types of changes, stored procedures provide the best protection.

For example, if a field is moved from storage in one table into another one, you could simply change the stored procedure to keep pace with the changing database. If your data service components were built to take advantage of stored procedures, then a shifting database definition would go unnoticed. Your components would continue to send values into stored procedure parameters and receive data in return, blissfully ignorant of those annoying, frequent changes. Sure, the use of stored procedures will force you to work when a cataclysm comes your way. But then again, you usually can see those types of changes coming much sooner than the casual addition, removal, or movement of a field.

In comparison, if you have coded for cataclysmic changes (in which case, you should begin to suspect that your boss/client subconsciously hates you), you would have to go back into your compiled code, make changes, recompile your code and resite it in MTS. Furthermore, even if you think you have coded your components to be database-nonspecific, you will often find that subtle changes in SQL syntax and other small vendor-specific oddities will unfortunately derail your best intentions. This type of change will force you into panicked, last-minute rewrites of components that you assumed were finished. (Sadly, this is the voice of experience talking here.)

The AddEditDeleteCustomer Stored Procedure

If you haven't worked much with TSQL stored procedures in the past, but you know SQL syntax, you will probably be able to make sense of this simple stored procedure used by the CustomerData object's AddUpdateDelete( ) method to make changes in the database. To begin, after the initial Create Procedure statement, there is a listing of all of the parameters that this stored procedure takes: their data types and their default values. As you will see in a moment, the CustomerData.AddUpdateDelete( ) method takes all of the data in the CustState( ) array passed to it from the client-side components and, in turn, passes it into this stored procedure's parameters.

The most programmatically important of these parameters is the @Action parameter, which drives the action (to INSERT, UPDATE, or DELETE) of the stored procedure on the database's base tables. The value that was originally set into the client-side Customer object's EditState attribute is eventually passed into this parameter. Therefore, if the EditState of the Customer object was ObjectAdd (i.e., an enumerated value equaling 0), an INSERT SQL statement will be run by the stored procedure. Likewise, if this value were ObjectEdit (i.e., an enumerated value equaling 1), then an UPDATE SQL statement would be run. If the @Action parameter were set to ObjectDelete (i.e., 2), a DELETE would be issued. Therefore, not only does the CustState( ) array carry the client-side Customer object's data, but it also carries instructions about what should be done with the data once it reaches the database.

```
Create Procedure AddEditDeleteCustomer
( /*These are the Parameter Definitions*/
@Moniker VarChar(50) = NULL, @Name varchar(75) = NULL,
@ContactName varchar(30) =NULL, @Phone varchar(12) = NULL,
@Fax varchar(12) = NULL, @Address1 varchar(50) = NULL,
@Address2 varchar(50) = NULL, @City varchar(30)= NULL,
```

(*continues*)

(Continued)

```
@State varchar(2) = NULL, @PostalCode varchar(10)= NULL,
@LastUpdated datetime = NULL, @CreditLimit money = NULL,
@Lockedby char (10) = NULL, @LockDate datetime = NULL,
@Action Int = 1, /* 0 = Insert, 1 = Update, 2 = Delete*/
@UpdateID Int = 1
)
As
/*This is where the Logic of the SP is run*/
IF @Action = 0 /*Insert New Record*/
    INSERT INTO Customers
        (cuCustomerID, cuCustomerName, cuContactName,
        cuContactPhone, cuContactFax, cuAddress1,
        cuAddress2, cuCity, cuState, cuPostalCode,
        cuLastUpdated, cuCredit, cuUpdateID)
    VALUES (@Moniker, @Name, @ContactName, @Phone, @Fax,
        @Address1, @Address2, @City, @State,
        @PostalCode, GetDate(), @CreditLimit, @UpdateID)
ELSE IF @Action = 1 /*Update Existing Record*/
    UPDATE Customers
SET cuCustomerID = @Moniker, cuCustomerName = @Name,
        cuContactName = @ContactName,
        cuContactPhone = @Phone, cuContactFax = @Fax,
        cuAddress1 = @Address1,
        cuAddress2 = @Address2, cuCity = @City,
cuState = @State, cuPostalCode = @PostalCode,
cuLastUpdated = GetDate(),
        cuCredit = @CreditLimit
cuLockDate = NULL,
        cuUpdateID = (@CurUpdateID + 1)
        WHERE cuCustomerID = @Moniker
ELSE IF @Action = 2
    DELETE FROM Customers WHERE cuCustomerID = @Moniker
RETURN
```

Working with the Command Object

Now that you have seen the stored procedure that the CustomerData object's AddUpdateDelete() method uses, it is time to examine the Visual Basic code in the method call. Once again, we are looking at another pretty simple routine. Basically, all that the AddUpdateDelete() does is to pass parameters to the AddEditDeleteCustomer stored procedure, execute the stored procedure, and then catch any errors.

In order to work with the stored procedure, the AddUpdateDelete() method makes use of the ADO Command object. Remember from Chapter 2 that an ADO Command object is used to issue SQL statements and make calls to stored procedures. One way to pass values to the ADO Command object is to create ADO Parameter objects and then append them to the Command object before you call the Command's Execute method. The basic syntax for creating and appending a Parameter object is as follows:

```
      'To create a parameter object pass these values to the Command's
      'CreateParameter method.
Set ParameterObject=CommandObject.CreateParameter(Name, _
Type, Direction, Size, Value)
'Use the Command object's Parameter's collection's Append method
'to add the new parameter
CommandObject.Parameters.Append ParameterObject.
```

Working with the Command object and its Parameters collection definitely has its advantages. For one, when you pass parameters, you don't have to worry about passing single quotes in your strings, thereby avoiding the situation with inline SQL in which the single quote in, for example, O'Conner or Joe's is taken by the SQL language parser to be the end of a quoted string. Another advantage of the Parameters collection is that you can use them to pass long text values or binary information to a database.

Of course, you pay a price for these advantages in the form of additional coding overhead due to the fact that you will need to research your stored procedure to determine the name, type, direction, and size of each parameter as you create. Although this might sound fairly trivial, it can become a brutal coding process if you are working with a stored procedure like AddEditDeleteCustomer, for which you would have to endure the creation and appending of 15 individual parameters.

The DebugPrintParams Code Builder

It is with the DebugPrintParams( ) utility that the niceties of ADO and being a big cheater pay off. We'll explain how in a minute, but first this background information. Once you associate a Command object with a database connection and a stored procedure name, its collection of Parameters can be *read*. Since each of the Parameter objects has properties that contain all of the values that you need to pass to the CreateParameter method, it is a fairly simple matter to build a string containing all of the CreateParameter and Append statements. After this string is built, you can simply spit it out to the immediate window, where it can be cut and pasted into a code window. The practical results of "cheating" like this is a major reduction in coding time and generally more accurate code.

The function of the DebugPrintParams( ) utility is to execute just such a cheap trick. The function that follows accepts the connection string to your database (e.g, "Driver={SQL Server};Server=(Local);Database=Pubs;UID=sa"), the name of the Command object that you are using in your code (e.g., objMyCommand), the name of the temporary parameter that you are using in your code (e.g., objMyParameter), and the name of the stored procedure that you wish to build against (e.g., AddEditDeleteCustomer). Then it uses these values to make a connection to your database, create a Connection object, and iterate through the Connection object's Parameters collection. As it iterates, it builds a string of CreateParameter( ) and Append( ) method calls, which it will print out to the debug window for your use.

```
Public Function DebugPrintParams(strConnection As String, _
   strCommandObjectName As String, strTempParameterName As String, _
   strProcName As String) As String
```

(continues)

(Continued)

```
Dim objCommand As ADODB.Command
Dim objParam As ADODB.Parameter
Dim strParameters As String

    'Create Command Object
Set objCommand = CreateObject("ADODB.Command")

    'Set up the connection to the database and specify the SP name
objCommand.ActiveConnection = strConnection
objCommand.CommandText = strProcName

    'Iterate through the collection of parameters that ADO
    'reads from the stored procedure and create a string that
    'can be cut from the VB immediate window and pasted into a procedure
    'that will correctly create and append parameter objects to the
    'passed Command object.
For Each objParam In objCommand.Parameters
        'Read parameter name, type, and size from the current
        'Parameter object and build a CreateParameter statement
    strParameters = strParameters & vbCrLf & "Set " & _
        strTempParameterName & "=" & _
        strCommandObjectName & ".CreateParameter(" & """" & _
        objParam.Name & """" & ", " & objParam.Type & _
        ", adParamInput, " & objParam.Size & ", "
        'Request input for the value or variable name that the
        'Parameter object will carry to the database
    strParameters = strParameters & InputBox( _
        "What Value Would You Like to Pass to " & objParam.Name) & ")"
        'build the Append statement
    strParameters = strParameters & vbCrLf & strCommandObjectName & _
        ".Parameters.Append " & strTempParameterName
Next objParam
    'Print all of the CreateParameter() and Append code to the immediate
    'window where it can be cut and pasted into a code window
DebugPrintParams = strParameters

End Function
```

AddUpdateDelete()

Now that we have a helper routine for building parameter objects, the creation of the AddUpdateDelete() method is a piece of cake. This function begins by accepting the Cust-State() array coming from the client-side Customer component, establishing a connection to the database, and creating a Command object that executes against the AddEdit-DeleteCustomer stored procedure. What follows are 15 individual CreateParameter() and Append() method calls, which were built by running the DebugPrintParameters() utility against the AddEditDeleteCustomer stored procedure (it's a lot of code, so for the sake of space, we don't list it all here). Finally, the procedure calls the Command object's Execute method and checks for errors coming back from the stored procedure. Notice that the

CustData enumerator, which we discussed in the client-side Customer object, is also included in the general declaration section of the server-side CustomerData object. Thus, in the following code, the members of the passed array (i.e., aParams) are referred to using their enumerated values.

```
Public Function AddUpdateDelete(ByVal aParams As Variant) as Boolean
Dim objConnection As ADODB.Connection
Dim objCommand As ADODB.Command
Dim objTmpParam As ADODB.Parameter

On Error GoTo ERR_AddUpdateDelete

    'Establish connection to the database
    Set objConnection = CreateObject("ADODB.Connection")
    objConnection.Open "Data Provider=MSDASQL;Driver={SQL Server};" & _
            "Server=(Local);Database=Pubs;UID=sa"

'Create command
    Set objCommand = CreateObject("ADODB.Command")

    'Set Command object to execute against the SP
    objCommand.ActiveConnection = objConnection
    objCommand.CommandText = "AddEditDeleteCustomer"
    objCommand.CommandType = adCmdStoredProc

    'Start adding the parameters (referencing into the aParams array
    'using the element's enumerated values (e.g., MonikerValue = 0)
    Set objTmpParam = objCommand.CreateParameter("@Moniker", 200, _
            adParamInput, 50, aParams(MonikerValue))
        objCommand.Parameters.Append objTmpParam
    Set objTmpParam = objCommand.CreateParameter("@Name", 200, _
            adParamInput, 75, aParams(NameValue))
        objCommand.Parameters.Append objTmpParam

'********Code snipped here for the conservation of space on the page
(CreateParameters and Appends go on for a long, long time)******

    'Execute the command
    objCommand.Execute

    'Check for Errors and raise them back to the client
    If objConnection.Errors.Count = 0 Then
        AddUpdateDelete = True
    Else
        AddUpdateDelete = False
        With objConnection.Errors(0)
            Err.Raise .Number, .Source, .Description
        End With
    End If

    'Call SetComplete to release the MTS object
```

(continues)

(Continued)

```
   mObjCtxt.SetComplete
   AddUpdateDelete = TRUE
   Exit Function

ERR_AddUpdateDelete:
     MObjCtxt.SetAbort
     AddUpdateDelete = False
     Err.Raise Err.Description, "Database", Err.Description

End Function
```

It is important to note that not all errors coming from ADO will be raised to a general Visual Basic exception. Because of this, it is essential that you check your Connection object's Errors collection and raise any errors that you find there back to Visual Basic. If you don't, you might fool yourself into thinking that your code actually worked.

Adding a New Customer

That brings us to the end of a first look at the code that goes into saving a record to the database. Although it takes a lot of hops between the user and the database, it's a fairly simple path once you get your head around it. What is most important about this structure is how easy it makes working with customer information from any client application. Since all of the complexity is hidden, look at how simple it is to create and add a new customer to the database from a client application.

```
Private Sub InsertTrashCustomer()
Dim objCourier As New Transport.Messenger
Dim objFactory As New BusinessServices.Factory

        'Establish the initial connection to the server
    Set mobjFactory.Messenger = objCourier

        'Create a new Customer object
    Set mobjCustomer = objFactory.CreateCustomer()

        'Add some test data to the object's properties
    mobjCustomer.Name = "Test Customer"
    mobjCustomer.CreditLimit = 2000

        'Save the new customer to the database
    mobjCustomer.Commit

End Sub
```

Retrieving Customers

In our sample application, there are two basic ways to retrieve information: The first is an object-specific retrieval and the second returns a mix of object attributes. In either case, a search is always based upon a stored procedure and a disconnected ADO Recordset.

The best place to start this discussion is with the simple retrieval of information and the creation of an object that happens when a client application requests an instance of a Customer object from the Factory object. Remember that the idea behind business objects is to hide complexity and to make things easy on the application that uses them. As such, the following code is all that is needed to retrieve an existing Customer object from the database.

```
Public Sub GetMeCustomer()
Dim objCourier As New Transport.Messenger
Dim objFactory As New BusinessServices.Factory
        'Establish the initial connection to the server
    Set objFactory.Messenger = objCourier
        'Create a Customer object (passing one of those weird
        'WinNT generated Monikers)
    Set mobjCustomer = _
objFactory.GetCustomer("CAA1E308-50D8-11D2-9BEA-545CB")
End Sub
```

The Factory Object's GetCustomer( ) Method

As are most of the methods of the Factory object, the GetCustomer( ) method is rather simple. It takes two optional parameters that will be used to establish the state data for the retrieved object. If an ADO Recordset is passed into this procedure, the Factory object instances a Customer object and then passes the Recordset into the object's Set-State( ) method. However, if only a Moniker (CustomerID) is passed to the GetCustomer( ) method, then a query must be run to establish the data for the manufactured Customer object.

If only a Moniker is passed, this method first dimensions a four-element array. Then it sets the value of the Moniker to the first element in the array and calls the Messaging object's FetchCustomers( ) method, passing the new array. Eventually, the FetchCustomers( ) method will return a Recordset that will be passed into the SetState method of the Customer object.

```
Public Function GetCustomer(Optional strMoniker As String, _
    Optional objRS As ADOR.Recordset) As Customer
Dim objCustomer As Customer
    'Make sure that a Messaging object has been established
    'for the Factory (remember)
If Ready() = False Then Exit Function

    'Create a new Customer object and establish a pointer
    'to the shared messaging component
Set objCustomer = New Customer
Set objCustomer.Messenger = mobjMessenger
```

(continues)

(Continued)

```
    'Test to see if a moniker has been passed
    If Len(strMoniker) > 0 Then
        ' Dimension an array that will be used as
        'a parameter
        Dim aParams(4)
        'Set the passed moniker into the first element of the
        'array

        aParams(0) = strMoniker
        'Call the messenger's FetchCustomers method and
        'pass the resulting recordset to the Customer object's
        'SetState method
        objCustomer.SetState mobjMessenger.FetchCustomers(aParams)
    ElseIf Not objRS Is Nothing Then
                'If a recordset exists, just send it into the
                'Customer's SetState
            objCustomer.SetState objRS
    End If
        'Return the manufactured customer
    Set GetCustomer = objCustomer
End Function
```

Once the control passes to the Messaging component, it works in its traditional role as a relay to the server-side DataServices' CustomerData object.

```
Public Function FetchCustomers(aParams() As Variant) As ADOR.Recordset
    Set FetchCustomers = mobjCustomer.Retrieve(aParams())
End Function
```

The RetrieveCustomerByMonikerOrName ContactName Stored Procedure

The array that was passed to the server-side CustomerData object by the Messaging object is eventually destined for the RetrieveCustomersByMonikerOrNameContact-Name stored procedure. This mouthful of a procedure does exactly what its name implies: Accepts either a moniker value, the name of a customer, and/or a contact name of a customer and returns a result set.

As you can see in the following Create Procedure script, this stored procedure takes three parameters that all have a default value of an empty string. In the body of the procedure, you can see that the values of these parameters are tested to determine the WHERE clause of the SQL statement that will be run. If the @Moniker parameter has been passed, (which is the case when the Factory object retrieves object state data), then the WHERE clause limits the query to returning the one record whose cuCustomerID field value matches the value of the passed parameter.

Notice that in all of the SQL statements in this procedure, the field names are aliased by inserting the name of the field to be returned to a results set to the right of the table's field name. For example, since the name Moniker is inserted after the field name cuCustomerID, the cuCustomer field value will be returned to the result set, but the name of the column in the result set will be named Moniker. By using this field-aliasing technique, you encapsulate the actual field names in the database tables from your application. Then, if field names in the database are changed, or fields are moved from one table to another, the stored procedure can be edited and none of your compiled code needs to change. That's what we're shooting for with this methodology: easy maintenance through single points of change.

```
Create Procedure RetrieveCustomersByMonikerOrNameContactName
    (
        @Moniker Varchar(50) = '',
        @Name varchar(75) = '',
        @ContactName varchar(30) = ''
    )
As
IF NOT @Moniker = ''
    SELECT cuCustomerID Moniker, cuCustomerName Name,
        cuContactName ContactName, cuContactPhone Phone,
        cuContactFax Fax, cuAddress1 Address1,
        cuAddress2 Address2, cuCity City, cuState State,
        cuPostalCode PostalCode, cuLastUpdated LastUpdated,
        cuCredit CreditLimit, cuLockDate LockedDate,
        cuLockedBy LockedBy, cuUpdateID UpdateID
    FROM Customers
    WHERE cuCustomerID = @Moniker
ELSE IF @Name <> ''
    IF @ContactName <> ''
        SELECT cuCustomerID Moniker, cuCustomerName Name,
            cuContactName ContactName, cuContactPhone Phone,
            cuContactFax Fax, cuAddress1 Address1,
            cuAddress2 Address2, cuCity City, cuState State,
            cuPostalCode PostalCode, cuLastUpdated LastUpdated,
            cuCredit CreditLimit, cuLockDate LockedDate,
            cuLockedBy LockedBy, cuUpdateID UpdateID
        FROM Customers
        WHERE cuCustomerName LIKE @Name + '%'
        AND cuContactName LIKE @ContactName + '%'
    Else
        SELECT cuCustomerID Moniker, cuCustomerName Name,
            cuContactName ContactName, cuContactPhone Phone,
            cuContactFax Fax, cuAddress1 Address1,
            cuAddress2 Address2, cuCity City, cuState State,
            cuPostalCode PostalCode, cuLastUpdated LastUpdated,
            cuCredit CreditLimit, cuLockDate LockedDate,
            cuLockedBy LockedBy, cuUpdateID UpdateID
        FROM Customers
        WHERE cuCustomerName LIKE @Name + '%'
ELSE IF @ContactName <> ''
    SELECT cuCustomerID Moniker, cuCustomerName Name,
        cuContactName ContactName, cuContactPhone Phone,
        cuContactFax Fax, cuAddress1 Address1,
```

(continues)

(Continued)

```
        cuAddress2 Address2, cuCity City, cuState State,
        cuPostalCode PostalCode, cuLastUpdated LastUpdated,
        cuCredit CreditLimit, cuLockDate LockedDate,
        cuLockedBy LockedBy, cuUpdateID UpdateID
    FROM Customers
    WHERE cuContactName LIKE @ContactName + '%'

    Return
```

The CustomerData Object Retrieve() Method

The CustomerData object's Retrieve( ) method makes a call to a stored procedure, so part of it is very much like the same object's AddUpdateDelete( ) method. That is, it works with an ADO Command object to send parameters to a stored procedure.

However, in this procedure, the stored procedure returns an ADO Recordset when the Command object's Execute method is called. Eventually, this aliased Recordset will be passed all the way back to the client-side Factory object. In order to do this, the Recordset must first be disconnected from the connection to the database so that it can be marshaled over the network as a powerful, robust data-handling structure.

An ADO Recordset can only be marshaled if it uses a local client cursor (i.e., a result set that is moved to the calling application rather than remaining on the database server). As you can see in the following code listing, setting the Connection object's CursorLocation property to adUseClient does this.

```
objConnection.CursorLocation = adUseClient
```

After this change is made, the Command object's Execute method returns a set of data into a cursor in the DataServices component's memory. Since this Recordset is going to travel back to the client-side BusinessServices component, it must first be disconnected from the database connection by setting the Recordset's ActiveConnection property to Nothing. Once this is complete, all that has to be done to marshal the Recordset is to set the Retrieve( ) function (which returns a marshalable ADOR.Recordset) to be equal to the newly retrieved, aliased, disconnected Recordset.

```
Set objRS.ActiveConnection = Nothing
Set Retrieve = objRS
```

The entire CustomerData object's Retrieve( ) method is as follows:

```
Public Function Retrieve(ByVal aParams As Variant) As _
    ADOR.Recordset

Dim objConnection As ADODB.Connection
Dim objCommand As ADODB.Command
Dim objMoniker As ADODB.Parameter
Dim objName As ADODB.Parameter
Dim objContactName As ADODB.Parameter
Dim objRS As ADODB.Recordset
```

```
Set objConnection = CreateObject("ADODB.Connection")
objConnection.Open "Data Provider=MSDASQL;Driver={SQL " & _
    "Server};Server=(Local);Database=Pubs;UID=sa"

Set objCommand = CreateObject("ADODB.Command")

objCommand.ActiveConnection = objConnection
objCommand.CommandText = _
    "RetrieveCustomersByMonikerOrNameContactname"
objCommand.CommandType = adCmdStoredProc

    'Ensure that the array has a 0 element
If Ubound(aParams) >= 0 Then
  If Len(aParams(0)) > 0 Then
    Set objMoniker = objCommand.CreateParameter("Moniker", _
        adVarChar, adParamInput, 50, aParams(0))
    objCommand.Parameters.Append objMoniker
  End If
End If

'Ensure that the array has a 1st element
If Ubound(aParams) >= 1 Then
  If Len(aParams(1)) > 0 Then
    Set objName = objCommand.CreateParameter("Name", _
        adVarChar, adParamInput, 75, aParams(1))
    objCommand.Parameters.Append objName
End If
End If

'Ensure that the array has a 2nd element
If UBound(aParams) >= 2 Then
  If Len(aParams(2)) > 0 Then _
    Set objContactName =
    objCommand.CreateParameter("ContactName", _
        adVarChar, adParamInput, 30, aParams(2))
    objCommand.Parameters.Append objContactName
  End If
End If

Set objRS = CreateObject("ADODB.Recordset")
objConnection.CursorLocation = adUseClient

Set objRS = objCommand.Execute

Set objRS.ActiveConnection = Nothing
Set Retrieve = objRS

'Call SetComplete to release the component
mObjCtxt.SetComplete

End Function
```

If the procedure of using Command objects to create disconnected Recordsets was simply to create a Recordset based on a Command object alone, the Recordset could not be made to disconnect and marshal over the network. Only if you explicitly create an ADO Connection object as the Command object's ActiveConnection and manipulate the type of cursors that are used with the Connection can the Recordset be made to marshal.

The Customer Object's SetState Method

After the CustomerData object's Retrieve( ) method returns a disconnected Recordset, the Recordset is sent back to the Messaging object and then on to the Factory object's GetCustomer( ) method. Once it gets back to the Factory object, the following line of code is run to establish the manufactured Customer object's state data:

```
objCustomer.SetState mobjMessenger.FetchCustomers(aParams)
```

The purpose of the business object's SetState( ) method is to take a Recordset and set its values to be equal to data in the Customer object's CustState( ) array.

```
Friend Function SetState(objCursor As ADOR.Recordset) _
    As Boolean

On Error GoTo Err_SetState

    If Not objCursor Is Nothing Then
        With objCursor
            If .State = 1 And Not .EOF Then
                CustState(MonikerValue) = _
                    objCursor("Moniker")
                CustState(NameValue) = objCursor("Name")
                CustState(ContactNameValue) = _
                    objCursor("ContactName")
                CustState(PhoneValue) = objCursor("Phone")
                CustState(FaxValue) = objCursor("Fax")
                CustState(Address1Value) = _
                    objCursor("Address1")
                CustState(Address2Value) = _
                    objCursor("Address2")
                CustState(CityValue) = objCursor("City")
                CustState(StateValue) = objCursor("State")
                CustState(PostalCodeValue) = _
                    objCursor("PostalCode")
                CustState(LastUpdatedValue) = _
                    objCursor("LastUpdated")
                CustState(CreditLimitValue) = _
                    objCursor("CreditLimit")
                CustState(ObjectEditValue ) = _
                    ObjectNoChange
```

```
                Else
                    GoTo Err_SetState
                End If
            End With
        Else
            GoTo Err_SetState
        End If


    Exit Function


    Err_SetState:
        Err.Raise vbObjectError + 1, "BusinessServices", _
            "Object Data Could not be Retrieved from the Database"


    End Function
```

 Notice that this SetState( ) function is declared as a Friend. In Visual Basic, that means that only code inside the same component can see this function. Declaring sensitive or fragile functions like this one (e.g., passing an inappropriate Recordset from outside the component) as Friend is good practice because it would be dangerous to expose it to code outside of the component, where you have little control.

Editing and Deleting Objects

Now that you have been through the addition and retrieval of Customer data, you can probably guess how editing and deleting customers will be done. Remember the Edit-State value in the Customer object that is passed to the AddEditDeleteCustomer stored procedure by the CustomerData object's AddUpdateDelete( ) method and used to determine whether the customer data being sent to it was to be used in an INSERT, UPDATE, or DELETE statement? Well, you guessed it, the EditState property is what governs edits and deletes. Whenever you change any property of a Customer object, the property let procedure first calls the ProcessCheck( ) procedure. This procedure first checks to see if the Customer is currently being added to the database; if not, it changes the EditState of the Customer to show that it has been edited.

```
Function ProcessChange() As Boolean
    If Not CustState(ObjectEditValue ) = ObjectAdd Then
        CustState(ObjectEditValue ) = ObjectEdit
    End If
End Function
```

Next, when the object's Commit( ) method is called, the EditState data is sent along with the rest of the Customer object's data and is eventually used by the AddEdit-DeleteCustomer stored procedure to guide its decision to commit an UPDATE statement rather than an INSERT or DELETE statement against the database.

Deleting a Customer is equally as unchallenging. Simply put, when the Customer object's MarkForDelete( ) method is called, the following code is run:

```
Public Function MarkForDelete() As Boolean
    CustState(ObjectEditValue ) = ObjectDelete
End Function
```

Of course, this value is eventually used by the AddEditDeleteCustomer stored procedure to issue a DELETE statement this time.

Returning Sets of Information

Now you know how an individual object's data can be brought back and forth from the database. But being able to retrieve only a small amount of data from the database at a time would make developing a large application a very painful process. As you no doubt know, if you have ever developed a database application, you simply need to fetch data from the database in sets.

This is where the importance of the disconnected ADO Recordset comes back into play. For example, if you were only to access your data without sets, then to fill a grid with attributes from a number of objects, you would have to retrieve each object that was showing a single attribute in the grid. As you can imagine, working without a set is code-intensive and incredibly slow. In contrast, if your business objects are made to return ADO Recordsets, then you can retrieve the set of information that you want from your business tier (where the structure of the database is encapsulated) and then (in VB 6) simply bind the Recordset to a grid control.

The Search Object

The client-side BusinessServices component's Search object exists to return disconnected Recordsets from the server-side DataServices component. This object has a number of methods for returning full sets of same-object data. For example, the Fetch-Customer( ) method of the Search object returns a specific set of customer-only data from the database. It also has one method called, simply, DoSearch( ) that returns a mixed (i.e., attributes from different objects) set of data.

Returning Object-Specific Sets of Data

Let's start the discussion of returning sets of data with the retrieval of object-specific Recordsets. If a client application of the BusinessServices component wanted to return a set of customers, it would have to use the Search object's FetchCustomer( ) method. For example, to return a Recordset of customers whose Name attribute began with the letter B, a client of the BusinessServices component would have to issue something like the following code:

```
Function GetCustomerB() as ADOR.Recordset

'Fictional function that returns customers whose Name attribute
'begins with the letter "B"

Dim objFactory as New BusinessServices.Factory
Dim objMessage as new Transport.Messenger
Dim objSearch as BusinessService.Search
Dim aParams(4)

'Set up Factory to use a certain messenger
Set objFactory.Messenger = objMessage
Set objSearch = objFactory.CreateSearch ()

'Populate the appropriate element in the parameter array
aParams(2) = "B"

'Make the Call to the Search object and return a Recordset
Set GetCustomerB = objSearch.FindCustomers(aParams())

End Function
```

By this time, you have already seen much of the code that makes this type of interaction possible. In fact, the Search object uses all of the same server-side DataServices object method calls that the Factory does when it retrieves a single object's data from the database.

When the Search object's FindCustomers( ) method is called, it calls to the FetchCustomers( ) method of its assigned Messaging component.

```
Public Function FindCustomers(aParams() As Variant) _
    As ADOR.Recordset
Set FindCustomers = _
mobjMessenger.FetchCustomers(aParams())
End Function
```

Predictably, the Messaging component simply relays the call and parameters to the server-side DataServices component.

```
Public Function FetchCustomers(aParams() As Variant) _
    As ADOR.Recordset
Set FetchCustomers = mobjCustomer.Retrieve(aParams())
End Function
```

In our earlier discussion of the Factory's GetCustomer( ) method, you saw the complete code in the CustomerData object's Retrieve( ) method, along with the stored procedure that it calls. This method simply makes a call to the RetrieveCustomersBy MonikerOrNameContactName stored procedure and passes it parameters. The only difference between the Search object's use of this method and the Factory's is that instead of a Moniker being passed as the only parameter, either a Customer's Name or Contact-Name is passed to the stored procedure. Since either of these parameters will return a set of records, it is likely that a Recordset containing more information than one record will be passed back to the client.

Creating Object Instances with Object-Specific Recordsets

One of the niceties of returning an object-specific Recordset is that it can be used directly to create instances of business objects without having to make a return trip to the database. Since an object-specific Recordset is exactly the same Recordset that the Factory uses to create objects, it is a simple matter to use the Factory object's GetCustomer() record to manufacture a new Customer object based on the current row in a Recordset.

```
Public Function GetCustomer(Optional strMoniker As String, _
    Optional objRS As ADOR.Recordset) As Customer

Dim objCustomer As Customer

'Make sure that a Messaging object has been established
'for the Factory (remember this?)

If Ready() = False Then Exit Function
    'Create a new Customer object and establish a pointer
    'to the shared Messaging component
    Set objCustomer = New Customer
    Set objCustomer.Messenger = mobjMessenger

    'Test to see if a moniker has been passed
    If Len(strMoniker) > 0 Then
        ' Dimension an array that will be used as
        'a parameter
        Dim aParams(4)
        'Set the passed moniker into the first element of the
        'array
        aParams(0) = strMoniker
        'Call the messenger's FetchCustomers method and
        'pass the resulting recordset to the Customer object's
        'SetState method
        objCustomer.SetState
        mobjMessenger.FetchCustomers(aParams)
    ElseIf Not objRS Is Nothing Then
        'If a recordset exists, just send it into the
        'Customer's SetState
        objCustomer.SetState objRS
    End If

'Return the manufactured customer
Set GetCustomer = objCustomer

End Function
```

Once the Recordset that is passed to the Factory's GetCustomer( ) method is passed into the manufactured Customer object's SetState( ) method, the object takes its state data from the current row in the Recordset. Because the SetState( ) method does nothing other than assign the values of the Recordset's fields to the Customer object's Cust-State( ) array, it doesn't care that it is assigning these values from a Recordset containing thousands of rows rather than from the Recordset of just one row that the Factory uses in its GetCustomer() method. In other words, all that the Customer object's SetState( ) method cares (or knows) about is the current record in the Recordset that it is passed.

So, if a client of the BusinessServices component wanted to retrieve a set of all of the customers whose names begin with the letter B and then change the Customer object's Address2 attribute to the string "a B company", the client application could create a routine like the one that follows:

```
Private Sub UpdateCustomerB() as Boolean

'Fictional procedure that could be found in
'an application that uses the BusinessServices
'Component.  This procedure changes
'the Address2 attribute of all customers whose Name attribute
'begins with the letter "B" To be equal to '"A 'B' Company"

Dim objFactory as New BusinessServices.Factory
Dim objMessage as new Transport.Messenger
Dim objSearch as BusinessServices.Search
Dim aParams(2)
Dim objRS as ADODB.Recordset
Dim objCustomer as BusinessServices.Customer

Dim inCounter as Integer

'Set up Factory to use a certain messenger
Set objFactory.Messenger = objMessage
Set objSearch = objFactory.CreateSearch

'Populate the appropriate element in the parameter array
aParams(2) = "B"

'Make the Call to the Search object and return a Recordset
Set objRS = objSearch.FindCustomers(aParams())

Do until objRS.EOF
    'Create a new instance of the Customer object
    'Based on the Recordset Returned from the Search Object
    Set objCustomer = objFactory.GetCustomer(, objRS)

    'Sending single quotes won't mess anything up because
    'we are using Parameter objects, so
    'let's show off a little bit
    objCustomer.Address2 = "A 'B' Company"
```

(continues)

(Continued)

```
    'Save the Change to the database
    objCustomer.Commit

    'Move to the next record returned and repeat the process
    objRS.MoveNext
Loop

End Function
```

Retrieving Nonobject-Specific Sets

Many times, you simply need a set of data that comprises not just data elements from one type of object but from a number of different objects. There are two ways to approach this. The first, and most efficient way, is to add query-specific methods to the Search object. For example, if you wanted to add a query that would return some fixed set of data and would take a fixed number of parameters, you could create another method like FindCustomers( ) and write a stored procedure in the database to match it. This method allows you to work with stored procedures as quickly as possible, and it encapsulates any client application from having to know anything about the database.

However, sometimes it is really helpful to have some sort of method that can run any stored procedure in the database and return a Recordset. The Search object's DoSearch( ) method does exactly this. This method's parameters take the name of a stored procedure and an array of parameters to pass. In other words, you can use this one method to run any stored procedure in your database, pass it any parameters that it needs, and return a Recordset to the calling application. Now that's flexible!

```
Public Function DoSearch(strSearchName As String, _
    aParams() As Variant) As ADOR.Recordset

Set DoSearch = mobjMessenger.FetchRandom(strSearchName, _
    aParams())

End Function
```

After the Search object makes the call to the FetchRandom( ) method, the Messaging object routes the name of the stored procedure to be run and the array that carries any parameters that are needed for the stored procedure.

```
Public Function FetchRandom(strSearch As String, _
    aParams() As Variant) As ADOR.Recordset

Set FetchRandom = mobjSearch.RetrieveRS(strSearch, aParams())

End Function
```

Again, this RetrieveRS( ) method is dependent on the features of ADO to achieve its extreme flexibility. If you remember from the earlier discussion of the DebugPrint-Params( ) code-building utility, once a connection is set up and a stored procedure's name is given to an ADO Command object, the parameters that it takes can be read and manipulated. If this is the case, then a general-purpose stored procedure running routine can establish a Command object and assign values to whichever parameters present themselves when the Command object's Parameters collection is read.

That said, the basic action of the RetrieveRS( ) method is to establish an ADO Command object, associate it with the passed stored procedure, iterate through the stored procedure's Parameters collection, assigning the parameters values that are passed from the array, and execute the command.

```
Public Function RetrieveRS(strSPName As String, _
        ByVal aParams() As Variant) As ADODB.Recordset

Dim objConnection As ADODB.Connection
Dim objCommand As ADODB.Command
Dim objTmpParam As ADODB.Parameter
Dim objRS As ADODR.Recordset
Dim intIterator As Integer

Set objConnection = CreateObject("ADODB.Connection")
objConnection.Open "Data Provider=MSDASQL;Driver={SQL " & _
    "Server};Server=(Local);Database=Pubs;UID=sa"

'Create the Command object
Set objCommand = CreateObject("ADODB.Command")

'Associate the Command object with the Connection
'and a stored procedure name
objCommand.ActiveConnection = objConnection
objCommand.CommandText = strSPName
objCommand.CommandType = adCmdStoredProc

'Iterate through the collection of parameters
'and assign them with values from the passed array
For Each objTmpParam In objCommand.Parameters
    objTmpParam.Value = aParams(intIterator)
    objCommand.Parameters.Append objTmpParam
Next

'Construct a disconnectable recordset
Set objRS = CreateObject("ADODB.Recordset")
objConnection.CursorLocation = adUseClient

'Execute the stored procedure and assign the Recordset
Set objRS = objCommand.Execute

'Disconnect the Recordset and marshal to the client
Set objRS.ActiveConnection = Nothing
Set RetrieveCustomers = objRS

End Function
```

The Price You Pay

Of course, this wonderful flexibility comes at the cost of execution speed and architectural purity. As mentioned earlier, dealing interactively with ADO Parameter objects is a relatively costly operation. Further, this method essentially breaks the encapsulation between the client application and the database. That is, client applications need to know the names of the stored procedures.

Programmatic Duct Tape

Although this method of calling stored procedures is slower than adding query-specific methods to the Search object, and although it breaks the rule of encapsulation, by including one architecturally messy, compromised method like this one has proven itself over and over again to be as helpful as duct tape. In fact, you should treat it like duct tape; having a procedure like this is a lifesaver when you are pushed to make a quick-and-dirty change. But as soon as you have the time to add query-specific methods to the Search object, you should get rid of the duct tape and do your queries in a proper, speedy, and architecturally correct way.

Record Locking

One of the most problematic areas of database application development is record locking. Any application that will be used by more than one person at a time needs to devise some method of ensuring that users don't overwrite each other's work. If you haven't dealt with this subject in the past, here is the scenario:

- User 1 retrieves Record A, edits it, then gets involved in a prolonged rubber-band war with a co-worker.

- User 2 retrieves Record A after User 1 retrieves it. User 2 makes edits then diligently saves the changes back to the database.

- User 1 eventually shoots his or her entire stockpile of rubber bands and the war ends. Settling back to work, User 1 saves his or her changes to Record A and overwrites the labor of his or her more responsible co-worker.

There are a couple of ways to deal with this classic problem. You could write your application so that once User 1 retrieves the record, no other user can edit the record until User 1 releases it. This scheme is called *pessimistic locking*. Alternatively, you could create your application so that since User 2 changed Record A while User 1 had it, User 1 would not be able to update the record when he or she tried. This strategy is called *optimistic locking*.

Which is the right way? Well, it depends, because each method has advantages and disadvantages. If you elected to go with a pessimistic lock in this scenario, you could stop User 2 from doing any work while the User 1's rubber-band war rages on. On the other hand, if you decided to go with an optimistic lock, the situation could even be uglier. Let's say that when User 1 returned to work, he or she made lengthy changes to the record, which failed because User 2 got the changes to the database first. In this instance, User 1 could end up at your desk to express his or her disapproval by shooting you with the really thick, ultra-powerful rubber bands. The choice is up to you, and the decision that you make depends on your application. At any rate, you should know how to implement both locking methods.

Implementing Optimistic Locks

Of the two locking schemes, implementing optimistic locking is definitely the easier to do. In doing so, the crucial issue is finding some way to determine whether the object's data has been updated since it was fetched. The sample application deals with this problem by adding an UpdateID value to the business object's state data. Basically, optimistic locking works like this:

- When you retrieve the optimistically locked information, you retrieve an extra integer (UpdateID) along with the "real" data.

- When you save the information back to the database, a check is done to make sure that the incoming UpdateID value is equal to the one currently in the database. If the value in the database is greater than the value passed back from the client-side object, then someone has saved the data since it was retrieved and the incoming save will fail.

- If the incoming UpdateID value is the same as the one in the database, then the save will succeed, and the UpdateID value will be incremented by one to show any other pending updates that the data has changed.

There are relatively few changes that need to be made to the existing Customer object before implementing an optimistic lock. The first step is to save the UpdateID value already being returned from the server-side component into the CustState() array in the Customer object's SetState() method. This way, when the CustState() array is sent back to the server in the object's Commit() method, this value will be included.

```
If Not objCursor Is Nothing Then
    With objCursor
        If .State = 1 And Not .EOF Then
            CustState(MonikerValue) = objCursor("Moniker")
            CustState(NameValue) = objCursor("Name")
            CustState(ContactNameValue) = _
                objCursor("ContactName")
            CustState(PhoneValue) = objCursor("Phone")
            CustState(FaxValue) = objCursor("Fax")
            CustState(Address1Value) = _
                objCursor("Address1")
            CustState(Address2Value) = _
                objCursor("Address2")
            CustState(CityValue) = objCursor("City")
            CustState(StateValue) = objCursor("State")
            CustState(PostalCodeValue) = _
                objCursor("PostalCode")
            CustState(LastUpdatedValue) = _
                objCursor("LastUpdated")
```

(continues)

(Continued)

```
            CustState(CreditLimitValue) = _
                objCursor("CreditLimit")
            CustState(ObjectEditValue ) = ObjectNoChange
            'more elements to come~
            CustState(UpdateIDValue ) = _
                objCursor("UpdateID")
        Else
            GoTo Err_SetState
        End If
    End With
Else
    GoTo Err_SetState
End If
```

The next change that has to be made is in the server-side DataServices component's CustomerData object. In this case, you must make sure that in the AddUpdateDelete( ) method an @UpdateID Parameter object is created, set to the value of the fourteenth element of the array (remember that the enumerated value of UpdateIDValue is equal to 14), and appended to the Command object's Parameters collection.

```
Set objTmpParam = objCommand.CreateParameter("@UpdateID", 3, _
    adParamInput, 0, aParams(UpdateIDValue))
objCommand.Parameters.Append objTmpParam
```

The most significant change that has to be made to implement optimistic locking is in the AddEditDeleteCustomer stored procedure. First, the UPDATE statement should be changed so that it increments the value of the cuUpdateID field every time an UPDATE is successful (i.e., cuUpdateID = cuUpdateID +1).

Then, in the WHERE clause of both the UPDATE and the DELETE statements, the search should be expanded to look for both the matching cuCustomerID and cuUpdateID values (i.e., WHERE cuCustomerID = @Moniker AND cuUpdateID = @UpdateID). By doing this, UPDATE and DELETE statements that are being blocked by the optimistic locking scheme (i.e., passing an UpdateID value that doesn't match the record in the database) will simply "miss" and be unable to perform the UPDATE or DELETE.

Now that the basic mechanics of the optimistic lock are in place, it would be nice to let the client know when an UPDATE or DELETE has failed. In a stored procedure, you can test the success of a statement by checking the @@Rowcount variable after a SQL statement has been committed. This @ server variable reflects the number of records affected in the last statement. So, if the @@Rowcount variable is equal to 0 after an UPDATE or DELETE statement, you can be sure that the action was not successful.

Finally, as you can see in the full listing that follows, if the @@Rowcount value reflects a failed statement, an error is raised back to the calling program by issuing a RAISERROR from the stored procedure.

```
ELSE IF @Action = 1 /*Update Existing Record*/

    UPDATE Customers
```

```
    SET cuCustomerID = @Moniker, cuCustomerName = @Name,
        cuContactName = @ContactName, cuContactPhone =
        @Phone, cuContactFax = @Fax,
cuAddress1 = @Address1,
        cuAddress2 = @Address2, cuCity = @City, cuState =
        @State, cuPostalCode = @PostalCode, cuLastUpdated =
        GetDate(), cuCredit = @CreditLimit, cuLockDate = NULL,
        cuUpdateID = (cuUpdateID + 1)
    WHERE cuCustomerID = @Moniker AND cuUpdateID = @UpdateID
    IF @@ROWCOUNT = 0
        RAISERROR ('Customer data has been updated since
        fetched',1,1)
    ELSE IF @Action = 2
        DELETE FROM Customers WHERE cuCustomerID = @Moniker
        AND cuUpdateID = @UpdateID
        IF @@ROWCOUNT = 0
            RAISERROR ('Customer data has been updated since
            fetched',1,1)
```

Implementing Pessimistic Locks

The implementation of a pessimistic lock is a good deal more difficult than an optimistic lock because both the client-side component and the server-side component are involved in the behavior of this type of lock. In this sample framework, pessimistic locking works along the following lines:

- If a record is to be pessimistically locked, then a specific request must be made to the Factory object for the lock.

- When the Factory object makes its request to the server-side DataServices component, it appends a value, which is used to request a lock, and the current user's ID to the parameter array that will travel over the network. (The current user's ID is retrieved from Windows by using a Windows API call.)

- The DataServices component sends the value requesting the lock and the UserID value into a stored procedure used to retrieve data from the database.

- The stored procedure first tests to determine whether a record is currently locked (if the record's LockDate field is anything other than NULL, it is locked) or the lock is old enough to be ignored. If it is not locked or the lock has expired, then the record's LockDate field is updated to the current time, and the record's LockedBy field is updated to the current user's ID. Finally, a value indicating that the current user has achieved the lock is appended to the Recordset carrying the information that was queried from the database.

- When this Recordset arrives at the object that the Factory is manufacturing, its SetState() method takes the value indicating a successful lock and appends it to the object's state data array (e.g., CustState(GotLockValue)).

- The Factory object sets a flag on the created object to indicate that it should act in a pessimistically locked mode.

- Now that the object is in lock mode, whenever any change is made to the newly created object, a routine is run to determine if the object currently has a lock on its data. If it does not, then it will raise an error indicating that data cannot be updated.

- When the locked object's Commit( ) method is called, the value indicating that a successful lock was gained when the data was fetched is sent to the DataServices component.

- The DataServices component passes this value to a stored procedure, which will update the object's data only if a value indicating that the object has achieved a successful lock on the data has been passed.

- Since objects can interact with their data in both a pessimistically locked mode and an optimistically locked mode (one client may have a pessimistic lock and another may have an optimistic lock on the same object's data), the test that the stored procedure runs before performing an update or delete is expanded to test whether there is a current lock on the record or the lock has expired. By doing this, objects that do not have a pessimistic lock on the data can still update their data as long as there is no other instance of the same object that has gained a successful pessimistic lock.

See, we warned you that pessimistic locking was more complex.

Requesting a Lock from the Factory Object

When a client application makes a request for a pessimistic lock on an object, all it has to do is to pass a value of True into a third optional parameter of the Factory's Get-Client( ) method. For example, the following routine could be used by a client of the BusinessServices component to gain a lock on a Customer object.

```
Sub GetLockedCustomer(strMoniker as string) as Customer

Dim objFactory as New BusinessServices.Factory
Dim objMessage as new Transport.Messenger)

'Set up Factory to use a certain messenger
Set objFactory.Messenger = objMessage
Set objSearch = objFactory.CreateSearch

'Request locked customer object
Set GetLockedCustomer = _
objFactory.GetCustomer(_
"CAA1E308-50D8-11D2-9BEA-545CB",,TRUE)

End Function
```

After a call like this is made, the Factory object's GetCustomer( ) method checks to see if a TRUE argument has been passed. If it has, then it will set Customer object into "lock mode" by setting its WithLocks property to TRUE. Then, the Factory will set a

TRUE value in the third element of the aParams array and make a call to the Factory object's GetUserID( ) function to append the name of the user making the lock request into the array. Finally, the aParams array is passed to the Messaging object to be transported to the server-side DataServices component.

```
Public Function GetCustomer(strMoniker As String, _
    Optional objRS As ADOR.Recordset, Optional boolLock As
    Boolean = True, _
    Optional Batch As Boolean) As Customer

Dim objCustomer As Customer

'Check that the Factory has been passed a Messaging object
If Ready() = False Then Exit Function
    'Instance a new Customer object and assign it a pointer to
    'the Messenger
    Set objCustomer = New Customer
    Set objCustomer.Messenger = mobjMessenger

    If boolLock = True Then
        objCustomer.WithLocks = True
    End If

    If Len(strMoniker) > 0 Then
        Dim aParams(4)
        aParams(0) = strMoniker
        'If the boolLock parameter passed is true, then assign
        'a true value to the third element of the array and the
        'NT username to the fourth
        If boolLock = True Then
            aParams(3) = True
            aParams(4) = GetUserID()
            'Sets the Customer object into "lock mode"
            objCustomer.WithLocks = True
        End If

        'Get customer data with or without a lock
        objCustomer.SetState _
            mobjMessenger.FetchCustomers(aParams)

    ElseIf Not objRS Is Nothing Then
            'Only directly retrieved objects (not from an
            'existing recordset) can be locked
        objCustomer.SetState objRS
    End If
End If

Set GetCustomer = objCustomer

End Function
```

The GetUserID( ) function that is used in the Factory's GetCustomer( ) method simply retrieves the ID of the user from Windows. Using Windows' login user ID values in an application has the advantage of providing easily retrievable, more secure logins than is typically practical to build into a custom application. Also, this method has the advantage of not requiring users of a system to go through a login process when they start the application.

You can retrieve the value of the Windows username by making a GetUserName( ) Windows API call. This function will return the Windows username into a string passed to the function.

```
Private Declare Function GetUserName Lib "advapi32.dll" _
Alias "GetUserNameA" (ByVal lpBuffer As String, nSize _
As Long) As Long
```

The GetUserID( ) function makes use of this Windows API call first by passing the maximum length of the username string and a buffered (fixed length) string to the GetUserName function. Then, it uses the Visual Basic Left( ) function to strip off the extra buffered space from the passed fixed-length string. Finally, it returns only the portion of the passed string into which the API function wrote.

```
Private Function GetUserID() as String
    Dim strName As String
    Dim lngLen As Long
    Dim lngStatus As Long

    'set max length of string
    lngLen = 100

    'Buffer string to hold information entered into it from the
    'API call
    strName = String$(100, 0)

    'get the username using Win32 API
    lngStatus = GetUserName(strName, lngLen)

    'strip off the extra buffered space that was added
    GetUserID = Left(strName, lngLen - 1)

End Sub
```

Predictably, when the Factory's GetCustomer( ) method passes the aParams( ) array to the Messenger object , the Messenger simply relays the array to the server-side CustomerData object's Retrieve( ) method. If you remember from the earlier discussion, this method basically establishes an ADO Command object and passes parameters to a stored procedure named RetrieveCustomersByMonikerOrNameContactName.

So, to achieve a pessimistic lock on the Customer object's data, all that needs to be done in the Retrieve( ) method is to pass the new LockRequest and LockBy parameters to the procedure. As you can see in the following code excerpt, a test is first performed to determine if a pessimistic lock has been requested from the server. The LockRequest and LockBy parameters are then passed to the stored procedure.

```
~
If aParams(3) = True Then
    Set objContactName = objCommand.CreateParameter("LockRequest", _
    adInteger, adParamInput, 1, 1)
    objCommand.Parameters.Append objContactName

    If Len(aParams(4)) > 0 Then
        Set objName = objCommand.CreateParameter("LockBy", _
        adChar, adParamInput, 25, aParams(4))
        objCommand.Parameters.Append objName
    End If
End If
```

In the stored procedure into which these two new parameters are passed, a number of basic actions must be taken to effect a pessimistic lock. First, an UPDATE statement must be run against the Customer record to mark it as locked. It does this by setting the record's cuLockDate field equal to the time and date of the request (i.e, cuLockDate = GetDate( )) and the records cuLockedBy field equal to the user making the request (i.e., cuLockedBy = @LockBy). Finally, the variable named @Gotlock must be set equal to 1 and returned in the resultset. The value of the @GotLock variable will be used in the client application to determine if the requested lock was achieved.

The following Alter Procedure script begins by declaring the @LockDate and @Got-Lock variables that will be used in the locking mechanism.

```
DECLARE @LockDate as DATETIME, @GotLock as tinyint
```

Since a pessimistic lock in the sample application can only be achieved from this stored procedure a single record at a time, all of the locking code is enclosed in a test to determine if the calling procedure passed a Moniker (i.e., unique ID) value to the stored procedure.

```
IF NOT @Moniker = ''
```

After this initial test, the procedure goes on to determine if a lock request is being made. If the @LockRequest parameter is equal to 1, then the next step is to return the cuLockDate field value for the requested record into the previously declared @Lock-Date variable.

```
IF @LockRequest = 1
    SELECT @LockDate = cuLockDate
    FROM Customers
    WHERE cuCustomerID = @Moniker
```

As you will see later, this cuLockDate field is always set to NULL when a locked record is updated. The stored procedure can determine if there is already a lock on the record simply by checking to see if the @LockDate value is NULL. If this value is NULL, then the procedure updates the record's cuLockDate and cuLockedBy fields to reflect a lock. Finally, the procedure sets the value of the @GotLock variable to be equal to 1, thereby signifying a successful lock.

```
IF @LockDate IS NULL
    BEGIN
    UPDATE Customers Set cuLockDate = GetDate(),
        cuLockedBy = @LockBy
    WHERE cuCustomerID = @Moniker
    SET @GotLock = 1
END
```

Another condition under which a lock will be achieved is when the lock on a record is over an hour old. This rule is enforced by a second test that is run only if the @Lock-Date variable is not NULL. This test uses the SQL DATEDIFF function to compare the @LockDate value returned from the database against the current time in increments of hours (i.e., hh). If this function returns a value greater than 1, the record will be updated to reflect a lock.

```
ELSE IF DATEDIFF(hh, @LockDate, GetDate()) > 1
BEGIN
    UPDATE Customers Set cuLockDate = GetDate(),
cuLockedBy =  @LockBy
    WHERE cuCustomerID = @Moniker
    SET @GotLock = 1
END
```

Finally, the procedure will run a SELECT statement to return the Customer object's data. Notice in the full script that follows that the @GotLock variable is returned from the procedure as part of the resultset.

```
Alter Procedure RetrieveCustomersByMonikerOrNameContactname
    (
        @Moniker Varchar(50) = '',
        @LockRequest tinyint = 0,
        @LockBy char (25) = '',
        @Name varchar(75) = '',
        @ContactName varchar(30) = ''
    )
As

/*Declare variables*/
DECLARE @LockDate as DATETIME, @GotLock as tinyint

IF NOT @Moniker = ''
/*Only a request for a customer providing a moniker
(primary key) value is able to gain a record lock.
So, only one record per request can be locked.*/
IF @LockRequest = 1
```

```
    SELECT @LockDate = cuLockDate
    FROM Customers
    WHERE cuCustomerID = @Moniker

/* See if there is a current LockDate on the field. This
field is set to NULL during an update of a locked record.*/
IF @LockDate IS NULL
    /*If the record is marked as
    unlocked (cuLockDate = NULL), then mark
    the record as locked (cuLockDate as the
    current date and time) and set @GotLock = 1 to specify
    that the current request has the lock.*/
BEGIN
    UPDATE Customers Set cuLockDate = GetDate(),
        cuLockedBy = @LockBy
    WHERE cuCustomerID = @Moniker
    /*Set GotLock Variable so that it will be
    returned into the recordset with a value of 1
    Set @GotLock = 1
END
ELSE IF DATEDIFF(hh, @LockDate, GetDate()) > 1
/*If the lock on a record is more than an hour old,
then override the lock. (A business decision that
must not be made without considerable thought)*/
BEGIN
    UPDATE Customers Set cuLockDate = GetDate(),
        cuLockedBy = @LockBy
    WHERE cuCustomerID = @Moniker
    SET @GotLock = 1
END

/*Whether or not a lock request was satisfied, return record data.
Here, the GotLock field is used to communicate to the client application
if a lock has been achieved.*/

SELECT cuCustomerID Moniker, cuCustomerName Name,
    cuContactName ContactName, cuContactPhone Phone,
    cuContactFax Fax, cuAddress1 Address1,
    cuAddress2 Address2, cuCity City, cuState State,
    cuPostalCode PostalCode, cuLastUpdated LastUpdated,
    cuCredit CreditLimit, cuLockDate LockedDate,
    cuLockedBy LockedBy, GotLock = @GotLock, cuUpdateID
    UpdateID
FROM Customers
WHERE cuCustomerID = @Moniker

 /*Requests for the retrieval of customer data based on anything other
than the moniker value is not allowed to lock. So, the clipped portion
of this stored procedure (from here down)is exactly as you saw it earlier
in RetrieveCustomersByMonikerOrNameContactName Create Procedure script.*/
```

Once this resulting Recordset is marshaled back to the Factory, the Factory will pass it into the Customer object's SetState( ) method, where the Recordset data will be loaded into the CustState array. The only change in this method that must be made to accommodate a pessimistic lock is that the GotLock field value returned in the Recordset must be loaded into the thirteenth (i.e., the enumerated GotLockValue = 13) array element.

Once the success or failure of a lock is held in the CustState array, a routine can be written that will determine if the Customer object has gained a pessimistic lock on its data and thus can be updated. The LockCheck( ) function checks to see if the object is operating in "lock mode" (i.e., if the Factory set its WithLocks property to True), then tests to see if the thirteenth (GotLockValue) element of the CustState array is NULL. If the lock was successful, this value would be 1. If it is NULL, then the LockCheck( ) function raises an error, carrying the message that a lock has not been achieved for the object, and the object's data cannot be updated.

```
Private Function LockCheck() As Boolean
    If WithLocks  = True Then
        If IsNull(CustState(GotLockValue)) = True Then
            LockCheck = False
            Err.Raise vbObjectError + 10, _
                "Business Services", _

                "This record is currently unable" & _
                "to be locked for update."
        Else
            LockCheck  = True
        End if
    End If

End Function
```

Once written, this LockCheck( ) function is added to the ProcessChange( ) function that was placed at the beginning of each property let procedure. By doing this, an error will be raised any time a client application tries to make a change to an object that has been created by the Factory in lock mode but has not gained a lock on the record.

```
Function ProcessChange() As Boolean

    If LockCheck = True Then
        If Not CustState(ObjectEditValue ) = ObjectAdd Then
            CustState(ObjectEditValue ) = ObjectEdit
        End If
    End if

End Function
```

Saving a Pessimistically Locked Record

Except for changes to the stored procedure that commits adds, edits to, and deletes from the database, the action of saving a pessimistically locked record is really insignificantly different from saving an optimistically locked record. Remember that since the GotLocked value returned from the server was set into the Customer object's Cust-State() array, a value indicating the state of the record lock can be passed back into the AddEditDelete stored procedure. It is this GotLocked value that will be used to enforce the pessimistic lock.

To get this value to the stored procedure, the server-side CustomerData object's AddUpdateDelete() method must be changed again to pass the GotLock value originally defined by the RetrieveCustomersByMonikerOrNameContactName stored procedure.

```
Set objTemParam = objCommand.CreateParameter("@GotLock", 3, _
    adParamInput, 0, aParmams(13))
objCommand.Parameters.Append objTmpParam
```

For the AddEditDeleteCustomer stored procedure to handle a pessimistic lock, only a few changes need to be made. As you can see in the following full script, an IF condition is wrapped around the UPDATE and DELETE sections of the procedure. This IF condition will allow a change to be made to an existing record only if:

- The value of @GotLock = 1 (the current request holds the lock on this record).

- The value of the current cuLockedDate field retrieved into a @CurLockDate variable is NULL. (This means that the record is not locked and the current update is dependent on the default optimistic locking scheme.)

- The value of the current cuLockedDate field, retrieved into a @CurLockDate variable is more than an hour old (DATEDIFF(hh, @CurLockDate, GetDate()) > 1).

```
IF @GotLock = 1 OR @CurLockDate IS NULL
    OR DATEDIFF(hh, @CurLockDate, GetDate()) > 1
```

The other change to this procedure handles messaging an error back to the user if an update fails because the user trying to make the update is using an optimistic lock and the data in the database has been pessimistically locked. In this situation, the optimistically locked update will not clear the IF condition that has been added to the store procedure (this update would not have a @Gotlock value of 1, the @CurLockDate would be set to a value, and it would not be over an hour old).

In this case, a message (i.e., "The customer data is currently locked by") and the name of the user who currently has a lock on the record is selected and retrieved into the @CurLockedBy variable.

```
SELECT @CurLockedBy =
'The Customer data is currently Locked by ' + cuLockedBy
FROM Customers Where cuCustomerID = @Moniker
```

Then, this value is used to send the message back to the user through the use of a RAIS-ERROR statement.

```
RAISERROR (@CurLockedBy,1,1)
```

Finally, if an update request makes it through the new IF statement, the lock must be released. Since the whole pessimistic locking scheme basically hangs on the cuLock-

Date value of the record, the procedure's UPDATE statement must be altered so that this value is set to NULL. In other words, simply setting the cuLockDate value to NULL releases the pessimistic lock.

```
cuLockDate = NULL
```

The entire AddEditDeleteCustomer stored procedure with all of the changes to handle optimistic and pessimistic locking of Customer data is as follows:

```
Alter Procedure AddEditDeleteCustomer
(
@Moniker VarChar(50) = NULL, @Name varchar(75) = NULL,
@ContactName varchar(30) = NULL, @Phone varchar(12) = NULL,
@Fax varchar(12) = NULL, @Address1 varchar(50) = NULL,
@Address2 varchar(50) = NULL, @City varchar(30)= NULL,
@State varchar(2) = NULL,    @PostalCode varchar(10)= NULL,
@LastUpdated datetime = NULL, @CreditLimit money = NULL,
@Lockedby char (10) = NULL, @LockDate datetime = NULL,
@Action Int = 1, /* 0 = Insert, 1 = Update, 2 = Delete*/
@UpdateID Int = 1,
@GotLock Int = 0
)
As


DECLARE @CurLockDate Datetime
DECLARE @CurLockedBy Char

/*Retrieve UpdateDate Stamp on Current database Record*/

IF @Action = 0 /*Insert New Record*/
    INSERT INTO Customers
        (cuCustomerID, cuCustomerName, cuContactName,
        cuContactPhone, cuContactFax, cuAddress1,
        cuAddress2, cuCity, cuState, cuPostalCode,
        cuLastUpdated, cuCredit, cuUpdateID)
    VALUES (@Moniker, @Name, @ContactName, @Phone, @Fax,
        @Address1, @Address2, @City, @State,
        @PostalCode, GetDate(), @CreditLimit, @UpdateID)
ELSE


BEGIN
/*Retrieve a value into the @CurLockDate variable */
SELECT @CurLockDate = cuLockDate
FROM Customers
WHERE cuCustomerID = @Moniker

/*Test to see if the current request has the lock, if there is
no lock on the record or if the lock on the record is over an hour old*/

IF @GotLock = 1 OR @CurLockDate IS NULL
    OR DATEDIFF(hh, @CurLockDate, GetDate()) > 1
```

```
BEGIN
IF @Action = 1
/*Update Existing Record, inforcing a default optimistic
lock and setting the cuLockDate value to Null, thereby
releasing any pessimistic lock*/
    UPDATE Customers
    SET cuCustomerID = @Moniker, cuCustomerName = @Name,
        cuContactName = @ContactName,
        cuContactPhone = @Phone, cuContactFax = @Fax,
        cuAddress1 = @Address1,
        cuAddress2 = @Address2, cuCity = @City,
        cuState = @State, cuPostalCode = @PostalCode,
        cuLastUpdated = GetDate(),
        cuCredit = @CreditLimit, cuLockDate = NULL,
        cuUpdateID = (cuUPdateID + 1)
    WHERE cuCustomerID = @Moniker AND cuUpdateID = @UpdateID
    IF @@ROWCOUNT = 0
        RAISERROR('Data has been updated since fetched',1,1)
    ELSE IF @Action = 2
        /*Delete Existing Record and enforcing
        a default optimistic lock*/
        DELETE FROM Customers
        WHERE cuCustomerID = @Moniker
            AND cuUpdateID = @UpdateID
        IF @@ROWCOUNT = 0
            RAISERROR ('Data has been updated since
            fetched',1,1)
        ELSE
            /*Either no @Action parameter passed,
            or some mystery value was passed*/
            RAISERROR ('Incorrect parameter passed',1,1)

END
ELSE
BEGIN

/*If the record cannot be updated because it is locked, then find out
who has the current lock, create an error message containing the locking
user's name and assign it to a variable.  Then send the variable into a
RAISERROR statement to message the locking user's name back to the client*/
SELECT @CurLockedBy =
'The Customer data is currently Locked by ' + cuLockedBy
FROM Customers
WHERE cuCustomerID = @Moniker

RAISERROR (@CurLockedBy,1,1)

END
END
```

You don't have to use stored procedures to do this! As we said before, we elected to use stored procedures in this example because of their speed and ease of maintenance. However, if you can't use, or don't want to use, store procedures, the logic that they invoke to effect locking is pretty simple (once you get used to it). So, if you want to take the logic out of stored procedures and put it in your server-side business objects, it's up to you. However, you should expect a slight performance hit if you decide to do so.

Believe Us, It Gets Easier

So, where is the payoff for all of this hard, complex work? It comes whenever you work with business object data (in this example, customer data) in the future. Once a business object is built, all of the data-handling code from any application that uses the object is also done. What's more, if you find a problem with your data-handling code in one application, all you have to do is correct the problem in your business object and the problem is fixed everywhere.

Now, this is cheating! If you consistently implement business objects, you may get to a point where tasks can be accomplished very quickly, and code maintenance becomes easy. In fact, you may find yourself with the time to work on other projects, study, write books, or (if you're feeling slightly less ambitious) take long, restful afternoon naps underneath your desk.

From Here

In the last chapter of the book, we will explore the ability to handle complex transactions using ADO and MTS. To do this, the complexities of parent-child object relationships must be examined in the client-side BusinessServices component, and the details of using MTS transactions must be integrated into the server-side DataServices component. To close, you will see an example of the sort of data processing power the combination of ADO and MTS can provide.

Transaction Processing

In the previous chapter, you learned about a general framework for creating a distributed, ADO-based system. That gives you a basic understanding of how data travels between the database server, the middle tier, and the client business objects. This chapter builds on that knowledge. The basic patterns described in Chapter 10 will be expanded to include transaction processing.

To preserve the integrity of the data governed by the system, transactions will be necessary in this system when adding, deleting, or editing an order and its associated line items. However, to effect this necessary feature, the relationships among certain objects in the application must be more fully defined; unfortunately, this makes them more complicated.

What You'll Learn

In the following pages, you will learn the process of setting up client-side business objects to perform pretransaction behaviors (the client-side addition of line items to the order object's line item collection). You will explore the server-side behavior of making multiple calls to the database that can either be committed or rolled back in one step.

From a purely technical standpoint, you will learn about the following items:

- Saving a Recordset sent from the server to the client's disk.

- Using an ADO Recordset to hold the state data of multiple objects.

- "Shotgunning" a set of data across the network.

- Using multiple MTS-sited objects in the same transaction.
- Committing or rolling back transactions in MTS.

Parent Objects, Child Objects, and Transactions

In our sample application, the Order object and the LineItem object form a parent-child relationship. In Figure 11.1, you can see a graphical representation of this relationship.

Although the words used to describe this relationship can sound complex (transactions, object relationships, parents, and children), all we are really talking about here is saving the information that you typically see on an invoice. Common sense tells you that the Order object (represented in Figure 11.1 as the invoice) contains or has a collection of child LineItem objects (represented in Figure 11.1 as—of all things—line items). In a class diagram, we would represent this (Visual Basic) relationship between orders and line items in the following way: The diagram in Figure 11.2 indicates that the Order

Figure 11.1   An invoice is made up of an order and line Items.

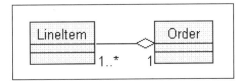

Figure 11.2   The modeled relationship between the Order object and the LineItem object.

object exists in a relationship of 1 to infinity LineItem objects (i.e., one Order to any number of LineItems).

Common sense also tells you that all the information contained on an invoice should be saved to the database at one time. That is, if you could not save a line item because stock levels did not allow for the addition of a line item to an invoice, then you should not save the whole invoice and charge the customer for something that they cannot get.

This is a pretty good example of a transaction. Simply put, a transaction is saving information to a data store in a batch. If any part of that batch process fails, then the whole process should fail. It's an all-or-nothing deal.

The Order Object

In the application, the Order object governs all of the information concerning (you guessed it) orders (see Figure 11.3). As such, its properties include a Moniker (unique identifier for the order), the date on which the order was placed, and the total cost of

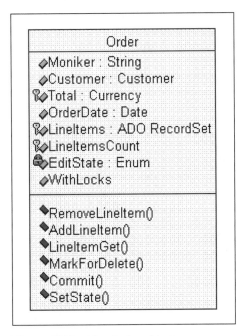

Figure 11.3   The Order object.

the order. Like the Customer object that was explored in the last chapter, the Order object too has a private EditState property that governs whether it is to be added, updated, or deleted in the database, and a WithLocks property that is used to govern the locking scheme being used (optimistic or pessimistic).

Following the pattern set forth in Chapter 10, this object maintains its state data in an array called OrderState( ). And as you saw with the Customer object, all of the property's let procedures in this object manipulate values stored in this array.

 We make the assumption here that you already have read Chapter 10 and have gained a basic understanding of how objects in this application manage data and send their data to the database. If you skipped Chapter 10, you should go back and read it before continuing here.

Aside from these (now) more familiar types of properties, the Order object also has a GetLineItem method that will return a LineItem object associated with the order, a LineItemsCount property that will return the total number LineItems in an order, and a LineItemsAdd method that will associate a LineItem object with the Order object. Later in this chapter, we will explore how these methods are used to implement the parent-child relationship between the Order object and its LineItem objects.

The Order's Customer Property: Implementing a Parent Object

Just as this Order object has child LineItem objects, it is, in turn, a child of the Customer object. To express this relationship, the Order object has a Customer property. If you look at the Order object diagram in Figure 11.3, you can see that the Customer property has a return type of Customer. That's right, this property will return a Customer object. This is a great example of how a child object (the Order) is able to reference its parent (the Customer).

This means that the Customer property get procedure is much different from the simple property get procedures that you saw in Chapter 10. In this case, it is not a simple value that is being returned, but a whole object with all of its data fetched from the database and assembled into a handy object instance.

You already know that the Factory object must be used to create any instance of an object. You also know that the Order object contains an array called OrderState( ) that holds all of the Order object's data. So, if the Order object's state array were to hold the Moniker (unique identifier) of its parent Customer object, then the Customer property get procedure could simply take this Moniker value and pass it to the Factory object's GetCustomer method to return the appropriate Customer object. Then, once this Customer object was created, the Order object should hold onto a pointer to the newly created object so that the next time it was asked for, the application would not need to requery the database and create a new Customer object.

In the following code snippet, you see that a module-level variable named mCustomer is established to hold a pointer to the parent Customer object once it is created. Then, in the property get procedure for the Order object's Customer property, a test is run to see if the Customer object has already been established for the Order. If the mCustomer variable is not equal to Nothing, then a previously established Customer object (mCustomer) is passed as the value of the property.

If the Order object does not yet have an instanced Customer object, a test is run to see if the OrderState array contains a Moniker value for the Customer associated with this order (i.e., "If Len(OrderState(1)) > 0"). If the Order object's state array does not contain its Customer's Moniker value, then the mCustomer variable is explicitly set to Nothing.

However, if the OrderState array does contain the Customer's Moniker, then a new, local instance of the Factory object is created and the mCustomer variable is set to be equal to the Customer object that is created by passing the Factory object's GetCustomer method the moniker of the Order's Customer.

```
    'Dimension a private variable for the Order's Customer object
    'once it has been established
Private mCustomer As Customer


Public Property Get Customer() As Customer
Dim objFactory As Factory
    'Test to see if the Customer object
    'for this Order has already been instanced
If mCustomer Is Nothing Then
    'Test to see if the OrderState array
    'contains a Moniker(id) value for the Order's
    'Customer
    If Len(OrderState(1)) > 0 Then
        'If there is a Moniker value for the Order's Customer
        'that has been retrieved from the database, then instance a new
        'Factory object and instance this Order's Customer by calling
        'the Factory's GetCustomer method
        Set objFactory = New Factory
        Set mCustomer = objFactory.GetCustomer(OrderState(1))
    Else
        'If there is no Moniker value in the OrderState array,
        'then explicitly set mCustomer to nothing.
        Set mCustomer = Nothing
    End If
End If
    'Set the value of mCustomer to the Property Get
Set Customer = mCustomer
End Property
```

If the Customer property get procedure returns an instance of the Customer object, then you should also be able to set the Customer for an Order by assigning an instance of a Customer object to the Order's Customer property. To do this, the following property set procedure must be added to the Order.

In the Customer property set procedure, the first thing that must be done is to ensure that only a Customer type object has been set to the property ("If TypeOf objCustomer is Customer"). After you are sure that a Customer object has been passed, the Customer object should be set to the mCustomer variable. The second thing that must take place is that the Moniker property of the passed Customer should be assigned to the Order-

State array. Since this array will later travel to the server to be persisted in the database (as you saw in the last chapter), this Customer object's Moniker (i.e., primary key) value in the Order's state array will establish a relationship between the Customer record and the Order record (primary key/foreign key) in the tables of the database.

```
Public Property Set Customer(objCustomer As Customer)

If TypeOf objCustomer Is Customer Then
    Set mCustomer = objCustomer
    OrderState(1) = objCustomer.Moniker
    'Method used to add this instance of an order to
    'the Customer object's Orders collection
    mCustomer.OrderAdd Me
Else
    Err.Raise vbObjectError + 1, "Business Services", "Please set only " & _
        "Customer obects to the Order object's Customer property."
End If

End Property
```

Managing Object Instances

Now you have seen how a parent (Customer) property can be implemented for a child (Order) object. The code looks basically sound, so you're probably thinking that the functionality of this relationship must be finished with its implementation, right? Well, think again.

Consider for a moment what would happen if you had a Customer object and you ran a query to return all of the Order objects that were owned by this Customer, and then you asked one of the returned Order objects for its Customer object. What would happen here is that the Order object would create another instance of the Customer object (same data, different object). In fact, each Order object returned by the query would create another instance of the Customer object. What a mess!

Obviously, there must be some mechanism in place so that instances of objects can be managed. This type of parent-child structure only makes sense when each child object points to the same instance of its parent. This is where an important, albeit complicating, object called the InstanceManager comes into play (see Figure 11.4).

This InstanceManager object is basically a wrapper around a Visual Basic Collection into which all of the objects that participate in a parent-child relationship will be placed. For any running instance of the client-side BusinessServices component, there will be one and only one active InstanceManager. To implement this, a global variable (don't worry, it's the only one) must be dimensioned as a new instance of this class in the BusinessService's modCommon general utility module.

```
Public gobjObjectPool As New InstanceManager
```

Since each object in the application has a Moniker (primary key) value that is unique both to its type and across objects of all types (this is where using the NT GUID monikers

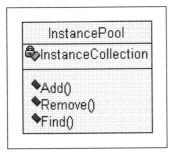

Figure 11.4 The InstanceManager is used to manage object instances that participate in parent-child relationships.

described in the last chapter pays off), any object can be thrown into the InstanceManager and then retrieved by its Moniker value. Internal to the InstanceManager class is a module-level instance of a Visual Basic Collection object used to store references to any type of object. So, to add a new instance of the object to the InstanceManager, you would simply call the object's Add( ) method and pass the instance of the object that you wished to add.

If you haven't worked with a Visual Basic Collection in the past, it is basically a smart array that can hold any type of information (strings, integers, pointers to objects); it knows the number of items in it and has methods to add, remove, and return items. Another interesting feature of the Collection is that when you add items to it, you can assign any item a Key value that can be used later to retrieve the item from the Collection. Although you can also return any item from a Collection as long as you know its position, there are obvious reasons why retrieving items by a Key value is much more handy. To take advantage of the capabilities of the Collection object, the InstanceManager's Add( ) method accepts any business object as a parameter and then adds it to its internal collection, using the passed object's Moniker property as the item's key.

```
Public Function Add(objBusinessObject As Object) As Boolean
    'The Add method takes two arguments 1) the thing to be added
    '2) the key for the item
    mCol.Add objNewMember, objBusinessObject.Moniker
End Function
```

Now that this object is in place and you know about its Add( ) method, all of the Factory object's methods that create or get instances of objects that participate in parent-child relationships must change. (Aren't you glad that you have a Factory now? Without having one point at which to accommodate this change, managing object instances would be even more nightmarish.)

The first change that must be instituted is that whenever the Factory object instances a new parent or child business object, it must now add it to the InstanceManager. For example, the Factory object's CreateCustomer( ) method should now be changed to add the newly created Customer object to the InstanceManager.

```
Public Function CreateCustomer() As Customer
Dim objCustomer As Customer
Set objCustomer = New Customer

    objCustomer.EditState = ObjectAdd
    objCustomer.Moniker = GetMoniker()
        'Add the new Customer object
        'into the InstanceManager to be managed
    gobjObjectPool.Add objCustomer

    Set CreateCustomer = objCustomer
End Function
```

Since the Factory is set up to place all new instances of parent or child business objects in this pool, there must also be an easy way to retrieve a pointer to one of these managed objects. This is where the InstanceManager's all-important Find() method becomes invaluable. For such an important function, it sure does some pretty simple stuff. In fact, all that this method does is to iterate through the InstanceManager's internal collection, looking for an object that matches the Moniker passed. If it finds a match, it returns a pointer to the found object.

```
Public Function Find(strMoniker As String) As Object
Dim intIterator As Integer
        'Iterate through the collection from the first item to the
        'number returned by the Collection's Count property
For intIterator = 1 To mCol.Count
    'Check to see if this item is a match
    If mCol(intIterator).Moniker = strMoniker Then
            'if it is a match, return it for the value of
            'the function and exit
            Set Find = mCol(intIterator)
            Exit For
        Else
        'If no match is found, set the function to return Nothing
            Set Find = Nothing
    End If
Next intIterator
End Function
```

Again, now that the InstanceManager's Find() method is in place, it can be used by the Factory to return a pointer to a business object, if the business object has already been instanced. For example, now in the Factory's GetCustomer() method, an attempt is first made to return the requested object from the InstanceManager. If the Find() method returns Nothing, then the method will go about returning an instance of a persisted Customer object and adding this new instance to the pool.

```
Public Function GetCustomer(strMoniker As String, _
    Optional objRS As ADOR.Recordset, Optional boolLock As Boolean = True, _
        Optional Batch As Boolean) As Customer
```

```
Dim objCustomer As Customer

If Ready() = False Then Exit Function
    'Attempt to return an existing Customer object that has
    'the passed Moniker from the InstanceManager
Set objCustomer = gobjObjectPool.Find(strMoniker)
    'Only if the InstanceManager returns nothing should a
    'retrieval from the database be done.
If objCustomer Is Nothing Then
    Set objCustomer = New Customer
    Set objCustomer.Messenger = mobjMessenger

    If boolLock Then
        objCustomer.WithLocks = True
    End If

        If Len(strMoniker) > 0 Then
            Dim aParams(4)
            aParams(0) = strMoniker
            If boolLock = True Then
                aParams(3) = True
                aParams(4) = mstrUserName
            End If
            objCustomer.SetState mobjMessenger.FetchCustomers(aParams)
        ElseIf Not objRS Is Nothing Then
                objCustomer.SetState objRS
            End If
        End If
        'Add the new instance to the pool
    gobjObjectPool.Add objCustomer
    End If

    Set GetCustomer = objCustomer
End Function
```

The Destroy Method of All Objects

That mess is now straightened out; the InstanceManager is in place and managing object instances, ensuring that there can be one and only one instance at any time of any business object that has the same moniker. Therefore, if multiple children objects were to be asked for their parent, each would be returned a pointer to the existing parent object from the Factory, thus solving our original problem of children creating multiple instances of the same parent object.

Unfortunately, there's more. Although this InstanceManager solves our original problem, it creates a huge, honking memory leak. The reason for this is that in COM and in Visual Basic, object instances are only released when there are no more references to them (i.e., when their reference count = 0). And now that this nice, handy InstanceManager object is holding a pointer to every object that is ever created, *no object instance is ever released*!

As you can imagine, not ever releasing your object instances is bad. It eats a lot of memory, and eventually your users will become angry when you crash their machines. Therefore, there has to be some way to release an object when you are done working with it. In the sample application, this is done by adding a method called Destroy() to every object that will be added to the InstanceManager. This simple method calls the Remove() method of the global instance of the InstanceManager class so that when a client application calls Destroy() on a business object and releases its reference to it, the object will actually go away.

```
Public Function Destroy() As Boolean
    gobjObjectPool.Remove Me.Moniker
End Function
```

In turn, the InstanceManager's Remove() method simply calls the Remove method of its internal collection and passes it the Moniker value as a key to use when finding the instance to remove it. Once the collection has removed its pointer to the business object, our memory leak problem is solved.

```
Public Sub Remove(vntIndexKey As Variant)
    mCol.Remove vntIndexKey
End Sub
```

The LineItem Object

Although the Customer object and the Order object also exist in a parent-child relationship with one another, the bulk of the remainder of this chapter will deal with the parent-child relationship between the Order object and the LineItem object. Therefore, you will need to learn the properties and methods of the LineItem.

As you can see in Figure 11.5, the LineItem object has an Order property that is implemented similar to how the Customer property was implemented in the Order object. The LineItem object also has a Product property that returns a Product object (contain-

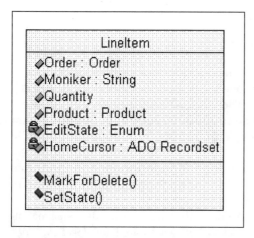

Figure 11.5 The LineItem Object.

ing a description of the product and the number in stock). This Product property is implemented in much the same way as all of the other parent-object type properties. (See a pattern beginning to emerge?)

The LineItem object also has a number of "normal" properties, such as Moniker and Quantity, that simply carry information. Other properties include the (hopefully) now familiar properties of WithLocks and EditState that are used to manage the record-locking behavior and editing state (whether a new object, an existing object that has been edited, or an existing object marked for deletion) of the object.

In terms of the object's methods, the now familiar Commit( ) method is present for saving the object's information to the database, as is the MarkForDelete( ) method that does what its name implies. One newer item on this object's method list is the Destroy( ) method that must be called by clients of the BusinessServices component to release the memory that instances of this object use.

All in all, this is a fairly run-of-the-mill object for this framework. Of course, this is a "typical" object except for that suspicious HomeCursor property that will be explained very soon.

The Order Object's LineItem Collection: Implementing a Child Collection

In a less structured application, you could return a set of LineItems for any given Order by sending an SQL statement to the database server and returning a set of records. Although this approach is very straightforward, it is also extremely brittle. For example, if there were a change to the structure of the database, or if the database were moved to another machine, then your entire application might have to be rewritten. Another disadvantage of this approach is that you might have to rewrite a SQL statement as many times as you intended to use it. Obviously, querying directly from the database to the client does not produce an application that is either durable or easily maintainable.

If you are thinking that these advantages could be gained in an application simply by creating shared routines, you are exactly right. In fact, one view of the business object approach is that it is a coding style that allows you to concentrate on creating reusable, shared code.

For these reasons and others, it is better to approach application development using business objects and centralized querying methods. Then, if a client application wanted to print out all of the LineItems in an Order to the Debug window, the following logically structured, simple lines of code could be run.

```
Private Sub DebugPrintLineItems(objOrder as Order)
Dim objLineItem as LineItem
Dim objProduct as Product
Dim intIterator as Integer

    'Iterate through the collection of the passed Order object's
    'LineItems (from one to the total #of LineItems)
For intIterator = 1 to objOrder.LineItemsCount
        'Get the current LineItem object by calling the
        'Order object's LineItemGet method and passing an
```

(continues)

(Continued)

```
        'item number
    Set objLineItem = objOrder.LineItemGet(intIterator)

        'Print the quantity of the Line Item and the LineItem's
        'related Product's Name
    Debug.print objLineItem.Quantity & " " & _
        objLineItem.Product.Name

        'Remember to call Destroy() on all created parent-child objects
        'when you are done with them to avoid the previously
        'mentioned memory leak.
    objLineItem.Destroy
Next intIterator

End Function
```

However, this simplicity can be provided in a client of the BusinessServices component only if some work goes into the Order object first. This work must be done whenever the Order object's AddLineItem or LineItemGet methods are called, or whenever the LineItemsCount property is requested. If any of these methods or properties that deal with the child LineItem collection are going to work, common sense indicates that the set of LineItems for this Order must first be retrieved from the database and stored somewhere in the Order object.

To meet the need for the retrieval of these LineItems from a number of different areas in the Order object, a general use, private function called GetLineItemsRS( ) will be added to the Order object. Before any of the previously mentioned methods that deal with the LineItems collection begin their work, they will call this method to either establish or get a reference to an (you guessed it) ADO Recordset. For example, in the following LineItemsCount property get procedure, you can see that the GetLineItemsRS( ) function is called to get a Recordset (or a pointer to an existing Recordset); it then returns a RecordCount property.

```
Public Property Get LineItemsCount() as Integer
    LineItemsCount = GetLineItemsRS.RecordCount
End Property
```

The GetLineItemsRS( ) Function

Basically, all this function does is run a very specific query and establish a module-level instance of a Recordset. Like every other query that is run in this sample application framework, the BusinessServices component's Search object executes a stored procedure. In this instance, the GetLineItemsRS( ) function first tests to see if a Recordset has already been returned. If the module-level variable mobjLIRS is not equal to Nothing, then the function will return a pointer to that variable. However, if mobjLIRS has not yet been established, then the GetLineItemRS( ) function makes a call to the Search object's FindLineItems( ) method and passes it a three-element array containing the Moniker of the Order object in its second element. This method will return an ADO Recordset, which the function will set as the value of the mobjLIRS variable.

```
Private Function GetLineItemsRS() As ADOR.Recordset
Dim objSearch As Search
Dim aParams(3) As Variant

If mobjLIRS Is Nothing Then
    Set objSearch = New Search
    aParams(2) = Me.Moniker
    Set mobjLIRS = objSearch.FindLineItems(aParams)
End If

Set GetLineItemsRS = mobjLIRS
End Function
```

As you have come to expect from this Search object in Chapter 10, the FindLineItems( ) method simply sends the parameter to the established Messaging component.

```
Public Function FindLineItems(aParams As Variant) As ADOR.Recordset
    Set FindLineItems = mobjMessenger.FetchLineItems(aParams)
End Function
```

Then the Messaging object simply relays the method call and the parameter to the server-side DataServices component, where all of the work is done.

```
Public Function FetchLineItems(ByVal aParams As Variant) As ADOR.Recordset
    Set FetchLineItems = mobjLineItem.Retrieve(aParams)
End Function
```

When the passed array finally makes it to the server-side LineItemData object, the values are used to create parameters to a stored procedure called RetrieveLineItems. Like the stored procedure that retrieved Customer information in the last chapter, this stored procedure enforces the requested locking scheme, then returns a Recordset to the client.

```
Public Function Retrieve(ByVal aParams As Variant) As ADOR.Recordset
    'Notice that the ADODB Recordset is cast into an ADOR.Recordset
    'so that it can be marshaled
Dim objConnection As ADODB.Connection
Dim objCommand As ADODB.Command
Dim objMoniker As ADODB.Parameter
Dim objName As ADODB.Parameter
Dim objContactName As ADODB.Parameter
Dim objRS As ADODB.Recordset

    Set objConnection = CreateObject("ADODB.Connection")
    objConnection.Open "Data Provider=MSDASQL;" & _
        "Driver={SQL Server};Server=(Local);" & _
        "Database=Pubs;UID=sa"

    Set objCommand = CreateObject("ADODB.Command")
```

(continues)

(Continued)

```
        objCommand.ActiveConnection = objConnection
        objCommand.CommandText = "RetrieveLineItems"
        objCommand.CommandType = adCmdStoredProc


        'Test to make sure you are not "walking off of the end"
        'of the passed parameter array.
        If UBound(aParams) >= 0 Then
            If Len(aParams(0)) > 0 Then
            'Sorry about the use of "magic numbers" here.  We used the
            'Parameter object Code builder covered in the last chapter
            'to build this code.
                Set objTmpParam = objCommand.CreateParameter("@Moniker", 200, _
                    adParamInput, 50, aParams(0))
                objCommand.Parameters.Append objTmpParam
            End If
        End If


        If UBound(aParams) >= 1 Then
            If Len(aParams(1)) > 0 Then
                Set objTmpParam = objCommand.CreateParameter("@OrderID", 200, _
                    adParamInput, 75, aParams(1))
                objCommand.Parameters.Append objTmpParam
            End If
        End If


        If UBound(aParams) >= 2 Then
            If Len(aParams(2)) > 0 Then
                Set objTmpParam = objCommand.CreateParameter("@ProductID", 200, _
                adParamInput, 30, aParams(2))
                objCommand.Parameters.Append objTmpParam
            End If
        End If


        If UBound(aParams) >= 3 Then
            If aParams(3) = True Then
                Set objTmpParam = objCommand.CreateParameter("@LockRequest", _
                        17, adParamInput, 0, aParams(3))
                objCommand.Parameters.Append objTmpParam


                If UBound(aParams) >= 4 Then
                    If Len(aParams(4)) > 0 Then
                        Set objTmpParam = objCommand.CreateParameter("@LockBy", _
                            200, adParamInput, 25, aParams(LockBy))
                        objCommand.Parameters.Append objTmpParam
                    End If
                End If
            End If
        End If


        'Set the RS up to be marshaled
        Set objRS = CreateObject("ADODB.Recordset")
```

```
          objConnection.CursorLocation = adUseClient

          Set objRS = objCommand.Execute

          'Disconnect and marshal the recordset
          Set objRS.ActiveConnection = Nothing
          Set Retrieve = objRS

          'Clean up and call SetComplete
          Set objMoniker = Nothing
          Set objContactName = Nothing
          Set objName = Nothing
          Set objCommand = Nothing
          objConnection.Close
          Set objConnection = Nothing
        mObjCtxt.SetComplete
End Function
```

Bouncing the Recordset Off the Client's Hard Disk: Creating Local Temporary Tables

Even after the Recordset has been returned to the client-side Order object's GetLineItemsRS( ) method, its trip is not over. Because this Recordset will be used to handle all additions, deletions, and edits to the Order's LineItem objects, it makes sense that the Recordset would have to be updateable. But the problem is that because of the way that the Recordset was created and marshaled, it is read-only.

The Order object will deal with this challenge by calling the Recordset's Save method to save the data to the client's disk. After that, the GetLineItemsRS( ) function will close the passed Recordset and set it to Nothing. Finally, the function will create a new Recordset and call its Open method using the saved file.

```
Private Function GetLineItemsRS() As ADOR.Recordset
Dim objSearch As Search
Dim aParams(3) As Variant

If mobjLIRS Is Nothing Then
    Set objSearch = New Search
    aParams(2) = Me.Moniker
    'Do the Search
    Set mobjLIRS = objSearch.FindLineItems(aParams)
    'Place the Temp file path and the Moniker name into
    'a string variable
'(i.e., "C:\Temp\CAA1E308-50D8-11D2-9BEA-545CB")
    mstrLineItemFile = Environ("TEMP") & "\" & Moniker
    'Remove any existing file of this name (explanation follows)
    KillFile
    'Save the Recordset's information to this file
    mobjLIRS.Save mstrLineItemFile
```

(continues)

(Continued)

```
    'Close and release the Recordset
    mobjLIRS.Close
    Set mobjLIRS = Nothing
    'Recreate the mobjLIRS object
    Set mobjLIRS = New ADOR.Recordset
    'Open this Recordset again using the temp file as a source
    'and using  a client batch cursor type,
    'enforcing a batch optimistic locking scheme
    mobjLIRS.Open mstrLineItemFile, , adUseClientBatch, _
        adLockBatchOptimistic
End If
    'Return the local recordset
Set GetLineItemsRS = mobjLIRS
End Function
```

Although this action certainly looks odd, essentially what it does is create a local temporary table into which all of the LineItem information related to the Order object can be written. If you have ever developed using either Visual FoxPro, Microsoft Access, or other file-server development tools, then you already know that the creation of local temporary tables is a proven practice for optimizing your application when dealing with sets of editable data.

If you choose to make use of local temporary tables in your application, then you must be careful to destroy your local file when the object hosting the temporary table is destroyed. In the sample application, this is handled in a private function called Kill-File( ). This simple function first checks to see if a file name for the object's Line Item Recordset has been established. Then it checks to see if the file already exists on the disk. If the file is found, then the Visual Basic Kill command is used to delete it.

```
Private Function KillFile() As Boolean
    'Check to see if the file name has been established
If Len(mstrLineItemFile) > 0 Then
    'The Dir() function will return
        'a string containing the path and file name
        'of a file if it is found
    If Len(Dir(mstrLineItemFile)) > 0 Then
            'Kill removes files from a disk
        Kill mstrLineItemFile
    End If
End If
KillFile = True
End Function
```

Of course, to keep the client machine's Temp directory uncluttered, the Order object's Class_Terminate( ) event-handling procedure makes a call to KillFile( ).

```
Private Sub Class_Terminate()
    KillFile
End Sub
```

The LineItemGet() and the LineItemAdd Function: Creating Transactional Child Objects Using a Local Data Store

In subsequent runs of the GetLineItemsRS() function, a local Recordset is established for all of the LineItem data. Just fetching the Recordset will be enough to satisfy the LineItemsCount() method that returns a count. However, to enable the Order object's RemoveLineItem(), AddLineItem(), or LineItemGet() methods, there must be some way to spawn object's from this Recordset.

Of course, you know from Chapter 10 that objects can be created from fetched Recordsets just by passing an object-specific Recordset to the Factory's GetLineItem() method. This isn't going to be enough in this situation. We want all of this information to go into the database at one time and either fail or succeed as a group, therefore changes to the LineItem objects should be made locally and then sent with all of the other LineItems and the Order object itself.

The HomeCursor Property

One of the cool things about business objects is that they don't really care where or how they keep their data. That said, the Order object's Recordset is as good a place as anywhere to store the LineItem's data and make any updates. In fact, it's the best place because after all of the additions, deletions, and edits to an Order's LineItems, the Recordset has a number of handy methods that allow you to pass an almost unlimited number of changes to the database in one method call (wait, you'll see).

Changes to the Factory Object

To create LineItem objects that write all of the changes to their properties to a local table, the Factory object and the LineItems objects themselves need to go through a couple of changes. Starting with the Factory object, one more optional parameter must be passed to its GetLineItem() method. As you can see in the following code, the Factory object's GetLineItem() method takes an optional Batch parameter. If this parameter is passed, the method will assign the passed Recordset to be equal to the created object's HomeCursor property and will establish the object's state information by passing the Recordset into the LineItem's SetState method. Finally, if the requested LineItem object is found to already exist, and a batch transaction is being requested, then the existing LineItem's HomeCursor property is set to the passed Recordset.

```
'(The following code appears in the Factory Class)
Public Function GetLineItem(Optional strMoniker As String, _
    Optional objRS As ADOR.Recordset, Optional boolLock As Boolean = True, _
        Optional Batch As Boolean) As LineItem
Dim objLineItem As LineItem
    'See if a Messenger has been passed to the Factory
    If Ready() = False Then Exit Function
    'Check to make sure that no prior instance of this LineItem exists
    If Not IsMissing(strMoniker) Then
    Set objLineItem = gobjObjectPool.Find(strMoniker)
```

(continues)

(Continued)

```
   End if

If objLineItem Is Nothing Then
    Set objLineItem = New LineItem
    Set objLineItem.Messenger = mobjMessenger
        'If a pessimistic lock is requested, then set
    'the new LineItem into Lock mode
    If boolLock Then
         objLineItem.WithLocks = True
    End If
            'Fetch the LineItems data from the passed RS
        If Not IsMissing(objRS) Then
        'If the Batch parameter to this method is True, then
        'a test is done to see if the passed Recordset supports updates
        'if it does, then the created object's HomeCursor property is
        'set to the Recordset and its Moniker is set equal to the
        'Moniker parameter that was passed

            If Batch = True Then
                If objRS.Supports(adUpdate) Then
                    Set objLineItem.HomeCursor = objRS
            ObjLineItem.SetState objRS
                Else
                    Err.Raise vbObjectError + 4, "BusinessServices", _
                        "Only Updateable recordsets can be passed"
                End If
            Else
        objLineItem.SetState objRS
            End If
        'Fetch the LineItem's data from the database
        ElseIf Len(strMoniker) > 0 Then
            Dim aParams(4)
            aParams(0) = strMoniker
            If boolLock = True Then
                aParams(3) = True
                aParams(4) = mstrUserName
            End If
          objLineItem.SetState mobjMessenger.FetchLineItems(aParams)
        End If
        gobjObjectPool.Add objLineItem
  Else
    'If Object exists, set its HomeCursor property to
    'the passed RS if Batch = True
    If Batch = True then
        ObjLineItem.HomeCursor = objRS
    End if
  End If

    Set GetLineItem = objLineITem
End Function
```

When the HomeCursor property is given a value, this simple property set procedure is run, and a private variable named mobjHomeCursor is set in the new LineItem object.

```
Private mobjHomeCursor As ADOR.Recordset

Friend Property Set HomeCursor(objRS As ADOR.Recordset)
    Set mobjHomeCursor = objRS
End Property
```

Back to the Order Object

Now that all of the work has been done in the Factory object and the LineItem object, implementing the Order Object's LineItemAdd and LineItemGet methods is a pretty simple task. All that the LineItemAdd method does is accept an instance of a LineItem Object, mark its (friend) EditState property as Add, and set its HomeCursor property as equal to the Order object's GetLineItemsRS( ) method.

```
Public Function AddLineItem(objLineItem As LineItem) As Boolean
    With objLineItem
        .EditState = ObjectAdd
            'Remember that if the RS for this object
            'has already been established
            'this function will only return a
            'pointer to the existing RS
        .HomeCursor = GetLineItemsRS()
    End With
End Function
```

The Order object's LineItemGet method is only slightly more complex. Like a Visual Basic Collection object, you are able to retrieve an item from it either by passing the item's ordinal position (e.g., LineitemGet 4 would retrieve the fourth LineItem) or by passing the item's key (i.e., Moniker). It follows that the LineItemGet function accepts a variant that is tested to determine its type.

If this value has a subtype of integer, then an ordinal argument has been passed to the function, and as such, the Recordset's Move method will be called to position it on the correct row. The Recordset will then be passed to the Factory object's GetLineItem method, and the current row's data will be set to the created LineItem object.

If the passed value has a subtype of string, then the Recordset's Find method will be used to position the Recordset on the requested record. After the Find method is called, a check on the EOF property of the Recordset is done to ensure that a record has been found. Finally, if a record is found whose Moniker value matches the passed value, then the newly positioned Recordset is passed to the Factory object's GetLineItem method to instance a new object.

```
Public Function LineItemGet(vntIdentity As Variant) As LineItem
Dim objRS As ADOR.Recordset
Dim objFactory As New Factory
```

(continues)

(Continued)

```
    Set objRS = GetLineItemsRS()
    objRS.MoveFirst
        'Remember that the NT GUIDs retrieved are converted into
        'Strings.  So if an integer is passed, then an object in an
        'ordinal position is being requested
    If VarType(vntItdentity) = vbInteger Then
        objRS.Move vntIdentity
        Set LineItemGet = objFactory.GetLineItem(, objRS, , True)
    ElseIf VarType(vntIdentity) = vbString Then
            'Find the Moniker passed in the RS
        objRS.Find "Moniker = '" & vntIdentity & "'"
            'If found objRS.EOF NOT = True
    If Not objRS.EOF Then
        Set LineItemGet = _
            objFactory.GetLineItem(vntIdentity, objRS, , True)
    Else
        Err.Raise vbObjectError + 1, "Business Services", _
            "LineItem could not be found"
    End If
    End If

End Function
```

Persisting Object Data to a Local Data Store

Once the HomeCursor property is set, nothing is different essentially from the way things worked in other business objects you have seen; that is, property values are set in an array, and when a property is changed or an object is marked for deletion, an Edit-State property is set to reflect the pending change.

The only changes that must be made to the generic business object pattern is in the LineItem object's Commit( ) method. First, if the HomeCursor property of this object is not Nothing, then the Commit( ) method will make a call to a private function called CommitLocal( ).

```
Public Function Commit() As Boolean
    If Not objHomeCursor Is Nothing Then
     Commit = CommitLocal
    Else
        Commit = mobjMessenger.CommitCustomer(CustState())
        mboolLocked = False
    End If
End Function
```

The CommitLocal( ) function takes whatever changes have been made to the object and saves them to the assigned HomeCursor, rather than sending them across the network to be persisted in the database. First, it checks the current value of the object's EditState (in the LineItemState array). If the object has been marked as new, then the Recordset's AddNew method is used to create a new row. Subsequently, the Commit-ToCursor function is called to populate this new row with values from the LineItem's

LineItemState( ) array. Finally, the EditState of the LineItem object is set to Object-NoChange. If the LineItem object was not new, the CommitLocal( ) function tests the state again to determine that there was a change made. If the LineItemState(EditState-Value) shows that something has been changed (i.e., = ObjectNoChange), it will begin the process of moving to the correct row in the HomeCursor Recordset.

```
If LineItemState(EditStateValue) = ObjectAdd Then
        mobjHomeCursor.AddNew
        CommitToCursor
    LineItemState(EditStateValue) = ObjectNoChange
```

This repositioning process begins with moving to the first record in the Recordset by calling its MoveFirst method. Next, it searches through the entire Recordset using the Find method to look for the record that has a Moniker field value equal to the LineItem's field value. If the Find method is successful, the Recordset will be positioned on that record, which means it can then be updated or deleted.

```
mobjHomeCursor.MoveFirst
mobjHomeCursor.Find "Moniker = " & LineItemState(Moniker)
```

If the record is not found, then the Recordset will be positioned on the last record. Therefore, you can check for the success of the Find method by testing if the EOF property of the mobjHomeCursor Recordset is true. If it is not true, then another test is done to determine if the LineItem is waiting to be edited (i.e., LineItemState(EditStateValue) = ObjectEdit). If this LineItem has been edited, then the CommitToCursor function is called again to set the LineItem's LineItemState array values to the field values in the current row in the Recordset.

```
If Not mobjHomeCursor.EOF Then
        If LineItemState(EditStateValue) = ObjectEdit Then
            CommitToCursor
        LineItemState(EditStateValue) = ObjectNoChange
```

Finally, a test is run to determine if the LineItem's EditState indicates that it has been marked for deletion (i.e., LineItemState(EditStateValue) = ObjectDelete). If this is the case, then the Recordset's Delete method is called to delete the current record. The entire CommitLocal( ) function is as follows:

```
Private Function CommitLocal() As Boolean
CommitLocal = True
    If LineItemState(EditStateValue) = ObjectAdd Then
        mobjHomeCursor.AddNew
        CommitToCursor
    ElseIf Not LineItemState(EditStateValue) = ObjectNoChange Then
        mobjHomeCursor.MoveFirst
        mobjHomeCursor.Find "Moniker = " & LineItemState(Moniker)
        If Not mobjHomeCursor.EOF Then
            If LineItemState(EditStateValue) = ObjectEdit Then
```

(continues)

(Continued)

```
            CommitToCursor
        ElseIf LineItemState(EditStateValue) = ObjectDelete Then
            mobjHomeCursor.Delete
        End If
    Else
        CommitLocal = False
        Err.Raise vbObjectError, "BusinessServices", _
            "The current object " & _
            "could not be found in the local data store.  " & _
            "Save not possible."
    End If
    End If
End Function
```

The CommitToCursor( ) function that you see called from the CommitLocal( ) function performs the simple action of taking the values in the LineItemState array and setting them to the appropriate field values in the current record. After the field values have been populated with the LineItem Object's property values, the Recordset's Update method is called to save the changes.

```
Private Function CommitToCursor() As Boolean
    With mobjHomeCursor
        .Fields("Moniker") = LineItemState(Moniker)
        .Fields("OrderID") = LineItemState(OrderID)
        'and so on
        .Fields("Lockedby") = LineItemState(LockedBy)
        .Fields("LockedDate") = LineItemState("LockedDate")
        .Fields("GotLock") = LineItemState("GotLock")
        .Fields("UpdateID") = LineItemState("UpdateID")
        .Update
    End With
End Function
```

"Shotgunning" a Client-Side Transaction Set to the Server

One of the general goals that you should try to achieve whenever you are developing distributed applications is to keep the cross-network calls to a minimum. Common sense tells you that one way to slow things down in a distributed application is to make information flow between the boundaries of both process and computer. With that in mind, we'll reveal a long-standing trick for optimizing performance in COM, DCOM, or MTS: Send a large number of parameters to any method. The logic behind sending as many arguments to a remote component's method is that the most expensive part of cross-process/cross-computer communication is establishing the connection between components. Once the connection has been made, sending information over that connection is comparatively inexpensive.

With that information, you might be able to guess where we're going with the Order object's LineItem Recordset. All of the changes that need to be sent to the server-side components are being stored in the client-side ADOR.Recordset object; therefore, we can load the add, edits, and deletes of an Order's LineItems into an array. Then, all of the information in the client's transaction can be sent across the wire in one call to the server-side component.

One way to describe this technique is using the shotgun metaphor: First, you pack your cartridge (the Order object) with many small pieces (client-side transactional components; i.e., LineItems) that you want to send to your target. With your payload ready and in place, you pull the trigger (call the server-side OrderData object's AddEditDelete method) and send all of the client-side information to the MTS server in one resounding blast.

Packing the Cartridge

The pieces that need to be packed into the client-side transaction fit into four basic categories: the Order object's data, the new LineItem data, the edited LineItem data, and the deleted LineItemData. You already know from Chapter 10 that the Order object's data is stored internally as a Variant array, as it is in (almost) all of the objects involved in this application, so sending the Order object's data is as trivial an affair as sending the Customer object's data. All you need to do is to pass this OrderState( ) array to the Messaging component, and it will travel to the server as a Variant, ByVal stream. (We are making the assumption here that you have a basic understanding from the previous chapter of how individual objects send their information to the server.)

The process of packing the client-side Order and LineItem information gets interesting in the creation of separate arrays for added, edited, and deleted LineItem information. Before any of these sections of the transaction are packed, we must establish the form in which they will travel. Before we can dig into the meat of the Order object's Commit( ) method, a number of arrays and Variant variables must be dimensioned. First, three dynamic arrays must be established: The aEdited( ) array and the aAdded( ) array will be used later to hold an array of Recordset bookmarks that will be used to filter the Recordset. Unlike these simple arrays, the aDeleteTransport( ) array is a multi-dimensional, dynamic array that will be used to actually transport the deleted LineItem data to the server. There are two other dimensioned Variant variables that will be used later to transport the edited and added LineItem data to the server.

```
Public Function Commit() As Boolean
ReDim aEdited(0) 'will hold bookmarks of edited records
ReDim aAdded(0)  'will hold bookmarks of added records
    'will act as the transport for deleted LineItems
ReDim aDeleteTransport(0, 8)
    'will act as the transport for edited LineItems
Dim aEditTransport As Variant
    'will act as the transport for added LineItems
Dim aAddTransport As Variant
```

After these variables have been established, the next thing to do is to place a filter on the Recordset so that only changed records will be manipulated. This is possible because, when the Recordset was opened, it was opened in a batch mode (i.e., adUseClientBatch and adLockBatchOptimistic options were passed to the Open method).

Because this Recordset is operating in a batched update mode, it is possible to use the Filter property of the Recordset to filter out all records except for those that have been edited, added, or deleted and not yet committed to the source file. All of the LineItem objects that use the Order object's LineItem Recordset as their HomeCursor write their changes to this Recordset, so applying an adFilterPendingRecords filter will filter out all of the LineItem records that do not need to travel to the server in this transaction.

```
    'Slap a Filter on the Recordset
    'so that you are only dealing with records that
    'need to be changed
mobjLIRS.Filter = adFilterPendingRecords
```

After the records have been limited to those that need to be packed (i.e., have changed in some way), then the Commit( ) method will loop through the entire Recordset and examine each record's Status property, which can be used to determine if the current record is one that has been added (Status = adRecAdded), deleted (adRecDeleted) or edited (adRecModified).

```
    'Loop through the local database until you are
    'at the end
Do Until mobjLIRS.EOF
        'Check the Status Property of the current row to
        'Determine where its information should go
    If mobjLIRS.Status = adRecDeleted Then
```

If the current record in the loop has been deleted, then the aDeleteTransport( ) array must be changed to include the information needed to delete the record. The first thing that must be done is to determine if the adDeleteTransport( ) array has to be resized to hold the information. A local variable is set to be equal to the upper bound of the array. If there is a value in the first element of this array, the array is resized (preserving the values already present) as one larger than it is currently.

```
        'Find the upper boundary of the delete array
    intCurMax = UBound(aDeleteTransport)
    If Not Len(aDeleteTransport(0, 0)) = 0 Then
        intCurMax = intCurMax + 1
        ReDim Preserve aDeleteTransport(8, intCurMax)
    End If
```

After the aDeleteTransport( ) array is resized to hold the new LineItem's values, its columns are populated with the deleted record's values. Notice that these values cannot be directly accessed because when the record is deleted, all of its values are destroyed. However, the field object's UnderlyingValue properties still contain the deleted record's values.

```
'Populate the row in the array with the values from the deleted records
    aDeleteTransport(intCurMax, 0) = _
mobjLIRS("Moniker").UnderlyingValue
```

```
aDeleteTransport(intCurMax, 1) = _
mobjLIRS("OrderID").UnderlyingValue
aDeleteTransport(intCurMax, 2) = _
mobjLIRS ("ProductID").UnderlyingValue
aDeleteTransport(intCurMax, 3) = _
mobjLIRS ("Quantity").UnderlyingValue
aDeleteTransport(intCurMax, 4) = _
mobjLIRS ("Lockedby").UnderlyingValue
aDeleteTransport(intCurMax, 5) = _
mobjLIRS ("LockedDate").UnderlyingValue
aDeleteTransport(intCurMax, 7) = _
mobjLIRS ("UpdateID").UnderlyingValue
aDeleteTransport(intCurMax, 8) = _
mobjLIRS ("GotLock").UnderlyingValue
```

Getting the values from the edited and added records into an array is a much easier process than that for deleted records. The reason is that the Filter property of the Recordset can be used to limit the records to only those that have been added or edited. Thereafter, the Recordset's GetRows( ) method can be used to populate an array.

Although getting these records with this method is easier, it's not as easy as it would be to simply set the Filter property of the Recordset to some value like adFilterEdited-Records (at the time of this writing, this still was not possible, but check your version of ADO in case things have changed). So, to filter out all of the records that have not been edited, you need to first build an array of bookmarks. Remember from earlier in the book that a bookmark is simply a placeholder in a Recordset. If you build an array of these bookmarks, you can set the Filter property of the Recordset to be equal to this array and it will filter out all those records that cannot be identified by one of the bookmarks.

```
    ElseIf mobjLIRS.Status = adRecModified Then
            'If it is a record that has been
            'Modified, then bookmark it and save
            'That bookmark to an array that will be used
            'to define a filter later on... (you'll see that it's much
            'better than what was done with the deletes)
        AssignBookMarkArray aEdited, mobjLIRS
    ElseIf mobjLIRS.Status = adRecNew Then
            'Do the same with added records as with edited records
        AssignBookMarkArray aAdded, mobjLIRS
    End If
        'Go to the next record in the RS and loop
    mobjLIRS.MoveNext
Loop
```

As you can see in the previous code snippet, the Order object's Commit( ) method uses a utility function called AssignBookMarkArray( ) to build an array of bookmarks. This simple function accepts an array and a Recordset (i.e., aEdited and mobjLIRS) as parameters. All it does is to make sure that the passed array is large enough to hold the new bookmark and then to pass the current record's bookmark into the array.

```
Private Function AssignBookMarkArray(ByRef aArray() As Variant, _
                                     ByRef objRS As ADOR.Recordset)
Dim intCurMax As Integer
      'Find out the upper boundary of the passed array
    intCurMax = UBound(aArray)
    If Not Len(aArray(0)) = 0 Then
        'If this is not the first bookmark added, then
        'resize the passed array (preserving existing values
        'and add the bookmark value into this row
        ReDim Preserve aArray(intCurMax + 1)
        aArray(intCurMax + 1) = objRS.Bookmark
    Else
        'If it's the first bookmark, then just add it in
        aArray(intCurMax) = objRS.Bookmark
    End If

End Function
```

Once these arrays of bookmark values are built, the Commit( ) method first tests to see if the individual bookmark arrays have been created, then it uses them to create a filter that will either return all of the records that have either been edited or added in the Recordset. After one of these edit or add filters is enforced on the Recordset, simply calling the GetRows method on the filtered Recordset can create arrays of added or edited record values.

This Recordset method will return a two-dimensional array in which the first dimension will hold the value of the field in a record and the second dimension will hold the row number of the record. For example, when the aEditTransport array is built with this method, the value of aEditTransport(1,0) will hold the second field value (OrderID) for the first (i.e., the first zero-based position) record in the Recordset. (Note: This is exactly the reverse of what was built earlier for the aDeleteTransport array, where aDeleteTransport(1,0) would be the first field value (Moniker) in the second record.)

```
    'Test to see if there have been values placed in the aEdited array
If Not aEdited(0) = "" Then
    'If so, then apply the filter
    mobjLIRS.Filter = aedited
    'Populate an array using the GetRows method
    aEditTransport = mobjLIRS.GetRows
End If

    'Same tests as in the edited array
If Not aAdded(0) = "" Then
    mobjLIRS.Filter = aAdded
    aAddTransport = mobjLIRS.GetRows
End If
```

Pulling the Trigger

Now that everything is packed into the "cartridge," pulling the trigger on the transaction is easy. As you might suspect, the Transport component's Messaging object has a CommitOrder( ) method that accepts the LineItem arrays as parameters. As mentioned, everything involved in this transaction gets blasted over the wire in one big, packaged shot.

```
'pull the trigger and send (a lot) of information
'(the Order object data and the data of any LineItem
'object that has been added, edited or deleted)
        'to the server
Commit = mobjMessenger.CommitOrder(OrderState, aDeleteTransport, _
aEditTransport, aAddTransport)
```

 Why not just send the Recordset? For two good reasons: First, the Recordset does not travel as gracefully or quickly to MTS as a simple Variant (aTransactionTransport); second, the decomposition of the Recordset into sets of records to be added, edited, and deleted has to be done somewhere. The architecture of this framework assumes a middleweight client machine, so the already beleaguered server application can be relieved of this simple data shuffling and reorganizing against a local data store. In other (slightly more fancy) words, there is more *processing opportunity* on the client machine than on the server for this operation.

The entire Order object's Commit( ) method is as follows:

```
Public Function Commit() As Boolean
ReDim aEdited(0) 'will hold bookmarks of edited records
ReDim aAdded(0)  'will hold bookmarks of added records
    'will act as the transport for deleted LineItems
ReDim aDeleteTransport(0, 8)
    'will act as the transport for edited LineItems
Dim aEditTransport As Variant
    'will act as the transport for added LineItems
Dim aAddTransport As Variant
Dim aTransactionTransport(3)

'Slap a Filter on the Recordset
        'so that you are only dealing with records that
        'need to be changed
mobjLIRS.Filter = adFilterPendingRecords

    'Loop through the local database until you are
    'at the end
Do Until mobjLIRS.EOF
        'Check the Status Property of the current row to
        'Determine where its information should go
    If mobjLIRS.Status = adRecDeleted Then
    'Find the upper boundry of the delete array
        intCurMax = UBound(aDeleteTransport)
        If Not Len(aDeleteTransport(0, 0)) = 0 Then
```

(continues)

(Continued)

```
                    intCurMax = intCurMax + 1
                    ReDim Preserve aDeleteTransport(8, intCurMax)
          End If
'Populate the row in the array with the values from the deleted records
     aDeleteTransport(intCurMax, 0) = _
mobjLIRS("Moniker").UnderlyingValue
aDeleteTransport(intCurMax, 1) = _
mobjLIRS("OrderID").UnderlyingValue
aDeleteTransport(intCurMax, 2) = _
mobjLIRS ("ProductID").UnderlyingValue
aDeleteTransport(intCurMax, 3) = _
mobjLIRS ("Quantity").UnderlyingValue
aDeleteTransport(intCurMax, 4) = _
mobjLIRS ("Lockedby").UnderlyingValue
aDeleteTransport(intCurMax, 5) = _
mobjLIRS ("LockedDate").UnderlyingValue
aDeleteTransport(intCurMax, 7) = _
mobjLIRS ("UpdateID").UnderlyingValue
aDeleteTransport(intCurMax, 8) = _
mobjLIRS ("GotLock").UnderlyingValue
     ElseIf mobjLIRS.Status = adRecModified Then
               'If it is a record that has been
               'modified, then bookmark it and save
               'that bookmark to an array that will be used
               'to define a filter later on
          AssignBookMarkArray aEdited, mobjLIRS
     ElseIf mobjLIRS.Status = adRecNew Then
               'Do the same with added records as with edited records
          AssignBookMarkArray aAdded, mobjLIRS
     End If
          'Go to the next record in the RS and loop
     mobjLIRS.MoveNext
Loop

     'Test to see if there have been values placed in th aEdited array
If Not aEdited(0) = "" Then
     'If so, then apply the filter
     mobjLIRS.Filter = aedited
     'Populate an array using the GetRows method
     aEditTransport = mobjLIRS.GetRows
End If

     'Same tests as in the edited array
If Not aAdded(0) = "" Then
     mobjLIRS.Filter = aAdded
     aAddTransport = mobjLIRS.GetRows
End If

'Pull the trigger
Commit = mobjMessenger.CommitOrder(OrderState, aDeleteTransport, _
AEditTransport, aAddTransport)
```

```
'Error Handling can (should) be added here
End Function
```

The Server-Side OrderData Object

As you already know, all communication with the server-side business objects is first routed through the Messaging object. This case is no different; when the call is made from the client-side component, the parameters are relayed to the server with the following procedure:

```
Public Function CommitOrder(OrderState, aDeleteTransport, _
AEditTransport, aAddTransport) As Boolean
    CommitOrder = mobjOrder.AddUpdateDelete(OrderState, aDeleteTransport, _
aEditTransport, aAddTransport)
End Function
```

The OrderData Object's AddUpdateDelete( ) Method

Like the Customer object's AddUpdateDelete( ) method, the function of this server-side method is to use ADO Command objects to act upon a stored procedure, which will persist the object's data in the database. However, this method is different from that of the Customer object because it also needs to take care of the persistence of its child LineItem objects.

Of course, if anything happens during the persistence of the Order object's data or of any of the LineItem's data, then the entire action against the database should fail. This is where Microsoft Transaction Server really shows its muscles. Because the server-side OrderData and LineItemData objects are both created to take advantage of MTS transitions, the job of sending all of this information to the database in an all-or-nothing batch is easy. As you will see in the forthcoming code, if an error is raised by any action of any object in the method, the error trap will call the Order object's MTS context's SetAbort( ) method and all of the changes will be rolled back.

The OrderData object's AddUpdateDelete( ) method accepts four ByVal variant parameters. The first of these is the data being stored for the Order object; the second, third, and fourth contain deleted, edited, and added child LineItem data, respectively.

```
Public Function AddUpdateDelete(ByVal aOrderState As Variant, _
        ByVal aLIDelete As Variant, _
        ByVal aLIEdit As Variant, ByVal aLIAdd As Variant) as Boolean
```

 Remember to use ByVal parameters with MTS. And to avoid network round-trips when speaking to an MTS component, pass all parameters ByVal. By doing this, you will send a copy of all of the values to the server in one shot.

Processing the Order Object's Data

The first thing that the AddUpdateDelete( ) method does is to process the changes to the Order object's data. As far as this action is concerned, this method is very much like the Customer object's method of the same name. First, an ADO Connection object is established. Second, a Command object is created, its ActiveConnection property is set to be equal to the established Connection, and its CommandText property is set to the name of the stored procedure used to persist the object's data. Third, the values passed in the OrderState array are appended to the Command object as members of its Parameters collection (this is not shown in the following code for the sake of space). Fourth, the Command object's Execute method is called to run the stored procedure using the passed parameters. Finally, the Connection object's Errors collection is checked for any nonreported errors.

```
Public Function AddUpdateDelete(ByVal aOrderState As Variant, _
          ByVal aLIDelete As Variant, _
          ByVal aLIEdit As Variant, ByVal aLIAdd As Variant) as Boolean
Dim objConnection As ADODB.Connection
Dim objCommand As ADODB.Command
Dim objLineItem As LineItemData
Dim aLineItemDataArray(8) As Variant
Dim intIterator As Integer
Dim boolSuccess As Boolean

Dim objTmpParam As ADODB.Parameter

On Error GoTo ERR_AddUpdateDelete

    Set objConnection = CreateObject("ADODB.Connection")
    objConnection.Open "Data Provider=MSDASQL;Driver={SQL Server};" & _
            "Server=(Local);Database=Pubs;UID=sa"

    Set objCommand = CreateObject("ADODB.Command")

    objCommand.ActiveConnection = objConnection
    objCommand.CommandText = "AddEditDeleteOrder"
    objCommand.CommandType = adCmdStoredProc

    'Append all the params passed in the OrderState() array
    'This is not shown here for the sake of space. If you
    'are unclear about using Parameter objects, please reference
    'the code in Chapter 10

    objCommand.Execute

    If objConnection.Errors.Count = 0 Then
        AddUpdateDelete = True
    Else
        AddUpdateDelete = False
        With objConnection.Errors(0)
            Err.Raise.Number,.Source,.Description
```

```
        End With
    End If
```

Notice at the beginning of the procedure that an error trap is set. This is so if an error is returned to the Connection object's Errors collection, an error will be raised that will be caught in the trap. The action of the trap is to GOTO a line in the method where SetAbort is called, and an error is raised back to the client-side application. By raising errors in this way, the transaction is aborted before any more unnecessary processing is done.

Processing LineItem Data

As you already know, three separate arrays of LineItem data were passed to this method. Since the LineItem data has been predigested into arrays of information to be added, edited, and deleted, sending this information to the database will be relatively simple. You might have already guessed that this information will be processed by the LineItemData object. Like the other server-side objects in this application, this object has an AddEditDelete( ) method that accepts an array as a parameter, then uses an ADO Command object to execute a stored procedure. This simple method is so similar to the AddEditDelete( ) method in the CustomerData object, as is the code used to persist Order information in the OrderData object, this method will not be shown here. Besides, more interesting than its use of the Command object is the way that the array it accepts is populated.

But before working with this LineItemData object, the OrderData object's AddEdit-Delete() method must create an instance. You have seen this type of thing earlier; to be able to transact all of the actions performed by this method, the LineItemData object must be created in the same MTS context as the OrderData object. This is done by using the OrderData object's MTS Context object, which sets to a module-level variable (mob-jCtxt) in the OrderData object's ObjectControl_Activate( ) event procedure. This Context object has a CreateInstance method that can be used to instance other objects using the same MTS context as the creating object. By doing this, when the SetComplete or SetAbort method of the Context object is called, the transaction will be enacted on the actions of both the OrderData and the LineItemData objects.

```
'using the mobjCtxt var, instance a LineItemData object
    Set objLineItem = mObjCtxt.CreateInstance("DataServices.LineItemData")
```

Now that an instance of the LineItemData object has been instanced, processing the passed LineItem arrays can begin. To maximize the accuracy of any transaction, the method will first process the LineItem records to be deleted because the action of deleting a line item will logically increment the number of product units in stock. For example, if a LineItem for 20 widgets were removed from an order, there would be 20 more widgets available for another order.

At the beginning of the method, an eight-element array named aLineItemDataArray was dimensioned. This array is populated with values from each of the three LineItem arrays and then used as a parameter to the LineItemData's AddEditDelete( ) method. As you can see in the following code, the OrderData object's AddEditDelete( ) method first checks the first element in the passed aLIDelete array to see if it contains information.

If it passes that test, the method iterates through the array. On each iteration, the aLineItemDataArray( ) array is populated with information from the next row in the aLIDelete array. The LineItemData object's AddUpdateDelete( ) method is then passed to this newly populated array. Finally, if the LineItemData object's AddUpdateDelete( ) method does not return as TRUE, the method will GOTO the error handler, where the transaction will be aborted (i.e., mObjCtxt.SetAbort).

```
'Process the Delete Array
    If Len(aLIDelete(0, 0)) > 0 Then
        For intIterator = 0 To UBound(aLIDelete)
            aLineItemDataArray(Moniker) = aLIDelete(intIterator, 0)
            aLineItemDataArray(OrderID) = aLIDelete(intIterator, 1)
            aLineItemDataArray(ProductID) = aLIDelete(intIterator, 2)
            aLineItemDataArray(Quantity) = aLIDelete(intIterator, 3)
            aLineItemDataArray(LockedBy) = aLIDelete(intIterator, 4)
            aLineItemDataArray(LockDate) = aLIDelete(intIterator, 5)
                'This is the Delete array, so insert the Action param
            aLineItemDataArray(Action) = 2
            aLineItemDataArray(UpdateID) = aLIDelete(intIterator, 7)
            aLineItemDataArray(GotLock) = aLIDelete(intIterator, 8)
            'Pass current record to the LineItemData object
            boolSuccess = objLineItem.AddUpdateDelete(aLineItemDataArray)
            If boolSuccess = False Then GoTo ERR_AddUpdateDelete
        Next
    End If
```

Much the same thing is done for the aLIEdit and aLIAdd arrays. But because these arrays were created on the client using the Recordset's GetRows method, their structure is different from the aLIDelete array. Therefore, when the iteration is performed on these arrays, the second dimension of the array is used to determine the number of records in the array.

```
'Process the Edit Array
    If Len(aLIEdit(0, 0)) > 0 Then
            'Unlike in the Delete array, the number of the record is
            'stored in the second element of the aparams(2) array
        For intIterator = 0 To UBound(aLIEdit, 2)
            'See, the reference is switched from the order of the
            'Delete array
            aLineItemDataArray(Moniker) = aLIEdit(0, intIterator)
            aLineItemDataArray(OrderID) = aLIEdit(1, intIterator)
            aLineItemDataArray(ProductID) = aLIEdit(2, intIterator)
            aLineItemDataArray(Quantity) = aLIEdit(3, intIterator)
            aLineItemDataArray(LockedBy) = aLIEdit(4, intIterator)
            aLineItemDataArray(LockDate) = aLIEdit(5, intIterator)
                'This is the Edit array, so insert the Action param
            aLineItemDataArray(Action) = 1
            aLineItemDataArray(UpdateID) = aLIEdit(6, intIterator)
            aLineItemDataArray(GotLock) = aLIEdit(7, intIterator)
```

```
        'Commit the current LineItem data to the database
            boolSuccess = objLineItem.AddUpdateDelete(aLineItemDataArray)
            If boolSuccess = False Then GoTo ERR_AddUpdateDelete
        Next
    End If


'Process the Add Array
    If Len(aLIAdd(0, 0)) > 0 Then
    For intIterator = 0 To UBound(aLIAdd, 2)
            aLineItemDataArray(Moniker) = aLIAdd(0, intIterator)
            aLineItemDataArray(OrderID) = aLIAdd(1, intIterator)
            aLineItemDataArray(ProductID) = aLIAdd(2, intIterator)
            aLineItemDataArray(Quantity) = aLIAdd(3, intIterator)
            aLineItemDataArray(LockedBy) = aaLIAdd(4, intIterator)
            aLineItemDataArray(LockDate) = aLIAdd(5, intIterator)
                'This is the Add array, so insert the Action param
            aLineItemDataArray(Action) = 0
            aLineItemDataArray(UpdateID) = aLIAdd(6, intIterator)
            aLineItemDataArray(GotLock) = aLIAdd(7, intIterator)
            boolSuccess = objLineItem.AddUpdateDelete(aLineItemDataArray)
            If boolSuccess = False Then GoTo ERR_AddUpdateDelete
        Next
    End If
```

What About Stock Levels? The AddEditDeleteLineItem Stored Procedure

All of this packaging and MTS marshaling stuff is neat, but what about incrementing stock levels? In this application, the decision was made to handle the incrementing and decrementing of stock levels in a stored procedure to enable the application to meet a high level of consistency and speed.

In some ways, this stored procedure is like the AddEditDeleteCustomer stored procedure that you saw in the last chapter. It handles locking (both optimistic and pessimistic) in the same way and is able to perform INSERTS, UPDATES, and DELETES against a base table just like the AddEditDeleteCustomer stored procedure. What is different is that this stored procedure automatically handles the adjustment of stock levels.

Let's start by examining what happens when this procedure is asked to add a new LineItem to the database. Logically, when a new LineItem is added, stock levels in the database must be reduced by the value of the LineItem. Also logically, this reduction of stock level should only be done if there is sufficient stock to fill the order. In the stored procedure code that follows, a check of stock levels is done first by querying the database to determine if the stock of a certain product (i.e., "Select iNumberInStock FROM Item WHERE iItemID = @ProductID") is greater than the amount requested ("@Quantity") in the new LineItem. If the stock level is sufficient, then the amount of stock noted in the database is reduced by the number requested and the new LineItem data is inserted.

```
IF @Action = 0 /*Insert New Record*/
    /*Only do the insert if there is sufficient stock
from which to pull*/
  IF (SELECT iNumberInStock FROM Item
WHERE iItemID = @ProductID) >= @Quantity
  BEGIN
    /*Adjust Stock Levels*/
  UPDATE Item SET iNumberInStock = (iNumberInStock - @Quantity)
  WHERE iItemID = @ProductID
    /*If there were any problems, raise an error*/
  IF @@ROWCOUNT = 0
  RAISERROR ('There was a problem communicating with the datbase',1,1)

/*Add the new LineItem*/
  INSERT INTO LineItems
    (liLineItemID, liOrderID, liQtyOrdered,
    liProductID, liUpdateID)
  VALUES (@Moniker, @OrderID, @Quantity, @ProductID,
      @UpdateID)
    /*Check For Problems*/
  IF @@ROWCOUNT = 0
    RAISERROR ('There was a problem communicating with the datbase',1,1)
  END
ELSE
    /*If not enough stock, return a meaningful error*/
  BEGIN
    SELECT @Message = 'Insuficient stock levels of ' + iDescription
    FROM Item
    WHERE iItemID = @ProductID
    RAISERROR (@Message,1,1)
  END
```

The action of deleting an existing LineItem is even simpler: Stock levels are incremented by the amount of stock that the LineItem held, then a DELETE is executed against the unwanted LineItem.

```
    /*Delete Existing Record enforcing a default optimistic lock*/
ELSE IF @Action = 2
 BEGIN
     /*Increment the stock that was consumed by the order about to
   be deleted and check for errors*/
  UPDATE Item SET iNumberInStock = (iNumberInStock + @Quantity)
  WHERE iItemID = @ProductID
    IF @@ROWCOUNT = 0
    RAISERROR ('There was a problem communicating
       with the database',1,1)

    /*Delete the Record*/
  DELETE FROM LineItems
  WHERE liLineItemID = @Moniker AND liUpdateID = @UpdateID
```

```
    IF @@ROWCOUNT = 0
      RAISERROR ('LineItem data has been updated since fetched',1,1)

  END
```

When an UPDATE of a LineItem is done, the logic concerning the adjustment of stock levels becomes more complex because you can't be sure if the stock level should be incremented (i.e., the LineItem now requires less stock) or decremented (i.e., the LineItem now requires more stock). This problem is solved by using variables and doing a little math.

First, the variable @CurItemQuant is set to be equal to the quantity of stock that currently exists for the LineItem about to be updated. Next, the variable named @NumItemInStock is set to be equal to the total number of the LineItem's requested Item in the database. Finally, the new stock level for the item in question is calculated by adding the @CurItemQuant variable to the @NumItemInStock variable and then subtracting the currently requested quantity of items from the sum.

```
/*Assign @CurItemQuant to be equal to the current value
      of the quantity ordered in the database*/
    SELECT @CurItemQuant = liQtyOrdered
FROM LineItems
WHERE liLineItemID = @Moniker
        /*Assign @NumItemInStock to be equal to
        the current number of items available*/
    SELECT @NumItemInStock = iNumberInStock
FROM Item
WHERE iItemID = @ProductID
    /*Assign @NewStock to be equal to the sum of the quantity in the
    order being changed and the total numberof items in the database
    minus the current quantity being requested- i.e., @NewStock =
    ((#InCurrent Record + #InDatabase) - CurrentRequest)*/
    SELECT @NewStock = (@NumItemInStock + @CurItemQuant) - @Quantity
```

In the full Create Procedure script that follows, you can see that the @NewStock variable is used to determine if there is sufficient stock for the update to succeed. As you read through this script, you will see a lot of code mirroring what you have seen earlier (i.e., locking and such); therefore, the procedure involved with the adjustment of stock levels has been boldfaced for easier identification.

```
Create Procedure AddEditDeleteLineItem
(
@Moniker VarChar(30) = NULL, @OrderID varchar(30) = NULL,
@ProductID varchar(30) =NULL, @Quantity Int = 0,
@Lockedby char (10) = NULL, @LockDate datetime = NULL,
@Action Int = 1, /* 0 = Insert, 1 = Update, 2 = Delete*/
@UpdateID Int = 1,
@GotLock Int = 0
)
As
```

(continues)

(Continued)

```
DECLARE @CurLockDate Datetime, @CurLockedBy Char
DECLARE @NumItemInStock Int, @CurItemQuant Int, @NewStock Int
DECLARE @Message Varchar(75)

IF @Action = 0 /*Insert New Record*/
    /*Only do the insert if there is sufficient stock
from which to pull*/
  IF (SELECT iNumberInStock FROM Item
WHERE iItemID = @ProductID) >= @Quantity
  BEGIN
    /*Adjust Stock Levels*/
    UPDATE Item SET iNumberInStock = (iNumberInStock - @Quantity)
    WHERE iItemID = @ProductID
    /*If there were any problems, raise an error*/
    IF @@ROWCOUNT = 0
    RAISERROR('There was a problem communicating with the datbase',1,1)

/*Add the new LineItem*/
    INSERT INTO LineItems
      (liLineItemID, liOrderID, liQtyOrdered,
      liProductID, liUpdateID)
    VALUES (@Moniker, @OrderID, @Quantity, @ProductID,
        @UpdateID)
    /*Check For Problems*/
    IF @@ROWCOUNT = 0
      RAISERROR  ('There was a problem communicating with the datbase',1,1)
  END
  ELSE
    /*If not enough stock, return a meaningful error*/
  BEGIN
    SELECT @Message = 'Insufficient stock levels of ' + iDescription
    FROM Item

    WHERE iItemID = @ProductID
    RAISERROR (@Message,1,1)
  END

ELSE
BEGIN
    /*Only assign a value to the  @CurLockDate variable if needed (Edit or
    Delete*/
  SELECT @CurLockDate = liLockDate FROM LineItems
  WHERE liLineItemID = @Moniker

  /*Test to see if the current request has the lock, if there is no
  lock on the record or if the lock on the record is over an hour old*/
  IF @GotLock = 1 OR @CurLockDate IS NULL
    OR DATEDIFF(hh, @CurLockDate, getdate()) > 1
  BEGIN
    /*Update Existing Record enforcing a default optimistic lock*/
    IF @Action = 1
```

```
    BEGIN
        /*Assign @CurItemQuant to be equal to the current value
        of the quantity ordered in the database*/
    SELECT @CurItemQuant = liQtyOrdered
FROM LineItems
WHERE liLineItemID = @Moniker
        /*Assign @NumItemInStock to be equal to
        the current number of items available*/
    SELECT @NumItemInStock = iNumberInStock
FROM Item
WHERE iItemID = @ProductID
        /*Assign @NewStock to be equal to the sum of the quantity in the
        order being changed and the total number of items in the database
        minus the current quantity being requested- i.e., @NewStock =
        ((#InCurrent Record + #InDatabase) - CurrentRequest)*/
    SELECT @NewStock = (@NumItemInStock + @CurItemQuant) - @Quantity

        /*If the @NewStock var is >=0, then there is enough
        stock to fill the order*/
    IF @NewStock >= 0
     BEGIN
        /*Update the number of available Items in the database
        and check for any errors that occur in doing so*/
        UPDATE Item SET iNumberInStock = @NewStock
        WHERE iItemID = @ProductID

        IF @@ROWCOUNT = 0
RAISERROR   ('There was a problem communicating with the
database',1,1)

        /*Once the stock is decremented, update the record
        and then check for any errors*/
      IF @@ROWCOUNT > 0
        UPDATE LineItems
        SET liLineItemID = @Moniker, liOrderID = @OrderID,
         liQtyOrdered = @Quantity, liLockDate = NULL,
         liUpdateID = (liUpdateID + 1)
        WHERE liLineItemID = @Moniker AND liUpdateID = @UpdateID
        IF @@ROWCOUNT = 0
        RAISERROR ('There was a problem communicating with
the database',1,1)
     END
    ELSE
     BEGIN
     /*If there was not enough stock to fill the order, then raise
      a meaningful error*/
     SELECT @Message = ' Insufficient stock levels of ' + iDescription
     FROM Item
     WHERE iItemID = @ProductID
     RAISERROR   (@Message,1,1)
    END
```

(continues)

(Continued)

```
    END
        /*Delete Existing Record enforcing a default optimistic lock*/
    ELSE IF @Action = 2
     BEGIN
            /*Increment the stock that was consumed by the order about to
        be deleted and check for errors*/
        UPDATE Item SET iNumberInStock = (iNumberInStock + @Quantity)
        WHERE iItemID = @ProductID
         IF @@ROWCOUNT = 0
           RAISERROR ('There was a problem communicating
              with the database',1,1)


         /*Delete the Record*/
        DELETE FROM LineItems
        WHERE liLineItemID = @Moniker AND liUpdateID = @UpdateID
         IF @@ROWCOUNT = 0
           RAISERROR ('LineItem data has been updated since fetched',1,1)


     END
    END


    ELSE
     BEGIN
        /*If the record cannot be updated because it is locked, then
         find out who has the current lock and return the user's name in the
         error message*/
    SELECT @CurLockedBy = 'The Customer data is currently Locked _
    by ' + cuLockedBy
        FROM Customers Where cuCustomerID = @Moniker
        RAISERROR(@CurLockedBy,1,1)
     END
    END
```

The Magic: To Commit or Roll Back?

If at any point the OrderData object's AddUpdateDelete method encounters an error, the error handler ("On Error GoTo ERR_AddUpdateDelete") will engage and route the execution to the very end of the method, where the OrderData's MTS Context (i.e., mobjCtxt) will be used to issue a SetAbort method. Since both the OrderData object and the LineItemData object share this Context, all of the actions completed by the method will be rolled back. But if the method executes without raising any errors, then the same Context object's SetComplete method will be called, and all of the method's changes to the database will be committed in a batch.

In the full text of the OrderData object's AddUpdateDelete method that follows, you can see how the MTS Context and the method's error handler stand guard while one Order object's data and countless LineItem objects' data go sailing into the database.

```
Public Function AddUpdateDelete(ByVal aOrderState As Variant, _
        ByVal aLIDelete As Variant, _
```

```
            ByVal aLIEdit As Variant, ByVal aLIAdd As Variant) as Boolean
Dim objConnection As ADODB.Connection
Dim objCommand As ADODB.Command
Dim objLineItem As LineItemData
Dim aLineItemDataArray(8) As Variant
Dim intIterator As Integer
Dim boolSuccess As Boolean

Dim objTmpParam As ADODB.Parameter

On Error GoTo ERR_AddUpdateDelete

    Set objConnection = CreateObject("ADODB.Connection")
    objConnection.Open "Data Provider=MSDASQL;Driver={SQL Server};" & _
            "Server=(Local);Database=Pubs;UID=sa"

    Set objCommand = CreateObject("ADODB.Command")

    objCommand.ActiveConnection = objConnection
    objCommand.CommandText = "AddEditDeleteOrder"
    objCommand.CommandType = adCmdStoredProc

    'Append all the params passed in the OrderState() array

    objCommand.Execute

    If objConnection.Errors.Count = 0 Then
        AddUpdateDelete = True
    Else
        AddUpdateDelete = False
        With objConnection.Errors(1)
            Err.Raise .Number, .Source, .Description
        End With
    End If

        'using the mobjCtxt var, instance a LineItemData object
    Set objLineItem = mObjCtxt.CreateInstance("DataServices.LineItemData")

        'Process the Delete Array
    If Len(aLIDelete(0, 0)) > 0 Then
        For intIterator = 0 To UBound(aLIDelete)
            aLineItemDataArray(Moniker) = aLIDelete(intIterator, 0)
            aLineItemDataArray(OrderID) = aLIDelete(intIterator, 1)
            aLineItemDataArray(ProductID) = aLIDelete(intIterator, 2)
            aLineItemDataArray(Quantity) = aLIDelete(intIterator, 3)
            aLineItemDataArray(LockedBy) = aLIDelete(intIterator, 4)
            aLineItemDataArray(LockDate) = aLIDelete(intIterator, 5)
                'This is the Delete array, so insert the Action param
            aLineItemDataArray(Action) = 2
            aLineItemDataArray(UpdateID) = aLIDelete(intIterator, 7)
            aLineItemDataArray(GotLock) = aLIDelete(intIterator, 8)
```

(continues)

(Continued)

```
            boolSuccess = objLineItem.AddUpdateDelete(aLineItemDataArray)
            If boolSuccess = False Then GoTo ERR_AddUpdateDelete
        Next
    End If
        'Process the Edit Array
    If Len(aLIEdit(0, 0)) > 0 Then
            'Unlike in the Delete array, the number of the record is
            'stored in the second element of the aparams(2) array
        For intIterator = 0 To UBound(aLIEdit, 2)
            aLineItemDataArray(Moniker) = aLIEdit(0, intIterator)
            aLineItemDataArray(OrderID) = aLIEdit(1, intIterator)
            aLineItemDataArray(ProductID) = aLIEdit(2, intIterator)
            aLineItemDataArray(Quantity) = aLIEdit(3, intIterator)
            aLineItemDataArray(LockedBy) = aLIEdit(4, intIterator)
            aLineItemDataArray(LockDate) = aLIEdit(5, intIterator)
                'This is the Edit array, so insert the Action param
            aLineItemDataArray(Action) = 1
            aLineItemDataArray(UpdateID) = aLIEdit(6, intIterator)
            aLineItemDataArray(GotLock) = aLIEdit(7, intIterator)
            boolSuccess = objLineItem.AddUpdateDelete(aLineItemDataArray)
            If boolSuccess = False Then GoTo ERR_AddUpdateDelete
        Next
    End If


        'Process the Add Array
    If Len(aLIAdd(0, 0)) > 0 Then
    For intIterator = 0 To UBound(aLIAdd, 2)
            aLineItemDataArray(Moniker) = aLIAdd(0, intIterator)
            aLineItemDataArray(OrderID) = aLIAdd(1, intIterator)
            aLineItemDataArray(ProductID) = aLIAdd(2, intIterator)
            aLineItemDataArray(Quantity) = aLIAdd(3, intIterator)
            aLineItemDataArray(LockedBy) = aaLIAdd(4, intIterator)
            aLineItemDataArray(LockDate) = aLIAdd(5, intIterator)
                'This is the Add array, so insert the Action param
            aLineItemDataArray(Action) = 0
            aLineItemDataArray(UpdateID) = aLIAdd(6, intIterator)
            aLineItemDataArray(GotLock) = aLIAdd(7, intIterator)
            boolSuccess = objLineItem.AddUpdateDelete(aLineItemDataArray)
            If boolSuccess = False Then GoTo ERR_AddUpdateDelete
        Next
    End If
        'Call SetComplete to send the transaction to the database
    mObjCtxt.SetComplete
Exit Function

ERR_AddUpdateDelete:
    AddUpdateDelete = False
    mObjCtxt.SetAbort
    Err.Raise vbObjectError + 1, "Transaction", Err.Description

End Function
```

From Here

Now your real learning curve begins: when you implement your own project. Hopefully, this book was helpful, giving you new knowledge and generating new ideas that will make your development life easier. As you work with this material, remember to be patient with yourself; this stuff may be really different from what you are used to.

We recommend that from time to time, you check in on this book's Web page, www.wiley.com/compbooks/martiner, where you can download the sample code included in the book. We will also post information there on any errata or to amplify points where greater clarification is found to be necessary.

Thanks from the three of us for buying the book. Writing it has been a great learning experience. We hope that reading it will be equally as enlightening for you.

Index